MW00396745

PRAYERS AND PROMISES OF THE BIBLE

the Smart Guide to the Bible™ series

BE SMART. BE INSPIRED.™

J. Heyward Rogers
Larry Richards, General Editor

THOMAS NELSON
Since 1798

NASHVILLE DALLAS MEXICO CITY RIO DE JANEIRO BEIJING

Prayers and Promises of the Bible
The Bible Smart Guide™ Series

Published in Nashville, Tennessee, by Thomas Nelson. Thomas Nelson is a trademark of Thomas Nelson, Inc.

Thomas Nelson, Inc. titles may be purchased in bulk for educational, business, fundraising, or sales promotional use. For information, please e-mail SpecialMarkets@ThomasNelson.com.

General Editor: Larry Richards
Managing Editor: Teri Wilhelms
Associate Editor: W. Mark Whitlock
Scripture Editor: Deborah Wiseman
Assistant Editor: Amy Clark
Design: Diane Whisner

Consultants: Eva Marie Everson—Prayers of the Bible
Rebecca Bertolini—Promises of the Bible

ISBN-10: 1-4185-1002-5
ISBN-13: 978-1-4185-1002-2

Printed in the United States of America
07 08 09 10 RRD 9 8 7 6 5 4 3 2 1

Introduction

Welcome to Prayers and Promises—The Smart Guide to the Bible™. This book is part of a series designed to bring God's encouragement and loving message to you in an easy-to-understand and relevant style.

Prayers. Promises. Our utterances to God. God's utterances to us. God's promises and our prayers constitute the life-long conversation between a believer and God. This book looks closely at about two hundred prayers and promises found in the Bible, providing you with the historical and scriptural context to gain a fuller understanding of what was going on and why when each prayer or promise was spoken. You'll also find a personal application for each prayer and promise, a way of making it relevant to the life you live.

When you examine the prayers of the Bible, you're struck by their variety. People pray out of joy, out of need, out of sorrow, out of relief. Sometimes prayer is the spontaneous overflow of a heart that is full of gratitude. Sometimes the prayer that pours out is a complaint, a venting of frustration to a God whose ways we humans don't always understand. Even giants of the faith have been known to pray such prayers. And that's okay too. The important thing is for prayer to be an outpouring of what's actually *in* the heart—offered up to the God who is forever faithful—and not an empty recitation of meaningless phrases and false sentiments.

There's a risk in that kind of honest prayer. You occasionally pray things you "should not" pray. You sometimes ask God to do things He simply won't do. It's a good thing He doesn't give you everything you ask for! But the real risk in honest prayer is this: it makes it hard for you to hold onto your old self. When you truly pour yourself out in prayer, it changes you from the inside out. You think you're asking God to change your situation, but you find that He frequently changes you instead.

Prayer is one of the principal means by which God fulfills His promise to make you look more and more like Jesus. Everything else here on earth is a moving target. Nothing ever stays the same. But if you are in Christ, you are locked onto the target of Christlikeness. God has begun the good work of making you look like Him, and He is going to complete it.

Which brings us to God's promises—the subject of the second half of this book. As much as we change—as much as we need to change—God never does. And if the variety of prayers in the Bible is striking, perhaps what's most striking about the promises in the Bible is their sameness. "Do not fear, for I am with you," God promises. He promises it over and over again. He promises to provide for our needs, physical, spiritual, emotional, and eternal. The same promise in many different ways. He promises that He will triumph over every enemy. He promises to love us with an everlasting love. A few of God's promises appear once and only once. But it's worth noticing how many of God's promises appear over and over again, from Genesis through Revelation. And why shouldn't those promises be the same? God never changes. He is forever true to Himself.

Why study the prayers and promises of the Bible?

BECAUSE . . . The Bible is God's love letter to us. When Jesus led His disciples in a final prayer before going to the cross, He declared to His Father, "Your word is truth." We can trust it, rely on it, count on it, live our lives by it, and know beyond the shadow of any doubt that what God says is true. God's promises to us are promises that will never be broken!

BECAUSE . . . For over 2,000 years, millions of people have improved their lives by following its wisdom. The Bible tells us repeatedly that when we study the Bible we will receive valuable blessings. When we study the prayers and promises of the Bible, we will discover principles and insights that will flood our lives with joy and peace.

BECAUSE . . . All of us want to respond to life's challenges in a godly way. The Bible offers answers to the difficult questions we face during the complex and demanding days that we live.

BECAUSE . . . Like no other book in the world, the Bible gives us hope.

It all comes down to God's faithfulness. We believe God's promises—and we pray with confidence and hope—because we know He is faithful, even when we are faithless.

We live in a changeable, time-bound world. God lives in eternal changelessness. How do we bridge those two realms? Our prayers. God's promises.

How to Use Prayers and Promises—The Smart Guide to the Bible™

You can read this book in one of two ways:

(1) Read through each prayer or promise in the order they are presented;

(2) Use the Chapters at a Glance section of the book to pick those prayers or promises that most particularly meet your specific needs.

Whichever way you choose, keep this book handy. Each day presents us with new challenges. A promise you might not need today may be "just what the doctor ordered" for tomorrow.

About the Author

J. Heyward Rogers is a freelance writer in Nashville, Tennessee. His other books include *Words to Live By for Teens*, *What Really Counts for Men*, *What Really Counts for Students*, and *Take a Closer Look for Teens*.

About the General Editor

Larry Richards has written over 175 books, including theories of Christian Education, studies of the Bible and theology, devotional and enrichment writings (*The 365-day Devotional Commentary*) and study Bibles (*The Nelson NKJV Student Bible*). His *A Practical Theology of Spirituality* has been translated into twenty-six foreign languages and is used by schools in Europe, Asia, South America, Asia, and the USA. Richards has served in the United States Navy and has a B.A. in Philosophy, a Th.M. in Christian Education, and a Ph.D. in Social Psychology and Religious Education. He is General Editor of The Bible Smart Guides ™ series. He resides in Hudson, Florida.

BE SMART • BE INSPIRED •

Understanding the Bible Is Easy with These Tools

To understand God's Word you need easy-to-use study tools right where you need them—at your fingertips. The Smart Guide to the Bible™ series puts valuable resources adjacent to the text to save you both time and effort.

Every page features handy sidebars filled with icons and helpful information: cross references for additional insights, definitions of key words and concepts, brief commentaries from experts on the topic, points to ponder, evidence of God at work, the big picture of how passages fit into the context of the entire Bible, practical tips for applying biblical truths to every area of your life, and plenty of maps, charts, and illustrations. A wrap-up of each passage, combined with study questions, concludes each chapter.

These helpful tools show you what to watch for. Look them over to become familiar with them, and then turn to Chapter 1 with complete confidence: You are about to increase your knowledge of God's Word!

Study Helps

The thought-bubble icon alerts you to commentary you might find particularly thought-provoking, challenging, or encouraging. You'll want to take a moment to reflect on it and consider the implications for your life.

Don't miss this point! The exclamation-point icon draws your attention to a key point in the text and emphasizes important biblical truths and facts.

death on the cross
Colossians 1:21–22

Many see Boaz as a type of Jesus Christ. To win back what we human beings lost through sin and spiritual death, Jesus had to become human (i.e., he had to become a true kinsman), and he had to be willing to pay the penalty for our sins. With his death on the cross, Jesus paid the penalty and won freedom and eternal life for us.

The additional Bible verses add scriptural support for the passage you just read and help you better understand the underlined text. (Think of it as an instant reference resource!)

How does what you just read apply to your life? The heart icon indicates that you're about to find out! These practical tips speak to your mind, heart, body, and soul, and offer clear guidelines for living a righteous and joy-filled life, establishing priorities, maintaining healthy relationships, persevering through challenges, and more.

This icon reveals how God is truly all-knowing and all-powerful. The hourglass icon points to a specific example of the prediction of an event or the fulfillment of a prediction. See how some of what God has said would come to pass already has!

What are some of the great things God has done? The traffic-sign icon shows you how God has used miracles, special acts, promises, and covenants throughout history to draw people to him.

Does the story or event you just read about appear elsewhere in the Gospels? The cross icon points you to those instances where the same story appears in other Gospel locations—further proof of the accuracy and truth of Jesus' life, death, and resurrection.

Since God created marriage, there's no better person to turn to for advice. The double-ring icon points out biblical insights and tips for strengthening your marriage.

The Bible is filled with wisdom about raising a godly family and enjoying your spiritual family in Christ. The family icon gives you ideas for building up your home and helping your family grow close and strong.

Isle of Patmos
a small island in the Mediterranean Sea

something significant had occurred, he wrote down the substance of what he saw. This is the practice John followed when he recorded Revelation on the **Isle of Patmos.**

What does that word really mean, especially as it relates to this passage? Important, misunderstood, or infrequently used words are set in **bold type** in your text so you can immediately glance at the margin for definitions. This valuable feature lets you better understand the meaning of the entire passage without having to stop to check other references.

the big picture

Joshua

Led by Joshua, the Israelites crossed the Jordan River and invaded Canaan (see Illustration #8). In a series of military campaigns the Israelites defeated several coalition armies raised by the inhabitants of Canaan. With organized resistance put down, Joshua divided the land among the twelve Israelite

How does what you read fit in with the greater biblical story? The highlighted big picture summarizes the passage under discussion.

what others say

David Breese

Nothing is clearer in the Word of God than the fact that God wants us to understand himself and his working in the lives of men.[5]

It can be helpful to know what others say on the topic, and the highlighted quotation introduces another voice in the discussion. This resource enables you to read other opinions and perspectives.

Maps, charts, and illustrations pictorially represent ancient artifacts and show where and how stories and events took place. They enable you to better understand important empires, learn your way around villages and temples, see where major battles occurred, and follow the journeys of God's people. You'll find these graphics let you do more than study God's Word—they let you *experience* it.

Chapters at a Glance

Part Two: PROMISES OF THE BIBLE

Part One:
PRAYERS OF THE BIBLE

Introduction

We study, talk, and read about prayer. *But do we pray?* And what, exactly, is prayer? Is it begging or just talking, and does it involve God talking back to us? Do we know how to pray? Do we call out to God first, or does God stir our spirits beforehand, beckoning us to come to Him?

Is there anything new to say about prayer . . . to write about . . . even to read about?

Solomon wrote, "That which has been is what will be, that which is done is what will be done, and there is nothing new under the sun" (Ecclesiastes 1:9 NKJV).

Great men and women who have marched across spiritual history have one very important thing in common: *they prayed!* They opened their hearts, minds, and souls to the One who knows them best and yet loves them most. They listened for His voice—they yearned for it. They sought out time to spend time alone with their Creator.

Within these pages are examples of biblical prayers, spoken by some of these very people. Here you will find some things to ponder, some things to remember, and words from others who have taken the journey toward understanding the very *complex*, very *simple* act of praying.

As you read this book, it is *our prayer* that you will learn about and know how to reach the very heart of God. And in return you will hear the voice of God, feel His Spirit stir you to come to Him often, and His Son will become more real to you.

Chapter 1: The Dynamics of Prayer

Chapter Highlights:
- Developing a God-ward vision
- God's transcendence
- God's faithfulness
- God's silence

God of All

1 Kings ***8:27 But will God indeed dwell on the earth? Behold, heaven and the heaven of heavens cannot contain You. How much less this temple which I have built!*** (NKJV)

When the temple was dedicated in Jerusalem, it represented the dawn of a new era in Hebrew history: generations of Israel's children had worshipped in a **tabernacle** but now a permanent house of worship was the new center around which national life would orbit. King Solomon stood before the people of Israel and made a short speech followed by a very long prayer. It was fitting that the world's wisest king should make so little of his address to his subjects and so much of his address to God. For that perspective, really, was the whole basis of his famed wisdom—a God-ward vision.

Solomon understood that if Israel was to be the nation he prayed it would be, it wouldn't do to have a God who dwelt only in the temple. "Will God indeed dwell on the earth?" he prayed. "Behold, heaven and the heaven of heavens cannot contain You. How much less this temple which I have built!" Bear in mind, this wasn't just any "house" that Solomon had built. The temple was the most magnificent place of worship ever built, before or since. But no house, no matter how spectacular, can contain God. If God is truly God, He has an impact on every corner of the life of His people.

go to

God is too big
Psalm 11:4

tabernacle
portable sanctuary—a tent containing the ark of the covenant

God is too big to be sequestered into any one place or any one area of life or any one day. He is "before all things, and in Him all things consist" (Colossians 1:17 NKJV). It is human nature to try to create little "God preserves"—places in your life where it's safe for God to stay, places where you can go to visit Him without having to worry about Him getting out and causing problems in the rest of your life. Sunday morning can be a "God preserve." So can certain friends with whom you exchange "God-talk" even though you carefully avoid the subject with other friends. Even a morning quiet time can be a God preserve. You pray, you spend time with God, and then, having checked that off your list, you get on with your day. Solomon's prayer demonstrates a very different attitude. He viewed the house of prayer as a beachhead from which God could invade every area of His people's lives. That's how effective prayer works: rather than checking God off your list or roping off limits, it invites God to expand into your whole life.

something to ponder

what others say

R. C. Sproul

When the Bible speaks of God's justice, it usually links it to divine righteousness. God's justice is according to righteousness. There is no such thing as justice according to unrighteousness. The justice of God is always and ever an expression of His holy character.[1]

Lord, Have Mercy

Nehemiah 1:6b ***[I] confess the sins of the children of Israel, which we have sinned against You. Both my father's house and I have sinned.*** *(NKJV)*

When Nehemiah prayed for the Jewish nation—for the relief of the people who still remained in a broken Jerusalem and for the return of the people who had been scattered—it's worth noting what he didn't pray. He didn't say, "Lord, the Jewish people have suffered enough. Cut them some slack. They aren't nearly as bad as the other people around here." Instead, he was perfectly honest about the sins of the people, including his own sins and the sins of his own family. "I confess the sins of the children of Israel," he said.

There would have been no point in Nehemiah trying to convince God that the children of Israel deserved any special privileges. They had been faithless. That was why they had been carried into exile in the first place. Even in exile they hadn't demonstrated any particular faithfulness. So Nehemiah appealed instead to God's faithfulness. Even though the people had forgotten the commands that God gave through Moses, Nehemiah asked God to remember the promise He had made through Moses. God had promised He would scatter the people if they were unfaithful. He had certainly kept that promise already. But He had also promised that He would gather them back together if they turned their hearts back to Him. Nehemiah prayed God's promises back to him. "These are Your people," he said.

go to

faithless
Psalm 78:57

"Have compassion on them for that reason, even if You can't reward their behavior."

Confession is an important part of your prayer life for a couple of reasons. It cleanses your heart and conscience before God. Just as importantly, confession also serves as a reminder that you aren't there to trade your good deeds for God's blessings. You are there to throw yourself on God's mercy and grace. What better way to put yourself into position to receive God's mercy than to reflect on your own need for mercy? Nehemiah's prayer is a little unusual; when was the last time you prayed to confess someone else's sin? But as his prayer shows, even when you're **interceding** for somebody you love deeply and think the world of, you're still making your request based on God's faithfulness, not on the merit of the person you're praying for. Isn't that a relief and a comfort? God blesses because He is God. That's what He delights to do. You can pray confidently for your loved ones because you can be confident in God's mercy.

confession
the act of admitting to sins and short-comings

interceding
praying on behalf of another person rather than for yourself

holiness
the state of perfect moral integrity; holiness implies separateness from that which is not morally perfect or pure

what others say

Stephen Richter

The shame and infamy that a person should strip himself before another human person, inform on himself and deride himself, what a precious piece of the Holy Cross! Oh, if we only knew what punishment is prevented by such voluntary blushing, if only we knew how merciful it makes God when man denies and humbles himself for His honor, we would exhume the practice of confession and travel a thousand miles to confess our sins.[2]

We Bow Down

PSALM 5:7 *But as for me, I will come into Your house in the multitude of Your mercy; in fear of You I will worship toward Your holy temple.* (NKJV)

Of all God's attributes, perhaps the one spoken of most often in the Bible is His **holiness**. In the book of Revelation, it's the one attribute of God that the angels in heaven tell of constantly: "They do not rest day or night, saying: "Holy, holy, holy, Lord God Almighty, Who was and is and is to come!" (Revelation 4:8 NKJV). To say that God is holy is to say that He is set apart, separate. As human beings, our own unholiness puts up a barrier that makes the holy God inaccessible to us. It was a glimpse of God's holiness that made the prophet Isaiah collapse when he saw Him, saying, "Woe is me, for I am undone! Because I am a man of unclean lips, And I dwell in the midst of a people of unclean lips; For my eyes have seen the King, The Lord of hosts" (Isaiah 6:5 NKJV). The gap between God and human beings isn't so much the gap between mortality and immortality or finitude and infinity, but the gap between holiness and unholiness.

go to

Isaiah
Isaiah 6

mercy
the attribute of God whereby He spares His people the punishment their sins would deserve

reverence
giving God the respect He deserves

That's why David marvels, "I will come into Your house in the multitude of Your mercy." A sinner simply cannot come into the presence of holiness except by the **mercy** of the Holy One. It is a good thing that the attribute of mercy isn't far behind the attribute of holiness in God's character. The holiness that takes offense at human sin is counterbalanced by the mercy that invites the sinner in. Because of God's mercy, we can, as the apostle Paul put it, "boldly approach the throne of grace" when we pray. David makes it clear, however, that the mercy that invites the sinner into God's presence doesn't negate the holiness of God. It is still a privilege to enter the holy place. Which is why David says, "In fear of You I will worship toward your holy temple."

something to ponder

If you were invited to dine at Buckingham Palace, you would feel honored. You wouldn't assume, however, that invitation gave you the right to eat with your elbows on the table. How do you strike a balance between boldness and **reverence** when you approach the throne? Perhaps the key is to remain thankful for God's mercy, and mindful that it is *only* God's mercy and love—not your own deserving—that makes it possible for you to come into His presence.

God's Mercy

Attribute	Scripture
God's name is synonymous with mercy	Exodus 33:19
God is mercy	Psalm 116:5
God's mercy cannot be exhausted	Lamentations 3:22

what others say

C. Samuel Storms

Why are we so lax in showing mercy? Why do we withdraw from the burdens of others rather than hasten to bear them? We are often slow to be merciful because we have forgotten how pitiful and wretched we ourselves once were. We have taken God's grace for granted. Forgiveness of our sins has made us forget just how far we have fallen. I'm not suggesting that we wallow in the sinful mud of our pre-Christian past. But our readiness to be merciful in helping others frequently depends on how well we remember how little we ourselves deserve. Although we were ungodly, unappealing and unfriendly, God was not put off. Instead, it was "at just the right time, when we were still powerless, Christ died for the ungodly" (Romans 5:6). How then can we possibly be hesitant in showing great mercy to others?[3]

God's Fatherhood
Romans 8:15–17

communing
communicating intimately with; being in a state of heightened, intimate receptivity

royal
having kingly ancestry

The Prayer of a Settled Heart

PSALM 89:26b ***You are my Father, my God, and the rock of my salvation.*** *(NKJV)*

You've heard of foxhole prayers—the one-off prayer of a person who wouldn't normally pray but finds himself in a bind (a soldier in a foxhole, for example) and so sends up a desperate prayer. David's prayer in Psalm 89, you might say, is the opposite of a foxhole prayer. It arises from a settled heart, a heart that is accustomed to **communing** with God and enjoying Him. David basks in the love of his heavenly Father: "You are my Father, My God, and the rock of my salvation." This is a prayer of spiritual health. David prayed his share of emergency prayers. But he also understood that what really nourishes the soul is quiet reflection on the goodness of God.

The Bible frequently speaks of the value of remembering. "Remember now your Creator in the days of your youth" (Ecclesiastes 12:1 NKJV). "Do not forget my teaching (Proverbs 3:1 NKJV). Peter said it was his intention "to stir you up by reminding you" (2 Peter 1:13 NKJV). We human beings have a bad habit of forgetting. We get out of the foxhole and forget who it was who delivered us—forget that we had ever prayed for deliverance.

What David remembered was the fact of God's Fatherhood. It is a glorious, soul-strengthening thing to remember that the Creator of the universe is also a Father. That means you are from a **royal** bloodline. It means you can go to Him as a son or daughter. You need not approach as a slave or beggar, asking for crumbs. You need not cower in the hallways of God's courts; you can approach His throne. There you can look up and know exactly who He is to you, and who you are to Him.

fortress
2 Samuel 22:2

adulation of his own people
1 Samuel 29:5

The prayer of a settled heart is just as vital to your spiritual life as the emergency prayer. David's prayer of praise reminded him who he was in relation to God. He was royalty, a son of the King of heaven. To rest in that truth is to build your life on a solid Rock. When David said, "You are my Rock," he used the Hebrew word *tsur*, which means something strong and secure as a fortress. That's a good thing to remember in your daily prayer life: you are making your home in the fortress of God's love. And a fortress is better than a foxhole any day.

what others say

Nick Harrison

Why should our prayers ever consist of begging? Are we beggars before God, or sons and daughters? Do the children of kings beg their father for their necessities? No, from their father they receive all the benefits of the kingdom.[4]

Mindful

PSALM 144:3 ***LORD What is man, that You take knowledge of him? Or the son of man, that You are mindful of him?*** **(NKJV)**

When David penned Psalm 144, he had already enjoyed a lot of success as a king and warrior. In fact, he enjoyed the kind of remarkable success that could easily make a man boastful and prideful. He had slain a giant. He had subdued whole nations. He had enjoyed the adulation of his own people. But David had sense enough to recognize that it wasn't all his doing. "Blessed by the Lord my Rock, Who trains my hands for war, and my fingers for battle. . . . Who subdues my people under me" (Psalm 144:1, 2 NKJV). Yes, there were nations subdued under his feet, but David understood that it was God who did the subduing.

The pagan kings of David's time had a bad habit of declaring themselves to be equals of the gods anytime they enjoyed some success. But David's success humbled him: "What is man, that You take knowledge of him, or the son of man, that You are mindful of him?" A human being is like a mere breath, he goes on to say—a passing shadow. And yet God is mindful of us. That's a great word, mindful. God's mind is full of His people. With all the things He has to manage, He remains mindful of the people He loves so dearly.

David, you will remember, started out life as an unlikely candidate for greatness. When the prophet Samuel came to the house of David's father Jesse looking for the next king, Jesse forgot all about his youngest son, out in the field tending sheep. But even if David slipped his earthly father's mind, David had a heavenly Father who had him in mind all along.

go to

bless you
Jeremiah 29:11

God has a plan for you. Not, perhaps, to subdue whole nations, but He does mean to bless you, and He means to use you to grow His kingdom. When you bow your head to pray, it is your goal, of course, to fill your mind and heart with God. It's good to know that God's heart and mind are full of you too. You call out to God, perhaps unaware that God is already calling out to you. That means He always listens. And He always has an answer to your prayer, even before you pray it.

something to ponder

It's an amazing thing to think about: God has you in mind. It's humbling. It's strengthening. And it changes the way you pray.

God Hears Our Prayers

Attribute	Scripture
The Spirit of God prays for us	Romans 8:26–30
Further assurance that God hears us when we pray	1 John 5:12–15
God knows our needs before we ask	Isaiah 65:24

what others say

Lloyd John Ogilvie

Simply stated, the truth is this: prayer starts with God. It is His idea. Our desire to pray is the result of God's greater desire to talk with us. He has something to say when we feel the urge to pray. He is the initiator. Our keen desire to being and end the day with prolonged prayer is His gift.[5]

He's Not the One Who Moved

ISAIAH 64:12 ***Will You restrain Yourself because of these things, O LORD? Will You hold Your peace, and afflict us very severely?*** *(NKJV)*

Isaiah lived in one of the most critical periods in all of Israelite history. Before Isaiah was born, David's kingdom had already split into the Northern Kingdom (which kept the name Israel) and the Southern Kingdom (known as Judah). During Isaiah's lifetime,

promises
Genesis 15:5;
Genesis 26:4;
Exodus 32:13;
Galatians 3:3

things went from bad to worse in his homeland. When the Northern Kingdom plotted to overthrown King Ahaz in the south, Ahaz unwisely turned to the Assyrians for help. He would have done better to leave them out of it. The ferocious Assyrians did major damage to the Northern Kingdom. Twelve years later, the Assyrians again attacked the weakened Northern Kingdom and carried its inhabitants into exile, effectively destroying ten of the twelve tribes of Israel. Twenty years later, Isaiah saw the Southern Kingdom attacked by the Assyrians, his own hometown of Jerusalem besieged before God miraculously delivered the city.

Isaiah witnessed the end of Israel as he had known it. It appeared that God's promises to the descendants of Abraham weren't going to be fulfilled after all. It was in that context that he cried out, "Will you hold Your peace and afflict us very severely?" To Isaiah, God seemed silent. He was holding His peace at a time when His people needed to hear from Him. He seemed very far away. But Isaiah understood that the people had moved away from God, not the other way around. They had gone complacent, had turned to idols, had busied themselves with other pursuits.

There's an old story about a couple of sweethearts who sat so close to one another in the car that it was hard to tell where his shoulder ended and hers began. Their closeness grew and they eventually married and had children. One day on their way to visit the grandchildren, the wife looked across the seat and sighed. She asked, "Do you remember when I used to sit right next to you?" Her husband nodded. "Why don't we do that anymore?" she asked. He turned to her and smiled: "Honey, I'm not the one who moved."

God hears you, even when you have slipped far from Him…when you're hanging onto the passenger side rather than rubbing shoulders with the Almighty. He not only hears you, He anticipates your call. When you feel the absence of God, ask yourself, "Who moved?"

A Promise Kept

Luke 2:29–32
Lord, now You are letting Your servant depart in peace,
According to Your word;
For my eyes have seen Your salvation
Which You have prepared before the face of all peoples,

A light to bring revelation to the Gentiles,
And the glory of Your people Israel. (NKJV)

There was a man in Jerusalem named Simeon, a righteous and devout man. He knew his sacred history. He knew how the Jews had been carried off into captivity in Babylonia and Persia. He knew how they had returned to Jerusalem, to walls rebuilt by Nehemiah and a temple rebuilt by Ezra—not nearly as magnificent as the temple that had been destroyed, but a temple nonetheless. He knew that it would not be many generations before they were subdued again in their own homeland, this time by the Romans. The Romans were still in charge in Simeon's time. It galled the Jews to see those idol-worshippers swaggering in the streets of Jerusalem.

Simeon also knew that God had promised a Messiah who would deliver His people, and Simeon longed for the coming of this Messiah. The Consolation of Israel, the Messiah was called. Most Jews assumed he would be a great military leader who would lead an uprising against the Romans. The Bible doesn't say what Simeon expected the Messiah would look like, but it does say that Simeon longed for the Consolation of Israel. As a reward for his faithfulness, the Holy Spirit revealed to Simeon that he would lay eyes on the Christ before he died.

Simeon came to the temple one day—"in the Spirit," as the Bible phrases it—and there he saw a young mother and father with an eight-day-old baby boy whom they had brought to be circumcised. The baby's name was Jesus. Simeon took the boy in his arms, and he knew that God's promise had been fulfilled. He was holding the Consolation of Israel. He offered up a prayer of thanks: "Lord, now You are letting Your servant depart in peace, According to Your word; For my eyes have seen Your salvation" (Luke 2:29–30 NKJV).

God always keeps His promises. You can imagine Simeon praying God's promise back to Him year after year until finally that prayer of supplication became a prayer of praise. We're quick to ask God to do great things—and God desires that we should. But we should be just as quick to give God thanks and praise when He keeps His promises to us.

We're often quick to ask God for things and should be just as quick to thank Him when He answers and keeps His promises to us.

God had promised a Messiah
Daniel 9:25–26

God always keeps His promises
1 Kings 8:23

hallowed
set apart as holy; greatly revered

what others say

Rebecca Barlow Jordan

It is impossible for God to break His promises. He and His Word are the same.[6]

God's Promises in the Old Testament

Promises	Scripture
God's promise to Noah	Genesis 9:12–17
God's promise to Abraham	Genesis 17:4–6
God's promise to Jacob	Genesis 28:13
God's promise to Moses	Exodus 3:17
God's promise to David	2 Samuel 7:8–16

Hallowed Be His Name

LUKE 11:2 *So He said to them, "When you pray, say:*
Our Father in heaven,
Hallowed be Your name." (NKJV)

The disciples frequently observed Jesus praying. Though they did not always understand what He was saying, or even who He was exactly, they could see that He was on very intimate terms with the Father. And they knew they wanted that kind of prayer life. So one day they asked Him, just after he had finished a session of prayer, "LORD, teach us to pray, just as John [the Baptist] taught his disciples. The sample prayer that Jesus gave in response is now known as "The Lord's Prayer."

Jesus came to earth in order to bridge the gap between God and human beings. He came to draw us near to God, to reestablish the terms of intimacy that should have marked our relationship with God all along. In light of those facts, the beginning sentence of the Lord's Prayer is a little unexpected: "Our Father in heaven, hallowed be Your name." Jesus came to show that the kingdom of God is here, in our midst. But we'd better not forget that our Father is a *heavenly* Father. He took on flesh and lived among us, "mixing it up" with human beings, but His name is still **hallowed**.

In his book *To Sir, With Love*, E. R. Braithwaite tells of his first year as teacher to a rough group of high school seniors. To establish both authority and respect, he told his students, "You will address me as

'Sir.'" He showed his students a great deal of love, but he required that they use a name of honor when they spoke to him.

Our relationship with God in prayer will grow more intimate when we first understand who God is. He is holy. He is perfect. He is gracious. He is in absolute authority over us. He, first and foremost, deserves our respect. This reverence from our lips to His ears echoes, "You are my Father. I am Your child." Even as we grow closer to Him, we should never forget to Whom we speak. He is God, Creator of heaven and earth.

go to

gracious
Exodus 34:6

As soldiers become familiar with their sergeants, they often slip from calling them "Sir" to a more relaxed "Sarge." We should never grow so accustomed to the majesty and authority of God that we forget He is holy. He is merciful, full of grace, slow to anger. . . . but He is first and foremost . . . always . . . *God*.

something to ponder

what others say

R. C. Sproul

God's holiness is more than just separateness. His holiness is also transcendent. To transcend is to rise above something, to go above and beyond a certain limit. When we speak of the transcendence of God, we are talking about that sense in which God is above and beyond us. . . . Transcendence describes God in His consuming majesty, His exalted loftiness. He is an infinite cut above everything else.[7]

A Word Before I Begin

ROMANS 1:7b ***Grace to you and peace from God our Father and the Lord Jesus Christ.*** *(NKJV)*

"Dear So-and-So," we begin our letters, "I hope this finds you well and happy," or "Dear So-and-So, How are you? I am fine." Paul, on the other hand, typically began a letter with a prayer for the people to whom he wrote. More than just hoping his correspondents were doing well, he invoked the power of the living God on their behalf. "Grace to you and peace," he usually said. To put it another way, rather than just hoping his friends were doing well, Paul was doing something about it, even if he was hundreds of miles away.

The Greek word translated "grace" is *charis*. In Vine's Dictionary, the relevant definition is "The friendly disposition from which [a]

peace
Philippians 4:7

friendship
Proverbs 18:24

kindly acts proceeds, graciousness, loving-kindness, goodwill generally." It is Paul's dearest hope for his brothers and sisters in Christ that they should experience the friendship of God. And they certainly needed it. They could use peace too. "Peace" in Greek is *eirene* The eirene Paul spoke of was a kind of peace that not only did not depend on earthly peace, but could flourish even in the least peaceful of earthly situations.

Many of the churches to whom Paul addressed his letters were experiencing little enough friendship and peace from the people around them. He was often writing to persecuted churches. Paul no doubt had a heart for persecuted churches, since he himself had been one of their persecutors before his conversion. He knew how much they needed God's grace and God's peace.

You can hear Paul's heart in the greetings he writes to his correspondents. Far from being a throwaway formality, his greetings set a loving tone for everything that followed. It's as if he was saying, "If you don't even read beyond the first paragraph of this letter, I want you to know this: I am praying God's blessings on you."

Think how many human interactions consist of mechanical, meaningless words. You ask people how they're doing as a greeting, but probably all you expect to hear back is "fine." What would you do if people actually told you how they were doing? Even among good friends, conversations can sometimes skim along the surface. Think what a difference it would make if your communications with your friends were bathed in prayer the way Paul's were. It could be an earth-shattering thing if believers everywhere took seriously their responsibility to lift one another up, to make prayer the basis of each interaction with one another.

what others say

John Wesley

God does nothing but by prayer, and everything with it.[8]

Always?

2 THESSALONIANS 1:11 ***Therefore we also pray always for you that our God would count you worthy of this calling, and fulfill all the good pleasure of His goodness and the work of faith with power.*** *(NKJV)*

Paul told his friends at Thessalonica that he was "always" praying for them. In another letter to the same church, he said that they should "pray without ceasing" (1 Thessalonians 5:17 NKJV). What could Paul have meant by such language? After all, he was doing a lot besides praying. He was preaching, traveling, getting beaten and stoned, and shipwrecked—not to mention writing a third of the New Testament. He wasn't "praying without ceasing," was he?

go to

thought life
Philippians 4:8

freely
Romans 8:32

To pray "always" or "without ceasing" is to turn every thought God-ward; it is to take your interior life out of the interior and reach it out to God in prayer. Instead of thinking good thoughts about a friend or loved one, you lift that person up to God. Every worry becomes a prayer for help. Every happiness becomes a prayer of thanksgiving. Every flash of anger or lust or pride gives way to a prayer of confession and repentance.

The idea here is to stop considering your thought life to be something that happens exclusively on the inside—or even mostly on the inside. An active prayer life extends you well beyond the limits of your self. Idle wishes become active prayers, transformed into something that is an actual force for good in the world. If you get in the habit of constant prayer, you are constantly bringing the power of an omnipotent God to bear on the world you live in, on the people you spend your time with. The truth is that your thought life is going to shape the rest of your life anyway. By praying, you are taking control of that interior part of your life—and the rest of your life too.

apply it

It's a scary thing, perhaps, to consider turning every thought into a prayer. You harbor secret thoughts that you would never speak to God as a prayer. But that's the point, isn't it? As you get in the habit of praying your thoughts, you begin to train your thoughts—like a vine trained along a trellis—to turn God-ward. You are reminded of the need to repent constantly. You are reminded just how much you need the mercy and grace of a God who gives them freely. If you pray your thoughts, you will no doubt pray some things you "shouldn't" pray. That's okay too. God doesn't mind answering "no" to such prayers. He can work with that kind of honesty.

Chapter Wrap-Up

- There is a holiness gap between God and human beings. But God has bridged that gap in Christ. That means you can enter into His presence with boldness.
- As you pour your desires out to God, He hears and responds to those desires. And yet prayer isn't a matter of bending God's will to your own.
- Prayer often changes your circumstances. Prayer *always* changes you.
- Your confidence in prayer derives from God's unchanging faithfulness.

Study Questions

1. How do you reconcile the seemingly contradictory ideas that you should address God with humility on one hand and with boldness on the other?
2. How can God's silence be an answer to prayer?
3. What is the difference between a "foxhole prayer" and a "prayer of a settled heart"?
4. What is a "God preserve," and why is it dangerous?
5. What does the phrase "good intentions" mean when you're talking about God?

Chapter 2: Prayers of An Awakened Heart

Chapter Highlights:
- Honesty with God
- Using prayer
- Trusting God
- Understanding God's love

Getting Real

EXODUS 33:18 *And [Moses] said, "Please, show me Your glory." (NKJV)*

intercede
try to reconcile differences between parties

tent of meeting
another name for the tabernacle

Moses was spiritually drained. Under the best of circumstances, it would be difficult to lead a whole nation of former slaves across a desert and into a land whose location was a little vague. But the hardheaded, faithless children of Israel were making things a lot harder than they had to be. When Moses got back from receiving the Ten Commandments on Mount Sinai, he was horrified to find that his people had turned to idolatry in his forty-day absence. They were dancing like pagans around a golden calf of their own making. In his rage, Moses shattered the two stone tablets on which God had carved the commandments.

Moses eventually cooled off and realized it was his responsibility to **intercede** on the people's behalf. He entered the tent of meeting, where "the LORD used to speak to Moses face to face, just as a man speaks to his friend" (Exodus 33:11 NKJV). Then he poured his heart out to God.

In the **tent of meeting**, Moses truly "got real" with God and vented some frustrations. "You have told me to bring up this people into the promised land...but You never really specified which people," he complained. "The idol worshippers? The troublemakers? Do I have to bring them to the promised land too? You say I've found favor in Your sight," Moses continued. "If that's still true, I need more guidance. I need some signs."

God promised to be always present with Moses and the Israelites, but Moses kept pushing. He felt he needed more than a promise this time. "Show me Your glory," he asked. It was an audacious request. Nobody could see God's glory and still live. But Moses needed to experience God with an intensity that would keep him going the next time the children of Israel made him feel like quitting.

go to

God's back
Exodus 33:23

transcendence
the state of living beyond and above earthly limits. Transcendence speaks of God's separateness or otherness from human beings

God couldn't show Moses the fullness of His glory. But He did lead Moses to a crack in a cliff, and when He passed over the cliff, Moses caught a glimpse of God's back as He passed.

God doesn't always give you what you ask for. But He always gives you what you need. There's real freedom in that realization. It means you're free to get real with God, to pour your heart out. Moses' request to see God was ridiculous when you think about it. But that was okay. God honored Moses' honesty nevertheless.

what others say

Dallas Willard

People who understand and warmly want to hear God's voice will want to hear it when life is uneventful just as much as they want to hear it when they are facing trouble or big decisions. As a part of their total plan for living in harmony with God, these believers adopt the general counsels of Scriptures as the framework within which they are to know His daily graces. These people will most assuredly receive God's specific, conscious words through the inner voice to the extent that it truly is appropriate in helping them become more like Christ.[1]

Experience the Reality of God

Reality	Scripture
God knows us well	Psalm 139:4–6
To know Christ is to know God	John 14:7
To know Christ is to know truth	1 Timothy 2:4

Near to His Heart

1 KINGS 8:59a ***And may these words of mine, with which I have made supplication before the LORD, be near the LORD our God day and night. (NKJV)***

Solomon's prayer of dedication for the temple began with the acknowledgement that God is bigger than heaven and earth put together. That is to say, he focused on God's **transcendence**. But by the time that long prayer ended, Solomon's focus had shifted to a different aspect of God's character: His tender, very personal love for His people. Solomon prayed, "May these words of mine…be near the LORD our God day and night." It's an incredible thing to think about: God Almighty, the One who set the universe into motion, the God who does whatever He pleases, is pleased to have your prayers before Him day and night.

You know of people who wield tremendous power. Presidents. Captains of industry. Oprah Winfrey. But probably none of those people hold you close to their heart on a personal level. On the other hand, you have people who hold you close to their heart and always want what's best for you—people who would do anything in their power to help you. But those people aren't all-powerful. Even kings and presidents can't make it rain or heal cancer or mend a broken heart. The miracle of prayer is that you come into the presence of a God who possesses all power *and* loves you intimately and deeply. You have a personal relationship with the Author of the universe. It's not the sort of thing that is easy to get your mind around.

heart
the center of emotions and spiritual activity

The people you love are never far from your **heart**. You think of them continuously, and when you know they are going through a particularly difficult time or have a need, you tend to think of them even more so. When you pray for those people, you are lifting them up to God and saying, "This person is close to my heart; would you hold her close to Your heart too?" It is good to know that God already holds that person close to His heart. He wants what's best for you. And He is omnipotent, which means He is able to carry through with His good intentions for you. That's a source of genuine confidence as you lift prayers up to God.

something to ponder

what others say

Lukas Vischer

The consideration of Christ has shown the central importance of his intercession for the life of the church. As with prayer in the widest sense, so with intercession in particular: either is possible only "in him." Intercession offered by individual Christians or even congregations for each other is, so to speak, a priestly act performed in his name. He has established for us access to the Father. He enables us to speak to the Father. He has led us into such intimate fellowship with the Father that his physical presence is no longer required; we are able to go to the Father in his name.[2]

No Goodness but God's

Psalm 16:1 ***Preserve me, O God, for in You I put my trust. O my soul, you have said to the Lord, "You are my Lord, My goodness is nothing apart from You."*** (NKJV)

go to

a plan for his life
Psalm 40:5

no goodness other than Him
Psalm 73:25

David's life was hard in ways that might make a person wonder what's the use in being good or faithful. He was fiercely loyal to his king, but the more faithfully he served Saul, the more Saul grew to hate him. He spent most of his young manhood on the run, living in camps and caves among ruffians and misfits. For a while he had to live among the Philistines, his nation's enemies, because that was safer than where his king could get at him. He had plenty of opportunities to overthrow Saul and put himself on the throne, but he always resisted the temptation.

What made David live the way he did? One clue, perhaps, lies in a prayer of David recorded in Psalm 16:1 (NKJV): "Preserve me, God, for I take refuge in You. I said to the LORD, 'You are my LORD. I have no goodness besides You." David understood that, even though he lacked the things he needed to live what the world might call "the good life," he had a very good life. He had a God who would always give him everything he needed. More than that, he had a God who had a plan for his life. And that plan would unfold in God's time, not David's. To jump the gun, to try to help God fulfill His promises, would only spoil the life of contentment he already led.

He might have prayed, "After all the effort I've put into being faithful, You could at least give me some peace." But he didn't. He learned what he was supposed to learn from his difficult situation: there's no counting on the things of the world to bring genuine happiness. Only God does that. We have no goodness other than Him.

When things don't go according to your plan, it's tempting to offer up prayers of complaint and questioning. David, as a matter of fact, prayed his share of those, as you can see by reading the Psalms. And it's better, by the way, to offer up a prayer of complaint than not to pray at all. But ultimately, you want to arrive where David arrived in Psalm 16, in an uncertain world, where unexpected troubles come and long-planned security may never arrive, God is the only good of which you can be sure.

something to ponder

When the world threatens you, your escape plan may or may not work, but God will always preserve you.

what others say

Billy Graham

There is no way to describe God. John could only describe the response to God...Even as he stood before Him, God remained a mystery to John and to us—the Mystery who was and is and will always be. We are the children of a great and wonderful God who even now sits in power accomplishing His purposes in His creation.[3]

exuberance
unrestrained enthusiasm or joy

anointed
to have placed oil on another's head as a sign of sanctification—in this case, as a sign that David is God's choice for Israel's king

The Good Work Begun in You

PSALM 18:28
For you will light my lamp;
The LORD my God will enlighten my darkness. (NKJV)

Psalm 18 actually appears twice in the Bible. It is a song of thanks that David offered up to God when he had at last been delivered from all his enemies and he could settle down to enjoy his kingdom. The song first appears near the end of Second Samuel, after David's last war with the Philistines was over. It was later collected in the book of Psalms. "For You will light my lamp; The LORD my God will enlighten my darkness. For by You I can run against a troop. By my God I can leap over a wall" (Psalm 18:28–29 NKJV).

Surely it was one of the great moments of David's life, as exhilarating as the day, decades earlier, when he slew a giant with a stone from a sling. His years and years of struggle were over. Or, in any case those particular struggles that had defined his life—with Saul, with the Philistines—were over. David's mind and heart turned immediately to the God to whom he owed his deliverance. His joy translated into a prayer of praise. His **exuberance**, in fact, led to a little joyful exaggeration. Could David actually leap over a wall? He felt as if he could do anything.

The joy David felt grew from his finally fulfilling the role God had for him. It had been decades since Samuel the prophet had **anointed** David as king. He had spent most of his life in that in-between phase, knowing he was destined to be king, but not yet enjoying the benefits of kingship. Now, at last, the promise had become a reality, and David couldn't contain his joy.

God calls you to a specific purpose, and He will keep working on you until you fulfill that purpose. As Paul said, you can be confident "that He who has begun a good work in you will complete it until the day of Christ Jesus" (Philippians 1:6 NKJV). God will provide for your needs, and He will raise you to the heights He has in mind for you. As you pray now, longing for the fulfillment of God's purpose for your life, know that your hope will one day give way to rejoicing, even exuberance of the faithfulness of the God who has promised to perfect His work in you. He will be your lamp along the dark way, and will give you strength to leap over every wall that stands in the way of your purpose.

apply it

People Called for a Specific Purpose

Person and Purpose	Scripture
Moses—to lead the Hebrews out of Egypt	Exodus 3:10
Joshua—to lead the Hebrews into the Promised Land	Joshua 1:2
Samson—to deliver the Israelites from their Philistine oppressors	Judges 13:5
Jonah—to preach repentance to the Ninevites	Jonah 1:2
Paul—to preach Christ to the Gentiles	Acts 9:15

what others say

Nick Harrison

When we walk in the Holy Spirit, we are led by God. He makes us into the kinds of people and personalities He wants us to be. He gives Himself as the flame for the candle.[4]

Cedar Houses

PSALM 30:2
O LORD my God, I cried out to You,
And You healed me. *(NKJV)*

When David dedicated his great house of cedar, he prayed a prayer of praise that comes down to us as Psalm 30. Secure in a strong and sturdy palace, he remembered the times past when he didn't even have a roof over his head and lived in constant danger of his enemies. "I will extol You, O LORD," he prayed, "for You have lifted me up" (Psalm 30:1 NKJV). He had indeed been lifted up. His feet had been placed on a foundation that was even more secure and sure than the one his palace sat on.

In his house of cedar, David had a retreat where he could rest and rejuvenate body and soul. He remembered, however, that true rest for the soul comes from quiet times of prayer. "LORD my God, I cried out to You, and You healed me" (Psalm 30:2 NKJV). As thankful as David was for his house of cedar, he realized that his true **refuge** was God. His soul-healing came from times of quiet with his Father.

You sustain a lot of dings and bruises in the course of everyday life. Little indignities chip away at your sense of self. Temptations pull you toward the ditches. Sheer busy-ness makes you lose your perspective on what really matters. Prayer is a kind of daily maintenance, healing what gets broken in the course of life's events, giving you a firm foundation on which to stand when life's storms come.

go to

life's storms
Matthew 7:24–27

refuge
protection or shelter, as from danger or hardship

idolatry
the worship of idols or false gods

You have "cedar houses" of your own—earthly structures that promise rest and healing. Houses. Jobs. Social networks. Those are all good things, blessings from God. He can and does use them to give you refuge. The problem with those "cedar houses," however, is that they ask you to place your trust in them. It's not always easy to maintain your focus on the Giver rather than on His gifts. Sometimes you spend so much time maintaining your cedar houses that you don't find time for the soul-maintenance of daily prayer.

something to ponder

Make time for the daily maintenance that is an active prayer life. That requires that you rearrange your schedule around a quiet time with God. It's that important. And while you're at it, get in the habit of praying in the car. Turn off the radio. What daily, mindless chores can you use instead as prayer time? Redeem that time. In the end, true refuge is to be found only in your relationship with God.

I Say, "Yes"

PSALM 138:1–2
I will praise You with my whole heart;
Before the gods I will sing praises to You.
I will worship toward Your holy temple,
Send praise Your name
For Your lovingkindness and Your truth;
For You have magnified Your word above all Your name.
(NKJV)

"Before the gods I will sing praises to you." In King David's world, there was nothing subtle about the temptation to **idolatry**. Throughout their history, the Israelites had been prone to wander from the unseen God of Abraham and follow the gods of their

above all others
Exodus 20:3

neighbors. They were petty gods, often cruel gods, but at least they were gods you could see. There were statues to bow down to, even statues you could carry around with you. Just like regular people, the pagan gods had specific jobs—gods of fertility, gods of war, nature gods. Yahweh was invisible, mysterious, and awe-inspiring. There was nothing very mysterious about the heathen gods.

The problem, of course, was that the heathen gods weren't real. They were the creations of human beings, not the other way around. As David knew, the worship of the true God was a matter of conforming himself to the truth of God, however invisible and mysterious that God might be, not creating a new god in his own image.

Nowadays, our false gods don't usually call themselves gods. And yet there is no shortage of idols that put themselves before God in our attentions—careers, comfort, convenience, material things, relationships, petty jealousies, anger, security, the pursuit of pleasure. It's quite natural to put any one of those things before God. There's nothing mysterious about the pursuit of self-interest, for example. But choosing to follow God at the expense of your evident self-interest? Not everybody is going to understand that. But that's what it means to say, "Before all gods I will praise You."

Cassie Bernall has become perhaps the most well-known victim of the 1999 Columbine school shootings. According to eyewitnesses, her killers pointed a gun at her and asked if she believed in God. "Yes," she answered, refusing to put even the god of self-preservation ahead of the true God. It was the last word she ever spoke.

David made a decision to proclaim his love for God before all others. Cassie Bernall made that same decision when she said "yes." Her fear of death was squashed by her fierce love for the God of eternity. Did you know that every day you face the same God vs. gods decisions? How you conduct yourself before your family, friends, coworkers, strangers, etc., is based on a decision to worship God. Saying yes to God above all others is your witness to the masses. It can change eternity.

Speechless

ISAIAH **38:15a–16**
What shall I say?...
O Lord, by these things men live;

And in all these things is the life of my spirit;
So You will restore me and make me live." (NKJV)

Hezekiah was one of the "good kings" of Judah in an era when most of Judah's kings were scoundrels and weaklings. He led his people away from idolatry; thanks to his prayerful leadership, God delivered Judah from invading Assyrians. So when he got sick, he must have been a little surprised at the news Isaiah brought to his sickbed: Hezekiah needed to get his house in order, because he was not going to survive this sickness.

go to

fifteen extra years of life
Isaiah 38:5

fancy language
Matthew 6:7

Hezekiah was a man of prayer, and his first reaction was to cry out to God to spare him. "Remember how I have walked before You with truth and with a whole heart," he pleaded. God heard his prayer, and Hezekiah recovered. Isaiah returned to the king and told him that God had granted him fifteen extra years of life.

Hezekiah was so overjoyed at the news that he lifted up a prayer of thanksgiving, which is recorded in Isaiah 38:10–20. Right in the middle of the prayer, verse 15, Hezekiah exclaimed, "What shall I say?" He's overwhelmed by the goodness and mercy of God. "What shall I say?" Perhaps it's the most honest prayer of praise you can offer. We human beings aren't really in a position to articulate the gratitude we owe to God. Yet God delights to hear our praise just as surely as a parent delights in the inarticulate babbling of a happy baby.

apply it

As Paul told the Romans, "The Spirit also helps in our weaknesses. For we do not know what we should pray for as we ought, but the Spirit Himself makes intercession for us with groanings which cannot be uttered" (Romans 8:26 NKJV). What a huge comfort! You don't know what to say to God? Pray anyway. The Spirit is there to hear and to "translate." God is not particularly impressed with fancy language anyway. He looks at the heart. And the heart that is full of praise may not be able to articulate that praise. The heart that is broken and most in need of help may not be able to articulate its need. If all you can do is groan to God, the Spirit intercedes with even deeper groans.

King Hezekiah was a man of prayer; he had plenty of practice. Even he didn't always know what to pray. Still, that didn't stop him from praying.

go to

Elisha and his servant
2 Kings 6:17

Prayers When People Didn't Know What to Say

The Person and the Prayer	Scripture
Job: "What shall I answer You?"	Job 40:4 (NKJV)
David: "I have become dumb."	Psalm 39:9 (NKJV)
Hezekiah: "What can I say?"	Isaiah 38:15 (NKJV)
The angels in heaven: their constant praise was interrupted by a half-hour's silence when the seventh seal is broken.	Revelation 8:1 (NKJV)

what others say

Janet Holm McHenry

I don't remember the day or the circumstance when I found myself in this type of silent, adoring prayer, but I do remember feeling so much love for God and His love for me that I simply ran out of words. It seemed as though everything I had—my limbs, my eyes, my pores even—were being spent worshiping the Lord who had created me and died for me. In my silent adoration I find true contentment and intimacy with my Savior...my sight has turned from outward to upward, overwhelmed by the knowledge that God *wants* to be with me.[5]

Open Eyes

EPHESIANS **1:18–20** ***[I pray] the eyes of your understanding being enlightened; that you may know what is the hope of His calling, what are the riches of the glory of His inheritance in the saints, and what is the exceeding greatness of His power toward us who believe, according to the working of His mighty power which He worked in Christ when He raised Him from the dead and seated Him at His right hand in the heavenly places. (NKJV)***

In the story of Elisha and his servant, Elisha prayed that God would open the eyes of his servant so he could see things in the spiritual realm rather than just in the earthly realm. The servant had awakened in the morning to see an enemy army surrounding the city. He was terrified. But when Elisha prayed for him, the servant was suddenly able to see the whole picture: yes, they were surrounded by soldiers, but the soldiers were surrounded by angels of God! The servant's situation hadn't actually changed; the angels had been there all along. But the fact that he could see them changed everything.

Paul's prayer for the Ephesians is very similar to Elisha's prayer for his servant. It is his desire that their eyes will be opened so that they can see the spiritual realities all around them. Which is to say, Paul isn't praying here that anything will change about the Ephesians' situation. In verse 18 he prays that they will have the "hope of [God's] calling"—eyes to see that the future holds the fulfillment of God's unshakeable promises. In verse 19 he moves from a future vision to a vision for the present. He prays that his brothers and sisters in Ephesus will see "the exceeding power of His greatness toward us who believe." Paul goes on to pray that the Ephesians will have an eye to that which has already been accomplished in the past—to be able to see and understand "the working of His mighty power which He worked in Christ when He raised Him from the dead and seated Him at His right hand in the heavenly places."

eyes to see them
Acts 26:18

The hope and vision to which Paul called the Ephesians had nothing to do with wishful thinking. It was all about seeing spiritual realities based in the fact of what God had already done on behalf of His people. With his own eyes, Paul had *seen* both the spiritual and physical manifestations of the power of God, and he wanted those he loved (among them the Ephesians) to "see" with their hearts rather than with their eyes. He was saying, "I want you to *get this*! I want you to *know that you know that you know* that you have eternal life because of the resurrection power of Jesus." Those same realities are true for you too. May God grant you eyes to see them.

To Know There Is No Other

EPHESIANS 3:16–19 ***[I pray] that He would grant you, according to the riches of His glory, to be strengthened with might through His Spirit in the inner man, that Christ may dwell in your hearts through faith; that you, being rooted and grounded in love, may be able to comprehend with all the saints what is the width and length and depth and height—to know the love of Christ which passes knowledge; that you may be filled with all the fullness of God. (NKJV)***

Ephesus wasn't the friendliest place for Christians. It was the site of the great temple of Diana (also known as Artemis), the goddess of the hunt, and her worshippers came from all over the known world to worship there. The Diana trade was big business for the Ephesians. The town's craftsmen sold Diana trinkets as fast as they could make them. So the Ephesians didn't appreciate anyone suggesting that Diana was a false god. It couldn't be good for business.

When Paul visited Ephesus, he chose not to keep his mouth shut. He did miracles, he baptized people, and he preached that there was no other god but God. The idol makers didn't appreciate him at all. In fact, they stirred up a riot with the intent of killing Paul, but he narrowly escaped.

Paul visited Ephesus
Acts 19:21–40

a rebuttal to the values of the world
1 Thessalonians 2:2

Surely Paul was thinking about the hostility he experienced in Ephesus when he wrote his letter to the Christians who still remained in that pagan city. He prayed that they would be spiritually strong and grounded in love, understanding Christ in all His fullness. Surrounded by so much falsehood, they needed the truth of Christ. Surrounded by so much hatred, they needed the love of Christ just to keep from being crushed under its weight.

You, too, live in a culture that is hostile to the values of Christ. Sure, there's plenty of talk about God. Most people don't think twice if you mention going to church on Sunday. Nobody's opposed to "Judeo-Christian ethics." But try living out Jesus' command to "turn the other cheek." Try living out your values when they conflict with your "self-interest." People look at you like you're crazy. Try living out your values when they conflict with somebody else's convenience. You might find you have a riot on your hands.

If you're following hard after God, your life will be a rebuttal to the values of the world around you—its self-indulgence, its self-reliance, its self-interest . . . self, self, self! Self is the great idol of our age—of the Ephesians' age too, when you think about it; the idol makers rioted because Paul was messing with their self-interest, not so much because he was messing with Diana.

That's why, like the Ephesians, you need to know the love of Christ—its width and length and depth and height. Otherwise, you're liable to forget who you are, and to Whom you belong.

what others say

John Gill

The love of Christ to His own, to His church and people, is special and peculiar; free and Sovereign; as early as His Father's love, and is durable and unchangeable; the greatest love that ever was heard of; it is matchless and unparalleled; it is exceeding strong and affectionate, and is wonderful and surprising.[6]

Overflow

1 THESSALONIANS 3:12 ***May the Lord make your love increase and overflow for each other and for everyone else, just as ours does for you And may the Lord make you increase and abound in love to one another and to all, just as we do to you.*** *(NKJV)*

your love for other people grows
1 John 4:19–21

Gnosticism
a body of heresies faced by the early church. Gnostic beliefs were broad and various, but they focused on a dualism that treated the flesh as bad and the spirit as good

Paul's love for his friends in Thessalonica shines though clearly in his First Epistle to the Thessalonians. They had their problems, but there's none of the scolding you sometimes find in Paul's letters to other churches. In First Thessalonians, Paul's strategy is to fill his readers so full of Christ that there's no room left for legalism or **Gnosticism** or any other –ism that might get them off track. His prayer in 1 Thessalonians 3 seems to derive from that same impulse. May you be so full of Christ's love, he prays, that it spills out all over the place.

Pour water into a glass until it is half full and then set it on a table. Watch it carefully. What does it do? It just sits there.

Take that same glass back to the kitchen sink and fill it almost to the rim of the glass. Turn off the faucet, take a step back, and look at it again. Stare as long as you want. Still, it just sits there.

But if you put the glass under the faucet and let it run, the water soon spills over the top of the glass and out into the sink and down the drain. From there it goes down the pipes, through the city water system, out into the river, and finally to the ocean, its ultimate home.

This is what happens when the love of Christ dwells within you and you allow that love to grow, when you commit yourself to grow daily in prayer and therefore closer and closer to God. As you experience the love of God, your love for Him grows, and your love for other people grows. Soon you can't hold it inside any longer. The result is *overflow*. Like the water in the glass, spilling out and pooling in the sink, flowing toward greater bodies of water, the love of God will reach a hurting world. Sometimes that love is required to go to undesirable places—the sewers of the world—but in the end it finds its way home to the great ocean depths of God's love.

When was the last time you prayed to the point of overflow? Prayer is the perfect opportunity to begin filling up and spilling over with the love of Christ. It is the place where God will call that love to go to places you never dreamed possible. You are the vessel by which the Living Water can flow to a parched and thirsty world.

sanctification
the process by which a Christian, having been saved, comes to look more and more like Christ in everyday holiness

justification
God's act of pardoning all the sins of those who believe in Christ, in which he accepts and treats them as righteous

Brotherly Love

Reality	Scripture
Brotherly love above self-love	Romans 12:10
Deep brotherly love is required	1 Peter 1:22
Brotherly love is next to godliness	2 Peter 1:5–7

Sanctified

1 THESSALONIANS 5:23 ***Now may the God of peace Himself sanctify you completely; and may your whole spirit, soul, and body be preserved blameless at the coming of our Lord Jesus Christ.*** *(NKJV)*

When he prayed for the **sanctification** of the Thessalonians, Paul chose an interesting epithet for God: "May the God of Peace Himself sanctify you (emphasis added). . . ." Sanctification is an uphill battle. You're trying to do better, be more righteous, but that old flesh of yours keeps dragging you down. Paul's prayer, however, is a reminder that sanctification is a work of God—the God of peace. That's not to say, of course, that sanctification isn't a struggle, nor is it to say that God does all the work. God does all the work of salvation, but the hard work of displaying more and more practical holiness each day is a joint venture between God and human beings.

Still, in all the struggle, the God with whom you are partnering is the God of peace. Sometimes God uses turmoil to increase your holiness. Still He's a God of peace. You may feel that you're at war with your old flesh and that your old flesh is at war with God. Even so, He is the God of peace.

key point

Here's the thing to remember about sanctification: it is a matter of becoming what you have already become. If you are in Christ, it's as if you are clothed in Him. When God looks at you, He sees the beauty and perfection of Christ. The theological term for that is **justification**. God looks at you just as if you had never done anything wrong.

But as you know, you have done wrong, you still do wrong, and you're going to do wrong tomorrow. That's where sanctification comes in. Sanctification is the process by which your daily life begins to look more and more like the perfection God sees in you. Justification happens all at once. Sanctification is a long, slow process.

Sure, sanctification is hard. But here's the good news. First, you're not in it alone. Sanctification is God's work too, and just as Paul prayed for the sanctification of the Thessalonians, God hears your prayers for sanctification. Second, the result is absolutely certain. The long, slow process will end in your perfection, no matter how things look today. One of these days you will be with Jesus, and you'll be like Him because you'll see Him as He is. And there, in the presence of the God of peace, you'll experience peace at last.

God's desire is to pour His peace and sanctification into our lives. Pray it for yourself. Pray if for others.

go to

see Him as He is
1 John 3:2

something to ponder

what others say

Matthew Henry

Where the good work of grace is begun, it shall be carried on, be protected and preserved; and all those who are sanctified in Christ Jesus shall be preserved to the coming of our Lord Jesus Christ.[7]

Chapter Wrap-Up

- Sometimes the value of prayer isn't in changing your situation, but in giving you the eyes to see the spiritual realities that have been there all along.
- Though few people literally bow down to idols, idolatry is as rampant now as it ever was. A robust prayer life guards you from idolatry.
- "Overflow" is an important concept when it comes to living a godly life. Daily prayer fills you with the things of God so that the things of God spill out of you.
- Sometimes we are tempted to put our trust in God's gifts rather than in God Himself.

Study Questions

1. Why is speechlessness an acceptable form of prayer?
2. David prayed, "All my goodness is in You." What did he mean by that?
3. What role does prayer play in the sanctification process?
4. How does intercessory prayer shape your relationships with the people you pray for?
5. What did Paul mean when he prayed that the eyes of the Ephesians' understanding might be opened?

Chapter 3: Prayers of Praise

Chapter Highlights:
- Trusting God's guidance
- Experiencing God
- Turning to God
- True healing

No One Better Than God

EXODUS 15:11
Who is like You, O LORD, among the gods?
Who is like You, glorious in holiness,
Fearful in praises, doing wonders? (NKJV)

After all the Hebrews had been through—generations of slavery under Pharaoh, the hope kindled by Moses' leadership, the Ten Plagues, the mad dash for freedom—it appeared the jig was up. For a while they thought Pharaoh, laid low by the plagues, would let them go without a fight. But then, before they had even made it as far as the Red Sea, they saw Pharaoh's army coming up behind them. Caught between an advancing army on one side and a sea on the other, they appeared to be doomed. There was nothing to do but pray, and that's what they did, fervently.

Then, to the Hebrews' amazement, the sea split apart when Moses stretched out his hand. They were able to walk to the other side on dry land. What's more, when Pharaoh's army pursued, the towering walls of water collapsed and drowned them.

On the far side of the sea, Moses sang a song of flabbergasted praise to his Deliverer: "Who is like You, O LORD, among the gods? Who is like You, glorious in holiness, Fearful in praises, doing wonders?" (Exodus 15:11 NKJV).

A young mother sat in the hospital's surgical waiting room as physicians operated on her badly injured daughter. Family members sat nearby, whispering about the hopelessness they'd heard in the voice of the chief surgeon before he'd gone into the operating room to scrub up. One or two talked openly about the marvel of medical science and the competency of the hospital staff. But the mother sat quietly, hands folded in her lap, eyes closed. She alone prayed to God asking Him to guide the hands of the surgeons…to work a miracle in her daughter in the presence of her unbelieving family. Hours passed. When the chief surgeon emerged from behind ominous double doors, he bore good news. Her daughter would be just fine.

go to

delights
Psalm 18:19

key point

On the other side of her daughter's deliverance, her mother whispered a prayer of praise: "Who is like You, O LORD, among the gods? Who is like You, glorious in holiness, Fearful in praises, doing wonders?" (Exodus 15:11 NKJV).

God still works miracles. He delights to do it. That's worth remembering. When life's problems seem insurmountable, it's easy to lose faith in God, or to call upon the reliability of human beings. But there's no one like God when it comes to problem solving. No earthly successes, drugs, or pagan beliefs can measure up to His provision and goodness. Never forget or be afraid to ask for His help.

what others say

Warren Myers

God honors prayer...He longs to demonstrate His power in the tremendous trials that jar us like thunder, and in the pinprick troubles that annoy us. Giant needs are never too great for His power; dwarf-sized ones never too small for His love.[1]

Honoring God for His Gifts

2 SAMUEL 7:18 ***Then King David went in and sat before the LORD; and he said: "Who am I, O Lord GOD? And what is my house, that You have brought me this far?"*** *(NKJV)*

David's palace was complete, and in his gratitude he wanted to build a house for God. Before long, the prophet came back with God's response to David's gesture. "No," God said, "you won't build Me a house. Instead, I'll build your house." God promised that He would bless David with a name that would be great throughout history, a son whom God would have a special love for, peace in the land, and a dynasty that would never end (a prophecy of the lineage of the Messiah). David was stunned . . . so much so he went into the temple and sat.

In ancient times to "sit" in worship typically meant upon one's heels. In other words, David kneeled in honor and reverence before God, his prayer full of awe and affection toward Him. Lifting up his voice in exaltation, David told God of the wonder of it all. He could not imagine anything he had done to deserve such a gift . . . such a heritage.

It showed a becoming humility, David's acknowledgement of the fact that he had done nothing to deserve such an honor. His subjects might have disagreed. After all, David had slain a giant. He had delivered the Israelites from the Philistines numerous times. He had shown incredible loyalty to Saul when Saul had long since stopped showing any loyalty to him. If David didn't deserve the honor of God, who on earth did?

grace
a favor bestowed by one who need not do so. Gifts freely given by God as a result of His kindness, not as the result of anyone's deserving

adoration
the act of honoring with admiration and devotion

That's just the point. Nobody deserves such honor as that bestowed by the God who knows even the number of hairs on your head. It's all about **grace**, not deserving—what God gives freely, not what we earn for ourselves. Even such good deeds as David's don't merit the amazing grace that God pours out on His people. For even those good deeds were the gift of God too, "prepared beforehand that [he] should walk in them" (Ephesians 2:10 NKJV).

The only response to the overwhelming blessings that God bestows is that of David: "Who am I that you have brought me this far?"

something to ponder

Perhaps we haven't been gifted with the type of legacy God gave to David, but that which God *has* given us should be enough to drop us to our knees in **adoration**. One of the first things we should do in our daily prayers is to humbly lift God in praise for all He has done, all He is doing, and all He will do for us and for those we love so dearly.

what others say

Alan C. Mermann, MD, M. Div.

Prayer is a process by which I review who I am, and what I have, what I do. This process confirms for me . . . that all I am and have—all that defines me to myself and to others—is a gift of God.[2]

David Is Blessed by God

Triumphs	Scripture
Victory over Goliath	1 Samuel 17:1–58
Victory over 200 Philistines to win the hand of Saul's daughter Michal	1 Samuel 18:20–30
Ascension to the throne of Israel	2 Samuel 2:1–7
Conquest of Jerusalem to make it the "City of David"	2 Samuel 5:6–10

go to

true Sovereign
Psalm 103:19

How Great Thou Art!

2 SAMUEL 7:22 ***Therefore You are great, O Lord GOD. For there is none like You, nor is there any God besides You, according to all that we have heard with our ears.*** **(NKJV)**

In 1885, a young Swedish preacher named Carl Boberg was walking home from church when he was suddenly caught in a thunderstorm. The power of the storm made a tremendous impression on Boberg, and when he made it home, he wrote out a prayer of praise to the God who made the thunder. That prayer became one of the most popular hymns of the last hundred years.

O Lord my God! When I in awesome wonder
Consider all the worlds thy hands have made,
I see the stars, I hear the rolling thunder
Thy power throughout the universe displayed.
Then sings my soul, my Savior God to thee;
How great thou art, how great thou art!

The Reverend Boberg, of course, wrote the words in Swedish. "O store Gud! O store Gud!" Years later, he heard his poem being sung to an old Swedish tune. An Englishman named Stuart Hine heard the hymn being sung in the Carpathian area of Russia where he and his wife were serving as missionaries. One day when caught in a rainstorm, Hine remembered the song and later wrote the English version. It was made popular when it was sung in the late 1950s and early 1960s by George Beverly Shea as part of evangelist Billy Graham's crusades.

Isn't it exciting to know what David and so many before and after him have known? *There is no god like our God! He is great! He is worthy to be praised!* David had ample opportunity to see the greatness of God. David's own greatness, in fact, was merely a reflection of God's greatness. So at those moments in his life when he experienced the greatest triumph, he was always faithful to praise God. When he was raised to the position of king, he didn't say, "How great am I!" but rather "You are great, O Lord GOD." David was sovereign over all Israel. But he knew who the true Sovereign was. He knew genuine greatness when he saw it.

something to ponder

God reveals Himself to His children in a variety of different ways. For David, it was hearing of the inheritance God had in store for his descendants. For Boberg and Hine, it was during storms. How has

God revealed His awesome sovereignty to you? How has He shown you, specifically, that there is no other god besides Him?

go to

no other god
Exodus 18:11; 1 Chronicles 16:25; Psalm 97:9

God didn't allow it
1 Chronicles 22:6–10

praise
an exuberant expression of worship

what others say

C. Samuel Storms

> In God alone are perfect order, harmony, magnitude, integrity, proportion and brilliance. In Himself, independent of any benefactor blessing of His which we might enjoy, God is beautiful. There are no random brush strokes in the Divine Being; no clash of colors or dissonant sounds. God is aesthetically exquisite. He is, if I may so speak, the one impeccable painting on display in His works and Word, to be observed and adored.[3]

Eternal Praise

1 CHRONICLES 29:11
Yours, O LORD, is the greatness,
The power and the glory,
The victory and the majesty;
For all that is in heaven and in earth is Yours;
Yours is the kingdom, O LORD,
And You are exalted as head over all. (NKJV)

David had hoped to build a great temple to God, but God didn't allow it. David had been a man of war for too long. God did many things through David and had received many an offering of thanks from him. But that particular offering—the offering of a beautiful temple—would be for somebody without blood on his hands. David was disappointed, but he learned that even though he wouldn't be allowed to build the temple, his son Solomon would be, and that was the next-best thing. He began gathering materials against the day when Solomon would start building. Then he led the people in a prayer dedicating the generous offerings they had given.

"Yours, O LORD, is the greatness and the power and the glory, the victory and the majesty; for all that is in heaven and in earth is Yours" (1 Chronicles 29:11 NKJV). David's declaration of **praise** is an example to anyone wanting to extend an offering of love to God. David openly prays from his heart, without reservation or fear. It's almost as if he will burst if the praises don't rise from the very depths of his soul and spill from his mouth. There is a sense of shouting

go to

at God's orders
1 Chronicles 22:8

adoration
the act of honoring with admiration and devotion

here, as though he had rushed to the top of a very high mountain, looked out over the lush hills and valleys of Israel and declared the eternal truths of God's awesomeness.

The truth of it is, David was drawing some of his last breaths. He was old and feeble. He had seen the better part of his life and had little time left before seeing God face to face. Yet in spite of his frailty, he called out a prayer of praise and **adoration**. His prayer is reverent, acknowledging God for who He is and all He has done and ever will do. It acknowledges God properly as the Creator, the one with all authority, as being beautiful and grand, and as being the King of the king's life. During his forty years as sovereign over Israel, David had surely seen some magnificent things, but nothing compared to the majesty of God.

something to ponder

Nothing or no one is greater, more wonderful, more glorious, more powerful or more majestic than God. Have you told Him just how much you adore Him lately?

what others say

Frances J. Roberts

Behold, you are in the hollow of My hand. Yes, in the moment that you lift your voice to cry out to Me, and when you raise your voice to praise and magnify My Name, *then* shall My glory gather you up. Yes, I shall wrap you in the garments of joy, and My presence shall be your great reward.[4]

For the Glory of the Lord

2 CHRONICLES 5:13c
For He is good,
For His mercy endures forever. *(NKJV)*

Pure gold and heavy bronze. Shiny silver, rich draperies, and tapestries. Seven and a half years of intense labor. These are but a few of the ingredients that went into the building of King Solomon's temple, once located at the present site of the Temple Mount in modern Jerusalem.

Solomon's father, King David, had drawn the blueprints to perfection, but had yielded the building of it (at God's orders) to his son. When it had been completed, Solomon called the elders of Israel to bring the ark of the covenant from Zion to Jerusalem. The

Ark, an oblong box made of acacia wood and covered within and without in pure gold, was the place where God's presence dwelled.

At Solomon's command, the ark was brought to the new temple and placed in the Most Holy Place between the wings of the gold cherubim by the priests. They withdrew, and having done so, the Levites began to offer up prayers of praise in the form of music and song. "He is good; His love endures forever."

As magnificent as that sounds, it's what happened next that should awe us the most. The temple, Scripture tells us, was so filled with God's glory that the priests couldn't complete their duties. They were simply unable to move.

"His love endures forever." In that massive, exquisite building, high on a hill, those celebrating priests may have thought that the temple, too, would last forever. It didn't. Solomon's temple was destroyed in 556 BC, rebuilt by Zerubbabel and later Herod, then destroyed for good in AD 70. But although those buildings didn't endure forever, God's love does. And God's temple, His dwelling place, is no longer in a building of stone and mortar. God's temple is His people! Your body is the temple of the Holy Spirit. As Peter phrased it, all believers together make up God's abode: "You also, as living stones, are being built up a spiritual house, a holy priesthood to offer up spiritual sacrifices" (1 Peter 2:5 NKJV). You are temple and priest both. The presence of God dwells with you, just as it dwelled in the ark of the covenant. It's enough to make you stop everything and stand in awe.

God's love endures forever, and you are living proof.

go to

temple of the Holy Spirit
Corinthians 6:19

what others say

Leon Morris

Each Christian is a *temple* in which God dwells. . . . The word is *naos*, referring to the sacred shrine, the sanctuary, not *hieron*, which includes the entire precincts. This gives a dignity to the whole of life, such as nothing else could do. Wherever we go we are the bearers of the Holy Ghost, the temples in which it pleases God to dwell. This must rule out all such conduct as is not appropriate to the temple of God. . . . Nothing that would be amiss in God's temple is seemly in the body of the child of God.[5]

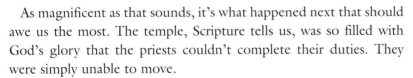

abundance
John 10:10

command that you praise Him
1 Thessalonians 5:18

One of Those Praise Days

Psalm 119:171
My lips shall utter praise,
For You teach me Your statutes. *(NKJV)*

You've had "one of those days." You open your eyes first thing to discover that the alarm clock had been set for p.m. rather than a.m. The toast burned rather than turning golden brown. You slipped behind the wheel of your car to discover you were low on gas—too low, in fact, to make it to your destination. Days like that start off wrong and end up worse. And they typically show up at the worst possible time, causing a day of aggravation, irrational thoughts, and negative words that spew from lips created to do otherwise. On days like that, negativity seems to be the natural overflow.

In Psalm 119, the psalmist talks about a very different kind of overflow—the overflow of praise from the lips of a person who has been filled with the word of God. Psalm 119 is unusual insofar as it focuses on the word of God—His decrees and laws—rather than the mighty acts of God, as so many of the Psalms do. And the more the psalmist filled himself with God's Word, the more he was inclined to overflow with praise for the God whose word he loved.

This idea of overflowing is all about abundance—of God giving more than you can possibly take in. There will be bad days; that's just a fact of life in a fallen world. But when you put yourself in a position to be filled and overfilled with the word of God, you'll react differently. When your days start out bad only to go downhill, or even when they begin in a happy mode, but take a sudden turn, praise and thanksgiving should not only be spoken from your lips, it should spill out. Sometimes you can only learn that principle when God taps you on the shoulder in a moment of discipline. To praise rather than spew is a difficult lesson to learn, but one with awesome results for both the giver and the Receiver.

It's natural to bemoan and complain over a hard day rather than to lift up praise to God during adverse circumstances. But God's decrees command that you praise Him, even then. An absence of praise brings a rebuke from God. But an overflowing of praise brings about a joy which cannot be contained. When life squeezes you, may prayer and praise come out.

what others say

Anonymous

Some people complain because God puts thorns on roses, while others praise God for putting roses among the thorns.

go to

Joshua finally led the children of Israel through the Jordan River
Joshua 4:1–7

Pass It On

Psalm 145:4, 5
One generation shall praise Your works to another,
And shall declare Your mighty acts.
I will meditate on the glorious splendor of Your majesty,
And on Your wondrous works. *(NKJV)*

intentionality
the quality of acting intentionally or proactively, not simply "going with the flow" or being reactive

When Moses gave the law to the people, he gave them a solemn admonition: "Diligently keep yourself, lest you forget the things your eyes have seen…and teach them to your children and grandchildren" (Deuteronomy 4:9 NKJV). It comes down to **intentionality**. We are a forgetful people, and if we aren't diligent to remember, the things of God just slip away. It's even more important that the people of God be intentional when it comes to the next generation. Our children and grandchildren must be taught if they are to know the God of their ancestors.

That's why David said, "One generation will commend your works to another." In biblical times, a father would teach the skills of his trade to his sons. It was—and still is—even more important that parents teach their children the "skills" of the spiritual life, prayer being chief among them. Children learn to honor God by seeing their parents honor Him by praising Him. They learn who God is by hearing their parents "tell of [His] mighty acts."

When Joshua finally led the children of Israel through the Jordan River and into the Promised Land, he instructed twelve representatives—one for each tribe—to pull a large stone out of the river. They stacked them into a kind of memorial. The point was that, in years to come, the descendants of the people who crossed the Jordan would ask what that pile of stones was for, and their parents would be prompted to tell of the mighty acts of God. It's a good practice, putting up little reminders of God's greatness that will cause your children to ask, "What does that mean?" We forget, and we need prompting sometimes.

meditation
continuous, deep contemplation on a subject—especially on the things of God

Notice how David concludes the thought about passing the story of God's greatness to the next generation: "I will meditate on your wonderful works." Meditation is a private thing, not something you think of doing with or for your children. But what truly puts you in a position to communicate the truths of God is for you to put those truths to work in your own life. It's not enough for you to tell your children—or anybody else—about the importance of prayer and the greatness of God. They need to see that dwelling in God's presence makes a difference in your life. To put it another way, you yourself need to be of memorial to the great deeds of God.

Memorials in the Bible

Stone Memorials	Scripture
"Jacob's Pillar" was a stone to commemorate his dream of angels ascending and descending.	Genesis 28:18
The Israelites stacked twelve stones for the twelve tribes to commemorate their crossing of the Jordan.	Joshua 4:3
After reading the law to the Israelites for the last time before he died, Joshua set up a stone memorial.	Joshua 24:27
David set up a stone called "Ebenezer" to commemorate the Israelites' victory over the Philistines.	1 Samuel 7:12

True Healing

JEREMIAH 17:14
Heal me, O LORD, and I shall be healed;
Save me, and I shall be saved,
For You are my praise. (NKJV)

To his fellow Israelites, Jeremiah frequently came across as a negative guy. He was always lamenting and mourning over his people—people who often felt that they were doing just fine, thank you very much. He always seemed to be predicting doom and gloom—even when everything appeared to be okay. But that was just Jeremiah's point: God's people appeared to be okay, but they were rotting from the inside out. They had lost their way, pursuing other gods. They had stopped taking care of their own, allowing the poor and oppressed to suffer at the hands of the rich and powerful. A big part of the Israelites' problem was self-sufficiency. They believed they had all the answers, and that was the first sign that they didn't have a clue.

Jeremiah's message, ultimately, wasn't doom and gloom, but hope. The Israelites were headed for disaster—Jeremiah was clear about that—but only if they continued relying on themselves and on the help of the world. If only they would turn to God, they would find themselves delivered from the dangers that loomed over them. There's no healing in self-help. There's no salvation in self-sufficiency. But a return to God—there's real healing, real salvation. That's why Jeremiah offered up prayers for healing: "Heal me. O LORD, and I will be healed; save me and I will be saved, for You are the One I praise" (Jeremiah 17:14 NKJV).

go to

a return to God
Jeremiah 3:1

prayers for healing
James 5:15;
Mark 11:24;
Daniel 6:10

Notice that healing and salvation here are the *result* of praise. That's what the little "for" indicates. You might expect Jeremiah to say, "I will praise You, for You heal me and You save me." That is to say, praise results from deliverance. Indeed, some prayers in the Bible work exactly that way. But Jeremiah's point here is just the opposite. Praise comes first, then healing and salvation. The people's peril comes from their refusal to worship God. It follows, then, that their salvation should come from a return to Him.

"Heal me, and I will be healed." There was plenty of false healing going around in Jeremiah's time, just as there is plenty going around now. Elsewhere, Jeremiah complained of people who "healed the hurt of [God's] people slightly, saying 'Peace, peace,' where there is no peace" (Jeremiah 6:14 NKJV).

something to ponder

False healing can be worse than no healing at all, if it causes the patient to stop seeking a cure. But where God heals, there is true healing.

To Whom We Pray

LUKE 1:46–47 ***And Mary said:***
"My soul magnifies the Lord,
And my spirit has rejoiced in God my Savior." (NKJV)

Mary was confused at first by the angel's news. How could she have a son? She was a virgin, still a girl in many ways. "Nothing is impossible with God," the angel said. As a matter of fact, Mary's cousin Elizabeth, at the other end of her childbearing years, was going to have a child in her old age.

go to

He can scarcely be grasped
Isaiah 55:8

Messiah
the long-awaited Deliverer and King of the Jews

When Mary went to visit Elizabeth, her old cousin affirmed her and her calling as the mother of the **Messiah**. And the baby in Elizabeth's womb—the baby who would someday be known as John the Baptist—leapt for joy to be near his kinsman Jesus. Mary was overcome with joy and with the realization of the responsibility she bore. The prayer she prayed at that moment became so famous that it has its own name. It is known as the *Magnificat*, after the first word in the Latin translation.

"My soul magnifies the Lord, and my spirit has rejoiced in God my Savior," Mary prayed, her heart unable to contain her joy. Notice that Mary calls God by three different names in that very first line: Lord, God, and Savior. Mary obviously knew the Father intimately. Lord, or *Kurios* in the Greek, means Supreme Being; one to whom a person belongs. God, or *Theos*, is the Greek word defining the Godhead, which is to say, Mary acknowledges God's transcendence. Finally, Mary refers to Him as her Savior. "*Soter*," she calls Him. *Deliverer*. Mary recognizes that while the Son of God will come from her womb, she is not the Savior, but *He is*. Mary probably was very young, but obviously she had a sense of the complexity of God and of her relationship to Him. He is her Deliverer. He is also her Master, and she his servant.

Children are known to call their parents many things. Toddlers refer to them as "Mommy" and "Daddy." Teenagers may say "Mom" and "Dad." In times of honor and respect, they properly call them, "Mother" and "Father." All titles are correct and show a level of intimate knowledge. They speak to the richness and complexity of the parent-child relationship.

something to ponder

To praise God properly is to acknowledge who He truly is and who you are before Him. He can scarcely be grasped by the human mind, and yet He invites you to know Him as intimately as Mary, whose soul magnified Him, and rejoiced in Him.

what others say

Corrie ten Boom

He is the same yesterday, today, and tomorrow. He never changes. He is the same now as he was in Israel two thousand years ago. He is a solid rock to stand upon. Talk much with Him. He is here now. He loves and understands you.[6]

Never-Ending Song

REVELATION 4:9–11 ***Whenever the living creatures give glory and honor and thanks to Him who sits on the throne, who lives forever and ever, the twenty-four elders fall down before Him who sits on the throne and worship Him who lives forever and ever, and cast their crowns before the throne, saying:***
"You are worthy, O Lord,
To receive glory and honor and power;
For You created all things,
And by Your will they exist and were created." (NKJV)

go to

no more self-interest
Philippians 2:5–11

enjoy Him
Philippians 2:18

It's hard to imagine praising God eternally. If we're being honest, it's hard to imagine that praising God eternally would be all that much fun. But according to the book of Revelation, that's exactly how you'll spend eternity if you're in Christ. If it's hard to imagine the soaring joy of eternal praise, perhaps it's because our flesh insists on putting itself first. It goes against the grain of our selfish natures to think of focusing all our energies on God. We've all heard about the importance of "taking a little time for yourself."

The human dilemma is that even while you're striving to put yourself first, you suspect you aren't good enough or smart enough or sufficiently worthy to deserve first-class treatment. When you have no more self-interest, no selfishness, you're also free from self-doubt. In the presence of the God who has accepted you fully, you can lose yourself in praise of the One who alone is worthy of all praise. You will finally get it right, and the glory of God will reflect back on you. It's one of the great paradoxes of the Christian faith: when we finally stop seeking glory for ourselves, we are covered up with glory.

One of the basic principles of Christianity is that we are here to glorify God and to enjoy Him forever. That's what is happening in Revelation 4. The angels and twenty-four elders are glorifying God, and they are enjoying Him. Forever.

Those who have made it to heaven are free from everything—ambition, worry, selfishness, anger—that keeps us human beings from fully enjoying God.

something to ponder

Prayer is a rehearsal for the glories of heaven. You practice the praise of God. You forget about yourself, focusing instead on the sufficiency of God. It's hard to imagine heaven. But as you get better at praising God, you get a little foretaste of the eternity that awaits.

what others say

Nick Harrison

Michelangelo didn't whip out his *David* in a week. Nor in a month. To be true to your art requires getting it right, no matter how long it takes...Prayer can be likened to an art in that the final result is a wonderful creation wrought through much sweat and labor. If you are a pray-er, then you are an artist of the finest sort.[7]

Chapter Wrap-Up

- God's enduring love is a cause for constant praise.
- You are living proof of God's goodness.
- God is the great Victor over all the universe, and He invites you to take part in His victory.
- Frequently we praise God as the result of some great work in our lives. But it also works the other way around: by praising God, we prepare ourselves to experience God's work in our lives.

Study Questions

1. What does it mean to be the temple of God's dwelling on earth?
2. Why did God forbid His people from making alliances with neighboring nations? How does that relate to your life today?
3. Why is self-sufficiency a major barrier to the praise of God?
4. How is prayer a rehearsal for heaven?
5. How does praise transform your experience of God in your everyday life?

Chapter 4: Prayers of Repentance

Chapter Highlights:
- Turning back to God
- Getting your heart right
- Taking sin seriously
- Regaining God's joy

Praying God's Forgiveness for Another's Sin

NUMBERS **14:19** ***Pardon the iniquity of this people, I pray, according to the greatness of Your mercy, just as You have forgiven this people, from Egypt even until now.*** *(NKJV)*

The Hebrews had made it through the desert and were knocking on the door of the Promised Land. There were so close they could taste it, and God, as they all knew, had promised to give the rich, fertile land to them. Moses had sent twelve spies into the land to scope things out before they crossed over the Jordan River.

When the spies returned, however, they had discouraging news. The land was indeed the promised land just as God had said. It was a rich and fertile land flowing with milk and honey, and there were bunches of grapes so huge that men had to carry them on poles held between them on their shoulders. There was just one problem: the cities were strong, fortified cities. And the men were giants. There was no earthly way the Israelites could conquer such people.

That's what ten of the twelve spies said. The minority report was offered by Caleb and Joshua. Yes, they said, there were giants in the land. But God had promised to give the land to the Israelites, and God cannot lie. God's promise was the most relevant fact, according to Caleb and Joshua. But the Israelites weren't ready to hear that. They were still thinking about those giants and those fortified cities. They refused to go in and lay claim to the land that was already theirs for the taking.

That kind of unbelief was a slap in the face of the God who delivered them from their Egyptian oppressors, who split the Red Sea so they could walk across on dry land, who provided them with manna in the desert. It was the worst kind of sin—the kind that leads eventually to every other sin. God was ready to punish the people according to their unfaithfulness. But as he had so many times before, Moses stepped in and prayed on behalf of the people God had given him to lead: "Pardon the iniquity of this people, I pray, according to

go to

the promised land
Exodus 3:8

God cannot lie
Titus 1:2

warfare
the struggle between the devil on your right shoulder and the angel on your left

stewardship
the management of resources entrusted to you by God

gluttony
the sin of eating and drinking to excess

the greatness of Your mercy, just as You have forgiven this people, from Egypt even until now" (Numbers 14:19 NKJV).

Here is a theme we've seen before: Moses appeals to God on the basis of God's character, not on the basis of any good that might be in himself or in the people he is praying for. Even today, God hears that kind of prayer, and He responds "according to the greatness of His lovingkindness."

what others say

Vickey Banks

Praying for others shouts "I love you" up and down the very halls of heaven. Praying for others is both a privilege and a responsibility. It is pure joy, and it is full-throttle **warfare**. It is one sure way to engage heaven in our earthly lives.[1]

A Vicious Cycle

JUDGES 10:10 ***And the children of Israel cried out to the LORD, saying, "We have sinned against You, because we have both forsaken our God and served the Baals!" (NKJV)***

The Book of Judges reveals a cyclical pattern in the history of the Israelites. The Israelites fall away from God and worship the idols of their neighbors. In order to bring the Israelites to their senses, God allows enemy nations to defeat and oppress them. Seeing the error in their ways, the Israelites repent and turn back to God. God raises up a "judge" who defeats the enemy and helps the Israelites get back on track. Once the crisis is over, however, the Israelites again grow complacent and, forgetting their need for God, turn to strange gods again. Which brings us back to Step 1 again (see chart that follows). This cycle repeated itself over and over again in the time of the judges.

The cycle still applies in many ways. When you depart from the good life God offers, you suffer the consequences. Bad **stewardship** of your resources, for example, leads to the oppression of financial trouble. Sexual infidelity leads to broken families and any number of serious problems. **Gluttony** leads to health troubles and low self-esteem. Sin carries its own punishment with it, and that punishment can be just as destructive as the Midianites or the Philistines who served as God's punishment on the wayward Israelites.

But when the consequences of our wrongdoing bring us to our knees in repentance, God hears our prayers and delivers. He doesn't always reverse the consequences of our actions—not immediately, anyway—but He does give a fresh start. The amazing thing is that, however many times God has heard the same old prayer of repentance, He always hears and forgives again.

something to ponder

The Israelites got it wrong a lot of times and in a lot of different ways. But here's what they did right: when things got really bad for them, they knew where to turn. Under the oppression of the Midianites or the Ammonites or the Philistines, they might have said, "God must not love us," or "The foreign gods must be stronger than our God after all." They might have blamed God for their troubles. But they had sense enough to see they had brought their troubles on themselves. And they had sense enough to turn back to God. "We have sinned against You," they cried. It was exactly what they needed to say. God, ever patient, heard their prayer of confession and repentance.

The Cycle of Punishment and Repentance in Judges

Step 1	The Israelites fall away from God and worship the idols of their neighbors.
Step 2	In order to bring the Israelites to their senses, God allows enemy nations to defeat and oppress them.
Step 3	Seeing the error in their ways, the Israelites repent and turn back to God.
Step 4	God raises up a "judge" who defeats the enemy and helps the Israelites get back on track.
Step 5	The crisis over, the Israelites again grow complacent and, forgetting their need for God, turn to strange gods again. Which brings us back to Step 1 again.

what others say

Billy Graham

Before I can become wise, I must first realize that I am foolish. Before I can receive power, I must first confess that I am powerless. I must lament my sins before I can rejoice in a Savior. Mourning, in God's sequence, always comes before exultation. Blessed are those who mourn their unworthiness, their helplessness, and their inadequacy.[2]

Remember Me

JUDGES 16:28 *Then Samson called to the Lord, saying, "O Lord GOD, remember me, I pray! Strengthen me, I pray, just this once, O God."* (NKJV)

Samson
Judges 13-16

Nazirite
a Jew bound by a vow to leave the hair uncut, to abstain from wine and strong drink, and to practice extraordinary purity of life and devotion, the obligation being for life, or for a certain time

Samson was a special child of God; from before the time he was born, God had special plans for him. Even before Samson was born, God instructed his parents to set him apart and raise him as a **Nazirite**. Samson grew to be a man of good looks, great athletic ability, and talents, full of God's blessings. He was a hero to his own people and a terror to the Philistines. But somewhere along the way, Samson got off track. He started using God's gifts for the gratification of his own desires, not for the fulfillment of God's purposes. He chased Philistine women, and he found himself ensnared by an especially nasty one: Delilah.

Delilah seduced Samson and manipulated him into giving up the secret of his supernatural strength. The Philistines shaved the hair that symbolized the vow that gave Samson his strength. They blinded him and put him to work as a slave—lower than a slave, actually. He did the work of a donkey, turning a grinder in the prison.

One day the Philistines were having a great festival in honor of their god Dagon, and it occurred to them to trot out the blind Samson. He was to perform for their entertainment. They could jeer and laugh at him—at the sight of the Philistines' greatest fear now reduced to being a blind, weakened slave. Samson stood in the midst of his enemies, beside the pillars that held up the temple where they had gathered. His life as he had known it—the life God had set him apart for—was over. So he prayed one last, desperate prayer. "Remember me, O God, and strengthen me just once more."

"Remember me." You can almost imagine Samson asking it as a question: "Remember me?" He could hardly remember himself. But he remembered that God had set him aside for a special purpose—to deliver Israel from the power of the Philistines—and he recognized this as one more chance, in spite of all his failures, to fulfill that purpose. God did remember Samson, and He answered his prayer. With one last burst of strength, Samson pulled the temple down on the Philistines, and on himself.

It's easy enough to get distracted by the things of the world, to get thrown completely off the purpose God has laid out for you. But it's never too late to return to Him. God remembers who He made you to be, even if you've forgotten. The way back begins with a prayer of repentance.

what others say

Cynthia Spell Humbert

One of the reasons God says He will never forget us is because He has engraved our name on the very palm of His hand. Now, if you know anything about engraving, it does not wash off. It's permanent. God says He thinks about you constantly because your name is always in front of Him. Every time God moves His hands, He sees your name and thinks loving thoughts about you as His precious child.[3]

go to

the laws regarding the ritual cleansing
Exodus 12:1–28

consecrated
dedicated to a sacred purpose—in this case, through special cleansing rituals

Dirty Feet and All

2 CHRONICLES 30:18B–19a ***May the good LORD provide atonement for everyone who prepares his heart to seek God.*** *(NKJV)*

When twenty-five-year-old Hezekiah became king he set about reestablishing the traditions of faith that his forerunners—his father, Ahaz, in particular—had neglected or actively opposed. He opened the doors of the temple that his father had closed. He ordered the priests to purify themselves before God and then to sanctify the temple. When that had been done, the long-forgotten sacrifices were made so that the "service of the house of the LORD was set in order" (2 Chronicles 29:35b NKJV). Pleased, Hezekiah sent letters throughout Judah and Israel, inviting all the people to come to the temple for Passover, something that hadn't happened for more than two hundred years.

Some of the people laughed, but others headed for Jerusalem. Nobody quite knew what to do, however, and the whole affair was sort of sloppy. Passover was supposed to happen in the first month of the Jewish calendar, but the priests couldn't get themselves **consecrated** in time, so they held the feast in the second month instead. Still, people came by the thousands from every corner of the kingdom to celebrate the Passover, eager to get right with God.

As might be expected, the people hadn't read the laws regarding the ritual cleansing that was required for Passover. And they certainly didn't know from experience. Many of them were technically "unclean" when they came before God. But their hearts were in the right place. They were coming before God with the desire of turning back to Him, even if they didn't have all their ducks in a row.

Hezekiah did know the laws of ritual cleansing. He looked at the dirty hands and dirty feet of his people and knew they were out of

go to

to reestablish a colony
Ezra 1–5

compliance with the laws, even if they didn't know it themselves. So he prayed God's mercy on them. "May the good LORD provide atonement for everyone who prepares his heart to seek God, the LORD God of their fathers, though he is not cleansed according to the purification of the sanctuary" (2 Chronicles 30:18b–19 NKJV). Hezekiah knew that God, in His goodness, would welcome and forgive those whose hearts were seeking Him.

something to ponder

It's the heart God sees, not fancy dress or ritual formality. There's nothing wrong with making things right and pretty. But preparing inwardly to meet God—and desiring to meet Him—is what really matters. God is more interested in the heart that seeks Him and earnestly searches for Him. He will welcome us; dirty feet and all.

what others say

Max Lucado

It makes me smile to think there is a grinning ex-con walking the golden streets who knows more about grace than a thousand theologians. No one else would have given him a prayer. But in the end that is all that he had. And in the end, that is all that it took. No wonder they call Him the Savior.[4]

Serious About Sin

EZRA 9:6 ***O my God, I am too ashamed and humiliated to lift up my face to You, my God; for our iniquities have risen higher than our heads, and our guilt has grown up to the heavens. (NKJV)***

Ezra was on a mission from King Artaxerxes of Persia. He traveled from Persia to Jerusalem to help rejuvenate the religious life of the temple there. Eighty years earlier, a group of 42,360 Jewish exiles had returned to Jerusalem to reestablish a colony there and rebuild the temple. But they were sort of limping along, not exactly thriving in the homeland. Artaxerxes, in an effort to "get in good" with the God of the Jews, had given Ezra everything he needed to build a first-rate temple in Jerusalem. He carried a great deal of gold and silver with which to enrich the temple, as well as bulls, rams, lambs, grain, and wine for sacrifices. He also brought over a thousand people, including priests and servants for the temple.

When Ezra and his caravan got to Jerusalem, they pulled out the treasure chests and showed the locals the riches they had brought.

Then they made sacrifices and worshipped God and presented the local authorities with the king's orders to treat them well and help them in their efforts to restore the temple. It must have been a great day for Ezra.

But after the worship service, some of the locals came to Ezra with alarming news. The people of the Jerusalem colony, it seems had not kept themselves separate from their pagan neighbors as God had commanded. They had married heathen wives—and the priests and leaders had been as guilty as anybody. Ezra was shocked. Perhaps he had envisioned the Jerusalem colonists as godly pioneer types, taking a stand in the face of the heathens' opposition. As it turned out, they weren't any different from the heathens—not even the priests. Ezra tore his beard and hair and "sat astonished."

as God had commanded
Genesis 28:1

But then Ezra got up and prayed: "I am too ashamed to lift up my head." Ezra took sin seriously. Looking at things from the outside, it looked as if Ezra was doing great. As the personal representative of the world's most powerful king, he was looking like a hero. What was the big deal? King Artaxerxes certainly wouldn't care about a little intermarriage with pagans. But Ezra understood that it was God, not Artaxerxes, who had given him his mission. And God was not pleased.

When things are going well, it's tempting to think of sin as no big deal. But Ezra had the spiritual sensitivity to see that without personal holiness, all the gold and silver and sacrifices in the world would mean nothing to God.

what others say

Matthew Henry

Holy shame is as necessary in true repentance as holy sorrow. Everyone in the church of God, has to wonder that he has not wearied out the Lord's patience, and brought destruction upon himself. What then must be the case of the ungodly? But though the true penitent has nothing to plead in his own behalf, the heavenly Advocate pleads most powerfully for him.[5]

Great Moments in Repentance

Incidents	Scripture
Jonah changes His mind about preaching to the Ninevites	Jonah 2:1–10
The Parable of the Prodigal Son	Luke 15:17–20

sets the captive free
Luke 4:18

slaves
those who are powerless over the authority of others

forsook
turned one's back on

Great Moments in Repentance (cont'd)

Incidents	Scripture
Jesus tells the woman, "Go and sin no more."	John 8:11
Saul, persecutor of the church, encounters Christ on the road and becomes the apostle Paul.	Acts 9:1–9
Our role and God's role in repentance	1 John 1:8–10

Voluntary Slavery, Involuntary Slavery

EZRA 9:9–10 ***For we were slaves. Yet our God did not forsake us in our bondage; but He extended mercy to us in the sight of the kings of Persia, to revive us, to repair the house of our God, to rebuild its ruins, and to give us a wall in Judah and Jerusalem. And now, O our God, what shall we say after this? For we have forsaken Your commandments.*** *(NKJV)*

The fact that the Jews were "**slaves**" was their own fault. They had disobeyed, and despite warning after warning from the prophets, they continued to make themselves the slaves of sin until God had no choice but to make good on His threat to subject them to the slavery imposed by the Assyrians and Babylonians. God gave them what they had chosen for themselves; they were slaves long before the foreign armies showed up. But as Ezra noted, even in that slavery, God never actually **forsook** His people. He was always there, always protecting, preparing them for the day when they would be released from slavery and ready to rebuild their temple and their homeland. And ironically, it was only in their slavery that the Israelites were able to come to terms with the goodness of God.

In his letter to the Romans, Paul wrote: "Our old man was crucified with Him, that the body of sin might be done away with, that we should no longer be slaves of sin" (Romans 6:6 NKJV). God sets the captive free. And that begins with being set free from our own worst tendencies. The old self that enslaved us has been crucified with Christ, and the life we live as Christ's servants is a life of freedom.

If you've been walking with God for any significant time, and if your walk began with a U-turn back to Him from a road of spiritual slavery you most likely can look back upon that part of your life lived BC (before Christ) and marvel at the way God kept you protected from your own stupidity and self-inflicted slavery. Praise God that even when we choose slavery, God is forever guiding us toward the new life of freedom for which He created us. Though we walk down a path that God did not intend for us, He never leaves us.

For Ezra, freedom from slavery didn't mean the freedom to lie around and do nothing. It meant the freedom to get to work rebuilding the temple of God. If you are in Christ, you are the temple of the Holy Spirit. Freedom in Christ all about the freedom to repair the ruins, to build your life into a proper dwelling-place for God.

something to ponder

> **what others say**
>
> **Allison Gappa Bottke**
>
> The Lord knew it would take a pretty miraculous scenario to catch my attention, and He did not let me down. He must have known how stubborn I was, how I would continue to keep walking the same dead-end paths if He didn't step in a and move me. And move me He did.[6]

David's Great Sin

Psalm 51:1–2, 8, 10
Have mercy upon me, O God,
According to Your lovingkindness;
According to the multitude of Your tender mercies,
Blot out my transgressions.
Wash me thoroughly from my iniquity,
And cleanse me from my sin…
Make me hear joy and gladness,
That the bones You have broken may rejoice…
Create in me a clean heart, O God,
And renew a steadfast spirit within me. *(NKJV)*

David was "a man after God's own heart." But even David fell into egregious sin. He saw a beautiful woman named Bathsheba bathing, and he wanted her. The fact that Bathsheba was married to one of David's most faithful captains didn't matter. He slept with her, impregnated her, and in an effort to cover up the whole affair, had her husband Uriah killed.

go to

"a man after God's own heart"
1 Samuel 13:14

prophet
a man or woman who is gifted by God with spiritual insight, especially when it comes to what's going to happen in the future

The **prophet** Nathan confronted David with his sin, and David repented with much grief and shame. Out of David's anguished repentance came Psalm 51, perhaps the greatest psalm of repentance ever written. "Have mercy upon me, O God," David prayed,

go to

separate us from our sins
Psalm 103:12

"according to Your lovingkindness; According to the multitude of your tender mercies, blot out my transgressions" (Psalm 51:1 NKJV). David appeals to God on the basis of God's character, not on the basis of David's own goodness. He doesn't justify himself, doesn't say "Have mercy on me because I'm never going to do this kind of thing again." His only hope is to throw himself on the mercy of the God who shows mercies by the multitude.

David, no doubt, had lost faith in his own ability to keep to the straight and narrow. But he still had full confidence in God's ability to forgive and to cleanse. "Wash me, and I shall be whiter than snow" (Psalm 51:1 NKJV). There's real faith in that prayer. God says He will separate us from our sins as far as the east is from the west. Who are we to doubt Him?

David's repentance led to a confidence in God's mercy, which ultimately gave way to hope and joy. He prayed, "Make me hear joy and gladness, that the bones You have broken may rejoice." Yes, David had been broken. He left God no choice but to break him. But that brokenness isn't the end of the story. Broken bones can heal, and broken spirits can rejoice again. That, in the end, is the purpose of repentance—a return to the fellowship whereby you can truly enjoy God and rejoice in Him.

key point

Repentance isn't a matter of beating yourself up. That's not the point at all. Rather, repentance is about availing yourself of the mercy of God, who promises to forgive and restore. Yes, God will break you if that's what you need. But if you turn to God in your brokenness, He will cause the bones He has broken to rejoice.

Send Me

Isaiah 6:8b *Then I said, "Here am I! Send me." (NKJV)*

In a vision, the prophet Isaiah entered into the throne room of God, where he was confronted for the first time with true holiness. He immediately understood how unholy he himself was, and he felt the "fear of the Lord." "Woe is me!" he said. "Because I am a man of unclean lips, and I live among a people of unclean lips." Bear in mind, Isaiah had already begun his career as a prophet at this point. He had already been telling people "Thus saith the Lord." But when he actually saw the Lord, he felt like a fraud. His lips were unclean, not worthy to speak what they had been speaking.

Then one of the **seraphim** attending at the throne of God flew to the altar and picked up a live coal. He touched the coal to the lips of Isaiah. The seraph assured the prophet that the coal from God's altar had purged the uncleanness from his lips.

Then God spoke: "Whom shall I send, and who will go for Us?" (Isaiah 6:8a NKJV) with no hesitation, Isaiah spoke: "Here am I! Send me" (Isaiah 6:8b NKJV). What a remarkable thing to say. Remember, just a minute ago, Isaiah was groveling before God, moaning about the uncleanness of his lips. But God had cleansed him, and Isaiah knew that the cleansing was effective. To put it another way, Isaiah took God at His word. God had declared Isaiah's lips clean. Isaiah could no longer wallow in his unworthiness. Instead, he answered God's call.

Coming to terms with God involves feeling your own unworthiness. But that's not where God leaves you. Your unworthiness isn't the point nearly so much as God's worthiness—and His ability to make you clean. God is able to cleanse even the most unclean of lips. And once He has cleansed you, you no longer have the option of saying you're not worthy to serve him. You may remember Peter's vision when God invited him to eat of the "unclean" animals. "Not so, Lord," said Peter. "For I have never eaten anything common or unclean" (Acts 10:14 NKJV). But God wasn't having any of it. He answered, "What God has cleansed, you must not call common" (Acts 10:15 NKJV). When God has cleansed you, you must not call yourself common. Once you get that straight, you're ready to answer God's call: "Here am I! Send me."

go to

Peter's vision
Acts 10:9–16

seraphim
plural of seraph, an angel with three pairs of wings

what others say

Beth Moore

The thought of speaking for God should scare us to death—death to ourselves, death to our own agendas, and death to our own ideas and concepts and religion. God forbid that flesh should enter in when it's time to speak the words of God! Yet so often we say things without much prayer or thought, supposedly speaking for Him.[7]

Count to Ten

JEREMIAH 10:24
O LORD, correct me, but with justice;
Not in Your anger, lest You bring me to nothing. (NKJV)

consuming fire
Deuteronomy 4:24

disciplines
trains by instruction and practice, especially to teach self-control

It almost sounds as if Jeremiah is trying to be funny: "O LORD, correct me, but with justice; not in Your anger, lest You bring me to nothing." You picture Jeremiah being vaporized like somebody in an old cartoon. But Jeremiah makes a good point in this prayer. The anger of God is not something to be taken lightly. If He were to vent His anger when He corrects us, we would be in major trouble.

Jeremiah took sin seriously—his own sin, not just the sin of other people. He understood that that holiness of God is so offended by the unholiness of human beings that it burns with a consuming fire—the kind that can bring you to nothing. The Bible speaks frequently of "the fear of the Lord." That's not just a figure of speech. The thought of God in His anger is a truly terrible thing to consider. But Jeremiah also understood God's grace. And the good news is that God deals with us out of His love and grace, not out of His anger. His correction is intended to bring you back into a right relationship with Him. Reducing you to nothing wouldn't accomplish that. That's why Jeremiah prayed the way he did.

Grace has been defined as God's act of bestowing goodness that we don't deserve. Conversely, mercy has been defined as God's act of *not* giving us what we *do* deserve. When Jeremiah asked God not to correct him in His anger, he was asking for mercy. This from the man who has been called "unquestionably the greatest spiritual personality in Israel [in his day]."[8] But even for great "spiritual personalities," grace and mercy are the very basis of our relationship with God, even when God corrects and **disciplines**. We have nothing to bring to God with which to earn his favor we have nothing of our own to bargain with. We can only give ourselves over to His grace and mercy and say, "If you must correct me, please correct me out of love and justice, not out of anger."

To submit to God is to be willing to receive His correction, to reenter a right relationship even if it is painful. And you can accept the pain of God's correction when you understand that He does it out of love—even if anger is what you deserve.

what others say

T. D. Jakes

God places his prize possessions in the fire...What a joy to know that He cares enough to straighten out the jagged places in our lives.[8]

Question and Answer

JEREMIAH 12:1, 4, 5
Righteous are You, O LORD, when I plead with You...
Why does the way of the wicked prosper?
Why are those happy who deal so treacherously?...
How long will the land mourn,
And the herbs of every field wither?...

If you have run with the footmen, and they have wearied you,
Then how can you contend with horses?
And if in the land of peace,
In which you trusted, they wearied you,
Then how will you do in the floodplain of the Jordan? (NKJV)

go to

threw him in a muddy cistern
Jeremiah 38:6

One of the chief jobs of the prophets was to be a voice for justice. They called their countrymen to account for society's injustices. "Thus says the Lord" Jeremiah intoned: "Execute judgment and righteousness, and deliver the plundered out of the hand of the oppressor" (Jeremiah 22:3 NKJV). The widows. The orphans. The aliens. The poverty-stricken. Jeremiah and his fellow prophets spoke up on their behalf and demanded justice.

It didn't make them the most popular people in their society. As a matter of fact, Jeremiah's neighbors once got so tired of hearing him that they threw him in a muddy cistern and left him there to die. It was a hard life for Jeremiah. The more he spoke out against injustice, the more it seemed he was a victim of injustice himself.

Then one day Jeremiah looked around and realized he was fed up. He wasn't just fed up with his fellow Jews. He had been fed up with them for years. No, Jeremiah was fed up with everything. He was beginning to wonder if God Himself was just. So he offered up a prayer of questioning. "Righteous are You, O Lord, when I plead with You," he began. "Yet let me talk with You about Your judgments." Seems polite enough. Then he launches into the heart of his complaint. "Why does the way of the wicked prosper? Why are those happy who deal so treacherously? You have planted them, yes, they have taken root; They grow, yes, they bear fruit" (Jeremiah 12:1–2 NKJV). Jeremiah feels that he's withering, dying on the vine. Yet the wicked prosper. Where's the justice in that, Jeremiah wants to know.

Jeremiah gets his answer from God: "If you have run with the footmen, and they have wearied you, then how can you contend

Trust Me
Psalm 9:10

with horses?" (Jeremiah 12:5 NKJV). In other words, "Do you really think you've got what it takes to run this universe better than Me?" In other words, "If you can't run with the big dogs, stay on the porch."

Do you ever feel like questioning God? Go ahead. You don't always have to be nice with God. If you've got questions, ask them. God can handle it. But be sure you're willing to hear the answer, even if it turns out to be, "Trust Me. You can't understand what I'm doing here."

Chapter Wrap-Up

- Just like the Israelites, we are still subject to the cycle of sin, punishment, repentance, deliverance, and sin again.
- To complain to God isn't necessarily a bad thing. God desires that you be honest with Him—as long as you're honestly seeking His face.
- Repentance is more than a commitment to try harder next time. It requires that you acknowledge your inability to mend your ways without God's help.
- The point of repentance isn't beating yourself up, but putting yourself in a position to be restored to a right relationship with God.
- Repentance leads to real joy.

Study Questions

1. What did David mean when he said, "Let the bones which You have broken rejoice"?
2. How does voluntary slavery lead to involuntary slavery?
3. Why did God overlook the ritual uncleanness of the Israelites when they came to that first Passover in Hezekiah's day?
4. Why doesn't a healthy "fear of God" lead to despair?
5. How is repentance different from self-punishment?

Chapter 5: Prayers of Personal Distress

Chapter Highlights:
- God provides
- The value of hardship
- God's grace
- Submitting to God
- Dealing with God

My Plate's Full, Lord

NUMBERS 11:14 ***I am not able to bear all these people alone, because the burden is too heavy for me.*** *(NKJV)*

God provided for His people when they were wandering in the desert. Every day the manna came, covering the ground like dew, and the people gathered it, prepared it, and ate it. But in time their gratitude for God's provision gave way again to grumbling. They started thinking about the variety of their diet back in Egypt: melons, leeks, onions, cucumbers, garlic. Sure, they were slaves, doing backbreaking labor, subjected to the oppression of cruel taskmasters, but at least they had some variety in their diet. In the desert it was just manna.

Their complaining angered God, and it angered Moses too. Moses complained to God: *Are these people my children?* he asked. *Why should I have to carry them all the way to the Promised Land?* Moses was feeling the burden of the people's expectations. He felt he was being crushed. "I am not able to bear all these people alone, because the burden is too heavy for me" (Numbers 11:14 NKJV).

God heard Moses' prayer and answered. He dealt first with Moses' leadership problem. God instructed Moses to appoint seventy elders from the twelve tribes to whom he could **delegate** his responsibilities. They would help bear his burdens. Then God made an astonishing promise: the people would have meat for thirty days straight. In fact that they would have so much meat that they would be sick of meat—"until it comes out of your nostrils and becomes loathsome to you" (Numbers 11:20 NKJV). Moses couldn't help but doubt. He was responsible for six hundred thousand men, plus all the women and children. Where would he ever find enough flocks and herds to feed (or overfeed) that many people for a month? But God reassured him. "Has the LORD's arm been shortened?" (Numbers 11:23 NKJV) he asked. God provided meat as He promised, but not in the way anybody expected. A wind blew quail by the millions into the camp. The people gathered baskets full of them.

go to

six hundred thousand men
Exodus 12:37

delegate
to commit or entrust a task or responsibility to another person

walls came tumbling down
Joshua 6

Notice that of God's two-part answer to Moses' prayer, the first part was very mundane, even obvious. You're feeling overwhelmed by your responsibilities? Delegate. God answered Moses' prayer by giving him the wisdom to see what he probably should have seen all along. but the second part of God's answer, who could have guessed? Millions of quail brought by the wind.

God's arm hasn't grown short. He still answers prayer, in a million different ways. Sometimes the answer is as mundane as a quickening of your common sense, and every now and again the answer is as spectacular as a great miracle.

God's Arm Is Not Short

Bible Personalities on God's Ability	Scripture
David: Power belongs to God . . . and mercy too.	Psalm 62
Jeremiah: Nothing too hard for the One who made heaven and earth with His hands	Jeremiah 32:17
Jesus: What is impossible with men is possible for God.	Matthew 19:26
Gabriel: Nothing is impossible with God.	Luke 1:37
Paul: God can perform everything He promises.	Romans 4:21

what others say

Oswald Chambers

"Cast thy burden upon the Lord"—you have been bearing it all. Deliberately put one end on the shoulders of God...and yourself with it, and the burden is lightened by the sense of companionship.[1]

Sin in the Camp

JOSHUA 7:7a *And Joshua said, "Alas, Lord GOD, why have You brought this people over the Jordan at all...to destroy us?" (NKJV)*

Their wandering in the desert was over. The children of Israel had paid their dues, and now it was time for them to enter the Promised Land under the leadership of Joshua. They marched on the fortified city of Jericho, and the walls came tumbling down. God was obviously with them on this campaign. If the mighty city of Jericho had fallen, how could the surrounding villages stand?

The next objective was the town of Ai. The spies scoped things out and came back with an encouraging report: Ai was a town of few people. There was no need to send the whole army against Ai, only two or three thousand soldiers. But when the soldiers went in for their easy victory, they were routed. Thirty-six men died, and the rest ran away demoralized.

treasury
a place in which riches are kept

There was no military explanation for the defeat, just as their had been no military explanation for the Israelites' victory at Jericho. Joshua, like everybody else, was perplexed by what had happened. *What's the deal, Lord?* he prayed. *Have you brought us all this way just to kill us off?* Joshua didn't know that there was sin in the camp. God had commanded that the Israelites not take any "accursed things" out of Jericho. The spoils of Jericho were to go into the Lord's **treasury** and were not to be taken by individuals. But an Israelite named Achan took some of the forbidden things and hid them in his tent. This hidden sin was the cause of the stunning defeat at Ai.

The sin had to be dealt with before the conquest could continue. After Achan and his family had been punished with death, the army marched again on Ai and won an easy victory.

It's puzzling when you think you are doing everything according to the will of God, but still things fall apart. You've prayed, you've marched ahead in what you believe God wants you to do, but the results are disappointing to say the least.

something to ponder

It's not uncommon for there to be "sin in the camp" of our lives…and oftentimes sin we are not aware of. When everything that should have been so right becomes so completely wrong, go to the Lord in prayer and ask Him, "What's the deal, God? Is there something I should know about? If so, how can I make it right?" Getting things right with God is the first step toward victory.

what others say

Andrew Murray

In the Christian life defeat is a sign of the loss of God's presence. If we apply this to our failure in prayer, we see that it is because we are not in full fellowship with God. The loss of God's presence is due to sin. Just as pain is nature's warning of a physical problem, defeat is God's voice telling us there is something wrong. He has given himself wholly to His people. He delights in being with them. He never withdraws himself unless they compel Him to do so by sin.[2]

Hannah's Heart-Filled Covenant

1 Samuel 1:11 ***Then [Hannah] made a vow and said, "O Lord of hosts, if You will indeed look on the affliction of Your maidservant and remember me, and not forget Your maidservant, but will give Your maidservant a male child, then I will give him to the Lord all the days of his life"*** *(NKJV)*

pour out herself
Philippians 2:17

Hannah wanted a child so badly she could taste it. She was one of two wives to Elkanah. The other wife, Peninah, had no trouble getting pregnant. She had several children, and there were a joy to her. More than that, Penina's children gave her something to lord over poor, barren Hannah. Hannah was Elkanah's favorite, and Peninah was jealous of her. She made Hannah's life miserable.

Every year the family went to the house of the Lord at Shiloh to pray and worship, and every year Peninah provoked Hannah so severely that Hannah couldn't eat for weeping. One year Hannah made an anguished, tearful prayer at Shiloh. If God would only give her a baby boy, she prayed, she would give him right back. As soon as the boy was weaned, she would send him to serve in the house of the Lord at Shiloh, the very place where she was standing.

The chief priest Eli saw Hannah standing there in the tabernacle with her eyes closed and her lips moving, and he figured she was drunk. He scolded her, but Hannah explained, "I am a woman of sorrowful spirit. I have drunk neither wine nor intoxicating drink, but have poured out my soul before the Lord" (1 Samuel 1:15 NKJV). It wasn't anything that she had poured *in* that made Hannah act so, but what she was pouring *out*.

The Hebrew word translated "poured out" is *shaphak*. It speaks of emptying or expending. It is used frequently to mean the shedding of blood. That gives you some idea of just how intense Hannah's prayer was. She was leaving her very lifeblood there in the tabernacle of the Lord. That word *shaphak* is specifically used to mean the pouring out of blood or wine or water on the sacrificial altar. Hannah's prayer was a kind of sacrifice. Indeed, she offered to give back the boy she hoped God would give her in answer to her prayer. How's that for sacrifice? Hannah had no authority to pour out a goat's blood or a flagon of wine as a sacrifice on God's altar. But she could pour out herself. God heard her prayer and answered it. The boy God gave Hannah turned out to be the prophet Samuel.

When was the last time you poured yourself out on the altar of prayer? Paul spoke of his desire to be a "living sacrifice." That begins with soul-emptying prayer like Hannah's.

go to

living sacrifice
Romans 12:1

dramatic efforts
1 Kings 18:26–29

what others say

Betty Robison

Whenever my heart is hurting over a troubling situation, I strive to remember that God has a plan and He sees the whole picture. He knows what I need and when I need it. Although it can be hard to wait on God, I cling to the truth that God wants to bless me with His best, in His perfect time.[3]

Barren Women Who Had Babies

Name	Scripture
Sarah	Genesis 21:1–6
Samson's Mother	Judges 13
Hannah	1 Samuel 1
Elizabeth	Luke 1:5–24

Lord, I Am Tired

1 Kings 19:4 ***[Elijah] came and sat down under a broom tree. And he prayed that he might die, and said, "It is enough! Now, Lord, take my life, for I am no better than my fathers!"*** *(NKJV)*

Elijah had been a party to an incredible triumph over God's enemies. It was a dramatic showdown—a kind of duel—between Elijah, the prophet of God, and 450 prophets of Baal. The people of Israel had been wavering between God and Baal, sometimes worshipping both. So Elijah proposed a challenge that would force the people to decide which was the true god. There were two bulls, one for Baal's prophets and one for Elijah. Each bull was placed on a pile of wood as for a burnt offering, but with no fire. The prophets of Baal would pray for Baal to send fire to consume their sacrifice, then Elijah would pray to God. Whichever deity came through would be proven true.

The prophets of Baal, of course, failed to attract Baal's attention, in spite of some very dramatic efforts. When Elijah's turn came, he soaked his sacrifice in water, just to be sure nobody could accuse him of trickery. He prayed, and fire from heaven fell and consumed the sacrifice, water and all. The people turned to God immediately. They seized the false prophets and put them to death.

despair
complete loss of hope

It was an exhilarating moment for Elijah. But he came down hard from his spiritual high. When wicked Queen Jezebel heard what had happened to her prophets, she threatened to have Elijah killed. And Elijah, for some reason, took her seriously. After all he had seen, he still was afraid of a mere human being. "It is enough," he moaned. "Now, LORD, take my life" (1 Kings 19:4 NKJV).

Elijah's **despair** seems odd so soon after his soaring victory. Surely it was just exhaustion speaking. Elijah lived a very stressful life, and the comedown from such a spiritual high must have been pretty abrupt. In any case, God heard Elijah's prayer. He didn't kill Elijah, as Elijah had prayed. Instead, God gave him comfort and relief and deliverance from danger.

apply it

Sometimes you just get tired. You feel like quitting, even when you've been affirmed in your calling. Sometimes, in fact, the low times come so soon after major victories that you can't even make sense of what you're feeling. That doesn't negate God's calling on your life. It's okay to be honest with God in those times. He will hear and give you what you need—even when you don't know yourself what you need.

what others say

Peter Marshall

God will not permit any troubles to come upon us unless He has a specific plan by which great blessings can come out of the difficulty.[4]

Stand Firm and Pray

2 CHRONICLES 20:9 ***If disaster comes upon us—sword, judgment, pestilence, or famine—we will stand before this temple and in Your presence (for Your name is in this temple), and cry out to You in our affliction, and You will hear and save. (NKJV)***

When King Jehoshaphat heard that the Moabites and Ammonites had entered into an alliance to attack Judah, he was afraid. Who wouldn't be? These enemies were famously cruel, and they had long nursed a hatred for the children of Israel, ever since the Israelites first entered the part of the world that the Moabites and Ammonites dominated. But even in that moment of fear, Jehoshaphat knew exactly where to turn. "Jehoshaphat was afraid and turned his attention to seek the LORD" (2 Chronicles 20:9 NKJV).

Jehoshaphat's world seemed very uncertain at that moment. He was aware that anything could happen. But he was also aware that, whatever lay ahead, God would never change. God was a firm foundation on which he could stand. He stood firm, and he prayed. Jehoshaphat's prayer springs from a confidence that went much deeper than self-confidence. His confidence lay in the God to whom he prayed; in 2 Chronicles 20:9 NKJV), Jehoshaphat asked, "O LORD God of our fathers, are You not God in heaven, and do You not rule over all the kingdoms of the nations, and in Your hand is there not power and might, so that no one is able to withstand You?"

God was a firm foundation
Psalm 46:1–5

nothing is impossible with God
Matthew 19:26

Jehoshaphat knew that his army didn't have the might to defend itself against the combined forces of the Ammonites and Moabites. That's why his first reaction was fear. But to pray is to avail yourself of the power of One whom "no one is able to withstand." Jehoshaphat knew what the apostle Paul knew: "If God is for us, who can be against us?" (Romans 8:31 NKJV). The prayer of Jehoshaphat took his focus off his own situation and focused him instead on the more important fact that nothing is impossible with God.

You don't know what the future holds for you either. The technology and conveniences of the modern world create the illusion that we human beings have everything under control. Retirement plans promise security and a sure future. But it's only an illusion. The world can still be a hard place to live, and no one is immune to hardships and suffering. Jobs go away. Natural disasters destroy worldly goods. Loved ones die. In those times of trouble, you have the privilege of placing your confidence in the God whose love and power overwhelm all. You can stand firm in the midst of trouble.

what others say

Bill Hybels

From birth, we have been learning the rules of self-reliance as we strain and struggle to achieve self-sufficiency. Prayer flies in the face of those deep-seated values. To people in the fast lane, determined to make it on their own, prayer is an embarrassing interruption . . . And yet somewhere, someplace, probably all of us reach the point of falling to our knees, bowing our heads, fixing our attention on God and praying.[5]

"Into Your hands I commit my spirit."
Luke 23:46

forever faithful
2 Timothy 2:13

In Distress, Grief, and Sorrow

PSALM 31:9, 14–16
Have mercy on me, O LORD, for I am in trouble;
My eye wastes away with grief,
Yes, my soul and my body!...
But as for me, I trust in You, O LORD;
I say, "You are my God."
My times are in Your hand;
Deliver me from the hand of my enemies,
And from those who persecute me.
Make Your face shine upon Your servant;
Save me for Your mercies' sake. (NKJV)

Psalm 31 is the outpouring of a heart in trouble. David had fallen into a trap laid by his enemies (v. 4), and he needed God's help to get out of it. He had been the victim of slander, the subject of schemes and plots (v. 13). His enemies had caused his friends to turn against him, and he felt that he was "repulsive to [his] acquaintances" (v. 11). David went so far as to say that he had been "forgotten like a dead man, out of hand" (v. 14).

Psalm 31 is classified as one of David's "psalms of complaint." There are more of them than you might expect. David poured out everything in his worship of God—his sorrows and disappointments as well as his joy and gratitude.

It's almost as if David's openness to complain to God made him all the more open to receive God's comfort. About halfway through this psalm, David's whole outlook changed. "But as for me," David prayed, "I trust in You, O LORD." David understood that in spite of all his troubles, he could trust in the God who holds all David's times in his hand (v. 15). The turning point comes when David takes his eyes off himself and locks them in on God.

On the cross Jesus cried, "Into Your hands I commit my spirit." He was quoting Psalm 31:5. There was nowhere else to turn; He could only give Himself over to God. In the end, that's all you have anyway—a God who holds your times in His hands, and who upholds up your spirit for safekeeping. When all else fails, when all your worldly supports have fallen away and your friends seem not to have kept faith with you, you have the comfort of knowing that your spirit is committed to the One who is forever faithful.

You experience the pain and sorrow of broken relationships, of slander and hostility. It hurts. There's no point denying it. There's certainly no point in trying to hide your hurt from God. Open yourself up to Him. Pour out your sorrow and disappointment before Him. But do so with the expectation of turning away from that big pile of heartache and turning toward the God who holds all your times in His hands.

Jesus Quoting the Psalms—A Partial List

Psalm Quoted	Scripture
Psalm 6:8—"Depart from me, all you workers of iniquity."	Matthew 7:23, 25:41 (NKJV)
Psalm 8:2—"Out of the mouth of babes and nursing infants you have ordained strength."	Matthew 21:16 (NKJV)
Psalm 22:1—"My God, My God, why have You forsaken Me?"	Matthew 27:46; Mark 15:34 (NKJV)
Psalm 37:11—"But the meek shall inherit the earth."	Matthew 5:5 (NKJV)
Psalm 69:9—"Zeal for Your house has eaten me up."	John 2:17 (NKJV)
Psalm 78:2—"I will open my mouth in a parable; I will utter dark sayings of old."	Matthew 13:35 (NKJV)
Psalm 110:1—"The LORD said to my Lord, 'Sit at My right hand, till I make Your enemies Your footstool."	Matthew 22:44; Mark 12:36, 16:19; Luke 20:42–43 (NKJV)
Psalm 118:22—"The stone which the builders rejected has become the chief cornerstone."	Matthew 21:42; Mark 12:10; Luke 12:10–11 (NKJV)
Psalm 119:142—"Your law is truth."	John 17:17 (NKJV)

Thirsting and Longing After God

PSALM 63:1
O God, You are my God;
Early will I seek You;
My soul thirsts for You;
My flesh longs for You
In a dry and thirsty land
Where there is no water. (NKJV)

If Bible scholars are correct, David wrote Psalm 63 while he was in the wilderness of Judah, having fled Jerusalem at the time of his son Absalom's rebellion. He would have been experiencing literal, physical thirst out there in the desert. The barrenness of the landscape would have symbolized for David the barrenness of his own

go to

nowhere else to turn
John 6:68

Living Water
John 4:10-15

seek Him
Deuteronomy 4:29; Luke 11:9

hunger and thirst for righteousness
Matthew 5:6

life at that moment. Family ties had broken apart. The power of the throne had let him down. God's protective hand seemed to have been lifted from him. The wilderness of Judah was a "dry and thirsty land" any way he looked at it.

But wilderness experiences have a way of stripping us down until the only things that are left are the things that are really important. When there's nowhere else to turn, even the most stubborn of us turn to God. Away from the kingly comforts that bred complacency, David's physical thirst reminded him just how much he thirsted for his heavenly Father. "My soul thirsts for You; my flesh longs for you." Ironically, the dry and weary land can turn out to be the best place to find the Living Water that quenches your deepest thirst.

When you find yourself in the wilderness—and everybody does from time to time—you have a choice to make. You may, if you choose, wallow in self-pity and focus on the thirst that makes you uncomfortable. Or you can turn back to God and say "This thirst, this longing for what I'm missing, is actually a longing for the God who alone can satisfy all my desires." Every desire, every longing ultimately points you toward God. Here on earth, there always seems to be some false satisfaction offering itself up as the answer to your longing. The wilderness may be hard, but at least there aren't so many false satisfactions getting in the way of your ability to receive the soul-quenching that God offers.

apply it

It's not long in David's psalm before thirst and dryness give way to abundance. "My soul shall be satisfied as with marrow and fatness" (Psalm 63:5 NKJV), he said. Here's the thing: when you thirst for God, you can be sure your thirst will be satisfied. You can't say that about any other desire. The desire for water doesn't guarantee that there's water to be had. The desire for status or security doesn't mean you're necessarily going to achieve those things. But if you long for God, you can be sure He'll satisfy that longing. Those who seek Him always find Him. Those who hunger and thirst for righteousness will always be filled.

what others say

Steve McVey

There have been times in my life when I was so busy trying to do things for God that I loss all sense of intimacy with Him. However, as a Christian moves from a legalistic, performance-based lifestyle into the grace walk, he will find an increasing interest in developing intimacy with Christ.[6]

But I Am a Man of Prayer

slander
a false and malicious statement or report about someone

PSALM 109:1–4
Do not keep silent,
O God of my praise!
For the mouth of the wicked and the mouth of the deceitful
Have opened against me;
They have spoken against me with a lying tongue.
They have also surrounded me with words of hatred,
And fought against me without a cause.
In return for my love they are my accusers,
But I give myself to prayer. (NKJV)

David was a casualty of a war of words. Wicked men lied about him; their words surrounded him like enemies Indeed, though David was seemingly invincible on the field of battle, he was very vulnerable to slander and lies on the home front. Some of it he brought on himself. Because he wasn't above reproach in all areas of his life, perhaps people were more willing to believe malicious falsehoods about him. In any case, there were people—David's son Absalom among them—who were willing to take David down with whispers and lies. And David didn't feel up to the task of defending himself. So he turned it over to God: "O God, whom I praise, do not remain silent."

David's approach to his **slander** problem is worth a closer look. When hurtful words are fired at you, it's tempting to shoot back, to create a crossfire. From David's complaint, you get the impression that he was under withering fire. But he doesn't fire back. It's not that he just sits there and takes it; he uses his words in a way infinitely more effective than simply talking back at (or about) his accusers. It's so quiet you can almost miss it: "But I am a man of prayer."

something to ponder

Words have tremendous power in this world where we live. But how much more powerful are words that are directed to God in prayer? A prayer reaches beyond the closed system of action and reaction, accusation and rebuttal, question and answer, and brings the power of God to bear to change the whole equation. To pray when you are under attack is to get out of a defensive posture and assume instead a posture of trust in the One who always delivers His people. God gives comfort to the accused. He can change the heart of the accuser. He can resolve an impossible situation in any number of ways.

go to

war of words
James 3:6

To pray instead of answering back is to change the terms of the conversation so completely that a slanderer can't possibly win.

That little statement, "But I am a man of prayer," says, "What matters is not what the world says or thinks about me, but what God says and thinks about me." A war of words, in the end, is a kind of spiritual warfare. To call on God is to bring an invincible power in on your side of the battle.

what others say

Barton Bouchier

The instruction to ourselves from these words is most comforting and precious. Are we bowed down with sorrow and distress? "I give myself unto prayer." Are we persecuted, and reviled, and compassed about with words of hatred? "I give myself unto prayer." Hope was left at the bottom of the casket, as the sweetener of human life; but God, in far richer mercy, gives prayer as the balm of human trial.[7]

David's Vulnerabilities

Troubles David Faced	Scripture
Saul's murderous rage	1 Samuel 18:10–16, 19:9–10
David's flight and exile	1 Samuel 20–31
Sin with Bathsheba, death of their baby	2 Samuel 11
Conflict among David's sons and daughters	2 Samuel 13
Absalom's revolt	2 Samuel 15–18

Racing Upward to High Places

HABAKKUK 3:17–19
Though the fig tree may not blossom,
Nor fruit be on the vines;
Though the labor of the olive may fail,
And the fields yield no food;
Though the flock may be cut off from the fold,
And there be no herd in the stalls—
Yet I will rejoice in the LORD,
I will joy in the God of my salvation.
The LORD God is my strength;
He will make my feet like deer's feet,
And He will make me walk on my high hills.
To the Chief Musician.
With my stringed instruments. (NKJV)

Like so many of the prophets of Israel and Judah, Habakkuk was active in a time of great uncertainty. The **Chaldeans** were on the prowl, conquering this little kingdom and that, and though they had not yet attacked Judah, it seemed only a matter of time before the Jews suffered the hardships that their neighbors had suffered at the hands of Chaldean invaders. It was a time when all the Jews' worldly supports—their wealth, their government, their military might—seemed very precarious. But that's not necessarily a bad place to be.

Habakkuk insists on praising God no matter how hard times get. No figs in the orchard or grapes in the vineyard? He will rejoice. The olive and grain crops fail? He will still be joyful in God's provision. No sheep in the pens or cattle in the stalls? God is still God. In that catalog of failure and hardship, everything Habakkuk lists is a man-made support. Orchards and fields and livestock pens are the work of human beings. And they can fail. But this is still God's world, and He is still in control even if all our efforts at security and prosperity fail.

"He makes my feet like deer's feet, and He will make me walk on my high hills." That's a great picture. The green valley—the world of human comfort and security—may turn brown and dead. And when it does, God gives you what you need to get by beyond that world where you felt so at home.

The high places are beyond the reach of human domestication. There the wild deer finds safety and provision. And there you find that you don't need everything you thought you needed. You will find that God is enough.

It is God who created the deer with the ability to climb in times of trouble and fear. By instinct, when fearful circumstances befall him, he runs for the heights rather than the lowlands. What about you? Do you put on the strength of God and run, by instinct to the high places? It can be hard up there. But there are times when the high places are the only places you can survive. And you may find that the high places have charms of their own. There you can look down on your everyday life and see things you never could have seen down in the valley.

go to

God is enough
Psalm 16:5

Chaldeans
an ancient nation of Mesopotamia. Abraham's hometown of Ur was in Chaldea

key point

what others say

Miriam Feinberg Vamosh

Thought it has a tremendous will to survive, the hart is often the victim of some hungry predator. Its only recourse is to

centurion
a commander of a hundred soldiers in the Roman army

intercession
prayer on behalf of another person

> escape and seek refuge, to wait for the time of strength and the season of rebirth that will replenish its depleted numbers.... [Israel] too waits, fallen and deserted, for the day of rebirth, of redemption.[8]

The Greatest Faith

MATTHEW 8:6 ***Lord, my servant is lying at home paralyzed, dreadfully tormented.*** *(NKJV)*

You think of Roman soldiers as being hard, pitiless men—men who rely on earthly power to get things done, not the sort to throw themselves on anybody's mercy. The Jews of Jesus' time certainly thought of their Roman rulers that way. But Jesus had an encounter with a Roman **centurion** that must have made His disciples wonder if He knew what He was doing.

Capernaum, on the Sea of Galilee, had a strong Roman presence. There was a Roman army garrison there, as well as a tax collector's office. But Jesus' reputation as a healer was known even to the Romans. When He visited Capernaum, a Roman officer came to Him with an urgent request: "Lord, my servant is lying at home paralyzed, dreadfully tormented." It was a simple **intercession**—if you can even call it an intercession; the centurion never got around to asking Jesus to do anything. He simply stated the problem. But Jesus understood. "I will come and heal him," Jesus said.

The Roman, in his humility, didn't consider himself worthy to have Jesus under his roof. Perhaps he felt the weight of the sins his people had committed against Jesus' people, the Jews. "Only speak a word, and my servant will be healed," he said. The Roman understood authority. He obeyed those who were in authority over him, and he knew that when he gave an order to the men under his authority, they obeyed. Jesus, he could see, had authority over the forces that plagued his servant.

Jesus marveled, "Assuredly I say to you, I have not found such great faith, not even in Israel." There was nothing fancy about the Roman's request or his faith either. He was quite matter-of-fact about things. He saw authority in Jesus, and he submitted himself to that authority. He had the earthly power to lord it over Jesus (indeed, other Roman soldiers would kill Him), but instead he accepted Jesus' Lordship. Being a Roman, he probably didn't understand very much about who Jesus was. But he did the best he could with the knowledge he had available to him, and Jesus declared him to be a man of great faith.

sovereign
possessing absolute power and full autonomy

An earnest prayer doesn't require that you say all the right things, or even that you understand exactly what you're doing. It comes down to your willingness to put your needs before a **sovereign** God and say, "I accept your authority over me, and I rejoice in your authority over the things that are troubling me."

something to ponder

what others say

Joni Eareckson Tada

That's what God did for me when he sent a broken neck my way. He blew out the lamps in my life which lit up the here and now and made it so exciting . . . You see, suffering gets us ready for heaven.[9]

Chapter Wrap-Up

- Even in times of hardship—especially in times of hardship—God is at work in your life.
- Prayer lifts you beyond the realm of the earthly troubles that afflict you.
- Sometimes having your earthly supports taken away is the best thing that could happen to you.
- God has authority over you; just as importantly, He has authority over everything that troubles you.

Study Questions

1. Even David's psalms of complaint end up with praise. What is the turning point?
2. If the Israelites' victory at Jericho was a sign of God's presence, why wasn't the defeat at Ai a sign of God's absence?
3. How is a prayer a kind of sacrifice?
4. Why did Elijah, after seeing God's power, collapse so completely when Jezebel threatened him? How did God respond to Elijah's lack of faith?
5. How can the difficulties of the "high places" or a "dry and thirsty land" be a blessing?

Chapter 6: Prayers of Petition

Chapter Highlights:
- Detailed prayers
- Being humble
- Trusting God
- Pleasing God
- Longing for God

God in the Details

> GENESIS 24:12a *Then he said, "Oh, LORD God of my master Abraham, please give me success this day."* (NKJV)

When it came time for Isaac to marry, Abraham wanted to be sure he didn't marry a woman from one of the neighboring tribes in Canaan. He wanted his son to take a wife from "back home"—from Ur in **Mesopotamia**, where Abraham and Sarah had originally come from. As is still the case in many Eastern countries, the parents typically took responsibility for finding spouses for their children. Abraham was too old to travel all the way back to Ur, so he sent his chief servant to find a wife for Isaac.

It was a very tall order for Abraham's servant. It would be hard enough to discern which young woman was the most suitable wife for his master's son. But then he would have to convince her (and her parents) to let him take her all the way back to Canaan to marry a man she had never seen. Abraham was adamant that Isaac not accompany the servant to Ur. He was afraid that Isaac would like Mesopotamia better than Canaan and stay there, negating the family's claim on the land God had promised.

The servant traveled to Ur and went to the well where the young women came to draw water. Standing there, he prayed a very specific prayer asking for a sign of guidance from God. As young women came to the well, the servant would ask each one for a drink. Should one of them not only give him a drink, but voluntarily offer to water his camels as well, he prayed, "Let her be the one you have appointed for your servant Isaac" (Genesis 24:14 NKJV). Before he had even finished saying the prayer, Rebekah, a beautiful young kinswoman of Abraham's, came to the well. When the servant asked for a drink, she offered water for his camels as well, and the servant knew he had found the one.

Abraham's servant prayed to a God of details. He knows the number of hairs on your head; He knows every time a sparrow falls to the ground. The servant's very specific prayer demonstrated a very full

go to

sparrow falls to the ground
Matthew 10:29-31

Mesopotamia
the area between the Tigris and Euphrates Rivers, in modern-day Iraq

Pharisee
a member of an ancient Jewish sect that emphasized strict interpretation and observance of the Mosaic law in both its oral and written form

Pentateuch
the first five books of the Old Testament

trust in God's provision, right down to the smallest item. It's one thing to pray in general terms—"God please grant me success." But to truly engage God is to pray through every little detail, acknowledging God's sovereignty over it all, and strengthening your faith to trust Him in all those details.

> **what others say**
>
> **Bruce Wilkinson**
>
> Let me tell you a guaranteed by-product of sincerely seeking His blessing: Your life will become marked by miracles. God's power to accomplish great things suddenly finds no obstruction in you. You're moving in His direction. You're praying for exactly what God desires. You're expecting to succeed.[1]

The Joys of the Humble Heart

LUKE 18:13 ***And the tax collector, standing afar off, would not so much as raise his eyes to heaven, but beat his breast, saying, "God, be merciful to me a sinner!"*** *(NKJV)*

Jesus told a story of two men who stood near one another praying in the temple. One was a **Pharisee**, the other a tax collector. They represented the two ends of the moral and religious spectrum to the Jews of Jesus' day. Pharisees had earned a reputation for incredible personal holiness—on the outside, at least, and that was all anyone could see. The Pharisees did an excellent job of keeping the complex dietary laws and laws of ritual cleanness in the **Pentateuch**, going well beyond what God required. The Pharisees were an intimidating presence on the religious scene.

Tax collectors, on the other hand, had earned a very different reputation. They were employees of the Roman government—government contractors, really. A tax collector was required to collect a set amount of money from the people in his jurisdiction, but he was also authorized to collect above that amount and keep the difference for himself. They became very rich by overcharging their neighbors in the name of Rome. A Jewish tax collector was the worst kind of collaborator in the eyes of other Jews. Tax collectors were excluded from almost all aspects of Jewish life, the lowest of the low.

In Jesus' story, the Pharisee prayed first: "God, I thank You that I am not like other men—extortioners, unjust, adulterers, or even as this tax collector. I fast twice a week; I give tithes of all that I possess" (Luke 18:11–12 NKJV). It's not at all clear what is the point of the Pharisee's prayer, other than self-congratulation.

The tax collector, on the other hand, wouldn't even raise his eyes from looking at the ground. He beat his breast and prayed, "God, be merciful to me, a sinner." It was this man, the tax collector, who was justified, according to Jesus. A whole lifetime of self-congratulatory prayers isn't worth a single prayer for mercy like that of this tax collector. The Pharisee, in his self-sufficiency, was a million miles away from God. But "the LORD is near to those who have a broken heart, and saves such as have a contrite spirit" (Psalm 34:18 NKJV).

something to ponder

You need to repent of your sin; everybody knows that. But did you ever consider the need to repent of your righteousness too? It was the Pharisee's righteousness—self-righteousness, to be more specific—that was keeping him from God. But the man who understood he had nothing good to recommend him—that man was counted as righteous.

what others say

Charles Haddon Spurgeon

> [Jesus] wears the glory of an Intercessor who can never fail, of a Prince who can never be defeated, of a Conqueror who has vanquished every foe. "Then shall He sit upon the throne of His glory." Oh, the splendour of that glory. It will ravish His people's hearts. If you would joy in Christ's glory hereafter, He must be glorious in your sight now. Is He so?[2]

Tax Collectors in the Bible

Who They Were	Scripture
The apostle Matthew	Matthew 9:9–13
Zacchaeus	Luke 19:2
The tax collector who prayed "God be merciful to me, a sinner!"	Luke 18:13

What Jesus Said About:

The Pharisees	Scripture
"Unless your righteousness exceeds the righteousness of the scribes and Pharisees, you will by no means enter the kingdom of heaven."	Matthew 5:20 (NKJV)
"Those who are well have no need of a physician, but those who are sick."	Matthew 9:12 (NKJV)

go to

fifty "runners"
1 Kings 1:5

order of succession
the rules for deciding who is the rightful king after a reigning king dies

What Jesus Said About: (cont'd)

The Pharisees	Scripture
"These people draw near to Me with their mouth, And honor Me with their lips, But their heart is far from Me."	Matthew 15:8 (NKJV)
"But woe to you, scribes and Pharisees, hypocrites! For you shut up the kingdom of heaven against men; for you neither go in yourselves, nor do you allow those who are entering to go in."	Matthew 23:13 (NKJV)
"You are like whitewashed tombs which indeed appear beautiful outwardly, but inside are full of dead men's bones and all uncleanness."	Matthew 23:17 (NKJV)
"Beware of the leaven of the Pharisees, which is hypocrisy."	Luke 12:1 (NKJV)

Wisdom for Today

1 Kings 3:9a ***[Solomon said,] "Therefore give to Your servant an understanding heart to judge Your people, that I may discern between good and evil." (NKJV)***

When David grew too old to govern, there was a great deal of intrigue and jockeying for position in the court. The **order of succession** wasn't very clear cut. Adonijah, who was probably David's eldest surviving son, began to put himself forward in ways very reminiscent of his rebellious brother Absalom. He rode around in a chariot with fifty "runners" for bodyguards, giving the impression that he was already in charge. He held a large sacrifice and feast in which he declared himself king.

Most of the court attended Adonijah's feast, but Adonijah didn't invite his younger brother Solomon, or any of Solomon's inner circle. He had good reason not to. David had already promised that Solomon would inherit his throne. When the prophet Nathan got wind of Adonijah's self-promotion, he recruited Solomon's mother Bathsheba to go to King David and remind him of his promise to Solomon. So goaded into action, David declared Solomon to be his true successor, and Adonijah was defeated.

Those were the circumstances under which Solomon became king—not the easiest waters to navigate. He wasn't especially powerful or assertive (it was Nathan and Bathsheba, after all, who put Solomon forward, not Solomon himself). He wasn't the eldest brother. And then there was another dilemma: it was by David's personal authority that Solomon was established as the rightful heir. But David would be gone when Solomon actually inherited the throne (by definition) and Solomon would have to stand on his own two feet.

So when God told Solomon to ask for whatever he wanted, Solomon knew what to ask for. "I am a little child," Solomon said. "I do not know how to go out or come in, and Your servant is in the midst of your people whom you have chosen, a great people, too numerous to be numbered, or counted (1 Kings 4:7b-8 NKJV). Solomon was in over his head. So he asked for wisdom: "Give to your servant an understanding heart to judge Your people, that I may discern between good and evil."

leprosy
a disease causing sores on the skin. Those who suffered with it were considered "unclean" and punished by God

You have a kingdom of your own—your home or perhaps your business. And sometimes you sense that you're in over your head. Pray for wisdom and discernment. "If any of you lacks wisdom," said James, "let him ask of God, who gives liberally and without reproach, and it will be given to him" (James 1:5 NKJV). God will delight to give you wisdom, as it's what He wants for you all along.

apply it

what others say

James Merritt

God is too wise to let man come to know Him by his own wisdom. Man cannot solve his problems because he cannot recognize their source, which is sin. 1 Corinthians 3:19 says "the wisdom of this world is foolishness to God." The Prophet Jeremiah said that the wise men "rejected the Word of the Lord." If a person is going to come to God, he or she will have to come as a little child.[3]

Enough for Today

MATTHEW 8:2 ***And behold, a leper came and worshiped Him, saying, "Lord, if You are willing, You can make me clean." (NKJV)***

Of all the social outcasts of Jesus' time, the lepers were probably the most thoroughly outcast. Their disease was physically disgusting and poorly understood. It was assumed that such a horrific disease could only be a punishment for some sin, and, indeed, on a number of occasions, God did afflict people with **leprosy**, as a punishment for sin. Lepers were forced to live in leper colonies beyond the boundaries of normal life. And, if ever they met anyone on the road, lepers were required to call out, "Unclean! Unclean!" as a warning to the other person.

God's goodness
Hebrews 11:6

After Jesus finished preaching the Sermon on the Mount, He was surrounded by great multitudes wanting to be healed or wanting to hear more of what this unusual man had to say. And among that throng of people was a leper. Word of the Healer must have reached the leper colony, and in his desperation this leper defied the laws that isolated him from everyone else. You can picture the crowd parting like the Red Sea to give way to the leper making his way to Jesus.

The leper worshiped Jesus and said, "Lord, if you are willing, You can make me clean." There's a remarkable mixture of faith and doubt in that prayer. The leper never doubted Jesus' ability. "You can make me clean," he said, unequivocally. However, he wasn't so sure Jesus would be willing to make him clean. Life had knocked this man down time after time. He probably had met very few people who would have been willing to do him a good deed. He was "unclean," after all, and he may have come to believe he was unworthy of healing. So even if he had no doubt about Jesus' abilities as a healer, he was plagued with the kind of self-doubt that made him wonder if Jesus would be willing to help.

Imagine the leper's joy and relief when he heard Jesus' answer: "I am willing; be cleansed." He was cleansed. He had a new lease on life.

One aspect of faith is believing that God truly can do everything. But true faith—saving faith—is believing in and resting in God's goodness as well. The leper knew about power. But nothing in his life to that point had prepared him for the love of a God who said, "I am willing." He is willing to do good on your behalf too.

what others say

Joni Eareckson Tada

I used to have this idea that God was leading me to some particular end in this life, some desired goal. I'd get too excited, so anxious, I would barely pay attention to the present moment. But I'm finding out more and more that reaching a particular earthly goal is merely incidental. It is trusting and obeying the Lord Jesus Christ in the mile of the journey right now that counts.[4]

Leprosy in the Bible

Victims	Scripture
Moses' sister Miriam punished with a temporary case of leprosy	Numbers 12:10
Naaman healed of leprosy	2 Kings 5:1–14
The four lepers of Samaria	2 Kings 7:3, 8
Ten lepers healed by Jesus	Luke 17:12–19

provision
that which is provided, in this case, by God

honorable
upright, moral, respectable

The Prayer of Jabez

> 1 CHRONICLES 4:9–10 ***Now Jabez was more honorable than his brothers, and his mother called his name Jabez, saying, "Because I bore him in pain." And Jabez called on the God of Israel saying, "Oh, that You would bless me indeed, and enlarge my territory, that Your hand would be with me, and that You would keep me from evil, that I may not cause pain!" So God granted him what he requested.*** *(NKJV)*

Never have two little verses and four short lines caused such a stir in the publishing world as they did just after the turn of the twenty-first century with a tiny book called *The Prayer of Jabez*.[5] You would have had to be living under a rock not to have heard of it. For two years it dominated the bestseller lists, won awards, stirred envy and controversy, and caused a lot of people who had never learned a prayer to do just that.

Some people, no doubt, bought *The Prayer of Jabez* because they thought it was some sort of biblically endorsed get-rich-quick scheme. *Pray this prayer, watch your territories enlarge, and live pain-free.* But that's not what author Bruce Wilkinson was talking about. *The Prayer of Jabez* is about trusting in God's **provision**, learning to move within the blessings of that provision and, in turn, blessing others. Lastly, it is about learning not to allow those blessings to put you in a place where you forget the Source, but instead keeping your focus always on the One from whom all blessings flow.

key point

Part of the prayer of Jabez is often overlooked. *Jabez was more honorable than his brothers* . . . God granted him what he requested. The prayer of Jabez is book-ended with a couple of things we should stop and notice. (1) He was **honorable** and that characteristic preceded his prayer. His prayer would have come from a right heart and right relationship with God. (2) God both heard his prayer and answered in the affirmative. God didn't answer his prayer because

Jabez said the right words to some success formula. Perhaps He blessed Jabez because He knew those blessings wouldn't be wasted.

go to

sign a decree
Daniel 6:7

It's true that God blesses those who don't deserve it. Actually, that's true all the time; that's what grace means. Nevertheless, character fits into the equation. A willingness to live honorably, to live for others and not just for yourself puts you in a position to receive the blessings of God. When we bring our petitions to God, He is aware of our character. Before we attempt to convince God of what He should bless us with, we should first ask for and work toward a godly nature. If you want to emulate Jabez, memorizing his prayer isn't nearly as important as living an honorable life like his.

apply it

As Was His Custom

DANIEL 6:10 ***Now when Daniel knew that the writing was signed, he went home. And in his upper room, with his windows open toward Jerusalem, he knelt down on his knees three times that day, and prayed and gave thanks before his God, as was his custom.*** *(NKJV)*

Daniel's enemies in the court of King Darius were sick of the favoritism with which the king treated Daniel, a Jewish foreigner. So they hatched a plan. They convinced Darius to sign a decree forbidding anyone to pray or make a request to anyone besides the king for thirty days. Anyone who violated the decree was to be thrown into the lions' den. Daniel's enemies knew that Daniel wouldn't go thirty days without praying to God. All they had to do was to catch Daniel at it, and Darius would have no choice but to throw his favorite into the lions' den.

Daniel knew about the king's decree. He also knew that his true allegiance lay with a king much higher than Darius. So he went home and knelt down to pray—three times that day—"as was his custom since early days." The Bible doesn't give any specifics on the nature of Daniel's prayers that day. You get the impression, however, that they weren't anything out of the ordinary. He "gave thanks." Maybe he prayed for deliverance or for wisdom in negotiating this difficult situation, but that's not what the Bible emphasizes. The Bible emphasizes that Daniel was just carrying on his everyday prayer life "as was his custom."

Daniel didn't even take the precaution of closing his window to pray. He was God's servant first, and he didn't care who knew it. His enemies couldn't believe their luck. They caught him the very first day. When they reported the situation to King Darius, the king "was greatly displeased with himself." He wasn't displeased with Daniel. Daniel, after all, was <u>just being Daniel</u>. Darius was displeased that he had allowed himself to be talked into such a rash decree. He tried to save Daniel, but he couldn't countermand his own decree, so Daniel was thrown into the den of lions. Darius commended Daniel to his God, then he stayed up all night fasting and worrying about his favorite courtier.

go to

just being Daniel
Daniel 1:8-21

It's worth noting that, for all King Darius' worry and concern, the Bible says nothing about Daniel worrying. Daniel simply trusted God, first to last. That trust surely came from a habit of daily prayer that was so ingrained that it wasn't even interrupted by a king's decree. There was nothing flashy about Daniel's faith. He simply went about his business, and God delivered him, as Daniel knew He would.

something to ponder

what others say

Nick Harrison

Why does God answer prayer? It's because He's instituted a new covenant with man, based on grace, not on law. Part of this new covenant is His commitment to the prayers of His people. He has given us promises regarding prayer that He *cannot* and *will not* break. God can do anything but lie. We have His word. Prayer is a granted privilege of His children. He is bound by His integrity to hear our prayers.[6]

My Mouth, Your Words

Psalm 19:14
Let the words of my mouth and the meditation of my heart
Be acceptable in Your sight,
O Lord, my strength and my Redeemer. *(NKJV)*

David understood the connection between the heart and the mouth. It does no good to pay lip service to God or to anybody else. It's not hard to tell when the words a person speaks don't match up with the things that are in that person's heart. Perhaps that's why David didn't just pray "Let the words of my mouth be acceptable in

go to

tamed
James 3:7–8

Your sight." He prayed, "Let the words of my mouth *and the meditation of my heart* be acceptable in Your sight."

There are two muscles that must be continuously spiritually tamed, the heart and the tongue. The best way to keep your words in line with your heart and your heart in line with what is pleasing to God is to spend time in His Word, meditating on the good things of *His* heart and asking Him to keep your heart and mouth pure. If you yield those powerful muscles to Him, He will help tame them.

David knew how to be sure his words were pleasing to God; the words of his mouth would be intimately related to the meditations of his heart. Therefore, part of his prayer was that the meditations, or those things he thought about, pondered, and considered, would be acceptable to God. In turn, his words would respond according to his thought.

apply it

When Jesus took on flesh to live as a man, He found Himself in a religious culture that was consumed with externals. What are the right words to say? What are the right things to eat? What is the procedure for eating that ensures you won't be "defiled"? Once when Jesus and his disciples sat down to eat without performing the accepted cleansing rituals, the religious professionals in the neighborhood were appalled. How could Jesus be a Man of God if He let Himself be defiled so? Jesus answered them in a way that turned their thinking inside out: "Whatever enters a man from the outside cannot defile him…what comes out of a man, that defiles a man" (Mark 7:18, 20 NKJV). For inside is the heart, and with all its jealousies and anger and lust and deceitfulness, it generates quite enough trouble without having to worry about the externals. As you get the heart under control—by meditating on things that are good and excellent, by filling it with God's Word—you find that the externals take care of themselves.

what others say

Prayers That Avail Much

> I will educate and train and develop my human spirit. The Word of the God shall not depart out of my mouth. I meditate therein day and night. Therefore, I shall make my way prosperous and I will have good success in life. I am a doer of the Word and put God's Word first. My spirit man is in the ascending.[7]

Remember Me, Remember Me Not

PSALM 25:7
Do not remember the sins of my youth, nor my transgressions;
According to Your mercy, remember me,
For your goodness' sake, O LORD. (NKJV)

If you've ever been to a high school reunion, you know what David meant when he prayed, "Remember not the sins of my youth." You hope people remember you, you just hope they don't remember you for the stupid things you did as a teenager.

David wanted God to remember him—he *needed* God to remember him—but he prayed that God wouldn't remember his youthful indiscretions. Notice, however, that he doesn't trot out a list of things for which he *does* want to be remembered. He might have said, "don't remember the sins of my youth, but do please remember my victories over the Philistines, and my loyalty to King Saul, and all those great Psalms I've written, and the way I've shaped Your people into a powerful nation."

"According to Your mercy remember me for Your goodness' sake" (Psalm 25:7 NKJV), David prayed. In the New International Version it's phrased, "Remember me, for You are good." Not "Remember me, for *I* am good," but "*You* are good." David may have been past some of the sins of his youth, but he realizes he's not good enough to merit God's favor without God's goodness thrown in.

The thief on the cross sheds some light on what David was saying in this prayer. Of the two thieves hanging on either side of Jesus, one said, in effect, *If You're so powerful, why don't You bust us out of here?* The other thief answered, *You and I are here justly. We deserve what we're getting.* Then he turned to Jesus and said, "Lord, remember me when you come into Your kingdom." Remember? Remember what? He had just admitted that he deserved to be crucified. He had done no good deeds worth remembering. But he trusted the goodness of Jesus. And that no-good thief is one person we know for sure is in heaven, for Jesus Himself said, "Today you will be with Me in paradise" (Luke 23:43 NKJV).

You need for God to remember you too. That can be a scary thought. No doubt you've done things you'd prefer not be remembered. Praise God that He remembers You not for the sake of *your* goodness, but for the sake of *His* goodness.

go to

thief on the cross
Luke 23:32-43

remember
Psalm 106:4

go to

impatient
1 Samuel 13:8–14

virtue
moral and spiritual merit, which when achieved, makes us more like God

what others say

Alan C. Mermann, MD, M. Div.

Prayer is a source of courage in my never-ending struggle to live a victorious life.[8]

Godly Impatience

Psalm 141:1
Lord, I cry out to You;
Make haste to me!
Give ear to my voice when I cry out to You. *(NKJV)*

Perhaps David hadn't heard what we've heard: Patience is a **virtue**. The apostle Paul said so in the letter he wrote to the Galatians: "But the fruit of the Spirit is love, joy, peace, longsuffering, kindness, goodness, faithfulness, gentleness, self-control" (Galatians 5:22 NKJV). Longsuffering, or patience, is something we are to aspire to.

Can impatience ever be a virtue? Consider this scenario. A newlywed couple gets back from their honeymoon. The first day they head back to their respective offices, they embrace in the doorway of their house and whisper, "Hurry home!" Throughout the day they call one another. "Hurry home! Can't wait to see you this evening." It's all they can do to keep from driving across town to meet for lunch.

That's the kind of impatience that David exhibits in Psalm 141. *I need You, God, and soon, I can't bear to be apart.* Saul, if you will remember, was also impatient when he prayed. But he was impatient to get the answer he needed. His impatience had nothing to do with a longing for God's presence, or for communion or fellowship with Him. That's the difference between godly longing and just regular, sinful impatience.

Impatient prayers aren't really that unusual. *Lord, I need the following things, and I need them now* . . . But how often do you feel the urgency in prayer that newlyweds feel for one another? That kind of longing, that kind of impatience is a pleasure to God.

something to ponder

God is as near as breath. And His answer to the prayer, "Come quickly," is "I'm already here." As you cultivate godly impatience, you learn not to wait to bring your burdens to God. How could you wait for tomorrow morning's quiet time? You'll bring everything to God *now*. No need to tell a friend "I'll pray for you." You're praying already! That kind of impatience will change your life.

David's Godly Impatience

His Pleas to God	Scripture
"But You, O Lord, do not be far from Me; O My Strength, hasten to help Me!"	Psalm 22:19 (NKJV)
"This You have seen, O Lord; Do not keep silence. O Lord, do not be far from me."	Psalm 35:22 (NKJV)
"Do not forsake me, O Lord; O my God, be not far from me! Make haste to help me, O Lord, my salvation!"	Psalm 38:21-22 (NKJV)
"But I am poor and needy; Make haste to me, O God! You are my help and my deliverer; O Lord, do not delay."	Psalm 70:5 (NKJV)
"Lord, I cry out to You; Make haste to me! Give ear to my voice when I cry out to You."	Psalm 141:1 (NKJV)

go to

fervor
James 5:16b

besetting sin
a "pet sin" that a person falls into over and over, seemingly never able to conquer it

what others say

Mark Hopkins

Our prayer and God's mercy are like two buckets in a well; while the one ascends the other descends.[9]

When the Answer Is No

2 Corinthians 12:8–9 ***Concerning this thing I pleaded with the Lord three times that it might depart from me. And He said to me, "My grace is sufficient for you, for My strength is made perfect in weakness." (NKJV)***

In his second letter to the Corinthians, Paul mentioned a "thorn in the flesh" that afflicted him. He wasn't specific about what this "thorn" was; he just said it was "a messenger from Satan to buffet me, lest I be exalted above measure." It might have been a health problem (perhaps bad eyesight) that hindered his ministry, or an enemy who made life difficult for him. It may have even been some **besetting sin** that endangered his witness and induced self-loathing.

Whatever this "thorn in the flesh" was, Paul prayed that he would be relieved of it. Actually, he "pleaded with the Lord" on three different occasions. But God didn't see fit to give Paul the relief he prayed for.

Sometimes you pray, and the answer is just "No." In Paul's case, it wasn't lack of fervor that kept him from getting what he prayed for. It didn't seem to be a lack of worthiness on his part. His "thorn in the flesh" didn't appear to be a punishment. It's just that God considered Paul's thorn, as uncomfortable as it was, to be doing

martyr
a person who dies for his or her faith

blasphemy
the sin of claiming for oneself the attributes and rights of God

more good than harm. The thorn in Paul's flesh forced him to rely on God's grace. It kept him from relying on his own strength. It kept him in a place where he could see God at work—His strength operating in spite of human weakness.

An answer of "No" from God isn't a sign that He doesn't love you or doesn't want what's best for you. And just because God answers "No" to a request, that doesn't mean you shouldn't have made the request. Sometimes you just have no way of knowing what's best for you. Paul would have never guessed that a thorn in the side was just what the doctor ordered. But the Great Physician saw that the suffering in Paul's life was leading to a glory that would be much greater than pain-free living on earth.

key point

Sometimes the answer is "No" because that's what it takes to make you trust in God's grace. Our desire is to be free from suffering and hardship and heartache. But that, as it turns out, may be what's best for us. It's hard to remember you need God when you're comfortable and successful. A thorn in the flesh may be a reminder of how much you need the grace of the One whose strength is made perfect in weakness.

Undefeated

Acts 7:59 ***And they stoned Stephen as he was calling on God and saying, "Lord Jesus, receive my spirit."*** *(NKJV)*

Stephen was the first **martyr** of the Christian faith. Christianity was just getting off the ground, just starting to cause a stir. Stephen, who was one of the first group of seven deacons in the early church, had been performing signs and wonders and causing quite a stir in Jerusalem and beyond. His enemies trumped up charges of **blasphemy** against him. He was found guilty and sentenced to death by stoning.

Stoning was a horrible way to die. It was painful, and it was slow, so it gave the victim ample opportunity to beg for mercy, or to take back everything he had said that got him in trouble, or otherwise behave in an undignified manner. But Stephen didn't. as the stones rained down on him, he prayed, "Lord Jesus, receive my spirit." Then, just before he died, he prayed for his executioners: "Lord, do not charge them with this sin."

Stephen, as those final prayers showed, was invincible. Sure, his body was broken and killed, but his spirit was undefeated. The terror of death didn't frighten him, but only served to usher him into the presence of God. The hatred of his attackers didn't induce him to hate; his dying words were a prayer for them. As you can see from those final utterances, Stephen was a man of prayer to the very end, and that put him beyond the reach of his enemies.

There's an old saying that "the blood of the martyrs is the seed of the church." Stephen's attackers sought to stop Christianity in its tracks. Instead, they hastened its spread. People who saw Stephen's prayerful end could tell that the faith that strengthened him was no ordinary religion. Even when persecutors succeeded in scattering Christians, the Christians only started new fellowships in the places to which they scattered. One of those onlookers was a man named Saul. He held the coats of the people who threw the stones. Soon he himself would earn a reputation as an active persecutor of Christians. But God would have the last laugh on Saul. Saul encountered the glorified Jesus on the road to Damascus and became Paul, the greatest missionary of the early church.

something to ponder

You, like Stephen, face opportunities to depict the true nature of your faith in front of the world. A quiet, prayerful composure in the face of hardship and opposition speaks volumes.

what others say

Max Lucado

Final acts. Final hours. Final words. They reflect a life well lived. So do the last words of our Master. When on the edge of death, Jesus, too, got His house in order. . . . Final words. Final acts. Each one is a window in which the cross can be better understood.[10]

The Sound of Silence

1 Samuel 14:37 ***So Saul asked counsel of God, "Shall I go down after the Philistines? Will You deliver them into the hand of Israel?" But He did not answer him that day.*** (NKJV)

The Israelites had won a major victory over the **Philistines**. The first thing King Saul did was to build an altar to God. After he had offered up a sacrifice, he offered up a prayer for guidance: "Shall I go down after the Philistines? Will You deliver them into the hand of Israel?"

Philistines
people from Ancient Philistia and age-old enemies of Israel

go to

inadvertently broken an oath of fasting
1 Samuel 14:27–30

But God chose not to give Saul an immediate answer. He was silent on the matter. That was a frustrating thing for Saul. After all, he seemed to have done everything right. He dropped everything. He worshipped God. He sought God's will rather than relying on his own understanding. That was Saul's view of things, anyway. So why didn't God answer him?

Saul was the kind of person who wouldn't take silence for an answer—not even silence from God. He was sure that some sin in the camp was the reason for God's silence, and he meant to take care of the matter. He cast lots to find out who the sinner was, promising to kill the man who was at fault. The lot fell to Saul's son Jonathan. Jonathan had inadvertently broken an oath of fasting that his father had imposed unwisely (and unnecessarily) on his men before the battle. Saul's foolish vow before the battle led later to his foolish vow to kill the sinner. Saul's men intervened and saved Jonathan's life. Saul's rash desire to control God had led to two foolish vows, both of which were broken.

It's not clear from the Bible whether Jonathan's misstep was actually the cause of God's silence. What is clear is that Saul made a royal mess of things because he believed that he could bend God to his will rather than bending his own will to God's. He would not accept the fact that God was not at his beck and call, the way one of his advisors or one of his generals would be.

something to ponder

Prayer isn't a matter of imposing your will on God. Saul didn't get that. He thought he could force God's hand by imposing this oath or that. But that's not how things work. Yes, God responds to the needs and hopes and desires expressed in prayer. But prayer, ultimately, is a recognition that God is in charge, not you. And that requires a willingness to receive God's answer, whether it's yes or no—or even if it's silence.

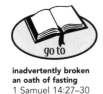

Chapter Wrap-Up

- A rich prayer life helps ensure that the rest of your life will be pleasing to God.
- Some of the best prayers are fueled by a "godly impatience"—a longing for God that won't wait.
- The experience of God brings you face to face with your own unworthiness; but it also brings you face to face with the God who cleanses you and makes you worthy.
- God always gives you what you need. Sometimes that means He says "No" to your prayers.

Study Questions

1. How can being a "Pharisee" be more dangerous than being a "sinner"?
2. What is the relationship between character and prayer?
3. How is "the blood of the martyrs the seed of the church"?
4. How does God use "thorns in the side" for the benefit of His people?
5. What does it mean to "repent of your righteousness"?

Chapter 7: Prayers of Intercession

Chapter Highlights:
- **The nature of benediction and blessing**
- **Pray for your leaders**
- **Pray for your children**
- **Pray for your enemies**

A Bold Approach

GENESIS 18:22B–23 ***Abraham still stood before the LORD. And Abraham came near and said, "Would You also destroy the righteous with the wicked?"*** *(NKJV)*

Abraham's prayer for Sodom and Gomorrah may be the most famous intercessory prayer in the Bible. You might say it was as much negotiation as intercession. God told Abraham He was going to destroy the wicked cities of Sodom and Gomorrah. But Abraham had family in Sodom—his nephew Lot and Lot's wife and two daughters. He didn't want to see the cities destroyed, so he entered into a lengthy (and very bold) negotiation with God. *You wouldn't destroy the righteous with the wicked, would you?* he asked. *If there are fifty righteous people in the city, would you spare the city for their sake?* God said that He would spare the city if he could find fifty righteous people. But Abraham thought again. Perhaps he had been to Sodom and Gomorrah and seen what those people were like. Fifty righteous people might be pushing it. *How about forty-five?* he asked. God said He would spare the cities for the sake of forty-five. The negotiation continued—forty, thirty, twenty, and finally ten. God said He would spare Sodom and Gomorrah if He found only ten righteous people there.

brimstone
an old name for sulfur, a flammable mineral that was found by the shores of the Dead Sea

In the end, God didn't find even ten righteous people in Sodom and Gomorrah, and the cities were destroyed in a rain of fire and **brimstone**. But God did spare Lot and his family. In that regard, God gave Abraham what he had asked for.

Abraham's prayer showed a combination of humility and boldness. "I who am but dust and ashes have taken it upon myself to speak to the Lord . . ." (Genesis 18:27 NKJV). "Let not the Lord be angry, and I will speak . . ." (Genesis 18:30 NKJV). It is clear from Abraham's language that there is some fear in his approach. He was taking a chance talking to God in the way he did. But Abraham loved his family enough to step in and speak to God on their behalf.

something to ponder

When we draw near to God we are approaching both the familiar and the heart-stopping. He is our heavenly Father and knows our every thought, our every need, our every care. He actually desires us to talk about these things. But He is also God. We should move toward Him with both reverence and boldness. It's okay to draw close, to lean in, to whisper in His ear. It's okay to speak to Him from the very depths of your heart, telling Him of your joys, your sorrows. He is waiting. He is listening.

what others say

Andrew Murray

We have confidence toward God in prayer when we are forgiven. We can be thankful every day of our lives because we are free and nothing stands between us and God. With the door open to communion with Him, God desires that we come boldly before the throne to spend time with Him each day as people whose sins are forgiven.[1]

What the Bible Says

Coming Boldly Before the Throne	Scripture
We have boldness and access thanks to the finished work of Christ.	Ephesians 3:11–12
We can come boldly because we have a High Priest (Jesus) who can sympathize with us.	Hebrews 4:16
We can be bold because our consciences have been sprinkled clean by the blood of Christ.	Hebrews 10:19–22

An Heirloom of Prayer

GENESIS **48:15–16** ***And he blessed Joseph, and said:***
"God, before whom my fathers Abraham and Isaac walked,
The God who has fed me all my life long to this day,
The Angel who has redeemed me from all evil,
Bless the lads;
Let my name be named upon them,
And the name of my fathers Abraham and Isaac;
And let them grow into a multitude in the midst of the earth."
(NKJV)

go to

draw close
James 4:8

Jacob had seen his share of family dysfunction in his life. He had his troubles with his brother Esau, troubles that were exacerbated by the favoritism of their parents, Isaac and Rebekah. In his own large family, factions and rivalries formed among the sons of Jacob's different wives and concubines, and Jacob did little to help the situation. In fact, the favoritism Jacob showed to Joseph yielded the most dramatic moment of family dysfunction in the whole story, when Joseph's brothers faked his death and sold him into slavery.

But at the end of his life, Jacob could see that God had redeemed all that strife and foolishness. What Joseph's brothers had meant for evil, God meant for good. He used Joseph's sojourn among the Egyptians as a means of rescuing Jacob's whole family. The family was reunited in Egypt, saved from ruin or dispersal. And after decades of mourning the loss of his favorite son, Jacob had Joseph returned to him, as if from the dead. Jacob's heart must have been full to bursting in his last days. Nothing about Jacob's parenting practices made him worthy of the happy result with which he found himself. Even on his deathbed, Jacob basked in God's grace.

Joseph brought his sons Manasseh and Ephraim to meet their grandfather Jacob on his deathbed, and the old man's joy was multiplied again. "I had not thought to see your face," he said to Joseph; "but in fact, God has shown me your offspring!" (Genesis 48:11 NKJV). The promise of his continued lineage stood before him in the persons of his grandsons. He placed his hands on them and prayed God's blessings on them: "Bless the lads; Let my name be named upon them, And the name of my fathers Abraham and Isaac; And let them grow into a multitude in the midst of the earth" (Genesis 48:16 NKJV).

Jacob was a rich man and was able to leave a great earthly inheritance for Joseph and his grandsons. In fact, he told Joseph just before he died that he had set aside a special inheritance for him, beyond even what his brothers were getting. But Jacob's great heritage to Joseph, Manasseh, and Ephraim was the blessing he prayed over them. Their future, their hope depended more on God's provision and blessing than on any wealth Jacob could bequeath them. It's an inheritance that any parent or grandparent can pass along to his or her descendants.

go to

favoritism Jacob showed to Joseph
Genesis 37:3

God meant for good
Genesis 50:20

what others say

Anita Corrine Donihue

Just as You prayed for me in the Garden of Gethsemane, I am assured that You accept my prayers for these, my children, my children's children, and on through the generations. I have no fear for their future, because I place them in Your loving care.[2]

Aaron and his sons
Exodus 28:3–4

Parents Praying for Their Children

Who Prayed	Scripture
Abraham prays for Ishmael.	Genesis 17:18
David blesses Solomon.	1 Kings 2:1–4
Job intercedes for his children.	Job 1:5
Jairus asks Jesus to save his dying daughter.	Luke 8:41–56

I Need Your Benediction

NUMBERS 6:24–27
"The LORD bless you and keep you;
The LORD make His face shine upon you,
And be gracious to you;
The LORD lift up His countenance upon you,
And give you peace."'
"So they shall put My name on the children of Israel, and I will bless them." (NKJV)

The word *benediction* literally means "good words" or "good speaking." A benediction is a blessing. God instructed Moses in the exact benediction He wanted the priests to speak over His people: "The LORD bless you and keep you; The LORD make His face shine upon you, and be gracious to you; The LORD lift up His countenance upon you, And give you peace" (Numbers 6:24–27 NKJV). It's a beautiful blessing, one that is still used as a benediction in many churches. It serves as a reminder that the greatest blessing of all is simply the presence of God—God's face shining like the sun on His people.

After giving that blessing, God made an interesting comment to Moses: "So they [the priests] shall put My name on the children of Israel, and bless them" (Numbers 6:27 NKJV). By that blessing—the promise of God's presence—the people would receive the name of God. That is to say, being the "people of God" means being people who live with a constant awareness of the presence and the blessing of God.

Another thing to note about blessings is their "other-focus." You don't usually think of a person speaking a benediction over himself or herself, but others—and especially others over whom that person exercises some authority. As priests, Aaron and his sons exercised power and authority over the people. They enjoyed a station in society from which they could "lord it over" their countrymen in many ways. Speaking a benediction transforms that authority into something more like a parent's love for a child. It says, "I'm going to use my position to be a blessing to you, not to use you for my own gain or gratification. By requiring the priests to repeat this blessing, God reminded them of their true role before the people. They were to be servant-leaders. The blessing also served as a constant reminder of who was the true Authority over the children of Israel.

You're in authority over somebody. How do you exercise that authority? Get in the habit of speaking a benediction over the people under your authority. They don't even have to know you're doing it. But as you call down the presence of God—the shine of God's face—on those people, you will be reminded of your true role in those people's lives, and your true standing before God.

go to

the shine of God's face
Psalm 36:16, 67:1, 80:19

Miriam saved Moses' life
Exodus 2:3–4

pillar of cloud
Exodus 13:21–22

what others say

Robert Benson

What binds us together is the prayer, the promise and the lifting of each other's burdens, the commitment we have made, and kept, to be companions to each other on the road that we share. What binds us together is the laying down of our lives for each other in a way that we cannot even explain.[3]

A Prayer for Healing

NUMBERS 12:13 ***So Moses cried out to the LORD, saying, "Please heal her, O God, I pray!"*** **(NKJV)**

There had been some strife within Moses' family. Aaron and Miriam were getting tired of playing second fiddle to their brother Moses. Remember, when Moses was a helpless baby Miriam saved Moses' life. She changed his diapers. And now Moses was the big hero, the prophet of God? She and Aaron grumbled, "Has the LORD indeed spoken only through Moses? Has He not spoken through us also?" (Numbers 12:2 NKJV).

God was not happy with the envious grumbling of Miriam and Aaron. He summoned the two of them to the tent of meeting, along with Moses. The pillar of cloud that represented God's presence overshadowed the tent and made things dark, creating an ominous mood. *There are prophets*, God said, *to whom I speak in dreams and visions. But Moses is in a different league. I speak to Moses face to face.*

go to

healing
James 5:15

"Why then were you not afraid to speak against My servant Moses?" (Numbers 12:8 NKJV).

The pillar of cloud went away when God finished speaking, and the tent grew light again. Moses and Aaron could see that Miriam's skin had turned white with leprosy. God had gotten the grumblers' attention. It's as if He were saying, "You want to present yourselves before the people as a prophet? See how willing they are to follow a leper."

But Moses prayed on his sister's behalf, "Please heal her, O God, I pray!" God did heal Miriam, though she had to stay outside the camp for seven days before she was deemed well and clean enough to reenter the community.

Moses might have held a grudge against his brother and sister. They represented a serious threat to his leadership and to the success of this huge undertaking. If his own brother and sister wouldn't follow Moses, it wouldn't be long before none of the other two million Israelites would be willing to follow him either. Moses might have prayed, "Thank you, Lord, for taking my side in this conflict. But did you forget about Aaron? He was grumbling too." Instead, he prayed for his sister. It took humility to do that, not to gloat over Miriam's getting what she had coming.

Did God heal Miriam? Absolutely. She was restored physically, spiritually, and within her role as sister, sister-in-law, and prophetess among the people. We serve a God who is interested in our physical healing—truly—but One who is even more concerned with the spiritual diseases that divide us from one another and from Him.

something to ponder

A few thousand years later, Jesus preached that we are to pray for our enemies. Moses practiced it before it was ever preached, laying aside a potentially dangerous sibling rivalry in order to recognize that Miriam was his sister first and foremost.

what others say

Richard Daly

Spiritual healing—a deeper reconciliation between God and man—is the highest and most complete form of healing one can receive.[4]

Praying for Our Leaders

NUMBERS 27:15–17 ***Then Moses spoke to the LORD, saying: "Let the LORD, the God of the spirits of all flesh, set a man over the congregation, who may go out before them and go in before them, who may lead them out and bring them in, that the congregation of the LORD may not be like sheep which have no shepherd."*** *(NKJV)*

go to

pray for kings
1 Timothy 2:1–2

representative government
government in which the leaders are chosen by popular election

Moses was getting old, and it was time to start thinking about who would lead the Israelites after he was gone. He prayed to God to identify a person who would be the kind of leader the children of Israel needed—"who may go out before them and go in before them, who may lead them out and bring them in, that the congregation of the LORD may not be like sheep which have no shepherd" (Numbers 27:17 (NKJV).

God heard Moses' prayer and answered it. Surely Moses was pleased to hear that the leader God had in mind for Israel was Joshua. He was Moses' right-hand man, and he was also one of only two spies out of twelve who insisted on trusting God and taking the promised land. After forty years, Joshua would get his chance to do just that.

Paul instructed Timothy to pray for kings and for those who are in authority. Moses' prayer provides a good model for those prayers. Moses prayed for a leader who would not simply look out for himself, but actually lead the people. Moses' ideal leader wouldn't leave the people to their own devices, like sheep without a shepherd, but would lead them out and bring them home again. Here's how C.S. Lewis described the ideal king in *A Horse and His Boy*: to be a king is "to be first in every desperate attack and last in every desperate retreat, and when there's hunger in the land (as there must be now and then in bad years) to wear finer clothes and laugh louder over a scantier meal than anyone in the land."

apply it

As you pray for your leaders, you're actually praying for your neighbors and fellow countrymen. As Paul said, the purpose of prayer for leaders is that "we may all lead a quiet and peaceable life in all godliness and reverence" (1 Timothy 2:2 NKJV). In a system of **representative government**, it's even more obvious that praying for the leadership means praying for the people. The leaders chosen by a community or nation say something about the character of that

right hand
Psalm 16:11

underneath His feet
Lamentations 1:15

nostrils
2 Samuel 22:9

community or nation. When you pray for your leaders, pray also for the people who elect them. Pray that your leaders will not be self-indulgent in their use of authority. At the same time, pray that the voters won't be self-indulgent either.

what others say

Stormie Omartian

Our nation was founded on prayer. The prophets of the Old Testament were thought of as watchmen . . . God has placed watchmen on the walls of our nation who see things we can't and who warn us of enemy encroachment. We have a new enemy we cannot always see . . . We know we need something greater than ourselves to defeat this enemy. We need the power of God. Because of that, we must make praying for our leaders/nation a habit.[5]

God's Eyes and Ears

1 Kings 8:52 ***[I pray] that Your eyes may be open to the supplication of Your servant and the supplication of Your people Israel, to listen to them whenever they call to You.*** *(NKJV)*

John 4:24 teaches clearly "God is a spirit." "He does not have a body like other men" is one of the basic religious principles taught to children.Throughout the Bible, the poets speak figuratively of God's body parts. At His right hand are pleasures forever. He has trampled His enemies underneath His feet. David even spoke once of God blowing smoke from His nostrils! But perhaps the most commonly mentioned body parts of God are His eyes and ears.

Solomon prayed that God's eyes would be open to the prayers of His people, and that He would be attentive to listen. Solomon knew, of course, that God didn't have eyes or ears, just as Solomon's father David knew it. But they spoke of God's eyes and ears because they knew first-hand how God watched over them and listened for them. He was more attentive and watchful than a person with eyes and ears could ever be.

key point

Every time you pray, it is your desire that God hear and see. That's the whole point of praying, isn't it? But remember that God hears and sees even when you're not praying. And that's a good thing. He holds your whole life in the palm of His hand. He never sleeps, but always watches. Of course, that can also be a scary thought—it's all the more reason to live the kind of life that pleases God! As you learn to live under the sight and in the hearing of God, you live differently.

supplication
the making of requests, especially to God

But if one purpose of prayer is to be seen and heard by God, another purpose is to see and hear God ourselves. We can't of course, see Him with our physical eyes, nor can we hear Him with our physical ears, but the practice of prayer makes us spiritually attuned to the things of God, and we perceive truths that we can neither see nor hear.

When we busy ourselves in our daily lives, God is listening. God is watching. Does that make you comfortable or uncomfortable?

something to ponder

what others say

Anonymous

Prayer based upon the Word rises above the senses, contacts the Author of the Word and sets His spiritual laws into motion. It is not just saying prayers that gets results, but it is spending time with the Father, learning His wisdom, drawing on His strength, being filled with His quietness, and basking in His love that bring results to our prayers.

Looking Forward, Looking Back

1 Kings 8:56–58 ***Blessed be the Lord, who has given rest to His people Israel, according to all that He promise. There has not failed one word of all His good promise, which He promised through his servant Moses. May the Lord our God be with us, as He was with our fathers. May He not leave us nor forsake us, that He may incline our hearts to Himself, to walk in all His ways, and to keep His commandments and His statutes and His judgments, which He commanded our fathers.*** *(NKJV)*

You typically think of prayers—especially prayers of **supplication** or intercession as being forward-looking: *Lord, I have this problem right now, but I hope you'll provide me with a solution in the not-too-distant future.* Prayers of thanksgiving are often more backward-looking: *Lord, thank you for what you did for me in the past.* Solomon's prayer at the dedication of the temple demonstrates how past, present, and future—as well as supplication and thanksgiving—all get blended together in our prayers.

"God be with us," Solomon prays. That's a prayer for the present or the future. The dedication of the temple marks the start of a new

go to

his heritage
Psalm 16:6

made their requests known to Jesus
Philippians 4:6

Sermon on the Mount
Matthew 5-7

era for the Israelites. They have a bright future ahead of them, but it won't mean anything if God isn't with them. Look at the basis of Solomon's confidence: "May the LORD our God be with us, *as He was with our fathers* (italics added)." Solomon has hope for the future because he knows what God has been like in the past. Looking back at the sweep of Israelite history, Solomon saw a pattern: God promised, and God delivered on His promises. No wonder he's so confident. He knows that God was with his ancestors, so why wouldn't God be with him now? He's looking forward and backward at the same time, and what he sees is God's faithfulness.

Solomon has chosen his words carefully in this prayer. He prays "May He not leave us nor forsake us." He's got to feel good about his chances of getting an affirmative on that one. For he's only praying back the promise that God gave to Solomon's people generations earlier: "Be strong and courageous. Do not be afraid or terrified because of them, for the Lord your God goes with you; he will never leave you nor forsake you." Solomon is very strong, very courageous as he looks ahead to the future of his kingdom. That's because he knows his heritage. He remembers God's faithfulness.

something to ponder

How has God shown His faithfulness in your life? Looking back, where can you see that He has protected you, strengthened you, provided for you in ways that were so obviously God that they can't possibly be explained away? Consider how God has shown Himself faithful to His church through the years. All those past victories are the basis for a future hope. Pray with one eye to the past and one eye to the future.

Short and Sweet

JOHN 11:3 *Lord, behold, he whom You love is sick. (NKJV)*

Lazarus lay dying in Bethany. His sisters went to find Jesus and said urgently "Lord, behold, he whom You love is sick." It was a very simple request. In fact, strictly speaking, it wasn't a request at all. They simply made their needs known to Jesus They used no flowery language, nor did they use any formulas. They didn't even say 'amen.' They just spoke to Jesus, as a friend to a friend—which, of course, Jesus was to Martha and Mary and to Lazarus too.

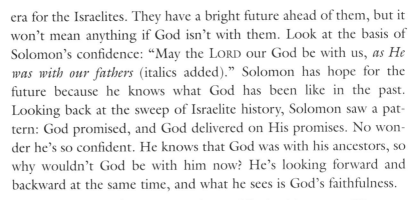

The simplicity of the sisters' prayer must have pleased Jesus. In the Sermon on the Mount, Jesus said, "When you pray, do not use vain

repetitions as the heathen do. For they think that they will be heard for their many words" (Matthew 6:7 NKJV). Vain repetitions. Excessive words. The prophets of Baal, you will remember, shouted themselves hoarse trying to get their god's attention, but Elijah prayed a short, comparatively quiet prayer that was shockingly effective. It's not just the heathens who fall into the trap of vainly repetitive prayers. The formulas change from group to group and from era to era, but Christians can't help coming up with new formulas to repeat to seem more reverent or more earnest or more holy in their prayers. God isn't especially impressed with formulas. He already knows your needs before you articulate them. By praying them, you're not so much informing God or trying to get His attention as you are putting yourself into a position to rest in His care.

Think how Martha and Mary's prayer might have been expressed today: "Dear Lord, we just acknowledge right now that you are the great Healer. And we lift before you right now our brother Lazarus. We pray that you would give the doctors wisdom and discernment, and that You would guide their hands as they minister to our brother Lazarus . . ." There's nothing inherently wrong with most of the formulaic language you hear in prayers. The problem is that it is often used for the purpose of impressing human listeners; sometimes it has little or nothing to do with the true purpose of supplication—letting go of your needs and concerns, and laying them at the feet of God. There's real beauty in the short, sweet prayer of Martha and Mary: "Lord, behold, he whom You love is sick."

go to

his cloak and some scrolls
2 Timothy 4:13

It's All About Jesus

> HEBREWS 13:20–21 ***Now may the God of peace who brought up our Lord Jesus from the dead, that great Shepherd of the sheep, through the blood of the everlasting covenant, make you complete in every good work to do His will, working in you what is well pleasing in His sight, through Jesus Christ, to whom be glory forever and ever. Amen.*** (NKJV)

Most of the books of the New Testament started out life as letters from real people to other real people. They were personal communications, and they often contain personal details that you would expect in a letter between friends. Paul asked Timothy to bring his cloak and some scrolls that he had left with a friend named Carpus.

go to

advice regarding his digestion
1 Timothy 5:23

supremacy
the state of being the greatest in importance, significance, rank, power, and authority

In another letter to Timothy, he gave advice regarding his digestion. In his letter to the Philippians, Paul called out two women by name—Euodia and Syntyche—and told them to stop quarrelling.

The personal relationship between the correspondents in the epistles of the New Testament adds another dimension to the beautiful blessings with which so many of the epistles conclude. The writer of Hebrews remains anonymous, but his love for the people to whom he wrote is evident in the closing paragraph of his letter. "May God make you complete in every way," he prayed. But notice what that completion, that fulfillment meant to this writer. He didn't say, "May your every dream come true" or "May you find what you're looking for." His prayer for his friends was that they would be made complete so that they could do the things that please God.

The writer of Hebrews prayed that his friends' lives would be swallowed up by the life of Christ. He could offer no better blessing. His fondest hope for them was that they would be lost in the glory of the Christ who died and rose again to redeem them.

The writer of Hebrews was himself consumed with the **supremacy** of Christ. It was all he could talk about. It was all about Jesus, first and last. This closing blessing sums it all up. He speaks of God the Father as the One "who brought our Lord Jesus from the dead." And the completion he prayed for his friends would be accomplished "through Jesus Christ, to whom be glory forever."

The glory of Christ. In the end, all the glory you could hope for yourself or for those you love is to be swallowed up and lost in the glory of Christ. He is our hope and our glory, first and last.

what others say

Eugene H. Peterson

It seems odd to have to say so, but too much religion is a bad thing. We can't get too much of God, can't get too much faith and obedience, can't get too much love and worship. But religion—the well-intentioned efforts we make to "get it all together" for God—can very well get in the way of what God is doing for us . . . Our main and central task is to live in responsive obedience to God's action revealed in Jesus...and we are free once more for the act of faith, the one human action in which we don't get in the way but on the Way.[6]

Pure and Blameless

PHILIPPIANS 1:9–10 ***And this I pray, that your love may abound still more and more in knowledge and all discernment, that you may approve the things that are excellent, that you may be sincere and without offense till the day of Christ.*** **(NKJV)**

Paul's prayer for the people of Philippi was a prayer for balance. He prayed that their love would abound. As Jesus said, "By this all will know that you are My disciples, if you have love for one another" (John 13:35 NKJV). But even as love abounded, Paul prayed the Philippians' love would be accompanied by knowledge and **discernment**. Love is an opening of the self; it's risky, and involves being exposed and vulnerable. Love "believes all things." That is to say, love is inclined to see the best in people. But the Philippian Christians lived in a community hostile to them. If they were to be faithful disciples of Christ, they had no choice but to love others, even their enemies. But that love needed to be tempered by a measure of knowledge and discernment if they were to survive as a body. They needed some "street smarts" to get by in Philippi.

Paul didn't promote knowledge and discernment ahead of love. It wasn't knowledge and discernment that would change the world; only love could to that. But Jesus Himself urged the disciples to be "wise as serpents and harmless as doves" (Matthew 10:16 NKJV).

When abounding love is tempered by knowledge and discernment, the result is the habit of "approving things that are excellent." That word "approve" is the Greek word *dokimazo*. It means "test, examine, scrutinize," or "recognize as genuine" or "deem worthy." It's one thing to disapprove of things that are wicked. But the true Christian witness has the ability to recognize the good life when we see it. It takes more than worldly wisdom to do that. It takes a godly love to truly appreciate—approve—the things that are excellent.

Paul actually goes a step further. It's not enough to approve or recognize the good life. Love and discernment make it possible for you to *live* the good life. The goal is to be "sincere and without offense" until the day of Christ. Paul intercedes on behalf of his brothers and sisters in Philippi, that they might be that kind of people. It is each believer's responsibility to discern right and wrong, and to pray for the strength to do so, but what strength is there when brothers and sisters in Christ commit to pray that for one another!

go to

Love "believes all things"
1 Corinthians 13:7

hostile
Acts 16

discernment
the ability to tell the difference between right and wrong, or even between good, better, and best, even when the difference is not obvious

what others say

George Hakewill

> The first thing he vows touching himself, is wise behavior . . . not wise contemplation, but wise action. It is not wise thoughts, or wise speaking, or wise writing, or wise gesture and countenance, will serve the turn, but wise behavior.[9]

Chapter Wrap-Up

- God's past faithfulness is a source of confidence and future hope as you pray.
- To pray for government leaders is to also pray for the people who are governed by them.
- One of your responsibilities as a person of authority is to pray for and bless the people you have authority over.
- To speak a blessing or benediction is to forget yourself and be other-focused.

Study Questions

1. What is an intercessory prayer?
2. How is pronouncing a benediction a kind of servant leadership?
3. Why is it important to look backward *and* forward when you pray?
4. What does it mean to "approve the things that are excellent"?
5. Why does love need knowledge and discernment?

Chapter 8: Prayers for Guidance

Chapter Highlights:
- Seeking God's will
- Hearing God's voice
- Doing God's will
- The Fatherhood of God
- God's guidance

Traveling Mercies

NUMBERS 10:35b ***Rise up, O LORD! Let Your enemies be scattered, And let those who hate You flee before You.*** *(NKJV)*

manna
a miraculous food gifted to the Hebrews by God and provided daily, except on Sunday

Anytime the children of Israel broke camp and moved during their wanderings in the wilderness, it was a huge production. After all, there were two million of them, of all ages. Of all the things they carried, the most vital was the ark of the covenant, a gold-covered box topped with two angels facing each other with outstretched wings touching tip-to-tip. Attached poles enabled the men to pick it up and carry it as they moved through the desert. The ark carried three sacred objects: the tablets containing the Ten Commandments, a portion of saved **manna**, and Aaron's rod, which had grown buds and leaves in Egypt. The ark was also associated with the presence of God. Indeed, to the traveling Hebrews, it *was* the presence of God. Unless it was with them to protect them from harm, they weren't going anywhere.

Before they moved the ark, the people of Israel always prayed, "Rise up, O LORD! Let Your enemies be scattered, And let those who hate You flee before You" (Numbers 10:35b NKJV). It's as if God is a football blocker, clearing a path for the Israelites to run, knocking opponents out of the way. Or maybe a better image is the Secret Service, securing every place the President might go, providing a bubble of protection in a hostile world.

The dangers of traveling were very obvious to the Israelites. They were traveling through deserts, after all, and there was always the possibility of dehydration, heat stroke, snake bites, attacks by enemies, and other dangers. There were going into the unknown, so it was very apparent to them that they needed God's help—his mercy.

In our world, travel doesn't seem nearly so big a deal. With air-conditioning and power steering and antilock brakes, we can go a very long way without feeling any discomfort, much less danger. You can leave New York and fly to London in six hours or so. With trav-

go to

makes a path
Job 41:32;
Psalm 16:11;
Psalm 27:11;
Psalm 119:1, 5

"least" in the family
Judges 6:15

prayer of safekeeping
asking God to keep us safe and in His care

eling conditions like that, it's easy to forget that we still need God's traveling mercies.

We set out on journeys using all sorts of transportation—car, bus, cab, subway, boat, or train. Regardless of our mode of travel we should begin and end each journey with a **prayer of safekeeping**, and then thanking Him for our safe travels when we've arrived.

We still live in a hostile world, no matter what our technological advances and civilized comforts might tell us. That's why it's so important to acknowledge the One who is our only help. We need God to go before and beside and behind. Of course people travel safely without ever praying or ever even acknowledging God. But physical safety isn't really the point. The point is going through this world—this life—under the guidance and guardianship of the God who makes a path for us.

Was That You, God?

JUDGES 6:17 ***Then [Gideon] said to Him, "If now I have found favor in Your sight, then show me a sign that it is You who talk with me." (NKJV)***

Gideon was a poor Israelite belonging to the weakest clan in Manasseh. He was the youngest son; in those days he was considered to be the "least" in the family. There was nothing remarkable about him. In the eyes of the world, his family, and even himself, he wasn't much to write home about.

But that's not what God saw when He looked at Gideon. God delights in doing great things with seemingly weak vessels. He used Moses, a stutterer, to speak the truth to Pharaoh. He used Rahab, a heathen prostitute, to rescue the twelve spies and preserve the Israelite cause. He used a boy with a slingshot to defeat a Philistine giant. And when He took on human flesh, God was born to peasants, not to a king and queen, and was laid to rest in a feed trough for animals.

So perhaps it shouldn't be too surprising that God should go to a person like Gideon when He was looking to raise up a champion to lead the Israelites against their Midianite oppressors. Nevertheless, Gideon was very surprised when an angel said, "The LORD is with you, you mighty man of valor" (Judges 6:12 NKJV). You can under-

stand if Gideon turned around to see if the angel might be talking to somebody else. And when the angel said, "Go in this might of yours, and you shall save Israel from the hand of the Midianites" (Judges 6:14 NKJV), you can understand Gideon's answer—in effect, "Might? What might?"

go to

chose not to lean on his own understanding
Proverbs 3:5

Gideon wanted to be sure he wasn't imagining things, so he asked God to give him a sign. The angel instructed Gideon to prepare a goat and some bread and broth, the components of an offering. When Gideon brought them, fire appeared to consume the offering, and the angel disappeared. Gideon knew he had heard from the Lord. The rest, as they say, is history.

Asking for signs from God can be a tricky business. We can't after all, understand all of God's ways, and we owe God obedience with or without signs. Gideon's request for a sign appears at first blush to be a challenge to God: Prove it! But in fact, there was real humility in Gideon's request. He chose not to lean on his own understanding. He *thought* he was hearing from God, but he wanted to be sure before he stepped out. When he was sure, he obeyed without hesitation.

something to ponder

God's Signs to His People

Sign	Scripture
Noah's Rainbow	Genesis 9:13-17
The Burning Bush	Exodus 3:2-6
Signs for Pharaoh	Exodus 4:1-9
Gideon's Fleece	Judges 6:36-40
The Star of Bethlehem	Matthew 2:1-10

what others say

Dallas Willard

I believe we, as disciples of Jesus Christ, cannot abandon faith in our ability to hear from God. To abandon this is to abandon the reality of a personal relationship with God, and that we must not do.[1]

Your Servant Is Listening

1 Samuel 3:10b ***Samuel answered, "Speak, for Your servant hears." (NKJV)***

It had been a spiritual dry spell in Israel. The priesthood had fallen into corruption, and the people had fallen away from God. When

go to

Hannah prayed
1 Samuel 1:9–17

Be still
Psalm 46:10

the devout Hannah prayed in the temple—her lips moving silently in the intensity of her prayer—the chief priest Eli, the highest-ranking religious professional in the land, thought she was drunk. Had he never seen such heartfelt prayer?

That's the spiritual context in which Samuel grew up. He was literally the answer to his mother Hannah's prayer—the prayer she offered up in Eli's temple. But when Hannah handed her boy over to Eli, she was leaving him in a world where God had seemingly gone silent. "The word of the Lord was rare in those days; there was no widespread revelation" (1 Samuel 3:1 NKJV).

God didn't remain silent, however. He spoke to the boy Samuel in the dead of night. Three times Samuel heard the voice of God calling him audibly, and each time he ran to Eli, thinking the old priest had called for him. By the third time, however, Eli understood that it must have been God calling Samuel, and he instructed Samuel to lie back down and, should he hear the voice of God again, pray this expectant prayer: "Speak, Lord, for your servant hears" (1 Samuel 3:9 NKJV). The Lord spoke a fourth time, and Samuel prayed as Eli instructed him. The Lord spoke, Samuel heard, and thus began the prophetic career of Samuel. Under his spiritual leadership, Israel came out of its spiritual depression and entered into its golden age—the era of King David, whom Samuel himself anointed.

key point

If you want to know the heart of God, be sure your prayer life includes time for listening, not just talking. Prayer is communication. And communication isn't just a matter of one person spouting off a monologue at another person. Be still. Trust God to speak. For He does speak to those who say "Your servant hears." He probably won't speak audibly. But in the silence, He will bring to mind the truths you know you can build a life on. He will shape your desires and check the desires that don't accord with His will. He will prepare your heart and mind to see His clear guidance in the everyday events and conversations of life. Listen. God still speaks.

what others say

Mother Teresa

Listen in silence, because if your heart is full of other things you cannot hear the voice of God. But when you have listened to the voice of God in the stillness of your heart, then your heart is filled with God.[2]

Details, Details

1 Samuel 23:10–11 ***"O Lord God of Israel, Your servant has certainly heard that Saul seeks to come to Keilah to destroy the city for my sake. Will the men of Keilah deliver me into his hand? Will Saul come down, as Your servant has heard? O Lord God of Israel, I pray, tell Your servant." And the Lord said, "He will come down."*** *(NKJV)*

go to

loyalty
1 Samuel 24:10

As usual, David was on the run from King Saul. Yet his loyalty to Saul remained strong, and his loyalty to Saul's kingdom of Israel was even stronger. When the Philistines marched on the Israelite town of Keilah, David realized that he and his men, not Saul's army, would be in the best position to rescue their countrymen. He prayed for guidance. God answered, "Go and attack the Philistines, and deliver Keilah." In earthly terms, it was a crazy idea. David and his men weren't a real army. If the Israelites were being attacked, shouldn't that be the king's problem? Why should they do the work of the king who was trying to kill them? Furthermore, it was possible that King Saul was already heading for Keilah to address the problem. Assuming David and his men *didn't* get slaughtered by the Philistines, they might find themselves facing Saul's fresh troops as soon as they were finished with the Philistines. So David prayed again, just to make sure, and God assured him that he should go to Keilah.

David's men conquered the Philistines, but their difficulties weren't over. When Saul heard that David was inside a walled, double-gated city, he was delighted. "God has delivered him into my hand," he crowed. He left immediately for Keilah, at the head of a besieging army.

David got word of Saul's plan, and again he prayed for guidance. "Is Saul truly headed this way?" he asked. "Yes," was God's answer. "And will the citizens of Keilah betray us into Saul's hands?" "Yes." David and his six hundred men left immediately, escaping Saul once again.

Notice how David prayed for guidance at every point. When he got his answer, he prayed again, just to make sure. Also notice what Saul said when he discovered that David was in a trap. He "spiritualized" the matter, declaring that God had given David into his hands. But the Bible never says he actually prayed. He never asked,

"What is God's will here?" He saw what he wanted to see. Saul got it wrong because he was interested in God's plan only insofar as it seemed to justify his own.

something to ponder

There is a difference between looking for signs and actually praying for guidance. The "signs," in fact, can't make much sense unless you approach them from a place of prayerfulness.

what others say

Matthew Henry

David's address to God is very solemn, also very particular. God allows us to be so in our addresses to Him; Lord, direct me in this matter, about which I am now at a loss. God knows not only what will be, but what would be, if it were not hindered; therefore He knows how to deliver the godly out of temptation, and how to render to every man according to his works.[3]

Trusted Father

2 SAMUEL 7:28 ***And now, O Lord GOD, You are God, and Your words are true, and You have promised this goodness to Your servant.*** *(NKJV)*

Even when he was at the zenith of his career, David was still a little child before God. He came before his heavenly Father with all the trust of a child who takes his earthly father's every word for the gospel truth. "Your words are true," he prayed, "and you have promised this goodness to Your servant." This is the continuation of the prayer discussed in "Honoring God for His Gifts." Still marveling at the promises God made regarding David's heritage, David is struck anew by the fact that God keeps His promises. He is forever trustworthy.

David's prayer is fueled by the fact of God's faithfulness. It gives him the security and confidence to make his request known to God. As Paul told Timothy, "If we are faithless, God remains faithful, for He cannot deny Himself" (2 Timothy 2:13 NKJV). God's faithfulness is not a response to your **faithfulness**; it doesn't rise and fall with your emotional state or your recent performance. God is faithful because that's who He is. He cannot deny Himself. Once you understand the fact of God's unchanging character, it changes your approach to everything. You don't have to look at the ever-changing

faithfulness
reliability; steadfast adherence, as to the teachings of the Christian faith

facts of the world around you in order to knew where you stand. Rather, you can look at God's promises.

The result of that shift in thinking is a trust and rest very similar to that of a child who rests in the love and provision of a parent. "Surely I have calmed and quieted my soul," wrote David in Psalm 131. "Like a weaned child with his mother, like a weaned child is my soul within me." That's a beautiful picture of what it means to trust God's faithfulness.

It's true that a small child lives in a world full of potential danger and hardship. It's true that a child is utterly incapable of taking care of himself in the world at large. And yet those facts are very small compared to the fact that he has a parent who shields him from the dangers of the world and takes care of his needs. That's why a child rests rather than worrying where his next meal is coming from or fretting about the mortgage.

You can rest and rejoice in the faithfulness of God, who always, always keeps His promises.

go to

worrying
Matthew 6:25

what others say

Hank Hanegraaff

As the father of eight children, I can tell you that I sometimes know what my children need before they ask me. However, what I, as an earthly father, only sometimes know, our eternal father always knows. The fact that I often know what my kids are going to say before they open their mouths does not mean I don't want them to ask. Rather, I long for them to verbalize their thoughts and feelings. That's how our relationship blossoms and grows. Likewise, if we are to nurture a strong bond with our Creator, we must continually communicate with Him.[4]

What the Bible Says About

The Spiritual Significance of Children	Scripture
"As a father pities his children, So the Lord pities those who fear Him."	Psalm 103:13 (NKJV)
[Jesus speaking]: "Unless you are converted and become as little children, you will by no means enter the kingdom of heaven."	Matthew 18:3 (NKJV)
[Jesus speaking]: "Let the little children come to Me, and do not forbid them; for of such is the kingdom of heaven."	Matthew 19:14 (NKJV)
"Do not be children in understanding; however, in malice be babes, but in understanding be mature."	1 Corinthians 14:20 (NKJV)

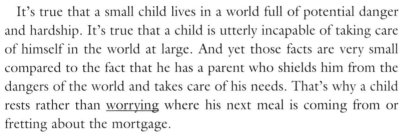

Light on the Path

2 Samuel 22:29
For You are my lamp, O Lord;
The Lord shall enlighten my darkness. *(NKJV)*

go to

dark places
Psalm 23:4

cares of today
Matthew 6:24

Thanking God for his deliverance from his many enemies, David prayed, "You are my lamp, O Lord. The Lord shall enlighten my darkness." David had known a lot of darkness, but now God had transformed it into light. And even before that when things were still dark, God lit David's way enough to get him where he was going.

Picture yourself walking down a long, narrow country road late one dark night. There are no street lamps glowing overhead to cast a shadowy path to follow. You have a pretty good idea as to *where* you are going, but the darkness is making the journey very difficult. Just when you wonder if you will make it at all, a gentle breeze pushes the cloudy veil from in front of the moon and for a time the road before you is illuminated.

In his prayer to God, King David is expressing the same sentiment that we might feel were we the dark night traveler. His words make up both request and praise. "I thank you for making the way clear for me and ask that you always will."

apply it

As you walk upon the road of life, you often find yourself in dark places . . . places where the path seems unclear and unsettled. There are ruts and debris and crossroads to consider. David understood this as well as anyone, having been pursued and unjustly persecuted for many years of his life. It isn't unusual that you sometimes feel exactly the same way. Jesus said, "I have come into the world as a light, so that no one who believes in me should stay in darkness" (John 12:46 NKJV). As you pray, you can call on the Lord to be a beacon for you.

David's word for "lamp" is translated "candle." When a candle is lit in a dark place, it illuminates only that which needs to be seen...only that directly around us. God's illumination is not to give us a magical view of the future, but to shine enough light on our cares of today. As we pray to God, praising Him for the light He brings to the paths we walk, remember to thank Him that you can see only what He needs you to see, so we may go only where He wants us to go.

what others say

Charles R. Swindoll

Think of some distinctive characteristics of light: 1. Light is silent. It's like a single lighthouse along a rugged shoreline. 2. Light gives direction. Jesus says that others "see our actions" but nothing is said of their hearing. 3. Light attracts attention. You don't have to ask people to look at you when you turn a light on in a dark room. It happens automatically.[5]

go to

never to trust in the heathen nations
Deuteronomy 17:16;
Isaiah 31:1;
Psalm 20:7

Commander of the Army

2 CHRONICLES 20:6b ***In Your hand is there not power and might, so that no one is able to withstand You? (NKJV)***

The Ammonites, the Moabites, and the people of Mount Seir together were descending on Judah. Three armies against one. It would seem to be good common sense, basic foreign policy for Judah's King Jehoshaphat to seek out an ally nation to join with Judah to help even up the odds—and quickly. There was just one problem with that plan. God had been very specific: His people were never to trust in the heathen nations for their deliverance. They were to rely only on the Lord.

So Jehoshaphat gathered his people together and prayed. They were going to take God at His word. "Do you not rule over all the kingdoms of the nations?" Jehoshaphat prayed, "And in Your hand is there not power and might, so that no one is able to withstand You?" Good start. Jehoshaphat, after his first, unavoidable flush of fear, was getting it right. He continued, "We have no power against this great multitude that is coming against us, nor do we know what to do, but our eyes are upon You" (2 Chronicles 20:12 NKJV).

The Lord answered through a prophet named Ahaziel. There was no need to be afraid, he said, no need to be dismayed, "For the battle is not yours, but God's." Go down to the place of battle, God instructed the people of Judah. They weren't actually going to battle, though. The prophet said, "You will not need to fight in this battle. Position yourselves, stand still, and see the salvation of the LORD!" (2 Chronicles 20:17 NKJV).

The next day the people of Judah went out ahead of the army, singing praises to God. And what they saw amazed them. The

exile
forced removal from one's country

Ammonites and Moabites turned on their allies from Mount Seir. And when they had slaughtered them, the Ammonites and Moabites slaughtered one another. The people gathered so many valuables from the bodies of the three armies that they could barely carry them. The Lord had indeed delivered, honoring their obedience in a difficult situation.

When you find yourself in trouble, pressed on every side by the troubles and dangers of the world, it's always tempting to place your trust in earthly allies. Financial troubles? There's always another credit card company offering an alliance. Difficulties at work? Why not play office politics to gain allies? But God desires to do His work in His way. He delights in the prayer that says, "I don't know what to do, but I know that the battle is the Lord's."

Miraculous Military Triumphs in which God's People Won the Battle without Fighting

Triumph	Scripture
The Egyptians drowned in the Red Sea.	Exodus 14
Gideon's three hundred men, armed only with lamps and trumpets, conquered the Amalekites and Midianites.	Judges 7
At the siege of Jerusalem, 185,000 Assyrians struck down in the night by an angel.	2 Kings 19

what others say

Watchman Nee

In our prayer we should pay attention to three things: 1) to whom we are praying, 2) for whom we are praying, and 3) against whom we are praying. All our prayers should fulfill God's will, afford others a profit, and inflict Satan with a loss.[6]

Get to Work

NEHEMIAH 1:6a *Let Your ear be attentive and Your eyes open, that You may hear the prayer of Your servant which I pray before You now, day and night, for the children of Israel Your servants.* (NKJV)

Nehemiah was one of the Jews who lived in **exile** in the decades after the Assyrians defeated Judah and sacked Jerusalem. He had never actually seen Jerusalem, having been born and raised in the lands controlled by the Persians. As a matter of fact, Nehemiah really had little practical reason to think about Jerusalem at all. He had a great job as an advisor to King Cyrus of Persia, one of the most powerful men in the world. He was doing just fine in Persia. To look back to Jerusalem might distract him from a pretty bright future right where he was.

> go to
>
> **God loved Jerusalem**
> Matthew 23:27

Even though it had been 160 years since the bulk of the Jews had been carried away from Jerusalem and Judah, each generation had taught the next that their true home was Jerusalem, hundreds of miles to the west. So when Nehemiah heard that the walls of Jerusalem had been torn down and the few Jews who remained were suffering, it broke his heart. He cried out to God to hear his prayer, to see what was happening to his beloved Jews.

The interesting thing about Nehemiah's prayer is that as he was begging God to hear his prayer, he was praying back the desires that God had obviously put on his heart. God loved Jerusalem even more than Nehemiah did, and Nehemiah's heart was broken for Jerusalem because God's heart was broken first. Of course God would answer such a prayer!

Which brings up a question: why pray? If God is simply going to work His will, what do our prayers have to do with it? The first way to answer that question is simply to say that the Bible commands us to pray. God works through the prayers of His people, and whether we human beings understand it doesn't really matter. A second thing to bear in mind is that your prayers often prepare you to be a part of God's answers to those prayers. When Nehemiah began praying day and night for Jerusalem, he probably had no idea that God had a plan for him to head up the rebuilding of the city. But as Nehemiah prayed his desires, it became apparent that he was the man for the job.

> something to ponder

Prayer often works that way: you think you're praying for God to get to work, and it turns out your prayer is really God's way of preparing you to get to work!

what others say

Richard W. DeHaan

God is interested in your prayers because he is interested in you . . . Come into my presence, says God. Talk to me. Share all your concerns. I'm keenly interested in you, because I'm your Father. I'm able to help, because all power in heaven and earth is mine. And I'm listening very closely, hoping I will hear your voice.[7]

go to

rebellion of his son Absalom
1 Samuel 15–18

hiding place
Psalm 32:7

Here an Enemy, There an Enemy

Psalm 3:3
But You, O Lord, are a shield for me,
My glory and the One who lifts up my head. *(NKJV)*

Of all the conflicts that troubled David in the course of his conflict-ridden career, surely the most heartbreaking was the rebellion of his son Absalom. This was no typical adolescent rebellion. It was a full-blown *coup d'etat.* It began with a whisper campaign in which Absalom "stole the hearts of the men of Israel" with lies about his father's regime. Eventually, Absalom raised an army, even drawing some of David's highest-level advisors to his side. David was forced to surrender Jerusalem and flee to the wilderness. He did more than retrench or plan a counter-attack. He wept. He went barefoot and covered his head, signs of mourning and contrition.

During that time of exile from his beloved Jerusalem and his kingly life, David wrote the psalm that comes down to us as Psalm 3. "Lord, how have they increased who trouble me!" he begins. "Many are they who rise up against me" (Psalm 3:1–2 NKJV). It must have been a very lonely feeling.

There is a big "but," however: "But You, O Lord, are a shield for me" (Psalm 3:3 NKJV). His enemies were indeed numerous, but in the big scheme of things, their power was nothing beside the power of God. When David said that God was his shield, it's worth noting what kind of shield David would have been most familiar with. He probably wasn't talking about the round shield held out in front with one arm. David would have been more familiar with the long, curved shield that wraps around a soldier—sort of a portable hiding place for the battle. God was that kind of hiding place for David.

David had enjoyed his share of glory, but he spoke this prayer at a moment of ignominy and shame. Nevertheless, in the absence of worldly glory, God remained David's glory. And David seemed to understand that even when he did enjoy all the earthly glory of a king, God was still his only glory.

something to ponder

Indeed, God lifts up the head of everyone whose head has been bowed by the attacks of enemies. You've probably experienced enemies who attack and undermine you. You may have experienced the betrayal of friends. At such times, remember that the power of God outweighs the power of the whole world put together. He is your glory, and the lifter of your head.

Help Me to Choose

Acts 1:24a ***And they prayed and said, "You, O Lord, who know the hearts of all."*** (NKJV)

It had been a trying few weeks. Their leader had been crucified, then raised again. But even after they knew Jesus had come back to life, the disciples still didn't necessarily know what to do with themselves. Some of them wandered back to their old lives as fishermen for a while before Jesus appeared to them personally and put them back on track. Thomas has gone down in history with a reputation for doubting, but surely all the disciples struggled with doubt after Jesus was no longer a physical presence to guide them. Peter, a great leader among the twelve, had denied Jesus in a moment of weakness. Judas had done worse, handing Jesus over to His killers in exchange for a pouch of silver. Besides self-doubt, what sort of doubts and suspicions must the disciples have harbored about one another?

In the forty days after Jesus' resurrection, however, the disciples managed to reassemble, encouraged by appearances of the risen Christ among them. He promised that a Helper, the Holy Spirit, would soon indwell them to strengthen and to guide. But until that happened, they would have to muddle through the best they could.

One of the first orders of business was to select a new disciple to replace Judas, who had killed himself. They had narrowed it down to Joseph Barsabbas and Matthias; now they had to make a choice. It must have been a paralyzing moment. There was so much at stake. They had to get this right. But how can you know what is inside another person? They had lived with Judas for three years, but none of them would have guessed at the darkness in his heart. How were they to know if either of these two men—or even both—were as bad as Judas? Though the disciples couldn't see the hearts of Matthias and Barsabbas, however, they knew that God could. So they prayed to God to reveal His will.

You are constantly being called upon to make judgment calls about people. But you can't judge another person's heart. The politician may say, "I will not fail the people," but only God knows the intent. The pastor may give testimony, but only God knows the real story. The young woman may say, "I'll love you without condition," but only God knows with absolute surety if her heart and the young man's heart will one day be able to beat as one.

go to

wandered back to their old lives
Luke 5

Judas
Matthew 27:3–10

apply it

With so many important choices to make, why do we attempt to make them alone? We can go to God and pray, "You know the heart of man," asking Him to guide us in our life choices. God will never get it wrong—he can't! Before voting for your next church or political official, pray. Before making choices dealing with personal relationships, pray. God alone knows the heart.

what others say

Richard W. DeHaan

We should come to the Lord with all our needs—material and physical, emotional and spiritual, large matters and small. Minor as they may seem to others or even to ourselves, the little things are important to God because He loves us. He's concerned about even the most minute details of our lives.[8]

Chapter Wrap-Up

- Sometimes when you pray for god to work. He's preparing your for the very work you're praying for.
- You can't truly know another person's heart when yo have to make a decision. but God does, and you can pray to Him for guidance.
- If you want to know the heart of God, your prayer life needs to include time for listening as well as talking.
- God gives us light for the path. Oftentimes He only gives light enough for the next step; but that's eenough.

Study Questions

1. If God is going to work His will anyway, why bother praying?
2. How does God make His voice heard in everyday life?
3. How does God use prayer to prepare us to "get to work"?
4. God commanded the Israeelites to be very wary of forming alliancees with other nations. How does that principle apply to Christians today?
5. What is the difference between Gideon's praying for a sign from God and Saul's belief that David's presence in Keilah was a sign from God?

Chapter 9: The Lord's Prayer

Chapter Highlights:
- Praying to the Father
- For God's kingdom
- Ask God's help
- Ask for provision
- Ask God's forgiveness

Pater, Father—The Lord's Prayer, Part 1

MATTHEW 6: 8B–9A ***For your Father knows the things you have need of before you ask Him. In this manner, therefore, pray: Our Father in heaven . . .*** *(NKJV)*

Jesus' best-known parable is usually called the Prodigal Son, but the real hero of the story is the father. His son betrayed him, insulted him, and broke his heart. And yet when the son came home a broken man, his inheritance wasted, his father ran to welcome him home, receiving him again into the household—not as a servant or hired hand, but as a fully restored son.

go to

Prodigal Son
Luke 15:11-32

accountability
responsibility to another person

The Bible talks about salvation in many different ways—as a debt repaid; as a legal problem resolved; as a transfer of sin from the guilty to the innocent. But the image that goes right to the heart is that old man running down the road to meet his ne'er-do-well son. When it comes to the kind of unconditional love that we all need, a parent's love is as close as we come on earth.

We all respond to the idea of a father's love. Either you know what it's like from experience, or you've felt the lack of it all your life. When Jesus gave His disciples a model for prayer, He could have addressed God in any number of ways: Our Creator, Our Redeemer, Our Provider, I AM. But He chose to address God as "Our Father." In doing so He was saying, "You have more than an **accountability** to this God. You have a relationship—an intimate relationship.

In his book *Invading the Privacy of God*,[1] Cecil Murphey tells the story of a trip he took to a place of Christian education. He was emphatically told that the word "Father" was not permitted there because many of the children related their earthly fathers with physical and emotional abuse or drug and alcohol abuse. Murphey suggested this might be a good reason to talk to them about God the Father, their heavenly "Daddy," the One who loves them above all others and would never hurt them.

go to

promised them a Messiah
Isaiah 9:6-7;
Micah 5:2;
Zechariah 9:9

The woman remained firm in her "no father" rule, but Murphey vehemently disagreed. He had grown up without the understanding of a good father, but his heavenly Father had seen to it that the first sermon he ever heard (he was in his twenties at the time) was about the fatherhood of God.

You were born feeling the need for a father's love. As the first words of the Lord's prayer remind us, you have a Father in heaven, and He desires a relationship with you.

To understand God the Father we should look at Him through the eyes of His Son. As Jesus taught His disciples the correct way to pray, He began by addressing God as "Father." The New Testament Greek reads: "*Pater*" (*pat-ayr*') and carries with it a tone of intimacy and purpose.

Jesus not only understood the intimacy God desires to have with His children, but also the intimacy we *need* to have with our heavenly Father. As you begin to speak to Him, first seek *who He is.* Set aside all negative thoughts you might have about fatherhood and allow Him to fill a place each of us has a need to have filled.

what others say

Cecil Murphey

Abba, Father, as I approach you, help me know that your hand holds mine, that you're always there for me to lean on because you hold me, that you're the True Father, especially when I'm afraid, alone, and troubled. Amen.[2]

The Lord's Prayer, Part 2

MATTHEW 6:10
Your kingdom come.
Your will be done
On earth as it is in heaven. (NKJV)

The Jews had longed for the promised Messiah for hundreds of years. Their history had been the story of one oppression after another; they got out from under one oppressor only to be oppressed by somebody else. Now it was the Romans who ruled over them, and the Jews despised them. But God had promised them a Messiah who would lead them to victory and to freedom. The Jews assumed this Messiah would be a great military and political leader who would rally them to fight the Romans and kick them out of Palestine. This Messiah, they believed, would set up a new kingdom in Israel, returning the nation to the glory it enjoyed under David and Solomon.

go to

not yet been revealed
Romans 8:18-23

In other words, the Jews weren't looking for Jesus. Jesus was, to be sure, overcoming the oppression under which the Jews had suffered, and He was setting up a new kingdom. But none of that had anything to do with politics or the military. "My kingdom is not of this world," He said (John 18:36 NKJV). And yet He also said, "The kingdom of God is within you" (Luke 17:12 NKJV).

The kingdom of God has no geographical boundaries, but is a spiritual state in which God's laws and purposes prevail in human affairs. Theologians speak of the kingdom of God as being "now and not yet." It is "now" insofar as it exerts itself any time the people of God are motivated by God's love, God's will rather than the will of the world. It is "not yet" because the kingdom of God has not yet been revealed in its fullness.

A great deal of Jesus' teaching in the Bible revolved around making people understand the kingdom of God (or kingdom of heaven). Many of his parables begin, "The kingdom of heaven is like . . ." Perhaps it is not surprising, then, that the first request in the Lord's prayer is "Your kingdom come." To pray that prayer is to look forward to the full establishment of God's kingdom at some time in the future. But just as importantly, that prayer is a commitment to help establish the kingdom of God *today* and every day as you do God's will.

Any time God's will is done, His kingdom has come a little closer. To pray for the coming of God's kingdom is to submit your will to the will of God.

something to ponder

what others say

Watchman Nee

There are three wills in the universe: God's will, man's will, and Satan's will. God does not remove Satan's will by Himself. He desires that man's will become one with His will, to deal with Satan's will. A spiritual prayer is an utterance of God's will. How useless is a prayer that merely utters one's own will! Our prayer cannot change God's will; it merely expresses His will.[3]

go to

go bad
Exodus 16:20

setting your eyes on a spiritual kingdom
2 Corinthians 4:18

What the Bible Says

The Kingdom of Heaven Is Like	Scripture
A man who sowed good seed in his field . . .	Matthew 13:24
A mustard seed . . .	Matthew 13:31
A treasure hidden in a field . . .	Matthew 13:44
A merchant seeking beautiful pearls . . .	Matthew 13:45
A landowner who hired laborers for his vineyard . . .	Matthew 20:1
A man traveling to a far country . . .	Matthew 25:14

The Lord's Prayer, Part 3

Matthew 6:11
Give us this day our daily bread. *(NKJV)*

When God provided manna for the Hebrews in the desert, He was very specific: the Hebrews were to gather enough bread for each day, and only for that day. If they gathered extra, it would go bad by the second day. Manna was "daily bread" in the truest sense. It came every day, and it lasted a single day. The people had no choice but to trust in God's provision every single day.

When Jesus taught us to pray for "our daily bread," He was teaching us to trust in God's provision every day. We human beings yearn for security; God made us that way. But in our sinful natures, we tend to look for security in things like full cupboards and full bank accounts. We want to have an ample stock saved for the future. That's not necessarily a bad thing. God in His mercy often provides for us in just that way. The danger of worldly plenty, however, is that it can sometimes give you the mistaken impression that you don't need God's provision each and every day.

God doesn't promise worldly riches to His people. He does, however, promise to meet your needs. In the Lord's Prayer, Jesus taught His disciples not only to trust in God's provision, but also to be content with it. He prayed for bread, not steak and caviar. As Paul said, "The kingdom of God is not in eating and drinking, but righteousness and peace and joy in the Holy Spirit" (Romans 14:17 NKJV). The world promises to give you joy and fulfill your longings. But it never does.

The kingdom of God is about setting your eyes on a spiritual kingdom even as you physically live among the kingdoms of the world. "Give us this day our daily bread" is a nod toward that physical realm; we have to be physically fed, and we can count on God to feed us. But the brevity of the request shows that Jesus' heart is elsewhere. Contentment comes down to being so thankful for the things God has given that you pay little attention to the things He has chosen not to give.

David rejoiced, "My soul shall be satisfied as with marrow and fatness" (Psalm 63:5 NKJV). In the end, God promises much more than daily bread. Spiritually we partake of the "Bread of Life," or Jesus Himself. As you learn to be content with daily bread in the physical realm, you prepare yourself for the marrow and fatness of the kingdom of God.

go to

Bread of Life
John 6:35, 48

story of a servant
Matthew 18:23-35

something to ponder

When we ask God for what we need physically and spiritually for *today*, we are reminding both Him and ourselves that we don't *need* most things. We should be content with what God gives us and we should be keenly aware that He never leaves us lacking. His provision is complete.

The Lord's Prayer, Part 4

Matthew 6:12
And forgive us our debts,
As we forgive our debtors. *(NKJV)*

Jesus told the story of a servant who owed his king ten thousand talents. That was an astronomical sum; it would take many lifetimes to pay it back. But when the servant begged for mercy, the king forgave the debt rather than throwing the servant and his family into debtor's prison.

It wasn't long, however, before that same servant was seen grabbing a fellow servant by the throat and demanding payment of a debt he owed. A man who had been forgiven millions of dollars in debt was ready to strangle another man over a few hundred dollars. When the king heard about it, he was furious. He said, "You wicked servant! I forgave you all that debt because you begged me. Should you not also have had compassion on your fellow servant, just as I had pity on you?" (Matthew 18:32-33 NKJV). He "delivered the man to the torturers" until his debt could be paid.

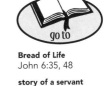

Jesus told this story in response to a question asked by Peter. "Lord, how often shall my brother sin against me, and I forgive him—up to seven times?" Peter thought he was being generous, offering to forgive the same sin seven times. By telling the story of the unforgiving servant, Jesus was saying, in effect, "You have need of limitless forgiveness; so why are you asking Me about the limit of the forgiveness you should offer?"

forgive others' debts
Ephesians 4:32; Matthew 18:27

Forgiveness
the act of letting go of your own anger (even righteous anger) over a wrong another person has committed against you

"Forgive us our debts, as we forgive our debtors," Jesus prayed. The grim story of the unforgiving servant shows just how much is at stake in that prayer. **Forgiveness** is at the heart of the Christian life. Because we have been forgiven, every human interaction should be marked by forgiveness. People have sinned against you. People owe you debts. It's human nature to want to grab those people by the throat and shake them until you get some satisfaction. But God's forgiveness pulls the rug out from under you. When you consider the debt of sin that God has forgiven, you can't possibly justify an unforgiving attitude toward anybody else.

You might view Jesus' prayer as a challenge. Are you truly willing to say, "God, forgive me in the way I've forgiven others"? Does the way you forgive others actually measure up to the forgiveness you need? Do we forgive others' debts—the big debts as easily as we forgive the smaller ones?

You still have to fall back on grace in the end. We'd all be in trouble if God only forgave us as much as we forgive each other. As you meditate on the greatness of God's forgiveness, may your own habit of forgiveness grow to overflowing.

The Lord's Prayer, Part 5

MATTHEW 6:13
And do not lead us into temptation,
But deliver us from the evil one.
For Yours is the kingdom and the power and the glory forever.
Amen. *(NKJV)*

It's not easy to make sense of Jesus' request, "do not lead us into temptation." Why would God lead His people into temptation? Why would God put us in a position to fail? In the cartoons, it's always the devil who leads a person into temptation. He sits on the person's left shoulder whispering bad ideas while the poor little good angel sits on the right shoulder waving his arms and shouting "No, don't do it!" But when Jesus said, "do not lead us into temptation," He was talking to God, not the devil.

It will be helpful to get a grasp on the word "temptation" as it is used in the Bible. In the Greek it's *peirasmos*, and it usually means "trial" or "test." And a test, as you know, is only a bad thing if you fail it. If you pass, it's a very good thing. It confirms that you are headed in the right direction, learning what you're supposed to learn. In the great majority of instances in the Bible, *peirasmos* is used in a positive or neutral sense. The disciples, for example experienced trials and tests (*peirasmos*) and were strengthened by them. Trials and tribulations produce perseverance, and perseverance produces character, and character produces hope.

go to

trials and tests
1 Peter 1:6; 4:12

tempted in the wilderness
Matthew 4:1–11

Jesus was tempted in the wilderness. That temptation was the last step in His preparation for public ministry. It was a kind of final exam, and Jesus passed with flying colors. He had been fasting in the desert for forty days when Satan appeared to Him, offering a whole new plan, an easier plan than what God had in mind for Jesus. He tempted Jesus to turn the stones at his feet into bread to ease His hunger. He tempted Jesus to throw Himself off a high place to prove that He was truly the Son of God. He tempted Jesus with the promise of worldly power. Jesus never rose to the bait. In each case he simply answered Satan with a word of Old Testament Scripture and kept to His path.

key point

No doubt that temptation was fresh in Jesus' mind when He prayed "do not lead us into temptation." It was a good thing in the end, but it was a very hard experience—the kind of thing He would prefer to avoid if possible. In the end, however, the important thing is that God is able to "deliver us from the evil one."

what others say

Bruce Chilton

Temptation was constant in Jesus' life, and he conveyed to his delegates the necessity of resisting it not simply with one's own strength but with prayer.[4]

Chapter Wrap-Up

- Our prayers to God are first and foremost prayers to a Father.
- Prayer is a means of bringing the kingdom of God to bear on the kingdoms of earth.
- Contentment begins with a willingness to rejoice in God's daily bread.
- Temptation is a test or trial; it is not sin.

Study Questions

1. What does it mean to say that God's kingdom is "now and not yet"?
2. How is submitting your will to God's will different from squelching your desires or pretending they don't exist?
3. How does "daily bread" relate to "marrow and fatness"?
4. How does God's forgiveness shape our relationships with other people?
5. How can temptation be a good thing?

Chapter 10: The Prayers of Jesus

Chapter Highlights:
- Unity in diversity
- Prayer for the persecuted
- Prayer of submission
- Jesus' prayer for those who crucified Him

Your Mission, Should You Decide to Accept . . .

LUKE 10:21 ***In that hour Jesus rejoiced in the Spirit and said, "I thank You, Father, Lord of heaven and earth, that You have hidden these things from the wise and prudent and revealed them to babes. Even so, Father, for so it seemed good in Your sight."*** *(NKJV)*

Jesus had an "advance team" who went ahead of Him to the cities where He would be visiting. Seventy disciples fanned out across Galilee and Judah in groups of two, preparing the people in every village and hamlet for the incredible things they were going to see when Jesus got there. They were to heal the sick and introduce people to the idea of the kingdom of God, about which Jesus would be preaching and demonstrating more fully.

"I send you out as lambs among wolves," Jesus said. Not the most reassuring pep talk ever given. He also told them not to take any money, but simply to rely on the generosity of the people in the villages they would be visiting. He warned that some cities would not receive them. In that case, they were simply to shake the dust of those places off their sandals and move on. It must have been a daunting task for those seventy disciples. Surely they went out with fear and trembling.

But when the seventy came back from their mission, they were overflowing with joy. They were pumped. "Lord, even the demons are subject to us in Your name," they marveled (Luke 10:17 NKJV). These were very common people. They weren't religious professionals. They probably weren't educated or wealthy (most of those people, after all, had other things to do besides serving as the street team for an itinerate carpenter-preacher). They probably weren't people who enjoyed a lot of authority in their everyday life. And yet they had exercised authority even over the demons! They had done things that the rich and powerful could only dream of doing.

Jesus rejoiced with the seventy disciples, and He led them in a prayer of thanksgiving: "I thank You, Father, Lord of heaven and earth, that You have hidden these things from the wise and prudent and revealed them to babes. Even so, Father, for so it seemed good in Your sight" (Luke 10:21 NKJV). Who would have thought it? Things that had been hidden from the wise were revealed to babies. That's what seemed good in God's sight. The foolishness of God is wiser than the wisdom of human beings.

God continues to amaze. He continues to produce beauty out of ashes, to come through when hope seems lost. We can rejoice in those beautiful, unexplainable moments, marveling all the while, "so it seemed good in Your sight!"

A Prayer for Unity

> **JOHN 17:11b** ***Holy Father, keep through Your name those whom You have given Me, that they may be one as We are. While I was with them in the world, I kept them in Your name. Those whom you gave me I have kept.*** **(NKJV)**

Jesus was coming to the end of His time on earth. For three and a half years the twelve disciples had been with Him and with each other almost constantly. But within twenty-four hours, Jesus would be gone and His disciples would be on their own.

The twelve came from different walks of life. Matthew had been a tax collector. Luke was a physician. What did they share with the fishermen in the group? They didn't all share the same politics; Simon, for instance, had been known as "the Zealot," one of a party of political extremists. Their personalities didn't always mesh. Peter was a headlong enthusiast, always speaking first and thinking later, sometimes leading by example, sometimes serving as the example of what not to do. Thomas, on the other hand, was somewhat **melancholy** obedient, and more resigned than enthusiastic. Soon he would achieve his unfortunate fame as a doubter. What hope existed for this motley crew without the Leader who held them together? That question must have been in Jesus' mind as he prayed to His Father to preserve their unity: "Holy Father, keep through Your name those whom You have given Me, that they may be one as We are" (John 17:11b NKJV).

God gave these disciples to Jesus, and here, less than a day before His return to His Father's side, Jesus gave them back. Jesus had been the mortar that held these very different men together. Even after

the foolishness of God
1 Corinthians 1:25

beauty out of ashes
Isaiah 61:3

Thomas
John 11:16

melancholy
predisposed to a gloomy frame of mind

He died, He would still be holding them together, for He wouldn't stay dead, but would return to "the right hand of God the Father Almighty" (as the **Apostles' Creed** puts it) and there, as part of the **Godhead**. He would answer His own prayer.

Later in the same prayer, Jesus clarified what He was really getting at. "I do not pray for these alone, but also for those who will believe in Me through their word; that all may be one, as You, Father, are in Me, and I in You" (John 17:20–21 NKJV). Why was it so important that God maintain the twelve in unity? Because the twelve represented the beginning of a worldwide movement that continues today. Consider the diversity of those who enjoy the unity of Christ today: from the unity of twelve very different men has grown the unity of millions of people representing every tribe and language and nation.

Apostles' Creed
a Christian creed traditionally ascribed to the twelve apostles and often used in public worship

Godhead
the God of the Bible, especially the Trinity

what others say

Matthew Henry

The prosperity of the soul is the best prosperity. He pleaded with his holy Father, that he would keep them by his power and for his glory, that they might be united in affection and labours, even according to the union of the Father and the Son. He did not pray that his disciples should be removed out of the world, that they might escape the rage of men, for they had a great work to do for the glory of God, and the benefit of mankind. But he prayed that the Father would keep them from the evil, from being corrupted by the world, the remains of sin in their hearts, and from the power and craft of Satan.[1]

A Prayer Before Dying

JOHN 17:13 *But now I come to You . . . (NKJV)*

In his book *The Game*, Robert Benson explains that life is a lot like baseball. The point of living, as in the point of baseball, is to somehow get the ball off the bat and into the field and then run the bases toward home. The greater point is to make it to home without being tagged or called "out." The victory comes in holding your head up high and pushing your body as hard as it will go until you get home and hear the word, "Safe!"

The runner's time is over when he crosses the plate, but oh, what a glorious moment it was! Safe at home, he is welcomed by his teammates, praised in the dugout, and handed a cup of Gatorade.

citizenship is in heaven
Philippians 3:20

stranger and a traveler
1 Peter 2:11

It will be like this for all of us one day if, as they say, "Jesus tarries." We will all breathe our last breath on this earth as we run toward "home plate," where teammates and coaches from throughout the years await us. They watch in anticipation, and as they see us heading home from third base, they begin to jump up and down, waving us in. If we are actually able to see through the sweat in our eyes and hear over the crowd, we just may offer up the same type of prayer Jesus prayed shortly before His death. "Now I come to You."

Jesus had a keen understanding that this earth was not His home. As He finished his time here as a man, he looked with eagerness toward his true home. And he called out with joy to His Father, "Now I come to You." This earth isn't your home either. Your citizenship is in heaven. Sometimes that can be easy to forget. After all, you've never lived anywhere else but this earth. But you're just a stranger and a traveler here. No wonder you sometimes feel so out of place! But one of these days you're going to be safe at home—the true home for which you were made.

Your time out here on the base paths is sometimes exhilarating, sometimes frightening, sometimes exhausting. Ultimately, however, the goal isn't to run the bases, but to get safely home—to see the Coach waving you in and say, "Now I come to You!"

what others say

Robert Benson

Sid Bream steams around third and heads for the plate. . . . The third-base coach for the Braves is standing in his coach's box, making a big circle with his right arm . . . and he is shouting what all of us are shouting—"Slide, Sid, slide!" Slide he does, and the umpire calls him safe and Sid lies back on his back in the dust and begins to laugh. His teammates pile on top of him in celebration. On this day Sid has slid in safe at home and brought a whole lot of us home with him.[2]

In the World, but Not of It

JOHN 17:15–16 *I do not pray that You should take them out of the world, but that You should keep them from the evil one. They are not of the world, just as I am not of the world.* (NKJV)

It was a hostile world that Jesus walked in. He was the light of the world, but most of the world preferred the darkness, thank you very much. While He was on earth, He bore most of the brunt of the world's hatred. His disciples didn't experience nearly as much persecution as He did. John the Baptist was a notable exception; he was killed by King Herod. But for the most part, the enemies of Jesus took their anger out on Jesus Himself. Jesus understood, however, that after He was gone, His enemies would turn their attention to His followers. His death on the cross would mean neither the end of His following nor the end of persecution for His followers.

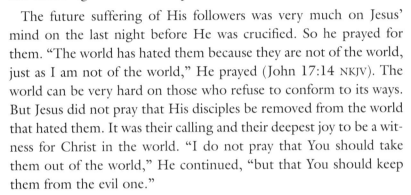

light of the world
John 1:9–11

killed by King Herod
Matthew 14:1-12

The future suffering of His followers was very much on Jesus' mind on the last night before He was crucified. So he prayed for them. "The world has hated them because they are not of the world, just as I am not of the world," He prayed (John 17:14 NKJV). The world can be very hard on those who refuse to conform to its ways. But Jesus did not pray that His disciples be removed from the world that hated them. It was their calling and their deepest joy to be a witness for Christ in the world. "I do not pray that You should take them out of the world," He continued, "but that You should keep them from the evil one."

Jesus prayed for His followers' protection, not for their ease and comfort. After all, they were foot soldiers. To be set apart from the world is not the same as being taken out of the world. The disciples would still be rubbing up against the world they were called to reach. That would be uncomfortable at times. At times it would be worse than that. For some of them, being faithful to Christ would mean torture, imprisonment, even death.

Even more frightening was the possibility that the world might seduce Jesus' followers to forsake their Master for the comforts of the world. They needed to be protected from the evil one's "comforts" as much as the evil one's "threats." Jesus wanted what was best for His disciples. That didn't involve ease or comfort. What was best for them was to fulfill the purpose of their lives.

What the Bible Says

Regarding Persecution	Scripture
"Blessed are you when they revile and persecute you, and say all kinds of evil against you falsely for My sake. Rejoice and be exceedingly glad, for great is your reward in heaven, for so they persecuted the prophets who were before you."	Matthew 5:11–12 (NKJV)

disciples specifically, the twelve men who made up Jesus' inner circle of friends

What the Bible Says (cont'd)

Regarding Persecution	Scripture
"If you are reproached for the name of Christ, blessed are you, for the Spirit of glory and of God rests upon you. On their part He is blasphemed, but on your part He is glorified."	1 Peter 4:14 (NKJV)
"[Jesus speaking] If they persecuted Me, they will also persecute you . . . But all these things they will do to you for My name's sake, because they do not know Him who sent Me."	John 15:20–21 (NKJV)
"The reproach of Christ [is] greater riches than the treasures in Egypt."	Hebrews 11:26 (NKJV)

Separate, Sanctify, and Specify Truth

JOHN 17:17 *Sanctify them by Your truth. Your word is truth. (NKJV)*

As Jesus was nearing the conclusion of his prayer for the **disciples**, He asked God to *sanctify* them. The word in the original text Greek is *Hagiazo*. It means "to set apart"—specifically, to set the disciples apart from the wicked things of the world and into a dedicated and intimate relationship with God. Jesus has asked the Father to purify these men in a very special way. He asked God to purify them by His very word, which is truth.

The apostle John was obsessed with the idea of truth. Whereas Matthew, Mark, and Luke used the word "truth" a total of eleven times in their three Gospels combined, John used the word twenty-seven times in his Gospel! John's Gospel starts with the idea of Jesus as the Truth—the Word of God: "In the beginning was the Word, and the Word was with God, and the Word was God" (John 1:1 NKJV). Jesus *was* the Truth, the very Word of God become a Man. John recorded many of Jesus' sayings about truth. The most well-known, perhaps, was "You shall know the truth, and the truth shall make you free" (John 8:32 NKJV). In a world of falsehood and deceit, Jesus brought the Truth that could transform people.

The Apostle John was sitting right next to Jesus at the Passover meal the night before He was crucified. He was right there when Jesus prayed for His disciples. You can be sure he sat up and took notice when Jesus returned to John's favorite subject. "Sanctify them by Your truth," He prayed. It must have come to no surprise to John when Jesus identified truth as the means of sanctification.

Falsehood and deceit cause the ground beneath us to turn to shifting sands, but truth is a solid rock on which to stand. Truth is something you can build a life on—a life that pleases God. And the most reliable source of truth is the Word of God: "Your word is truth."

When we speak the Word of God, we speak the **truth.** That's why it's important to pray back the Scriptures to God whenever possible. As we pray for both ourselves and others, we can pray that the Word will go deep into and from the heart, out of the mouth in prayer.

Had I But One Prayer for You

JOHN 17:24 ***Father, I desire that they also whom You gave Me may be with Me where I am, that they may behold My glory which You have given Me; for You loved Me before the foundation of the world. (NKJV)***

The "Upper Room Discourse" was Jesus' earthly farewell to a group of men He loved very much. His face was set to do what He had come to do—to die for the sins of the world—but that didn't make His farewell to the Twelve any easier. The tenderness in His words is striking. Jesus didn't pray to remain with the disciples. It wouldn't do any good to keep things as they were; Jesus had come, after all, to make everything different. Instead, He prayed that the disciples might join Him where He was going.

The disciples had seen the glory of God in the person of Jesus. But they hadn't seen His full glory. Jesus' prayer for them was that they might be able to see the fullness of His glory, bestowed by the Father who had loved Him since before the foundation of the world. It's not so much that Jesus needed the disciples to be impressed with Him. It's not that He needed their *ooh*s and *ahhh*s. He enjoyed the pleasure and <u>approval of the Father</u>; He didn't need affirmation from any other source. No, He wished for the disciples to see His full glory because He wanted them to feel the fullness of their joy in Him.

The disciples were men of faith. But as singer-songwriter Andrew Peterson puts it, "faith is a burden." To live in faith is to live in the gap between what you see with your eyes and what you know to be true. That's stressful. Faith is a gift, certainly, and it's the best we limited human beings can do. But still, it's a temporary solution. One of these days we'll see God face to face, and there will be no need for faith, for we will <u>see Him as He is</u>.

go to

approval of the Father
Matthew 3:17; 17:5

see Him as He is
1 John 3:2

truth
any word spoken by God or written by men from God

Garden of Gethsemane
a garden east of Jerusalem near the foot of the Mount*

Jesus' prayer for His disciples was for the day when they would see Him in the fullness of His glory. Swallowed up in God's love, they would know that they had invested their lives in something that was truer and more real than the world they had lived in.

something to ponder

It's not easy to live a life of faith. Doubts attack every day. And even when you aren't doubting, you're still yearning for something you can't quite get your hands on. But one of these days you're going to behold the glory of Christ, and your joy will be complete.

what others say

Andrew Murray

As a part of our daily fellowship with God, let us "pray" that we may be "one". Just as we say "Father" with the thought of our love to Him, we can say "our" with the childlike affection for all the saints whoever and wherever they be. The prayer that "we may be one" would then bring joy and strength, a deeper bond of fellowship with Christ Jesus and all His saints, and an offering of sweet savor to the Father of love.[3]

Cup of New Covenant

Matthew 26:39 He went a little farther and fell on His face, and prayed, saying, "O My Father, if it is possible, let this cup pass from Me; nevertheless, not as I will, but as You will." *(NKJV)*

Hebrews 4:15 speaks of Jesus as our High Priest, who sympathizes with our weaknesses, who "was in all points tempted as we are, yet without sin" (NKJV). That's hard to get your head around. The church taught that Jesus was fully God and fully man. But if Jesus was fully God, how can He sympathize with human weakness? If God cannot sin, how could He have been tempted just like we're tempted?

Jesus' prayer in the **Garden of Gethsemane** gives us a picture of His humanity. He was just hours away from His crucifixion. It was the reason He came here, to be the perfect Lamb whose sacrifice would make atonement for the sins of the world. But that didn't mean He liked the idea. Crucifixion was a gruesome way to die. It was torture. When Jesus looked ahead to it, His flesh recoiled in horror. So He prayed about it. "O My Father, if it is possible, let this cup pass from Me." That was His human nature talking. It was there, making itself heard. What human being could possibly embrace a death as horrible as crucifixion?

But Jesus' human nature didn't carry the day. Jesus submitted it to the will of God: "Nevertheless, not as I will, but as You will." That's the most obedient prayer possible. *"Here, Lord, are my desires. I offer them up to You. But You are God, not me. And my greatest desire is to see Your will done in this and every situation."*

It is a comfort to know that our great High Priest, our representative before God's throne, knows what it's like to be saddled with a human nature. Being a follower of God doesn't mean you become a robot with no will or desires of your own. It doesn't even mean you make an effort to squelch your desires or pretend they don't exist. It simply means that in the grand scheme of things, you realize that your desires aren't the be-all, end-all. Or to put it another way, all your smaller desires are **subordinate** to your greatest desire, which is to see the will of God done in your life.

Here's the thing about your will: the more practice you get submitting your will to God's will, the more frequently you find that your will actually matches up with the will of God.

go to

John the Baptist
John 1:29

subordinate
to rank or order as less important; to assign a lower priority

atonement
the reconciliation of God and humans brought about by the redemptive life and death of Jesus

apply it

The Ultimate Forgiveness

> LUKE **23:33–34** ***And when they had come to the place called Calvary, there they crucified Him, and the criminals, one on the right hand and the other on the left. Then Jesus said, "Father, forgive them, for they do not know what they do." And they divided His garments and cast lots.*** *(NKJV)*

John the Baptist called Jesus "the Lamb of God, who takes away the sins of the world." The sins of the world. How do you even begin to form a mental image of "the sins of the world"? It's sort of like the national debt—a figure so big you simply can't make any sense of it. Your next mortgage payment is a bigger deal to you than the national debt—first, because you're personally responsible for it, and second because it's a real number to you. You can at least imagine how many hours you have to work to make your mortgage payment.

According to the same principle, it's easier to make sense of the **atonement** if you think in terms of specific sins rather than "the sins of the world." Consider one of the last sayings of Jesus. He had been nailed to the cross, and as He hung there dying, he prayed, "Father, forgive them, for they do not know what they do" (Luke 23:34

Psalm 22
is a prayer of David, which begins with Jesus' words from the cross

forsaken
abandoned or left altogether

NKJV). He was being tortured to death, yet He prayed that His torturers would be forgiven—while they were still at it! That's God's love in a nutshell. The "sins of the world"—every single one of them—are committed against God. He feels all the suffering—and the anger—of One who has been sinned against. And yet He died for the forgiveness of sinners.

Jesus stormed through the temple, turning over tables and swinging a scourge, furious at the people who had turned His Father's house into a street bazaar. Then He died so that those very people's sins might be forgiven. He is the Judge. He set the penalty for sin (and set it high). Then He paid the penalty Himself!

What's the most shameful thing you've ever done? What past mistakes make you blush? What errors do you simply choose not to remember? Jesus died for those sins too. Now He stands before the throne of God and says, "Forgive this one whom I love."

something to ponder

It wasn't just the people who pounded the nails through Jesus' feet and hands who crucified Him. It wasn't just the people who shouted "Crucify Him!" and set a murderer free in His place. All our sins sent Jesus to the cross. And from the cross Jesus prayed, on our behalf, "Forgive them, for they do not know what they do."

The Ultimate Heartbreak

MARK 15:34 ***And at the ninth hour Jesus cried out with a loud voice, saying, "Eloi, Eloi, lama sabachthani?" which is translated, "My God, My God, why have You forsaken Me?" (NKJV)***

The physical sufferings of Christ on the cross would have been excruciating. But perhaps most excruciating of all was the sense of loss and abandonment He felt as His Father turned His face away from His suffering. "My God, My God, why have you forsaken Me?" he cried as foretold in **Psalm 22**. He turned his blood-stained face toward heaven and, for the first time in His life, He couldn't find God. All the sins of the world were on Him. He needed the Father more than ever. But the Father couldn't look on that kind of sin.

The Son of God **forsaken** by the Father. It looked like an absurd end to a beautiful life. An onlooker couldn't be blamed for thinking it was just another instance of senseless violence in a meaningless world. This Jesus claimed to have a better way, claimed to have a direct line to God. He had said, "The kingdom of God is among you." But in the end, even He felt abandoned and neglected by God—if indeed there was a God.

Only that wasn't the end. Christ died, but He didn't stay dead. He rose again from death into life, in order to make a way for us to follow Him from death into life. Satan thought he had won. But the joke was on him. The foolishness of God is wiser than the wisdom of the world. Even His defeats are shattering victories.

When Jesus died on the cross, He was the perfect sacrifice for our sins. As the writer of Hebrews said, the blood of goats and bulls in the old sacrificial system just wasn't sufficient to cleanse us of our sins. Those sacrifices were merely a shadow-picture of the true sacrifice of the Lamb of God. It was a terrible thing, all that ugliness, all that nastiness heaped on One so pure. The sky turned dark in the mid-afternoon. The earth shook with horror. And God turned His face away from the suffering of His Son. But this was what Christ had come to earth to do. God turned away once, but only as a result of Christ's sacrifice. He has never turned away since.

Final Words

The Last Seven Things Jesus Spoke Before Dying	Scripture
"My God, My God, why have You forsaken Me?"	Matthew 27:46 (NKJV)
"Father, forgive them, for they do not know what they do."	Luke 23:34 (NKJV)
[To the thief on the cross]: "Assuredly, I say to you, today you will be with Me in Paradise."	Luke 23:43 (NKJV)
"Father, into Your hands I commit My spirit."	Luke 23:46 (NKJV)
[To Mary]: "Woman, behold your son!" [To John]: "Behold your mother!"	John 19:26-27 (NKJV)
"I thirst."	John 19:28 (NKJV)
"It is finished!"	John 19:30 (NKJV)

The Ultimate Release

LUKE 23:46 ***And when Jesus had cried out with a loud voice, He said, "Father, into Your hands I commit My spirit." Having said this, He breathed His last.*** (NKJV)

Jesus' last words as a human being were a prayer yielding that life-giving part of Himself—His spirit—to God, once and for all. The Greek word Jesus used for "commit" is *paratithemi*, meaning, "to entrust" or "to deposit," as you might make a deposit at a bank. He

go to

entrusting
1 Corinthians 9:17

gave His spirit to God as a trust or for protection.[4] The word translated "spirit" is *pneuma*, which has many meanings, but here means "the vital principle by which the body is animated." It has another, more detailed, meaning as well: "the disposition or influence which fills and governs the soul of any one; the efficient source of any power, affection, emotion, desire, etc."[5] In other words, Christ was entrusting to God all that He had embodied as a human being. The totality of His life He handed back to the Father.

As He often did, Jesus was using a quotation in this prayer rather than saying something completely original. He was quoting a traditional Jewish bedtime prayer. Mothers taught their children to pray, "Into Your hands I commit my spirit" as the terrors of the night approached. Maybe Mary taught Him that prayer when He was little. In any case, as the darkness closed in around Jesus on the cross, He spoke the prayer again. As always, Jesus imbued the quoted phrase with a new intensity of meaning. But it's worth noting that the prayer started out life as a daily prayer. Committing your spirit—that is to say, the wholeness of your life—into the hands of God is something to do every day, not just at the end. Jesus certainly committed His spirit to God every day of His life on earth.

Paul urged the Romans, "present your bodies a living sacrifice, holy, acceptable to God" (Romans 12:1 NKJV). That's what it means to commit your spirit into God's hands: your life for your sake is over. You've given all your vital energies over to God. He will surely guard the life you deposit with Him and pay you back with interest.

apply it

Think what would happen if the last prayer of Jesus became your daily prayer. "Father, into your hands I commit my spirit—all my energies, all my desires, the totality of my life." With a prayer like that, your life becomes a living sacrifice.

what others say

Robert Benson

When the disciples asked Jesus to teach them to pray, he responded with a prayer that was largely constructed from phrases taken from Jewish liturgical prayers. The words He groaned from the cross as He died—"Into your hands I commit my spirit"—were quoted from the end of the traditional prayers that had been said at sundown by the faithful for centuries.[6]

A Benediction

2 Thessalonians 2:16–17 ***Now may our Lord Jesus Christ Himself, and our God and Father, who has loved us and given us everlasting consolation and good hope by grace, comfort your hearts and establish you in every good word and work.*** *(NKJV)*

go to

good works
Ephesians 2:10

the power of prayer
James 5:16

As you continue to pray, may God give comfort to your heart, and may He "establish you in every good word and work." To put it another way, may you feel good, but more importantly, may you *do* good. Prayer isn't an end unto itself. It makes its way into all of your life, causing you to speak good words and do good works. As Garrison Keillor puts it, "Be well, do good work, and keep in touch." Keeping in touch with God is one of the best ways to ensure that you are staying well and doing good work.

We pray boldly because God loves us. We pray reverently because He is God. We pray confidently because He is forever faithful, even when we are faithless. We don't deserve the blessings that God bestows. But that was never the point anyway. The point is that God loves us better than we love ourselves, with a love far deeper even than the love of a parent for a child.

The key, of course, is grace. As Paul said in his blessing on the Thessalonians, God's "consolation and good hope" come to us by His grace. The grace of God makes us channels of grace for others. God's promises make you strong and hopeful, and they put you in a position to offer strength and hope to others.

It's nice to be thought of. But through the power of prayer your desires become something infinitely more important than thoughts or wishes. They become instruments of the will of God on earth. It's a great mystery. God is not at our beck and call; and yet somehow He shapes the course of human affairs according to the desires of the faithful as they are breathed up to Him in prayer. Prayer changes many things. One of the most important things a prayer changes is the person who prays. As you communicate your will to God in prayer, you find that He is communicating His will to you, shaping your will into conformity with His own.

Paul's prayer for the Thessalonians gives you all the reason you need to "keep in touch" with God through prayer. God loves you. He has given you everlasting consolation through His grace. The result is hope, comfort, and a life well-lived.

Chapter Wrap-Up

- To speak God's word is to speak truth.
- Our joy in Christ derives from a vision of His glory. Prayer is an important means of seeing more of His glory.
- Through prayer, we can commit our spirits into the hands of God every day.
- Prayer changes many things—and it always changes the person who prays.

Study Questions

1. Why did the disciples need to be protected from Satan's "comforts" even more than they needed to be protected from Satan's "threats"?
2. What does it mean to say "faith is a burden"?
3. On what basis do we know that Jesus was talking about us—and not just the people who physically crucified Him—when He said "Father, forgive them, for they do not know what they do"?
4. If Jesus was fully God, how could He have experienced temptation as we do?
5. "Through prayer, your desires become something infinitely more important than thoughts or wishes." What does that mean?

Part Two:
PROMISES OF THE BIBLE

Introduction

The second half of this book will place at your fingertips promises that God has made to you, about you—timeless truths that are guaranteed to bring peace, certainty, and comfort to you and your loved ones. God has pledged to us "to do or not to do" specific things. He has given us grounds for "the expectation of success or improvement" in our lives. In short, He has lovingly committed Himself to care, provide, protect, and guide us in the days ahead.

As you read through this book and claim each promise as your own, you will gain the strength and knowledge you will need to face the future with confidence. In writing this book, we offer a straightforward understanding of Biblical truth. Here you will find clear, concise, and readily understandable information about what God has promised to you.

God gave us these promises for one reason: He loves us. More to the point: God loves you. He longs to flood your troubled soul with "the peace of God, which surpasses all understanding," a peace that "will guard your hearts and minds through Christ Jesus" (Philippians 4:7 NKJV). As you study these promises, you will experience God's peace—peace that will sustain you no matter what challenges life may send your way. Each of these promises is for you, from God's heart to yours. Count on the fact that God will fulfill every promise in this book in ways that you can't even imagine. Your life will change as you read *Prayers and Promises—The Smart Guide to the Bible*™ series. And that's a promise!

Chapter 11: Promises Concerning Our God

Chapter Highlights:
- God's faithfulness
- God's promise
- God's ever-renewed mercies
- God's power

Holding on to Hope

HEBREWS 10:23 *Let us hold fast the confession of our hope without wavering, for He who promised is faithful.* (NKJV)

The writer of Hebrews issued a challenge to his readers. "Hold fast," he said. "Without wavering." Consider his audience. He was writing to a church of Jewish Christians who had experienced persecution. The whole point of persecution, of course, is to cause its victims to waver, to let go instead of holding fast. In the early church, however, persecution rarely succeeded in shutting Christians up. The calm and peace with which the early martyrs accepted their fate only served to draw people to the faith that so strengthened them. And even when persecutors succeeded in scattering believers, the result was that the gospel grew in those places where they scattered.

go to

persecution
Hebrews 10:32–39

The Hebrews, however, surely faced a challenge that may have been even more insidious than active persecution. No doubt these Jewish Christians had to face their Jewish family members, friends, and neighbors who didn't understand why they had "turned their backs on" a very rich religious tradition that had nurtured them from birth. It's hard enough to face down a persecutor; for many people, it would be even harder to face down a disappointed mother: *So this life, this faith I raised you in wasn't good enough for you?* No wonder the writer of Hebrews reminded his readers to "hold fast."

But the Jewish Christians had an advantage that the Gentile Christians didn't have. From before they could remember, they had heard stories of the God who had made outrageous promises to His people, and then kept them. So when the writer said, "Hold fast, don't waver," he wasn't simply telling the Hebrews to show some character and self-discipline. He was saying, "You know God is faithful. You know He keeps His promises. So you know that you *can* stand firm without fear. Whatever happens to you—even if it's death—God can make it good."

Ultimately, the ability to stand firm for God doesn't come down to character. It comes down to whether or not you actually believe that God will keep His promises. You can hold fast without wavering. That's why you need to keep the promises of God in your heart. It's not just that you'll feel better (though, of course, you will), more importantly, you'll live better when you realize you've got nothing to fear from the uncertainties and hostilities of the world.

something to ponder

Because God is faithful, you can afford to be faithful. We can trust God to fulfill His every commitment and keep His every promise, and that He will never let us down.

> **what others say**
>
> **Joni Eareckson Tada**
>
> Have you found yourself comfortable with good health, secure in a loving relationship, or fulfilled in a steady job, only to have the props unexpectedly knocked out from under you? You and I don't need an earthquake to remind us that our confidence and hope must always rest in the One who never changes.[1]

God's Photographic Memory

ISAIAH 49:15

Can a woman forget her nursing child,
And not have compassion on the son of her womb?
Surely they may forget,
Yet I will not forget you. (NKJV)

Israel had a very big problem. The Israelites suffered from doubts that caused them to wonder whether or not God had forgotten them. In one sense, they had reason to doubt. They seemed to be constantly under assault by their enemies. Worse than that, they seemed to be constantly defeated by their enemies. It felt to the Israelites as if God had simply gone away and left them to their own devices.

This was the historical moment in which Isaiah wrote to the children of Israel. He warned them that through their stubborn disobedience they had forced God's hand in judgment. His words cut like a two-edged sword. On the one side, when the people failed to heed God's warning, God lifted His protective hand and allowed their enemies—principally Assyria and Babylon—to have their way with them. Blood flowed in the streets. The wails and cries of the punished people reverberated off the cities' walls. Their suffering seemed insurmountable.

Yet, on the other side, to the faithful **remnant** Isaiah offered comforting words of encouragement. The faithful few lamented, "The LORD has forsaken me, and my Lord has forgotten me" (Isaiah 49:14 NKJV). Isaiah had to convince them that despite their sufferings God had *not* forsaken them. He had not, indeed He would not ever forget them. Their pleas would be heard. Their faithfulness would be honored. Their prayers would be answered, their pains would end, and the bliss of God's blessing would flood their lives once again.

Isaiah painted a poignant picture of a loving mother tenderly nursing her newborn child. "Can a woman forget her newborn child?" he asked. You expect the answer to be, "No, of course a woman can't forget her newborn child." But that's not what Isaiah said. He said, "Surely they may forget." If anything on this earth were certain, surely it would be the love of a mother for her child. Even that's not certain. Isaiah follows up, however, with a very big "Yet." "Yet I will not forget you." God would *never* forget His people. He even engraved their image on the palms of His hands so that they would remain before Him every minute of every day.

Your name, too, has been engraved on God's hands. Every earthly support may fall away. In the end, however, your support doesn't come from this world. It comes from God. And God is forever faithful.

go to

the palms of His hands
Isaiah 49:16

remnant
small number of people who continue to obey God despite the cultural pressures to compromise their convictions

what others say

George Matheson

O Love that wilt not let me go,
I rest my weary soul in Thee;
I give Thee back the life I owe,
That in Thine ocean depths its flow
May richer fuller be.[2]

Lest We Forget

Forgetting in the Bible	Scripture
God doesn't even forget the sparrows' needs—much less yours.	Luke 12:6
Israel forgot God—and was punished.	Hosea 8:14
When God restored His people, their former troubles were forgotten.	Isaiah 65:16
The needy are not forgotten.	Psalm 9:18
Paul encouraged believers to forget about the past and press on for the goal.	Philippians 3:13

Open-Heart Surgery

everyone
Romans 3:23

contrition
sincere remorse for wrongdoing; repentance

Psalm 51:17
A broken and a contrite heart—
These, O God, You will not despise. (NKJV)

King David seemed like a man who had temporarily lost his mind. How else can you explain his bizarre behavior? Things had been going beautifully for David. He enjoyed unprecedented popularity as the leader of God's people. He had position, power, and possessions beyond imagination. But for some reason, David craved something that wasn't his to have.

David's sadly sensual story begins with the ominous words "It happened in the spring of the year" (2 Samuel 11:1 NKJV). As commander-in-chief, he placed himself in the wrong place at the wrong time, choosing to stay home when he should have been with his men on the battlefield. He next chose to look upon something he never should have seen: a naked Bathsheba, bathing on the rooftop next door. He then took something he never should have. He slept with Bathsheba, the wife of another man. When he learned that Bathsheba was pregnant with *his* child, David launched a nationwide cover-up that included the murder of her husband.

Not until the prophet Nathan confronted him did David's hard heart break. But when David's heart finally broke, it shattered. Psalm 51 is the resulting wail of a deeply repentant man. Every word of his prayer bespeaks the gut-wrenching sorrow of a man who knows he failed himself, his nation, and most importantly, his God.

But amid the dung heap of David's sin gleams the jewel of God's grace. God responded to David's brokenness, his **contrition** David may have despised himself at that point, but God did not despise him. No amount of self-justification could have accomplished for David what his simple confession accomplished: "Against You, You only have I sinned" (Psalm 51:4 NKJV). No matter how horrible a person's sin, God is always willing to embrace the repentant sinner with outstretched arms of forgiveness and grace.

Everyone has sinned. Everyone has fallen short. The question is, how will you respond when you realize you have done wrong? Seek to justify your sin or try to ignore it, and you are on your own. But if you are willing to admit you're wrong and desire a better path, the promise of God is straightforward: He will not despise those who humble themselves in contrition. God never turns away a broken heart. No matter what we have done, when we confess our sins to God with the same brokenness and contrition as David, God forgives us too.

go to

mournful language
Jeremiah 8:22; 14:17; 15:18; 20:14

what others say

A. W. Tozer

It is one of the supreme tragedies in religion that so many of us think so highly of ourselves when the evidence lies all on the other side; and our self-admiration effectively blocks out any possible effort to discover a remedy for our condition.[3]

Contrite Hearts in the Bible

Whose Heart	Scripture
Jonah	Jonah 2
Levi (Matthew)	Mark 2:14–17
Zaccheus	Luke 19
Paul (Saul)	Acts 9

New Every Morning

LAMENTATIONS 3:22–23
Through the LORD's mercies we are not consumed,
Because His compassions fail not.
They are new every morning;
***Great is Your faithfulness.* (NKJV)**

Jeremiah had a rough time of it. Nicknamed "The Weeping Prophet," Jeremiah's mournful language sounds much like the language of a person struggling with depression. Jeremiah's message was largely one of impending judgment. He took no joy, no smug satisfaction from telling others how wrong they were or what their comeuppance would be. No, his unenviable job was to warn of judgment and destruction that would fall upon the places and people he loved the most. The children of Israel were abandoning God in droves. Moral decay had become the order of the day. The storm clouds of God's wrath were building up on the horizon, and there was nothing Jeremiah could do to stop it. No wonder he got depressed.

The fateful day finally arrived. The barbarous Babylonians conquered the country. Men were killed. Women were raped. Children

lamentations
cries of sorrow and grief

were led away in chains. And the city of Jerusalem, the very heart of the Jewish nation, race, and religion, fell to famine and fire. The Book of **Lamentations** records Jeremiah's personal lament or "mournful wail" over the collapse of the Holy City.

Yet, against the black backdrop of Lamentations, hope continues to burn. At points along his tattered tale, Jeremiah looks backward, inward, outward, upward, and forward. Consider Lamentations 3:19–24 (NKJV), Jeremiah looks backward: "Remember my affliction and roaming." Then he looks inward: "My soul still remembers and sinks within me." Things begin to look better, however, when he takes his eyes off his troubles and begins to look outward: "This I recall to my mind, therefore I have hope." Then Jeremiah begins to look upward, focusing on the promises of the amazing faithfulness of God: "Through the LORD's mercies we are not consumed, because His compassions fail not. They are new every morning; great is Your faithfulness." And finally, right in the middle of his lamentation for a people who seemed to have no future, Jeremiah was able to look forward: "'The LORD is my portion,' says my soul, therefore I hope in Him!"

something to ponder

As you face troubles in your life, it always helps when you can get your eyes off yourself and onto God. No matter how dark and desperate your trials may be, no matter how downcast you might feel, you need never be consumed by your circumstances. God's compassion floods the lives of His people . . . daily. His mercies are renewed every single morning of every darkened day. Therefore, like Jeremiah of old, you have the promise of hope!

what others say

Corrie ten Boom

Once, while we were on roll call, a cruel guard kept us standing for a long, long time. Suddenly a skylark began to sing in the sky, and all the prisoners looked up to listen to that bird's song... God sent that skylark daily for three weeks, exactly during roll call, to turn our eyes away from the cruelty of men to the ocean of His love.[4]

Mission *Not* Impossible

LUKE 1:37 ***For with God nothing will be impossible.*** (NKJV)

Elizabeth harbored in her heart an unfulfilled longing. She desperately wanted a baby. At the time, to be barren was culturally, almost superstitiously, considered a disgrace, as if she bore the brand of a scarlet "B" upon her clothing, a mark of God's disfavor upon a married woman. A woman's self-worth was tied directly to her ability to bear children in that culture, with little or no thought of the husband's role in the whole thing. Read the stories of Sarah, Hannah, and the like, and you can practically feel their pain coming through the pages of Scripture. We've come a long way in our understanding of human reproduction, but in biblical times, a woman's greatest fear was that her womb would remain barren.

go to

Sarah
Genesis 16:1–2

Hannah
1 Samuel 1:10

impossible for God to lie
Hebrews 6:18

How shocking it must have been to Elizabeth when, "in her old age" (Luke 1:36 NKJV) she became pregnant. She would give birth to John the Baptist! And when the bearer of good news, Gabriel, announced to Mary that her cousin Elizabeth was with child, he dared to make one of the most dramatic predictions possible: Mary would have a child without ever having relations with a man—the virgin-born Son of God. In *that* context, Gabriel announced to a waiting world, *nothing* is impossible with God.

key point

Actually, there are a few things that *are* impossible for God. It is impossible for God to lie, for instance. It is impossible for God to die or sin or change. Or break a promise. But those are all limits that God imposed on Himself. What the angel Gabriel meant was that when it comes to the limits that are imposed on us human beings, nothing is impossible with God.

Part of being a human being is learning to live within our limitations. Sometimes we have to learn the hard way. But when you're dealing with God, however, it's just the opposite. Knowing God means understanding that He lives outside our limitations. It's impossible for a barren old woman or a young virgin to have a baby. And yet both of those things happened. It is impossible for incurable cancers to be cured. That happens, too, when God sees fit to show Himself strong in that way. It is impossible for sinners to be reconciled to a holy God. But God delights to do the impossible, to blow away our expectations. It's just what God does.

go to

demon-possession
Matthew 8:16

herd of pigs
Matthew 8:32

what others say

Bill Bright

The church today can once again experience that same dynamic which characterized those first believers, if we, too, become totally absorbed in the character and attributes of our great God. It is then that we will truly begin to believe God for supernatural, impossible things.[5]

Power to the People

ROMANS 16:20a ***The God of peace will crush Satan under your feet shortly. (NKJV)***

"Be sober," wrote Peter, "be vigilant; because your adversary the devil walks about like a roaring lion, seeking whom he may devour" (1 Peter 5:9 NKJV). It's a frightening thing to think about—an enemy as powerful as Satan himself has it in for you. He's waiting for an opportunity to do you harm. "Resist him," continues Peter (2 Peter 5:10 NKJV). He seems confident that God's people have what it takes to resist Satan. Nevertheless, it's a sobering reminder of the threat posed by Satan.

Paul makes an even more confident promise in regard to our future dealings with Satan: "The God of peace will crush Satan under your feet shortly" (Romans 16:20 NKJV). That's an amazing thing to think about: God will one day crush Satan underneath your feet. You may not feel like a spiritual superstar. You may not even feel like a spiritual benchwarmer. But if you are in Christ, God is using you to do the most important work of the universe: defeating Satan and building God's kingdom.

Note, that Paul doesn't say, "*You* will crush Satan with God's help." No, as this passage makes clear, the victory is God's. God will crush Satan. And yet, He sees fit to include the most ordinary people in the victory. He will crush Satan underneath your feet.

During the time when Jesus was on earth, it seemed that Satan was particularly active. Jesus healed many people who suffered with demon-possession. He sent a legion of demons into a herd of pigs. John witnessed these and many other instances of Jesus' power first hand. So when John wrote, "He who is in you is greater than he who is in the world"(1 John 4:4 NKJV), he knew what he was talking about.

Satan and his demons do possess great power. Yet, add up all the power possessed by every one of them and it doesn't come close to the authority that resides in you by virtue of the Holy Spirit. You have more power at your fingertips than the devil could even dream of. Luke wrote, "But you shall receive power when the Holy Spirit has come upon you" (Acts 1:8 NKJV). That word translated "power" is *dunamis.* We get "dynamite" from the same word. It means "dynamic power." And dynamic power trumps demonic power every time.

something to ponder

I Am Convinced

Romans 8:38–39 ***For I am persuaded that neither death nor life, nor angels nor principalities nor powers, nor things present nor things to come, nor height nor depth, nor any other created thing, shall be able to separate us from the love of God which is in Christ Jesus our Lord. (NKJV)***

Paul was a stoic compared to many of the other biblical writers. No other writer displayed the level of raw intellect that Paul did. Many of his letters read like the carefully crafted legal transcript of a prosecuting attorney before a judge and jury. You won't sense the emotions of a David or the passions of a John, for instance, when you read Paul . . . except on the rarest of occasions. Romans 8:38–39 is one of those occasions. As he reflected on the love of God, he dropped the careful argument that marked so much of his writing and grew downright lyrical.

If someone were to read the text to a musical accompaniment, melody, tempo, and volume would start out subdued and slowly build until it reached a cymbal-crashing climax at the words, "nor any other created thing." You can sense Paul reaching for superlatives to describe how secure we are in our relationship with God.

"I am persuaded," Paul wrote. He used the word *peitho.* It literally meant "to come to a conclusion by the influence of reason." Paul, the <u>intellectual</u>, had considered the evidence and the sheer force of the facts persuaded him beyond the shadow of a doubt that he was loved. Like a brilliant burst of instantaneous insight, Paul suddenly realized that God loved him so totally, completely, and unconditionally that nothing ever could or would diminish that love.

go to

intellectual
Acts 22:3

go to

"chief" among sinners
1 Timothy 1:15

Bear in mind, at this point in the book of Romans, Paul is only one chapter away from his desperate self-complaint, "For what I will to do, that I do not practice; but what I hate, that I do . . . O wretched man that I am!" (Romans 7:15, 24 NKJV). Elsewhere he confessed that he was "chief" among sinners. Nevertheless, even more strongly than his own sin, he felt the love of God at work in his life.

something to ponder

The promise—that God loves you in spite of yourself—changes the way you view the world and your place in it. Self-doubt melts away beneath the warm sun of God's love and forgiveness. Sure, you've done things you wish you hadn't done. But sin is finite. God's love is infinite, reaching deeper than the darkest depths of the human heart. Nothing—not even our own stubbornness and bad habits—can separate us from the love of God. Paul was a very human, garden-variety sinner just like you and me. Yet he was convinced that God loved him to death, and even beyond.

what others say

Arthur W. Pink

There are many today who talk about the love of God, who are total strangers to the God of love.[6]

Paul's Shortcomings

Weakness	Scripture
Tendency toward pride	2 Corinthians 12:7
Volatile temper	Acts 15:39; 23:3; Galatians 2:11
Blood on his hands	Acts 8:1

Abounding in Love

PSALM 103:7–8
He made known His ways to Moses,
His acts to the children of Israel.
The LORD is merciful and gracious,
Slow to anger, and abounding in mercy. (NKJV)

David and Moses were separated by some five centuries of history. But when David composed Psalm 103, he had Moses very much in mind. Psalm 103 is a psalm of praise. It begins and ends with the same phrase: "Bless the LORD, O my soul!" David finds many different reasons to bless his Lord in this psalm, but one of the most interesting comes in verses 7–8, in which David borrows language from the Book of Exodus to express his love for God.

"He made known His ways to Moses," wrote David. He is referring specifically to the time that Moses came down from receiving the Ten Commandments on Mount Sinai only to find the children of Israel in the middle of a pagan worship service around the golden calf. Moses was so angry and discouraged that he didn't want to go on. But God gave Moses a special revelation of His glory, and He reminded Moses of a few things about Himself. "The Lord, the Lord God, merciful and gracious, longsuffering, and abounding in goodness and truth." That reminder was what Moses needed in order to carry on. The hope in that message—that he served a God who was slow to anger, abounding in goodness—made it possible for him to continue with the work that God had given him.

David, too, had his share of troubles as the leader of God's people. Perhaps, like Moses, he had times when he would have preferred not to bother with the calling God had given him. But like Moses, David gave more weight to the character of God than to his own feelings and frustrations. Perhaps that's why he quoted Exodus in Psalm 103 (NKJV): "The Lord is merciful and gracious, Slow to anger, and abounding in mercy."

key point

Remembering God's promises to Moses gave David strength. It gives us strength, too. No matter how painful our trials, how deep our depressions, or how paralyzing our fears, the promise of God's love is there for us, and He deserves our praise.

In spite of Israel's failure, and ours, God ever remains "merciful and gracious, slow to anger, and abounding in mercy"—so much so that, "For as the heavens are high above the earth, so great is His mercy toward those who fear Him" (Psalm 103:8, 11 NKJV). God's love encouraged Moses while in the depths of his despair. May His love ever encourage us.

what others say

Jerry Bridges

In 1 John 3:16 John says, "This is how we know what love is: Jesus Christ laid down his life for us." The key idea here is that *love gives, even at great cost to itself.* Jesus gave his life for us.[7]

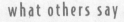

A Mighty Fortress

Psalm 46:1 ***God is our refuge and strength, a very present help in trouble.*** *(NKJV)*

Psalms 42–49 were composed by the "Sons of Korah." Korah was one of those men whose biography could appropriately be entitled, "Don't Let This Happen to You." In Moses' time, Korah was a spiritual leader of great influence, listed among the chief men of Israel. But Korah went rogue and led a mutiny against Moses that threatened to destroy the nation. So grievous were Korah's actions that God sent an earthquake to swallow him up. Yet, in spite of their father's defection, Korah's sons stayed faithful to God. David appointed men from the family of Korah to serve as choir leaders, and they continued to be temple musicians for hundreds of years.

The sons of Korah were still the temple musicians in 701 BC, when the Assyrian king Sennacherib brought an army to the very walls of Jerusalem in an attempt to conquer King Hezekiah and the Israelites. It has been suggested by some scholars that Psalm 46 is a commemoration of God's amazing victory over the Assyrians at that time. Known for their brute force, merciless tactics, and barbarian butchery, the Assyrians were a foe to be feared. For if the Assyrians remained true to form, the men of Jerusalem would be impaled on poles, the women and girls raped, and the boys enslaved to serve the sinister King Sennacherib. Only God could save the city.

And save it He did! "The angel of the LORD . . . killed in the camp of the Assyrians one hundred and eighty-five thousand . . . So Sennacherib king of Assyria departed and went away" (2 Kings 19:35–36 NKJV). At that moment, God was truly a "very present help in time of trouble." There seemed no hope for God's people, and yet God came through, as He does so often.

We also know that Psalm 46 inspired Martin Luther to compose the great hymn "A Mighty **Fortress** Is Our God." This hymn has given strength to believers for hundreds of years, a reminder of the strength of God even in our weakness. Psalm 46 ought to inspire us just as it inspired Luther. For our God *is* a secure place in which to rest, a source of strength and more than a match for any foe we may face. Even when our walls of protection fail us, God is a fortress. He is always there when we need Him, ever ready to rush to our aid.

go to

chief men of Israel
Exodus 6:21

threatened to destroy the nation
Numbers 16:1–35

Sennacherib
2 Kings 19

fortress
any place of exceptional security; stronghold

key point

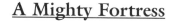

> **what others say**
>
> **Charles Haddon Spurgeon**
>
> It is all very well for me to stand here and talk about this, but the sweetness lies in getting under the refuge. It is of no use to know, when you are climbing the storm-beaten Alp, that there is a refuge on the hillside against the storm, unless you get into it. Beloved believer, get into your God![8]

go to

King Nebuchadnezzar
Daniel 3:1–6

adultery
literally, the sexual infidelity of a married person. Here it is used metaphorically to speak of the unfaithfulness of God's people

Hide and Seek

JEREMIAH 29:13 ***And you will seek Me and find Me, when you search for Me with all your heart.*** *(NKJV)*

In Jeremiah's time, the people had rejected God and chose instead to worship idols. They wished to live outside of the boundaries God had placed on them. So God gave them what they wished for. He allowed them to be taken far beyond their boundaries. When the Assyrians swept in, God lifted the hand that had protected the Israelites so many times before. Israelites died by the thousands, and thousands of the survivors were carried into captivity hundreds of miles away. The Jews had wanted to worship idols. They didn't like it so well when King Nebuchadnezzar set up a ninety-foot statue of himself and required them to bow down to it. Yes, the Jews had managed to get beyond the boundaries that God had set for them. They realized too late that those boundaries were intended to protect them more than limit them.

Though the nation as a whole descended into spiritual **adultery**, many followers remained faithful to God. Jeremiah wrote to encourage these beleaguered believers. He reminded them that God had not forgotten them, and that their exile would eventually end (Jeremiah 29:10–13 NKJV). He assured them that God had great and glorious plans to prosper them, to give them a hope and a future (v. 11). He encouraged them to pray to God, and affirmed that He would hear and answer their prayers (v. 12). And Jeremiah gave to every man and woman, every boy and girl, this promise from God: "You will seek Me and find Me, when you search for Me with all your heart" (v. 13).

something to ponder

After all their running from God, all their hiding from Him, Jeremiah reassured the people of Israel that God would always be there, ready to be found, when they were serious about finding Him.

go to

seeks that which is lost
Luke 19:10

something to ponder

As the writer of Hebrews put it, God "is a rewarder of those who diligently seek Him" (Hebrews 11:6 NKJV). The promise is not for those who try a little harder or do a little better. The promise is for those whose heart's desire is to know God. The reward is for those who are diligent in searching Him out.

God doesn't play hide-and-seek. No, seek-and-find is more His style. He seeks that which is lost. He always finds what He's looking for. And when you go looking for Him, He has promised you will always find Him.

Chapter Wrap-Up

- God promises never to despise or neglect the truly repentant and contrite.
- When you face troubles, it helps to get your eyes off yourself and onto God and His promises.
- God's mercies are new and fresh every day, even though we continue to sin.
- When you earnestly seek God, you will find Him every time.

Study Questions

1. What is the basis of your confidence in God's promises?
2. When it comes to standing firm for God, what is even more important than personal character?
3. What are some things that are impossible for God?
4. If "The God of peace will crush Satan under your feet," why do you still need to be wary of Satan?
5. What is your hope when you realize the depth and magnitude of your sin?

Chapter 12: Promises Concerning Our Future

Chapter Highlights:
- The return of Christ
- Our future in heaven
- The triumph of love
- Future judgment
- The death of death

He's Coming Back!

> ACTS 1:11 *This same Jesus, who was taken up from you into heaven, will so come in like manner as you saw Him go into heaven.* (NKJV)

The disciples were all alone—this time for good. Only recently they had heard the crowds welcome Jesus into the city, heralding Him as their king. When the mob turned against Him and demanded His execution, they fled. Gazing into the empty tomb, they must have wondered at His resurrection. Now they watched helplessly as He ascended into heaven, leaving them all alone.

They would never see Jesus again. Or would they? A pair of angels appearing as two men in dazzling dress confronted the disciples, "Why do you stand gazing up into heaven?" (Acts 1:11 NKJV). The angels went on to remind the still-gawking men of the promise Jesus had offered them on the night before His crucifixion. He had assured them that they would not be left to find their own way. Jesus told them (and us, as His future followers): "I will come again and receive you to Myself" (John 14:3b NKJV). Even in the agony of the present, He made ample provision for their future.

For the early church, the thought of Jesus' return was a huge comfort. All the wrongs they were suffering, all the persecutions would be put right. Oppressed by this earthly kingdom, they longed for God's kingdom to be established in its fullness. When Paul wrote to the Thessalonians, he reminded them of the marvelous news that "the Lord Himself will descend from heaven with a shout . . . And the dead in Christ will rise first. Then we who are alive and remain shall be caught up together with them in the clouds to meet the Lord in the air. And thus we shall always be with the Lord" (1 Thessalonians 4:16-17 NKJV).

We Christians—especially Western Christians—can get pretty comfortable here in this world. We know we're supposed to be excited about the return of Christ, but on the other hand, we'd be

go to

the crowds welcome Jesus into the city
Mark 11

the night before His crucifixion
John 13–17

a little disappointed to miss seeing our children and grandchildren grow up, or miss drawing out all that 401(k) money we've been socking away. But the news of Christ's return is news of great comfort. It means you don't have to languish in light of the problems and pressures you face each day. Instead, you can live in the light of His return, knowing that someday soon you will see Him and be with Him forever. Everything you have been working toward and hoping for you will see in its fullness on that great day.

what others say

Herbert Lockyer

If we realize how He went away, then we know His return will correspond. Well, Jesus went away in the presence of His own—personally—visibly—suddenly—in a cloud., and His second advent will follow the same pattern, as the heavenly visitants affirmed.[1]

Charles R. Swindoll

Clearly, Christ is going to return. Our question is this: How can we best "stay ready 'til quittin' time?"[2]

Changed!

1 Corinthians 15:52b *For the trumpet will sound, and the dead will be raised incorruptible, and we shall be changed. (NKJV)*

"Behold," Paul wrote to the Corinthians—you just know he's about to say something important. "I tell you a mystery" (1 Corinthians 15:51 NKJV). Indeed, Paul is about to touch on one of the greatest of all mysteries: what happens to us after death? "We shall not all sleep," Paul continued, "but we shall all be changed."

Paul speaks one of the central truths of the Christian faith: We won't stay dead. We may go to sleep, but we won't stay asleep. But neither will we carry on with the same struggles and shortcomings that characterize our human condition. Instead, we shall be changed. Here on earth, we are constantly aware of the gap between who we are and who we were made to be. But one day a trumpet will sound, and we will be changed. We will be complete, we will be the people God meant for us to be all along.

Everything on earth is **corruptible**. Things break. Food goes bad. Relationships turn sour. Sometimes even people who appear to be of the highest character turn out to be corrupt. Perhaps the most dramatic instance of corruption is the rotting of bodies in their graves. But Paul reminds his readers that even that corruption, that rotting will be reversed and healed. "The dead will be raised incorruptible" (1 Corinthians 15:52 NKJV). No longer subject to the corruption of the flesh, the dead will be put back together. They will be set free not only from physical corruption, but also from the spiritual corruption that endangers us all.

go to

rotting
Matthew 23:27

corruptible
subject to corruption or spoilage

In one sense, change is what life on this earth is all about. Everything is in constant flux. But, as the saying goes, the more things change, the more they stay the same. We always seem to be struggling with the same habits and shortcomings with which we've been struggling forever. We're still fallen creatures, never quite able to be what we want to be.

But one of these days, we're going to be changed in a way that changes everything forever. We will be like Christ. As John put it, "We shall be like Him, for we shall see Him as He is" (1 John 3:2 NKJV). The corruptible will put on incorruptibility. One big change, and then we'll never change again. The gap between who we are and who we were made to be will be closed forever. Think of it!

something to ponder

what others say

Paul R. Van Gorder

That all Christians will not die was a new revelation . . . Whether we as believers die and are resurrected, or whether we are caught up to meet the Lord Jesus without dying, we shall *all* be changed!... In that day every believer will shout, "O death where is thy sting? O grave, where is thy victory?"[3]

You Can't Take It with You

Psalm 49:15
But God will redeem my soul from the power of the grave,
For He shall receive me. *(NKJV)*

Psalm 49—another "Psalm of the sons of Korah"—is unusual in that it is addressed not to God, but to "all peoples . . . all inhabitants of the world" (Psalm 49:1 NKJV). It is a psalm of hope, but it also contains a grave warning. "Hear this..." the psalm begins. The

amassing fortunes
Luke 12:20

ransom
a price paid to buy a person out of captivity and/or slavery

warning in Psalm 49 is directed at those who put their time and energy into amassing fortunes and seeking pleasure in the here and now. For in the end, those who think that fulfillment is found in fatter bank accounts and larger houses are in for a big surprise. "Do not be afraid when one becomes rich, when the glory of his house is increased; for when he dies he shall carry nothing away; his glory shall not descend after him" (Psalm 49:16 NKJV). In other words, "You can't take it with you."

"The redemption of [rich men's] souls is costly," wrote the psalmist, "and it shall cease forever" (Psalm 49:8 NKJV). That is to say, God cannot be bought off. When a person stands before the Maker, God will not ask the value of his or her portfolio. The accumulated wealth of the world isn't enough for anyone to buy his or her way into heaven.

That's the bad news. But here's the good: you don't need to buy your way into heaven. The psalmist rejoices that it is God who "will redeem my soul from the power of the grave, for He shall receive me" (Psalm 49:15 NKJV). You may not be received at the "best" parties or in the halls of power; but God will receive you. No wealth or earthly power or authority can redeem your soul from the power of the grave. But God can. More than that, He desires to, and has promised He will.

What *is* the value of one human soul? Just ask Jesus. He gave "His life a **ransom** for many" (Matthew 20:28 NKJV). Paul put it this way: Jesus "gave Himself for us, that He might redeem us" (Titus 2:14 NKJV). The sons of Korah lived centuries before Jesus. But their belief in the promised Messiah meant they could confront death with courage and confidence as they publicly proclaimed for "all inhabitants of the world" to hear: "God will redeem my soul from the power of the grave; for He shall receive me" (Psalm 49:15 NKJV). Place your trust in Christ and that same courage and confidence will be yours.

what others say

Robert W. Bailey

We who are in fellowship with Christ need be enslaved to the fear of death no longer, neither should we allow the false gods of death to separate us from God. While death is not removed, it is rendered impotent. Because of our relationship to God, we can die in peace.[4]

A Life-and-Death Situation

JOHN 11:25 ***Jesus said to her, "I am the resurrection and the life. He who believes in Me, though he may die, he shall live." (NKJV)***

go to

God's unique name
Exodus 3:14

resurrection
the act of rising from the dead

Jesus had enjoyed a special relationship with Lazarus and his two sisters, Mary and Martha. As a matter of fact, when Lazarus' sisters sent word to Jesus that His friend had become ill, they referred to Lazarus as "he whom You love" (John 11:3 NKJV). Jesus loved Lazarus so much that He placed His life at risk by traveling to Bethany, a tiny town just east of Jerusalem, knowing that there were those in the city who sought to kill Him. Jesus was a loyal friend.

As Jesus approached the town, Martha met Him on the road and broke the news: Lazarus had succumbed to his sickness and died. Second, Jesus comforted Martha with this promise: "I am the **resurrection** and the life. He who believes in Me, though he may die, he shall live" (John 11:25 NKJV).

When Jesus said, "I am," He declared His deity, taking God's unique name and applying it to Himself. "The resurrection and the life" is characteristic of God—He alone is the giver of life. Because of who Jesus is (God) and what Jesus does (gives life), Martha and Mary would see their brother again. His burial was not a final "Good-bye," but a "See you soon." Martha and Mary had no idea how soon.

Surely Lazarus and his sisters experienced overwhelming joy when they were reunited, Lazarus walking forth from the tomb still wrapped in his burial clothes. But in the end, Lazarus getting back his physical, earthly life isn't the point of this story. Lazarus, after all, had to die again. Jesus' miracle gave him a few more years, but Lazarus was no more exempt from bodily death than the rest of us. The real point of this story is that Jesus exercises power over death. He is the resurrection and the life. And those who believe in Him, even though they die, shall live. Jesus brought life not only to Lazarus, but to Martha and Mary too, and to everyone else who puts his or her trust in Him as the resurrection and the life.

something to ponder

For a follower of Jesus, death is not like hitting a wall, but more like walking through a door. Lazarus didn't stop living when he died; he did not really start living *until* he died. Even if you find it hard to welcome death, you can at least be joyful in the knowledge that even an enemy as frightening as death has been overcome by the One who loves you.

go to

questions about the future
Matthew 24:3; Acts 1:6

conflagration
a very large fire

> **what others say**
>
> **Marilyn Willett Heavilin**
>
> Your dreams have died or been altered. Life has not turned out exactly the way you planned. You are coming to terms with your vulnerability and the fragility of life. You don't know the future and neither do I, but God does.[5]

Back from the Dead

Resurrections in the Bible	Scripture
The widow of Zarephath's son (raised by Elijah)	1 Kings 17
The daughter of Jairus	Mark 5
The widow of Nain's son	Luke 7
Lazarus	John 11
Jesus	Matthew 28

Address Change

2 PETER 3:13 ***Nevertheless we, according to His promise, look for new heavens and a new earth in which righteousness dwells. (NKJV)***

Peter and the other disciples badgered Jesus with questions about the future. They *had* to know how things were going to end up. Peter, for his part, may have gotten more than he bargained for. Well after the death and resurrection of Jesus, this uneducated fisherman looked through the lens of prophecy to a time when the entire universe would literally melt down. It's a frightening picture: "the heavens and earth will pass away with a great noise, and the elements will melt with fervent heat; both the earth and the works that are in it will be burned up" (2 Peter 3:10 NKJV). In spite of the violence of the image, Peter says we should look for it, be eager for it. Why? Because out of that **conflagration** will arise the "a new heavens and a new earth." The ashes of the old earth will give rise to a new earth, a grand and glorious paradise restored.

The Bible doesn't say a great deal about our new dwelling place. It offers a few hints here and there, but we don't really get a detailed description until the last book of the Bible, Revelation. There we read about a place of unimaginable beauty, bliss, and blessing where

God will dwell with us forever. "God will wipe away every tear from their eyes; there shall be no more death, nor sorrow, nor crying. There shall be no more pain, for the former things have passed away" (Revelation 21:4 NKJV). We'll be happy; we'll never hurt again. No wonder the Bible ends with the words "Come, Lord Jesus!"

This world is not our home. This is not what we were made for. Sometimes, as in times of great sorrow, you feel that truth very keenly. At other times, you can feel quite comfortable here on earth. Even then, however, is it not because earth can remind us of heaven? When we are surrounded by loved ones, when our sorrows seem far away, the old earth feels a little bit like the new earth. As Peter taught, the new earth won't appear in its fullness until the old earth has gone away, burned up in the last day. That's something to look forward to, to long for. For you were made to be a citizen of the new heaven and the new earth. Here, you're just a **pilgrim** and stranger.

go to

stranger
1 Peter 2:11

pilgrim
a person who journeys, especially a long distance, to some sacred place as an act of religious devotion

something to ponder

what others say

D. L. Moody

We believe this is just as much a place and just as much a city as New York, London, or Paris. We believe in it a good deal more, because earthly cities will pass away, but this city will remain forever. It has foundations whose builder and maker is God.[6]

What the Bible Says

Regarding Heaven	Scripture
God fills heaven.	Jeremiah 23:24
Christ Rules in heaven.	Matthew 28:18; 1 Peter 3:22
God's people are rewarded in heaven.	Matthew 5:12
No hunger, no thirst, no tears in heaven.	Revelation 7:16–17

In My Father's House

JOHN 14:2–3 ***In My Father's house are many mansions; if it were not so, I would have told you. I go to prepare a place for you. And if I go and prepare a place for you, I will come again and receive you to Myself; that where I am, there you may be also. (NKJV)***

When Jesus and His disciples gathered to observe the annual Passover Seder, little did the disciples know that an evening that began in the Upper Room would end in a garden with Jesus under arrest, the disciples fleeing in fear for their lives, and their chief spokesman, Peter, swearing with an oath that he never knew Jesus. It was a dark night in Jerusalem, and it had nothing to do with the setting of the sun.

However, Jesus did know. He knew that His disciples were going to need all the comfort they could get. So He made them a promise: "I will come again and receive you to Myself" (John 14:3 NKJV). We have Jesus' promise that today, as we speak, Jesus is preparing our eternal dwelling place.

"In My Father's house are many mansions," Jesus observed. For the most part, the disciples were born and bred in Galilee. Houses in Galilee were of a particular kind, known as an *insulus*. You might remember when Jesus healed Peter's mother-in-law. She lived in an **insulus**, located in **Capernaum**. No doubt Jesus and His disciples visited Peter's home on numerous occasions, and may have even lived there during a large part of Jesus' Galilean ministry. Because of the layout of this particular type of dwelling, it was relatively easy for the head of the household to expand his home by adding rooms for his growing family as the need arose.

In a typical first-century Galilean home, one's extended family dwelt together—parents, grandparents, possibly sisters, brothers, and cousins, or in Peter's case, in-laws. The disciples could easily have pictured a heavenly dwelling with the intimacy of an insulus in which the heavenly Father would gather His own family to Himself to live with Him forever. The disciples had spent three years wandering the countryside with Jesus, with no real place to call home. But the Jesus who had called them away from the comforts of home now assured them that they would soon enough have a true home for all eternity.

Jesus' promises to His disciples extend to you too. If you are in Christ, you are a part of God's household. You can look forward to your very own place in your Father's house. As Jesus promised, He has gone ahead to prepare it for you. One of these days He will return to take you back to that place, where He will receive you with great joy and thanksgiving.

go to

Peter's mother-in-law
Mark 1:29-31

insulus
a large courtyard surrounded by rings of rooms

Capernaum
a large town near the Sea of Galilee. Peter's house in Capernaum served as Jesus' Galilean headquarters

key point

what others say

John F. MacArthur, Jr.

Some people believe heaven is an imaginary place. . . . But the Bible says that heaven is a place, the eventual dwelling of all who love God.[7]

legalist
a person who seeks to gain salvation by following laws and rules

seduce
to lead or tempt into sin

Love Overcoming

1 JOHN 5:4 ***Whatever is born of God overcomes the world. And this is the victory that has overcome the world—our faith*** **(NKJV)**

In his first epistle, the apostle John is simply consumed with the idea of love—the love of the Father for His people, the love of believers for one another and for God. For John, love is the basis of all right living. When you love people, you do right by them. When you love God, you live a life that pleases God. As John's friend Peter wrote, "Love will cover a multitude of sins," even when you mess up (1 Peter 4:8 NKJV).

"This is the love of God," John wrote, "that we obey His commandments" (1 John 5:3 NKJV). That sounds at first like the kind of thing a **legalist** might say. *Want to prove you love God? Obey a bunch of rules. Sacrifice your freedom. Take on a few extra burdens.* That's how the most religious people of John's Jewish tradition "proved" that they loved God. But that's not what John was talking about. "His commandments are not burdensome," he wrote. Love doesn't weigh you down with additional burdens. Love lightens your load. You obey God because you *want* to obey Him—because your desires match up with His desires. Martin Luther put it this way: "Love God, and do as you please." A heart that loves God is a heart that finds it easy to obey God's laws. Love changes you from the inside out, changes the things you want. You have a new self; you are "born of God." And "Whatever is born of God overcomes the world" (1 John 5:4 NKJV).

The world is forever trying to **seduce** you away from the things of God. A legalist deals with that seduction by putting up fences to keep the world at a distance. But if your heart hasn't been changed, the world will always figure out a way to climb the fence or dig under it.

apply it

A heart that loves God conquers the world because it doesn't want what the world has to offer. There's no victory in burdensome rules.

something to ponder

But a loving heart, on the other hand, is invincible. When you look at the violence in the world around you, it looks as if hate is a stronger force than love. John wasn't having any of that. Like the rest of the early Christians, John lived with the threat of violence and hatred hanging over him every day. Yet he still believed that love was the strongest force of all.

What the New Testament Says About

Burdens	Scripture
The Pharisees laid extra burdens on the people.	Matthew 23:4
Jesus' yoke is easy and His burden is light.	Matthew 11:30
God's commandments are not burdensome.	1 John 5:3
Believers are called to bear one another's burdens.	Galatians 6:2

Conviction, Not Condemnation

ROMANS 8:1 ***There is therefore now no condemnation to those who are in Christ Jesus.*** *(NKJV)*

Paul was keenly aware of his own sin. He felt it as a war within himself—the old self and the new battling it out. His new self wanted to do right, but his old self kept dragging him back down to the gutter. "The good that I will to do, I do not do; but the evil I will not to do, that I practice" (Romans 7:19 NKJV). It was a constant struggle, and it made Paul miserable: "O wretched man that I am! Who will deliver me from the body of this death?" But when Paul reached that crisis, he remembered the name of Christ, and immediately the crisis was resolved. "There is now no condemnation in Christ," Paul reassured himself (and us). Jesus brings peace and healing, not **condemnation**.

To be **convicted** of your sin is no fun. When you get serious about following Christ, you become more and more aware of the gap between the person you are and the person you need to be. That's a painful thing. Like Paul, you feel as if you're at war with yourself. You know what's right, you even desire what's right, but you find yourself doing wrong. Your old self, your flesh, is still trying to impose its old, invalidated claim on you. You try to do better; you fail; you begin to feel you're a hopeless case. Perhaps you remember what things were like before you received Christ. You didn't feel this bad, this condemned back then. What gives?

condemnation
a final judgment of guilt, and the punishment that is imposed

convicted
convinced that you have done wrong

That's when you turn again to Christ. He is the One who brings resolution. He bridges the gap between you and God. He brings peace in your inner self—where before there was only war. That bad feeling you get when God begins to work in your life—that's conviction, not condemnation. Conviction is constructive. It points you toward a future and a hope.

The war inside of you can make you feel as if condemnation is the inevitable result of your seemingly unconquerable sin. But there is no condemnation in Christ. His grace is greater than your sin. As long as you live in this body, your old self is going to try to drag you down. Soldier on. If you are in Christ, you can look forward to the day when that was with yourself will be over, and you will enter fully into the promised peace of the One in whom there is no condemnation.

go to

consume
Hebrews 10:27; Malachi 4:1

impenitent
not feeling regret about one's sin

Payday Someday

2 CORINTHIANS **5:10** ***For we must all appear before the judgment seat of Christ, that each one may receive the things done in the body, according to what he has done, whether good or bad. (NKJV)***

The writer to the Hebrews described the Bible as "sharper than any two-edged sword" (4:12 NKJV). That description certainly applies here. The description of Judgment Day in 2 Corinthians 5:10 slices two ways.

God does what is right every time, in every situation. He is merciful, but He is also just. And His justice demands that every human being stand before Him to be judged for the way he or she has lived. God warns the doers of evil, "In accordance with your hardness and your **impenitent** heart you are treasuring up for yourself wrath in the day of wrath and revelation of the righteous judgment of God" (Romans 2:5 NKJV). A just God can do no less than call into account the behavior of those who are stubborn and unrepentant toward Him. That judgment will consume God's enemies much as a raging fire consumes dried grass or a dead tree.

But those who love Christ—whose hearts are humble, broken, contrite, and repentant—are judged by a completely different standard. They are justified; when God looks at them in judgment, He sees the perfection of Christ, not the sins they have committed. Which is to say, if you are in Christ, your judgment is *not* one of punishment, but one of reward. We cannot be penalized because Jesus *already* paid the price to cover our punishment. To put it in legal terms, to punish us again after Christ had already received the punishment would be double jeopardy. And double jeopardy is just not just.

"We must all appear before the judgment seat of Christ" (2 Corinthians 5:10 NKJV). This double-edged promise should strike paralyzing fear into those whose hearts are hard. On the other hand, it should create an attitude of humble gratitude in those who have received Christ and rested in the work He accomplished on the cross. No one really deserves to share in the "joy of [our] lord" (Matthew 25:21 NKJV). We are all equally sinful.

something to ponder

The only difference between those who receive judgment and those who receive reward is that the first continue in their own stubborn ways and the others have thrown themselves upon God's mercy. If you've not yet experienced His forgiveness, pray this simple prayer: "God, be merciful to me, a sinner!" (Luke 18:13 NKJV). That's a prayer He will always answer!

what others say

Lewis Sperry Chafer and John Walvoord

There was no temporizing or partial dealing with sin at the cross. This great issue between God and man was there dealt with in a manner which is satisfying even to the infinite holiness of God, and the only question that remains is whether man is satisfied with the sacrifice which satisfies God. To accept the work of Christ for us is to believe upon the Savior to the saving of the soul.[8]

A Hand Full of Empty

ECCLESIASTES 12:13–14

Fear God and keep His commandments,For this is man's all.
For God will bring every work into judgment,
Including every secret thing,
Whether good or evil. (NKJV)

Solomon was a man to be envied. At least you'd think so. Raised in King David's home, Solomon knew a life of luxury from the moment he drew his first breath. He inherited his father's throne and an era of unprecedented peace in a unified land. He had the respect of his people and of leaders throughout the region. He built a temple unrivaled in its glory. Considered the wisest man who ever lived, he wrote the Book of Proverbs and two others: Ecclesiastes and the Song of Solomon. He also had a penchant for the ladies—so much so that he married *700* of them. What more could a man ask for? Yet, the Book of Ecclesiastes echoes with the hollowness of **disillusionment**. "Vanity of vanities," Solomon wrote, "all is vanity" (Ecclesiastes 1:2 NKJV).

go to

life of luxury
1 Kings 4:21–28

disillusionment
the state of having lost all sense of idealism

What went wrong? Just this: As Solomon filled his life with stuff and with worldly pleasures, he gradually squeezed God out. His became a life of continual compromise, so much so that when Nehemiah remembered him centuries later, this was his lasting legacy: "Among many nations there was no king like him, who was beloved of his God; and God made him king over all Israel. Nevertheless pagan women caused even him to sin" (Nehemiah 13:26 NKJV). Even the world's wisest man couldn't hold things together when he neglected to put first things first.

key point

In the book of Ecclesiastes, Solomon reflected on all the things with which he tried to fill his life, and in each case they came up lacking. But after roaming over the old, tired terrain of human pleasures and human endeavor, Solomon arrived at a simple, straightforward conclusion. The book ends with this plea to his people: "Fear God and keep His commandments, for this is man's all" (Ecclesiastes 12:13 NKJV). This from a man whose "all" seemed so much greater than the usual—all those palaces, all those riches, all those women. But even for Solomon, man's "all" was incredibly simple.

Fear God. Keep His commandments. Why? Because Solomon understood God's promise that "every work" will be brought into judgment, including "every secret thing, whether good or evil" (Ecclesiastes 12:14 NKJV). Solomon must have penned these words with great shame. He had to acknowledge in the end that living for God was a higher calling than living for himself. God is the only true source of happiness and fulfillment. Apart from Him, everything else *is* vanity.

what others say

Greg Johnson

"At the end of life, it's my closeness with God that means the most". . . The priorities that make life worth living are not work, pleasure, or accumulated "toys," but God, family, and friends.

How do your priorities stack up?[9]

Chapter Wrap-Up

- The promise of Christ's return means all will be put right someday.
- God has promised to change us from corruptible beings to incorruptible.
- The end of this world means the beginning of a new and glorious world.
- The future is indescribably bright for those who are in Christ.

Study Questions

1. What does it mean to say that Lazarus' physical resurrection isn't really the point of John 11?
2. How does love for God allow us to conquer the world?
3. What is the difference between conviction and condemnation?
4. What does "double jeopardy" have to do with Judgment Day?
5. What does it mean to be a stranger and pilgrim on earth?

Chapter 13: Promises Concerning Our Problems

Chapter Highlights:
- The certainty of difficulty
- God's deliverance
- Promise of eternity
- God's blessing

A Painful Promise

John 16:33b ***In the world you will have tribulation; but be of good cheer, I have overcome the world.*** *(NKJV)*

You're going to experience **tribulation** in this world. That's a promise. This may not exactly be what you were expecting to find in a book of Bible promises, but there it is: "In the world you will have tribulation." There's a kind of comfort even in that straightforward statement. No matter how much you are surprised by a loved one's death or a false accusation or a financial reversal, earthly trouble never takes God by surprise. He understands. Jesus, after all, experienced tribulation the likes of which none of us will ever know.

When you experience serious trouble, it can appear as if God isn't there, or maybe He's simply lost control. Or maybe He's not as powerful as the problems that plague this sin-cursed world. But Jesus immediately follows the promise of trouble with a promise of victory. "Be of good cheer," He said, "I have overcome the world." Jesus didn't eliminate earthly suffering and trouble. But He did change the equation completely. The defeats you suffer at the hands of the world are not final defeats. One of these days they will be swallowed by the eternal joy of heaven. The world has no final claim on you. Compared to heaven, these tribulations will seem as light as a feather.

Years ago there was a very popular book intended to give comfort to people who had suffered grief and loss. This book said, in effect, that there are dark corners of this chaotic universe where God does not exercise complete control. It said that's why we experience tribulation—because even though God wants to help, He can't stop every bad thing from happening. But that's not what Jesus said. Jesus said He had overcome the world. He said we could be of good cheer in spite of the fact that tribulations are inevitable.

David said, "Where can I go from Your Spirit? Or where can I flee from Your presence? If I ascend into heaven, You are there; If I make

go to

light as a feather
2 Corinthians 4:17

tribulation
trouble; hardship, distress, adverse circumstances

my bed in hell, behold, You are there. If I take the wings of the morning, And dwell in the uttermost parts of the sea, Even there Your hand shall lead me, And Your right hand shall hold me" (Psalm 139:7–10 NKJV). There isn't any corner where God isn't present or where God isn't in control. His ways are not our ways. But we can trust that He has overcome the world that constantly threatens to defeat us.

what others say

David A. Seamands

In a lifetime of listening to hurting people, I have heard many personal descents into hell with its abyss of emotional pain. Again and again, I have found that the most therapeutic turning point in the healing process is when people discover that God not only knows and cares but also *understands how they feel.*[1]

Personal Tribulations in the Bible

People Who Overcame Bad Times	Scripture
Joseph falsely accused, imprisoned	Genesis 39:20
Elijah becomes suicidal	1 Kings 19:4
Jeremiah beaten, confined	Jeremiah 20:2
Peter's moral crisis	Matthew 26:75
Paul's list of troubles	2 Corinthians 11:23–29
Mary watches her Son die	Luke 2:35

Delighting in Discipline

Proverbs 3:12
For whom the Lord loves He corrects,
Just as a father the son in whom he delights. (NKJV)

Peter blew it, and he knew it. Peter vowed that he would stand with Jesus and defend Him to the death. Yet, when the sparks started to fly, so did Peter. On the night Jesus was betrayed, Peter disowned Jesus three times. At the moment Jesus needed him the most, Peter collapsed like a house of cards. Not once, however, did Jesus disown Peter. Like Humpty Dumpty, Peter had a great fall. But Jesus was determined to put His fallen friend back together again.

"Operation Restore Peter" took place along the tranquil Galilean shore. Things were anything but tranquil for Peter on that morning.

You can only imagine the look on Peter's face when the resurrected Jesus showed up for breakfast. Three times Peter had denied Christ. So three times Jesus asked Peter, "Do you love Me?" (John 21:16–17 NKJV). Three times Peter said, "Yes, Lord . . ." sort of.

The first time Jesus asked "Do you love Me," the verb He used was *agape*, a selfless, sacrificial devotion. He was asking, in effect, "Peter, are you devoted to Me?" In his response, Peter used the word *phileo*, a friendship love—"Lord, we're good friends."

The second time, the same thing happened: "Friends, yes; devoted, not necessarily."

The third time, *Jesus* changed the verb to *phileo*, as if to say "Peter, are we even friends anymore?" Peter must have dropped his head in shame. Jesus had reason to doubt their friendship. How far Peter had fallen. Yet, at this moment of failure, Jesus lovingly called His wounded warrior back into the ministry. "Follow Me," He said. Those were the same words He used when He first called His disciples to a new life.

go to

first called
Matthew 4:19; 8:22; 9:9

chastens
inflicts suffering upon for purposes of moral improvement; chastises

Why did Jesus put Peter through all that pain? For the same reason He sometimes allows us to hurt. Disobedient disciples can sometimes be restored only through the loving hand of God's correction. That's why the verse preceding this promise in Proverbs encourages the reader not to "despise the chastening of the LORD, nor detest His correction" (Proverbs 3:11 NKJV). Why not? Because "whom the LORD loves He corrects, just as a father the son in whom he delights" (Proverbs 3:12 NKJV).

something to ponder

The writer to the Hebrews said the same thing: "Whom the LORD loves He **chastens**" (Hebrews 12:6 NKJV). No chastening or discipline is *delightful*. It helps to know, however, that God disciplines those in whom He *delights*. The discipline of difficulty is a sign that God is still working on you, not a sign that He's forgotten you.

what others say

Richard W. DeHaan

The story is told of an atheist whose pumpkin crop flourished while his Christian neighbor's froze. Taunting the believer, he asked, "Why did God let your pumpkins freeze? Mine are all right." The reply came, "God is not raising pumpkins. He's raising men!"[2]

go to

slow to anger
Exodus 34:6;
Nehemiah 9:17;
Psalm 86:15;
Joel 2:13

baby
2 Samuel 12:15b–23

Hebrew and Greek Words for *Love* (from *Vine's Dictionary*)

Word	Meaning
'ahab (Hebrew)	A strong emotional attachment to and desire either to possess or to be in the presence of the object; familial, romantic, or friendship . . . sometimes depicts a special strong attachment a servant may have toward a master under whose dominance he wishes to remain.
agapao (Greek)	Christian love, which "has God for its primary object, and expresses itself first of all in implicit obedience to His commandments." The opposite of self-will.
phileo (Greek)	"Tender affection." Unlike *agapao*, *phileo* does describe a feeling or an emotion.

"Good Morning"

Psalm 30:5
For His anger is but for a moment,
His favor is for life;
Weeping may endure for a night,
But joy comes in the morning. *(NKJV)*

David wrote Psalm 30 in celebration of the dedication of his palace in Jerusalem. After decades of running and hiding, sometimes triumphing, sometimes failing, sometimes making pretty big mistakes, he paused to praise the God who had seen him through. Looking back on all that struggle, here was one of the things that struck David: the promise that in the end, God's love always overcomes His anger. David had done plenty of things to incur God's anger. We mostly remember David's deeds of honor and bravery in that pre-king phase of his life, but he also made his share of mistakes. He threw his lot in with the Philistines at Ziklag. He could be bloodthirsty at times. But through all that, he came to understand that God overwhelmingly dealt with him in love, not in anger.

God is slow to anger. Being slow to anger, however, isn't the same thing as never getting angry. The Bible offers many examples of people who exceeded God's patience and were punished. Years after composing Psalm 30, David himself felt the brunt of God's anger when he committed adultery with Bathsheba. The baby they conceived died in infancy, and David's heart was broken.

There is great comfort, however, in the promise of Psalm 30: "His anger is but for a moment, His favor is for life" (Psalm 30:5 NKJV). That is to say, God doesn't hold a grudge. His anger is quickly spent. His love is eternal. Though God took one child from David, he gave

David and Bathsheba another son, Solomon, who grew up to be the hope of David's royal lineage.

"The fear of the Lord" isn't just a figure of speech. We human beings have reason to fear the power—not to mention the holiness and justice—of the Almighty. But if the thought of God's anger is overwhelming, what a comfort it is to know that His love overwhelms His anger. There's no contest, really. His love abounds.

God's punishments, when they come, bring a "dark night of the soul." That's not necessarily a bad thing. Sometimes it takes that kind of darkness for your eyes to adjust to see the spiritual things God would have you see. But, as David observed, however dark the night, "joy comes in the morning." The sun of God's love always shines again. There's the promise of hope and healing in that realization.

oxymoron
a combination of contradictory words, such as *"cruel kindness"*

key point

what others say

V. Raymond Edman

We can be so grieved by the mistakes and galled by the failures of the past that we have no heart for the present or the future. . . . It is gone, it is under the Blood, it is committed unto Him Who has said in His Word, " . . . he retaineth not his anger forever, because he delighteth in mercy."[3]

Lighten Your Load!

2 CORINTHIANS ***4:17 For our light affliction, which is but for a moment, is working for us a far more exceeding and eternal weight of glory. (NKJV)***

An **oxymoron** sits at the center of 2 Corinthians 4:17. Note the two words *light* and *affliction*. *Light* literally means "lacking weight"; *affliction* refers to "an intense or weighty pressure." So were Paul's troubles weightless, or were they weighty? Here's how Paul described his tribulations: "From the Jews five times I received forty stripes minus one. Three times I was beaten with rods; once I was stoned; three times I was shipwrecked; a night and a day I have been in the deep; in journeys often, in perils of water . . . robbers . . . my own countrymen . . . Gentiles, in perils in the city . . . in the wilderness . . . in the sea, in perils among false brethren; in weariness and toil, in sleeplessness often, in hunger and thirst, in fastings often; in cold and nakedness—besides the other things, what comes upon

go to

shipwrecked
Acts 27:13–44

me daily: my deep concern for all the churches" (2 Corinthians 11:24–28 NKJV). Sounds pretty weighty; they certainly outweigh the troubles we modern-day Christians experience. Paul's problems by far outweighed our own. When was the last time you were shipwrecked?

But from an eternal perspective, even such troubles as Paul's are mere trifles compared to the promise of "eternal glory" that awaits us in heaven. Troubles will be forgotten—or else remembered as souvenirs of God's grace in seeing us through. From the view of eternity, even the longest life here on earth is barely even a blip on the radar.

Consider the way an oyster makes a pearl. A little grain of sand gets inside and irritates the oyster, causing it pain. So the oyster coats the irritant with a layer of mother-of-pearl, then another layer, then another, until the grain of sand is long forgotten, buried in the middle of something far more beautiful and permanent even than the oyster itself! That's how suffering works in your life. It produces a glory, a beauty that renders the suffering irrelevant. It's a glory that far outweighs and long outlasts the whole of your earthly life. Indeed, when compared to eternity, our earthly trials are "momentary," a blink of an eye.

apply it

You're going to experience troubles in this fallen world. That's the sad fact of the matter. As long as your vision is limited to the world you can see, those troubles will weigh you down. But they don't get the last word in the life of a believer. If you can just look up, look ahead to the promised future that awaits you, you will see that in the grand scheme of things, those troubles are "momentary," and as light as a feather.

what others say

Charles R. Swindoll

Pearls are the product of pain . . . No wonder our heavenly home has as its entrance *pearly* gates! Those who go through them need no explanation. They are the ones who have been wounded, bruised, and have responded to the sting of irritations with the pearl of adjustment.[4]

Good as Gold

1 Peter 1:6b–7 ***You have been grieved by various trials, that the genuineness of your faith, being much more precious than***

gold that perishes, though it is tested by fire, may be found to praise, honor, and glory at the revelation of Jesus Christ. (NKJV)

Life under the Emperor Nero was a nightmare. When he assumed the reins of power, the Roman Empire quaked in fear. The man had no conscience. He was by all accounts a self-absorbed maniac. He murdered his mother, his brother, and his wife. He hated the Christians, who refused to worship the emperor as a god; refused to worship at pagan temples; refused to support the Roman ideals of self, power, and conquest; refused to accept Rome's hedonistic culture. When the city of Rome burned, Nero blamed the Christians. The vicious persecution of Christians throughout the empire forced scores of believers to abandon their homes and flee for their lives. Many ended up impaled on poles, covered with pitch, and burned alive to illuminate Nero's gardens at night.

go to

"pilgrims of the Dispersion"
1 Peter 1:1

"refiner's fire"
Malachi 3:3–3

These "pilgrims of the Dispersion" were the believers to whom Peter wrote. Theirs was the suffering of which Peter spoke. Theirs was the faith he described as "more precious than gold" (1 Peter 1:7 NKJV). When you consider Nero's burning of Christians, the believers to whom Peter wrote understood the metaphor of the "refiner's fire" in ways we never will. To these Christians, Peter offered the assurance that their faith would indeed result in "praise, honor, and glory" at the revealing of Christ. That promise made it all worthwhile.

The sufferings of the early church seem very far away. For that matter, the suffering still experienced by Christians in other parts of the world seems pretty remote from the comfortable, middle-class existence of so many Christians in North America. But our faith is inextricably tied to their faithfulness, to their willingness to press on in the face of persecution. Sometimes you're called upon to do something for the sake of your faith that makes you uncomfortable—to confront a person you don't feel like confronting, to take a stand when it would be easier to take a back seat. In light of the sufferings endured by our forebears, it's hard to justify our usual cop-outs.

something to ponder

The Roman Empire crumbled. It lies today in ruins. Nero is an historical footnote. But today, around the world, countless millions would die rather than deny their faith in Jesus Christ—a faith that is "more precious than gold." Peter was right. His readers' faith proved genuine. We are the beneficiaries of that faith. Like them, "having not seen [Him, we] love [Him]. Though now [we] do not see Him, yet believing, [we] rejoice with joy inexpressible and full of glory" (1 Peter 1:8 NKJV).

> **what others say**
>
> **H. A. Ironside**
>
> There are times when the tears will flow. But now God puts in contrast to the affliction which you have known down here the glory that is coming by-and-by, and if the affliction has oppressed your heart, how the glory will overwhelm you when you are at home with Christ.[5]

Pure Joy

JAMES 1:2–4 ***My brethren, count it all joy when you fall into various trials, knowing that the testing of your faith produces patience. But let patience have its perfect work, that you may be perfect and complete, lacking nothing.*** *(NKJV)*

James urged his readers to "count it all joy" when they experienced trials and hardships. That's an interesting word choice, "count it" joy. Some translations read "consider it" joy. In other words, examine your situation, investigate the evidence before you, and make a choice. It's up to you to decide whether or not you're going to be joyful. It's always up to you. To "consider" is to make a choice. James is talking about a state of mind that is quite independent of the circumstances in which you find yourself. Another writer might have said something like, "My wish for you is that you will have the things that make you happy." Not James. He says, in effect, "My hope for you is that you will choose joy, regardless of your situation."

When we face our problems and pressures with true joy, God promises that we will develop perseverance—the endurance to hang in there until the appropriate time for God to remove it. God then takes us to the next level where we become mature and complete—people who are whole, men and women of authenticity and integrity. That's what holiness means, by the way—wholeness, completeness. In the English language, *holy* and *whole* come from the same word. Holiness—now there's something you can rejoice in.

There's more here than finding the silver lining in every cloud. For James, it's not really a matter of finding joy in *spite of* trouble. It's a matter of understanding that without trials and tribulation, you will never become the kind of person who can experience true joy. You can't be perfected if you don't have patience. You can't cultivate patience if everything is going your way all the time. That's why you have to learn to *lean into* your difficulties. You don't have to be happy about them. You don't have to go seeking them out. You just have to choose joy even when the trials come. You have to choose to look beyond your problems to a God who is much bigger than the biggest problem.

Biblical joy is a determination of mind, a **resolution** of soul—the unshakable confidence that no matter what we are going through, God is in control. God's sovereignty thus becomes the stabilizing force with which we can confidently face any and all of life's challenges, no matter how hopeless they may seem.

what others say

Roy Hession

Since then I have seen others, who have been brought to the cross in a new way. . . . I have hated to see the pain of it, and in sympathy with a brother have said, "Oh, God, how long?" But we all emerged ultimately not only with a new experience in our hearts, but with a brand-new message on our lips.[6]

Search and Rescue Unit

2 TIMOTHY 4:18 ***And the Lord will deliver me from every evil work and preserve me for His heavenly kingdom. To Him be glory forever and ever. Amen!*** *(NKJV)*

Timothy was having a bad day. He seemed to have more than his share of bad days. With Paul in prison and his church in disarray, Timothy needed assurance. What could Paul do to embolden his struggling "son in the faith"? Paul did something that would mean more than anything else he might have done. He taught Timothy out of the framework of his own experience.

Paul knew there was only one way out of prison for him: death. He had come to the end of the line. In that place of vulnerability Demas deserted him; Alexander the coppersmith harmed him; no one stood with him; only Luke stuck by him. After a faithful ministry that

go to

patience
Ecclesiastes 7:8

Demas deserted him
2 Timothy 4:10

Alexander the coppersmith
2 Timothy 4:14

Luke
2 Timothy 4:11

resolution
determination, resolve

spanned decades and touched more than one continent, poor Paul faced the end alone. Or so it would seem.

Paul understood, however, that he wasn't as alone as he looked. "The Lord stood with me," he told Timothy, "and strengthened me" (2 Timothy 4:17 NKJV). He was confident that God would deliver him "from every evil work." Bear in mind, this was coming from a man who was under a death sentence from the Roman government. According to church tradition, Paul died at the hands of the Romans, crucified for his faith. That didn't look like deliverance to the casual observer. But Paul understood that even death was a kind of deliverance. Paul, you will remember, couldn't decide whether he wanted to live or die anyway. He wanted to continue God's work, but on the other hand, he longed to be with Jesus. The worst anybody could do would be to kill him. And should that happen, Paul knew that the Lord would "preserve me for His heavenly kingdom" (2 Timothy 4:18 NKJV). Death was a kind of rescue too. How do you imprison or control a person with an attitude like that?

Ultimate attack; ultimate rescue; ultimate victory in the face of certain defeat. That's an emboldening, freeing promise. It must have emboldened Timothy in the midst of intense problems and pressure, it certainly ought to embolden us to face life's challenges with the strength that the Lord Jesus will supply. You will be delivered. Nobody can do worse to you than was done to Paul—and yet Paul continued to luxuriate in God's promise of deliverance. For that assurance, God deserves "glory forever and ever. Amen!" (2 Timothy 4:18 NKJV).

key point

what others say

John R. W. Stott

Paul goes on confidently, 'the Lord will rescue me,' not indeed from death (for he is expecting to die, but 'from every evil' outside God's permitted will. He will also 'save me for his heavenly kingdom', though Nero may soon dispatch me from my earthly kingdom.[7]

Roger Palms

When the floods come upon me and I'm trying to get out, when the enemy is pressing behind me and I need a Red Sea miracle, when the flame is suddenly all around like a prairie fire on a hot, windy day and I have no safe place to go....That's when His promise means something . . .[8]

Our Ever-Present Help

Psalm 46:1–2a
God is our refuge and strength,
A very present help in trouble.
Therefore we will not fear. *(NKJV)*

If ever there was a psalm for **turbulent** times, Psalm 46 is it. The psalmist describes what life has become for so many today: "Even though the earth be removed, and though the mountains be carried into the midst of the sea; though its waters roar and be troubled, though the mountains shake with its swelling" (Psalm 46:2–3 NKJV). All stability rendered unstable. All strength rendered impotent. The earth and mountains are symbols of unshakable stability. The troubled sea represents all that is turbulent in life. Imagine it: when the mountains have been thrown into the sea, what on earth *can* you count on? The truth is, there's really nothing on earth you can count on in the end. If you're looking to the things of earth to give you stability and a firm footing, you're going to be disappointed. But "there is a river whose streams make glad the city of God" (Psalm 46:4 NKJV). What a promise! Let the ocean roar. Let the storms rage. There is still gladness to be had in God.

Though our symbols of stability should come crashing down, "we will not fear." Why not? Because whatever the uproar around us, the unshakable God promises to be our refuge. When friends run away, God promises to be an ever-present help. When we feel weak, God promises to be our strength. Times of upheaval are exactly the times to "'Be still, and know that I am God' . . . the LORD of hosts is with us; the God of Jacob is our refuge" (Psalm 46:10–11 NKJV). That's a fortress that can never collapse.

Psalm 46 was written for those whose foundations have cracked. It was written for people who feel overwhelmed by a troubled sea of circumstances over which they have no control. Can you relate? If so, you're not alone.

It wasn't very long ago that Americans felt invulnerable—so invulnerable that we gave very little thought to terrorism and war. Now we are constantly aware of threats to our security. Now we understand how easily the symbols of our strength and stability can collapse, falling victim to religious or political radicals. Should we quake in fear? Should we hide our heads? Certainly not! In times such as

go to

unshakable stability
Psalms 18:15; 30:7

troubled sea
Zechariah 10:11

turbulent
disruptive: characterized by unrest or disorder

something to ponder

just
guided by truth, reason, justice, and fairness

these we should hold on to the promise "God is our refuge and strength." He is our "very present help in trouble."

what others say

Alexander Solzhenitsyn

Instead of the ill-advised hopes of the last two centuries, which have reduced us to insignificance and brought us to the brink of nuclear and non-nuclear death, we can only reach with determination for the warm hand of God, which we have so rashly and self-confidently pushed away.[9]

Some "Fear Nots" in the Bible

Who Spoke	Scripture
God to Hagar	Genesis 21:17
God to Abraham	Genesis 15:1; 26:24
Joshua to the Israelites	Numbers 14:9
God to Joshua	Joshua 1:9
Hezekiah to his subjects	2 Chronicles 32:7
God to His people	Isaiah 41:10
The angel to Zacharias	Luke 1:13
The angels to the shepherds	Luke 2:10
Jesus to the synagogue official	Luke 9:50

Father Knows Best

HEBREWS 12:11 ***Now no chastening seems to be joyful for the present, but painful; nevertheless, afterward it yields the peaceable fruit of righteousness to those who have been trained by it. (NKJV)***

The real danger of suffering isn't so much what it might do to your body, but what it might do to your mind and spirit. Suffering is hard to understand. Those who suffer don't usually feel that they deserve what they're getting. If you're not careful, then, the next step can be the belief that God is not **just**, or that God isn't able to prevent suffering, or that God isn't there at all. Those aren't biblical views of suffering. The biblical view is this: when God allows suffering in the lives of those He loves, it is for the sake of some greater good. Suffering isn't random or meaningless, but productive.

God cares about our hearts. And pain is one of the ways God gets our hearts' attention. Sometimes we turn to Him only when we feel we have nowhere else to turn. C.S. Lewis remarked that pain was God's way of shouting at us, getting our attention when we're not otherwise inclined to listen. Discipline is never fun when you're in the middle of it. But the results are worth it. God promises the "peaceable fruit of righteousness" as the result of His discipline.

fruit
Galatians 5:22-23

Hebrews 12, God's "discipline chapter," is immediately preceded by Hebrews 11, "God's Hall of Faith." There, the writer enumerates believer after believer who suffered greatly for his or her faith, such as those who "had trial of mockings and scourgings, yes, and of chains and imprisonment. They were stoned, they were sawn in two, were tempted, were slain with the sword. They wandered about in sheepskins and goatskins, being destitute, afflicted, tormented" (Hebrews 11:36–37 NKJV). The Jewish Christians to which the book of Hebrews was addressed experienced plenty of suffering of their own. They desperately needed to be encouraged. The writer did just that. He promised them that their suffering would be productive. in the end "the peaceable fruit of righteousness to those who have been trained by it" (12:11 NKJV). Indeed—no pain, no gain!

You may not have "had trial of mockings and scourgings" for your faith. But life can still be hard. Your body may not have been beaten, but perhaps your heart has been broken. Whatever your grief, the promised blessing will follow, for God chastens us "for our profit" (Hebrews 12:10 NKJV). We can therefore "be in subjection to the Father of spirits and live" (Hebrews 12:9 NKJV).

what others say

Billy Graham

I think everything that comes to our lives, if we are true believers, God has a purpose and a plan. And many of these things are things that cause suffering or inconvenience or whatever. But it helps to mature me because God is molding and making me in the image of His Son, Jesus Christ.[10]

Some Members of the Hebrews 11 "Hall of Fame"

Name	Reason for Inclusion
Abel	Offered a more excellent sacrifice than Cain
Enoch	Taken away without experiencing death
Noah	Built an ark by faith, not by sight
Abraham	Followed God without knowing where he was going
Sarah	Bore a child as an old woman, because she believed God

nihilism
rejection of all distinctions in moral or religious ; a belief that nothing really matters because everything is random

persevere
to persist in anything undertaken; maintain a purpose in spite of difficulty, obstacles, or discouragement

Some Members of the Hebrews 11 "Hall of Fame" (cont'd)

Name	Reason for Inclusion
Moses	Refused to be called the son of Pharaoh's daughter, choosing instead to suffer with God's people
Rahab	Received the Israelite spies by faith

Blessings in Disguise

JAMES 1:12 *Blessed is the man who endures temptation; for when he has been approved, he will receive the crown of life which the Lord has promised to those who love Him.* (NKJV)

Try to name a man or woman in the Bible whom God used greatly, but who didn't suffer greatly. It's not easy. The Bible is full of suffering. The oldest book of the Bible—Job—is a story about suffering. Genesis carries on the tradition as it catalogs the sufferings of the likes of Noah (surviving a flood), Abraham (leaving everything behind and starting from scratch, with the death of his father thrown in for good measure), Isaac (offered up as a sacrifice by his own father), Jacob (marrying the wrong woman), Joseph (rejected by his brothers and sold as a slave), Hagar (thrown out on her own with a newborn son), and Tamar (abused by her father-in-law).

Genesis is not the only book in which the suffering of God's people is recorded. The Bible continues with others. Moses, Joshua, and Caleb suffered through forty long, seemingly endless years of wilderness wandering. Every one of the judges—Deborah, Barak, Samson, and company—suffered. The kings all suffered, including and especially the illustrious David. The prophets suffered (Jeremiah—beaten; Daniel—exiled; Hosea—dumped by his wife; just to name a few). The apostles suffered, with Paul spending more time in prison, it seemed, than in his own bed.

Suffering is as natural to life as breathing. As Moses confessed, "The days of our lives are seventy years . . . yet their boast is only labor and sorrow" (Psalm 90:10 NKJV). That's not to say, however, that we are doomed to misery and unhappiness, or doomed to a life devoid of joy. God offers us promises that render our sufferings meaningful, not meaningless. Those promises, as a matter of fact, are the difference between a godly view of hardship and mere **nihilism**.

For those who are in Christ, it's a win-win situation. God gives us the strength to **persevere** today, and rewards us with the "crown of life" tomorrow. Persevering under trial is just like taking a "test"—a test we are guaranteed to pass if we love Jesus. You've heard the cliché, "Whatever doesn't kill me will make me stronger." It has stayed around long enough to become a cliché because it's true. The promise of God isn't exemption from suffering, but the strength to grow from it.

Jesus Himself is the epitome of suffering—"a Man of sorrows and acquainted with grief" (Isaiah 53:3 NKJV). Why, then should any of us who are called by His name be exempt from suffering?

Chapter Wrap-Up

- Suffering need not be a sign of God's disfavor. God disciplines the people He delights in.
- God promises that His love outlasts and overcomes His anger.
- The Roman Empire—along with the other persecutors of the early church—lies in ruins, but the body of Christ continues its vibrant life 2000 years later.
- Joy is a choice.

Study Questions

1. Why does God allow suffering in our lives?
2. What does it mean to say that our present sufferings are "momentary, light afflictions"?
3. Why did Peter speak to the persecuted Christians about the refiner's fire?
4. What does it mean to "count it all joy"?
5. Paul's death at the hands of his Roman persecutors didn't indicate God's failure to deliver him. Why not?

Chapter 14: Promises Concerning Our Dependence

Chapter Highlights:
- Answers to prayer
- Promise to hold us
- Promise of provision
- Promise to be found by those who seek him
- Promise of a good life

A Confident Approach

Ephesians 3:11–12 ***Christ Jesus our Lord, in whom we have boldness and access with confidence through faith in Him. (NKJV)***

Ephesians
residents of Ephesus, a major city in Asia Minor, present-day Turkey

When he wrote his letter to the **Ephesians**, Paul was imprisoned in a Roman jail, an enemy of the state. Being an enemy of the state is never good—especially a state like Rome. The Romans, remember, used crucifixion as a routine punishment. They raised torture to new levels. They killed Christ, and had no sympathy for His followers.

Yet in Paul's letter to the Ephesian believers, he never complained about his own plight; he prayed only for them (Ephesians 3:14–21 NKJV). The Ephesians were free; he was imprisoned. Nevertheless, he did not ask what they could do for *him*; he was too busy asking God to do for *them*.

What gave Paul the courage to turn a blind eye to his own desperate needs and focus on the needs of others? Perhaps it was his faith and courage to approach God with absolute freedom. Imprisonment in a Roman jail is nothing compared to that kind of freedom—bold confidence. Paul had every reason to be tentative and fearful at that time in his life. Talk about uncertainty! But he was as sure of his place before God as he could possibly be.

Paul's unshakeable confidence in God's promise is shown in the next few verses of Ephesians 3:

- The confidence that God tenderly loved him as a perfect father perfectly loves his son (v. 14);
- The confidence that he was a part of a special family that stretched from heaven to earth (v. 15);
- The confidence that God would strengthen him with a dynamic power (v. 16);
- The confidence that this power dwelt right inside of him in the person of the Holy Spirit (v. 16);

go to

boldness
Hebrews 4:16

fervent
having or showing great warmth or intensity of spirit, feeling, enthusiasm

- The confidence that Christ was his constant companion (v. 17);
- The confidence that he was loved in ways he couldn't even begin to comprehend (v. 19);
- The confidence that God could do "exceedingly abundantly above all" Paul could ask or even imagine (vv. 20–21).

This same confidence can be yours. You may feel as though you are a prisoner of your circumstances, locked up behind bars of adversity, illness, ill-treatment, rejection, betrayal, disappointment, discouragement, depression, shattered dreams, or broken promises. But whatever your difficulties, you have this promise: you can approach God with "<u>boldness</u>" and "confidence"—the confidence that God will do for us all that he did for Paul, and "exceedingly abundantly above all" that we could ever ask or even dream.

what others say

R. A. Torrey

But when we really come into God's presence, really meet Him face to face in the place of prayer, really seek the things we desire *from Him*, then there is power.[1]

Prayer Power

James 5:16 ***The effective, fervent prayer of a righteous man avails much. (NKJV)***

When James wrote that "the effective, **fervent** prayer of a righteous man avails much," he offered up Elijah as an example. "[Elijah] prayed earnestly that it would not rain; and it did not rain on the land for three years and six months. And he prayed again, and the heaven gave rain, and the earth produced its fruit" (James 5:17–18 NKJV). It seems almost unfair that James, in urging his readers to pray, should bring up a spiritual giant like Elijah. Just because Elijah got big prayers answered, it doesn't necessarily follow that the rest of us would. It's as if he's saying, "Get out there and dunk a basketball; Michael Jordan used to do it all the time!"

But James is careful not to leave us that excuse. He says, "Elijah was a man with a nature like ours" (James 5:17 NKJV). If you remember the story of Elijah, you will remember that he was much as we are. Sure, he single-handedly took on the 450 false prophets of the god Baal and brought them to their knees. Indeed, at the very mention of Elijah's name, wicked King Ahab quaked in his sandals. But the next thing we hear about Elijah is that he fell into deep fear and depression when Queen Jezebel threatened his life. In fact, Elijah prayed that he might die: "It is enough! Now, LORD, take my life" (19:4 NKJV). Elijah looked invincible on the outside. But on the inside, he was as fragile as the rest of us.

Elijah's reputation as a great prophet grew from the fact that when he prayed, God answered. He prayed for drought to get his countrymen's attention, and God sent a drought. He prayed for relief from the drought three and a half years later, and God sent rain. Elijah was in touch with God's will; when he prayed God's will back to Him, he got results. But notice what happened when he prayed for God to take his life. God ignored that prayer. He lost touch, lost sight of God's plan. That prayer, "Take my life," arose out of Elijah's overwrought emotions.

Elijah was indeed "a man with a nature like ours." His emotions failed him from time to time, but his God did not. His God keeps his promises to answer the prayers of the righteous. Like Elijah, you can expect to see your prayers accomplish incredible, world-changing things when you stay in touch with God—when you want what God wants.

key point

what others say

Beverly LaHaye

> Remember James 5:16: "The effective, fervent prayer of a *righteous* man avails much" (emphasis added). A righteous person is one who has a right relationship with God that comes from submission and obedience. . . . Only if one knows God personally can he have a right to expect God to hear and answer his prayers.[2]

A Few of Elijah's Dramatic Deeds

Miracles Performed With God's Help	Scripture
Creating the drought	1 Kings 17:1
Multiplying the widow's oil and meal	1 Kings 17:10–17
Raising the widow's son from the dead	1 Kings 17:17–24
The showdown with the prophets of Baal	1 Kings 18:20–36
Ending the drought	1 Kings 18:37–45
Elijah parts the Jordan River	2 Kings 2:8

Things You Didn't Know

JEREMIAH 33:3 ***Call to Me, and I will answer you, and show you great and mighty things, which you do not know.*** *(NKJV)*

go to

call of God
Jeremiah 4:19; 20:9

captivity
Jeremiah 25:8–11

Nebuchadnezzar
Babylonian king during the Jews' Babylonian captivity

Things were not looking good for the weeping prophet. Jeremiah had hit rock bottom in his personal and spiritual life. For years, he had been dutifully proclaiming God's coming judgment on His unrepentant people, not a pleasant task by anyone's imagination. The people remained unmoved by his impassioned pleas. For his efforts, Jeremiah was beaten, imprisoned, and abused—physically, mentally, and emotionally. "Cursed be the day in which I was born," Jeremiah groaned . . . "Why did I come forth from the womb to see labor and sorrow, that my days should be consumed with shame?" (Jeremiah 20:14, 18 NKJV).

Jeremiah was ready to give up and go home. But he couldn't. The call of God in his life was just too strong (20:9). He felt trapped, compelled from within to do something that only brought him unending misery. Jeremiah *couldn't* change his mission, and yet the people *wouldn't* change direction. Now they all faced the bleak prospect of seventy years of captivity at the hands of the vile and wicked **Nebuchadnezzar**. As he delivered this bad news, Jeremiah must have wondered if God had at last abandoned them for good.

God made a promise to Jeremiah: "Call to Me, and I will answer you, and show you great and mighty things, which you do not know" (Jeremiah 33:3 NKJV). God would restore His people to their land. A new generation would arise that would faithfully follow God's Law. The future for Israel burned brightly. Though His people had abandoned Him, God would never abandon them.

something to ponder

Does your future seem bleak and hopeless? Do you ever get the feeling that God has abandoned you? God knows things that you don't know. From here, we can see only a few little tiles in the mosaic, and they look rough around the edges. But God sees the big picture. He sees how your life fits into something beautiful. Call to God in your confusion and sorrow. Spend time in His Word. Wait for God to tell you "great and mighty things, which you do not know." That's not to say He'll tell you everything you wish to know; His ways aren't our ways, and His thoughts aren't our thoughts.

Sometimes, if you're listening very carefully, God tells you things you didn't know before, things you would have had no way of knowing. He gives you a new way of seeing things, something closer to the way He sees things, and it makes a world of difference. Call to him. He has promised to answer.

go to

Beatitudes
Matthew 5:3–10

> **what others say**
>
> **George Mueller**
>
> Under every trial and difficulty, we find prayer and faith to be our universal remedy; and, after having experienced for half a century their efficacy, we purpose, by God's help, to *continue* waiting upon Him, in order to show to an ungodly world, and to a doubting church, that the Living God is still able and willing to answer prayer.[3]

His Hand Is Open

PSALM 145:14
The LORD upholds all who fall,
And raises up all who are bowed down. *(NKJV)*

"The LORD upholds all who fall." What an incredible promise. We live in a success-oriented culture. We have somehow gotten the idea that success is an indicator of how much we're pleasing God. After all, why would God allow you to fail if He really loves you? When things aren't going well, we have a tendency to ask, "What have I done wrong?" or "What have I done to deserve this?"

But the Bible is quite clear: God has a special place in His heart for those who fail. We human beings admire success, self-confidence, rugged individualism. But look at the Beatitudes in Jesus' Sermon on the Mount. Jesus said "Blessed are the poor in spirit . . . blessed are those who mourn . . . blessed are the meek." And blessed are those who fall down; God is there to pick them up. There are many, many ways to fall. Your finances could take a dive. Your family situation could deteriorate. You could be stuck at the bottom of the corporate ladder. You could fall into serious sin. Even so, God promises to uphold you. He "raises up all who are bowed down."

key point

Why does God allow His people to suffer? God doesn't promise that we'll understand that. Sometimes you can look back on a time you've fallen and see how you were strengthened and made more into the person God wanted you to be. Perhaps you can look back and see how you learned to trust in God rather than your own righteousness or your own success. Perhaps you can look back and see

go to

fall down
Proverbs 24:16

apply it

that relationships were strengthened. Sometimes, however, you simply can't make any sense of your hardships—especially when you're in the middle of them. In that case, you have to fall back on the promise of God: "The LORD upholds all who fall, and raises up all who are bowed down."

When you fall down—especially when there are people around to see you fall—you feel like a loser. It can be heart-breaking to realize your own weakness. Thankfully, "The LORD is near to those who have a broken heart" (Psalm 34:18 NKJV). Jesus didn't come to recruit a team of all-stars and first-round draft picks to His side. No, as Jesus said, "[God] has sent Me to heal the brokenhearted" (Luke 4:18 NKJV). Do you feel you stumble and fall more often than you succeed? You're just the sort of person God is looking for—and the sort He has promised to help.

what others say

Herbert Lockyer

God never withholds any good thing from those who seek Him aright. There are times, however, when granted answers appear to be most unfavorable to our finite understanding....Has God forgotten to be gracious? Of course not! Because of His infinite wisdom He knows what is best for his own.[4]

The Beatitudes (Matthew 5:3–12 NKJV)

The Blessed	The Blessing
The poor in spirit.	Theirs is the kingdom of heaven.
Those who mourn.	They shall be comforted.
The meek.	They shall inherit the earth.
Those who hunger and thirst for righteousness.	They shall be filled.
The merciful.	They shall receive mercy.
The pure in heart.	They shall see God.
The peacemakers.	They shall be called sons of God.
The persecuted.	Theirs is the kingdom of heaven.
You, if you are reviled for Christ's sake.	Your reward in heaven is great.

Ask and It Will Be Given

MATTHEW 7:7 ***Ask, and it will be given to you; seek, and you will find; knock, and it will be opened to you.*** (NKJV)

The "multitudes" followed Jesus. The word "multitudes" signifies, of course, a huge number of people. But it also distinguishes those people from the elite. Sometimes that word "multitude" is translated "common people." Regular Joes, working people—they were the ones who responded most eagerly to the teachings of Jesus. The political and religious leaders of the time weren't so sure about this Jesus. But the common people were fascinated with Him. They had grown accustomed to an **authoritarian** religious system, in which their only access to God was through priests and rules and sacrifices. They had very little say in the matter. But here was this Man who said that God welcomed people like them—that God wasn't impressed with the pomp and ceremony of the religious professionals but instead dwelt with the lowly and humble. He said that they could bring their requests directly to God.

"Ask, and it will be given to you," Jesus said. The people must have been stunned at such a promise. They weren't used to people in power giving them anything. The Romans simply milked them for tax money and cheap labor. Very few of the Jews were even Roman citizens. They couldn't really ask the priests and Pharisees for anything. About all the common people could expect to get from the priests were more burdensome rules and regulations.

Perhaps, however, the people could relate to the idea of a father providing for his children. That's how Jesus made His hearers understand their relationship to the God who was the Giver of good gifts. The idea of asking good gifts from a judge or a king may not have made a lot of sense to these people, who were so remote from the power structure of their day. Even the idea of asking a favor of a priest may have seemed foreign to them. But the idea of a child asking a father—there was something they could relate to.

Jesus was talking about a completely new kind of kingdom, where the King was truly a Father to His people, where the people could feel free to ask for what they needed from Him. In this kingdom, the people served the King because they loved Him, not because they feared punishment. In this kingdom, love flows freely from the King to His subjects and back again, and the subjects are promised they will get what they need.

go to

Giver of good gifts
James 1:17

authoritarian
favoring complete obedience or subjection to authority as opposed to individual freedom

go to

never in a hurry
2 Peter 3:8

conditional
absolute; made or allowed on certain terms

Eagles Fly Alone

ISAIAH 40:31
But those who wait on the LORD
Shall renew their strength;
They shall mount up with wings like eagles,
They shall run and not be weary,
They shall walk and not faint. (NKJV)

To be in a waiting posture doesn't always feel like strength. It sometimes feels more like passivity, even weakness when you're forced to wait for God to make the next move. You want to do something—anything—just to feel that you're moving forward. It's hard to wait. But God assures us that having the strength to wait on Him is the first step toward having eagle-like strength to ride high above the concerns of earth.

Have you ever watched an eagle? They don't just fly; they soar. Eagles are to the sky what lions are to the jungle. They rule the heavens with regal authority. They don't fly in flocks. They don't need to. They soar and swoop with calm assurance. Never flustered, they use the turbulence of unsettled air to their advantage, riding the up and downdrafts with equal ease. Oh to be an eagle!

You can be, figuratively speaking. Life is filled with unpredictable updrafts and downdrafts. Left to face life's challenges alone, you might be spun out of control and slammed to the ground. But you have God's promise: when you place your hope in Him, He will renew your strength. He will not let you fall! The winds of adversity may knock you about, but they'll never knock you out.

something to ponder

The promise of Isaiah 40:31 is a **conditional** promise. It applies to those who "wait on the LORD." Some translations read "*hope* in the LORD." Hoping and waiting are really two sides of the same coin. Our hope is the confidence that God is big enough to handle our problems, and will use them for our good (Romans 8:28). When you have that hope, you can wait; you can live in the tension between the way things are right now and the way you know they're going to be someday.

key point

But it takes time. God is never in a hurry. It's hard to get comfortable with that fact. We are creatures who live in time; we don't share God's eternal perspective. In a way, when you learn to wait on God, you have already begun soaring above the earth. You have already been freed of the limited, time-bound perspective that makes life on earth so hard. Anxiety and uncertainty give way to eager expectation to see how God will act, in His way, in His time. So wait while hoping, and hope while waiting. God will give you the soaring strength of an eagle.

go to

leader of some note
Acts 15:13

what others say

Jerry Bridges

The cure for impatience with the fulfillment of God's timetable is to believe his promises, obey his will, and leave the results up to him. . . . I need to take to heart this admonition of the writer of Hebrews: "We do not want you to become lazy, but to imitate those who through faith and patience inherit what has been promised" (Hebrews 6:12 NKJV).[5]

Draw Me Nearer

JAMES 4:8a ***Draw near to God and He will draw near to you. (NKJV)***

The author of the Book of James, according to church tradition, was Jesus' half-brother James, the younger son of Mary and Joseph. He wasn't always on board with Jesus' program, however. Along with his other siblings, James refused to follow Jesus during His ministry on earth. As the apostle John reported, "even His brothers did not believe in Him" (John 7:5 NKJV). It's a dangerous sibling rivalry that would keep brothers from receiving the truth that was right there in their midst.

Apparently James's rejection of Jesus lasted to the end of Jesus' earthly life. When Jesus hung dying on the cross, His mother, Mary, was there, *alone*, with no family members. Her husband, Joseph, had most likely died. So just before He breathed His last, Jesus consigned the care of His grieving mother to the disciple John. By rights, in Jesus' absence, His younger brothers should have stepped up to the plate and offered to care for their mother. But James and company were nowhere to be found.

Eventually James did see the light, as evidenced by the fact that he became a leader of some note in the Jerusalem church. James had a unique opportunity to draw near to Jesus during Jesus' time on earth, but he wasted it. In the end, however he did choose to draw near, and he found that his older brother was faithful. Jesus drew near to James when James finally reached out to Him.

When James invited his readers to "draw near to God," he punctuated his point with the promise, "and He will draw near to you." James knew what he was talking about.

Perhaps James had noticed that, while He was on earth, Jesus never, *never* turned anyone away. Read through the Gospels and you will see that throughout His ministry Jesus always maintained an open-door policy. No one was more approachable. Lepers approached Him and weren't turned away. Prostitutes and tax collectors spent time with Him. Other people often urged Jesus to turn people away—sinners, children, and the infirm—but Jesus continued to welcome all who came to Him with open arms.

Those who seek God always find Him. You may choose, like James in his younger days, to keep your distance from God. But if you get serious about drawing near to God, you can be sure He will draw near to you. That's not to say that you get God on your own terms. If you truly desire **fellowship** with Him, you won't be disappointed.

go to

sinners
Mark 2:16–17

children
Matthew 19:13–14

infirm
Luke 18:39–40

scattered
1 Peter 1:1

pilgrims
1 Peter 2:11

fellowship
friendly relationship; companionship

something to ponder

what others say

Charles Haddon Spurgeon

If my Lord does cast out one poor soul that comes to him, let me know it, and I will give up preaching.[6]

Key to Contentment

HEBREWS 13:5 *I will never leave you nor forsake you.* (NKJV)

Jewish believers suffered greatly. Because of unrelenting persecution, many were forced to flee their homes and leave behind the lives they had known. Peter aptly referred to them as "scattered" and "pilgrims." With no jobs and little support, many of these believers began to doubt their faith and wondered if they'd made the right choice when they accepted Jesus as their Messiah. In the midst of such difficulty, you can understand their doubts. The Book of Hebrews attempts to answer the Jewish Christians' questions about Jesus by assuring them that they had indeed chosen well: Jesus was the Messiah for whom the Jews had been longing for centuries.

The writer of Hebrews reminded the Jewish readers of a promise they had known since they were babies: "I will never leave you or forsake you" (Hebrews 13:5 NKJV). He was quoting Deuteronomy 31:6. The Jewish Christians, perhaps, had begun to feel completely cut off from their past—not just their personal past, but their historical past. The writer of Hebrews offered a gentle reminder: the God of Abraham, Isaac, and Jacob was still their God. And He always kept His promises.

The context of this promise in Hebrews is interesting. "Let your conduct be without covetousness," the writer said. "Be content with such things as you have" (Hebrews 13:5 NKJV). That's in the same verse with the promise that God would never leave nor forsake. The two ideas don't seem an obvious fit at first. But God's presence truly is the answer to covetousness. God's presence is the source of true contentment. The Jewish Christians had so very little when it came to material things. No matter how strong your faith, living in poverty is difficult. But by reminding his readers of the presence of God, the writer of Hebrews is saying, in effect, "Don't you realize how rich you are? God is among you! You have the wealth of this long history with a God who made tremendous promises to your ancestors and kept them!"

When you look around and see people with more stuff than you, people who seem to have it easier than you, it's human nature to feel discontented and covetous. But consider your riches! God promised His perpetual presence—the same God who clothes the lilies of the fields and feeds the sparrows, also promises to clothe and feed us (Matthew 6:25–33). You have a God who will never leave you nor forsake you, no matter how dire your circumstances. You will never be left to suffer alone. God will be your constant companion—a haven of rest in times of trouble. That's worth so much more than worldly wealth.

Our Gift-Giving God

MATTHEW 7:11 ***If you then, being evil, know how to give good gifts to your children, how much more will your Father who is in heaven give good things to those who ask Him!*** *(NKJV)*

The people to whom Jesus preached the Sermon on the Mount were simple, earthy folk who worked the soil or fished the sea. Some were artisans who hewed stones or carved wood. But all of them were consumed with one all-encompassing desire: survival. They

carte blanche
a blank check; unrestricted power to act at one's own discretion

were subject to storms, drought, insect infestations, and various other calamities that could wipe them out overnight.

Then there was the ever-present military occupation by the ruthless Romans who made their lives miserable through unreasonable laws, outrageous taxes, and barbaric human-rights violations. For these dear people, just making it through the day with their families intact was a "good gift." Food on the table and clothes on the back were "good gifts." A warm fire in winter, a cool breeze in summer, the wonder of a rainbow, the singing of a bird, the hug of a friend, the laughter of one's children—these were all "good gifts." And they all came from God above.

Jesus put the promise of "good gifts" into perspective by comparing the heavenly Father's provision to the provision of an earthly father. "What man is there among you who, if his son asks him for bread, will give him a stone? Or if he asks for a fish, will he give him a serpent?" (Matthew 7:9–10 NKJV) Earthly fathers aren't perfect, but they do care enough about their children to try to give them what they need when they ask. How much more will God do so?

"Ask and it will be given to you" sounds a lot like a ***carte blanche***. You can see members in the crowd saying, *You mean I can get whatever I want? I want a nice farm out in the country* . . . But the Father analogy is helpful here. No father would give his son a poisonous snake if he asked for a fish. But if the son were to ask for a poisonous snake, the father wouldn't give it to him, no matter how badly the boy wanted it. As a matter of fact, he might give the boy the fish he should have asked for in the first place.

what others say

William Holmes McGuffey

You ask your friends for food, and drink, and books, and clothes; and when they give you these things, you thank them, and love them for the good they do you. So you should ask your God for those things which he can give you, and which no one else can give you. . . . You should thank him for all his good gifts.[7]

In our materialistic mind-set, where "good gifts" often mean the accumulation of "stuff," we can easily corrupt this promise to mean that God wants to load our lives with toys and trinkets. Not so! If you are sitting around, waiting for God to bestow His "good gifts" upon you, wait no longer. Look around—He already has!

A Woven Tapestry

ROMANS 8:28 ***And we know that all things work together for good to those who love God.*** (NKJV)

Romans 8:28 is one of those verses that is so used and overused that sometimes we forget its incredible power to give hope and encouragement. True, sometimes people rattle it off, cliché style, at the first sign of trouble, as if it is were an **incantation** to make people magically cheer up and smile. Familiarity can breed contempt, but this amazing promise is worth a fresh look.

Romans 8:28 is sometimes used as a shield from pain, but there are times in our lives when we need to hurt and really feel it! The biblical writers understood that we should not *avoid* pain, like some intruder, but rather *embrace* it as an honored guest. They understood that many of life's lessons we learn best through suffering. So how do you embrace pain as a positive thing rather than desperately trying to avoid or neutralize it as a negative thing? You embrace pain by embracing the promise of Romans 8:28: God will use all things in our lives for our good.

Life is like a woven **tapestry**. Look at one from behind and all you see are threads that have been pulled, stretched, cut, and woven together. Examine any one strand and it has no obvious purpose. But turn the tapestry over and you will see a beautiful picture to be admired by many.

In the tapestry of our lives, many things happen that seem to make no sense. That is because we are viewing the back side where we are pulled, stretched, cut, and pieced together. However, if you could look at the other side as God does, you would see the reason for our duress and discomfort and know that God is crafting a wonderful masterpiece. One of these days you'll see the masterpiece too. In the meantime, however, you just have to take God at His Word: He is working everything to your good and His glory.

What does that image on the "good" side of the tapestry look like? According to the very next verse (Romans 8:29), the image that God is creating is none other than the likeness of His Son, Jesus Christ. Jesus suffered too, and much more than any of us ever will. It's no easy thing to welcome pain as a friend. But it's one of the ways that God makes you into the person you born to be.

go to

suffering
James 1:12; Romans 5:3

incantation
words chanted to create a magical spell

tapestry
a heavy cloth woven with rich, often varicolored designs or scenes, usually hung on walls for decoration and sometimes used to cover furniture

what others say

Corrie ten Boom

My life is but a weaving, between my God and me. I do not choose the colors, He worketh steadily. Ofttimes He weaveth sorrow, and I in foolish pride, Forget He sees the upper, and I the underside.[8]

Chapter Wrap-Up

- Seeing God answer our prayers depends on our aligning our will with His.
- God isn't picking an all-star team; He has a special place in His heart for "losers."
- When it comes to God's work in our lives, waiting and hope are two sides of the same coin.
- Everyone who earnestly seeks God is going to find Him.

Study Questions

1. How do we know Elijah was "a man with a nature like ours?"
2. What is the true value of being shown "great and mighty things, which you do not know?"
3. How is waiting on God a kind of strength?
4. How does the promise of God's presence relate to covetousness and contentment?
5. How is life like a tapestry?

Chapter 15: Promises Concerning Ourselves

Chapter Highlights:
- Promise of new life
- Promise of abundance
- Promise to set us apart
- Promises to the powerless

Nobody's Fool

> 1 CORINTHIANS 1:27 *But God has chosen the foolish things of the world to put to shame the wise, and God has chosen the weak things of the world to put to shame the things which are mighty. (NKJV)*

Jesus reveled in **paradox**. The last shall be first. Blessed are the poor. If you want to find your life, you have to lose it. Jesus, you might say, *was* a paradox. He was 100 percent man and 100 percent God. He was the Immortal who died. He was rich beyond counting, but He became poor for our sake. He was the sinless One who took on our sin.

go to

hypocrites
Matthew 23

paradox
a statement or proposition that seems self-contradictory or absurd but in reality expresses a truth

If the Gospels were a drama being acted out on a stage, the Pharisees would be the villains in the story. No matter how hard a person tried, he or she could never live up to the outrageous standards of these self-righteous religious leaders. Neither could Jesus; the Pharisees were always finding fault with everything He did. But if Jesus couldn't live up to their laws, neither could they—something that did not escape Jesus' notice. He condemned them repeatedly and called them hypocrites.

When Paul proclaimed to the Corinthians the promise about God choosing the foolish and the weak, he understood it as few men ever would. You see, Paul had been a proud Pharisee until he met Jesus. After meeting Jesus, being a Pharisee meant nothing (Philippians 3:5–8 NKJV).

So perhaps we shouldn't be too surprised to hear Paul tell his friends in Corinth, "God has chosen the foolish things of the world to put to shame the wise, and God has chosen the weak things of the world to put to shame the things which are mighty" (1 Corinthians 1:27 NKJV). The Corinthian Christians seemed to be sort of a ragtag bunch. There were "not many wise" among them, according to Paul, "not many mighty, not many noble" (1 Corinthians 1:26 NKJV). *Thanks a lot*, the Corinthians must have thought when they got Paul's letter. But Paul's point was that God works through peo-

go to

splitting into sects
1 Corinthians 3:1–4

sexual immorality
1 Corinthians 5:1

ple who realize that their ability to be used by God has nothing to do with their worldly wisdom or worldly status. The Corinthian Christians weren't the pillars of the community in Corinth. They weren't running the city council or hosting debutante balls. No, they were just regular folks. Just the sort of people God uses.

By the way, there was more to the Corinthians' troubles than a lack of social standing. They had some pretty serious internal problems. They had a habit of splitting into sects and factions rather than displaying Christian unity. They had some issues with sexual immorality that would have been scandalous in even the most secular environments. But Paul didn't give up on them because God didn't give up on them. The Corinthians behaved themselves like fools. But God uses fools to shame the wise. He uses the weak to shame the strong.

In America we have grown accustomed to the idea of success-oriented Christianity. *If God wants to use me*, we think, *He can equip me with influence or wealth or wisdom.* Sometimes that's exactly how God works. You know of people who use their worldly success to further the kingdom of God. But that's not necessarily how it works. If you think that you aren't good enough, wise enough, or strong enough for God to use you, guess again. God delights in surprising us. When He works through the foolish and the weak, He leaves no doubt as to who is at work. God's fool is nobody's fool.

what others say

Dr. James Dobson

Let me stress again that the attributes which our society values most highly—beauty, intelligence, and money—must be seen from the Christian point of view. These are *man's* values, but not *God's* values. The Lord doesn't measure your worth the way people do.[1]

God's Lovable Losers

Nobody's Fools	Scripture
Gideon—the least member of the least family of the tribe of Manasseh	Judges 6:15
Saul—a member of the least family of Benjamin, one of the least tribes of Israel	1 Samuel 9:21
David—the forgotten youngest son of Jesse	1 Samuel 16:11
Matthew—a tax collector	Matthew 9:9
Zaccheus—another tax collector	Luke 19:1–10
The Adulterous Woman—A person of questionable morals	John 8:3-11

Tender Mercies

EZEKIEL 34:16 ***"I will seek what was lost and bring back what was driven away, bind up the broken and strengthen what was sick." (NKJV)***

lay in bed
Ezekiel 4:4-6

packed bags
Ezekiel 12:3-7

Old Testament prophets have gotten a bad rap. People think of them as fire-breathing and wild-eyed, shouting about God's judgment and coming doom. And there is certainly plenty of doom and judgment to be found in the Old Testament prophets. After all, the prophets were preaching to a nation that had forsaken God, a nation that had earned judgments far worse even than the ones the prophets warned them of. But for all the shouting and all the arm-waving, each of the prophets had a quieter side, even a tender side.

Ezekiel could be as fiery as anybody. He preached to a nation that was just about to be carried off into exile as punishment for their sins, and he did whatever he had to do to get their attention. Sometimes he came across as a little crazy. At God's command, he lay in bed on his right side for 390 days, then on his left side for forty days as a sign of the coming punishment. He walked around Jerusalem with packed bags to symbolize the people's upcoming departure from the land. Ezekiel was definitely a character.

But like the other prophets, Ezekiel wasn't gleeful in his pronouncements of judgment. The whole point was to call the people to repent and return to the God who wanted to have a relationship with them. So the heart of Ezekiel's message was one of love and tenderness, not punishment. Through Ezekiel, God promised His people, "I will seek what was lost and bring back what was driven away, bind up the broken and strengthen what was sick" (Ezekiel 34:16 NKJV). What a beautiful message. What a beautiful promise.

When you've messed up, when you feel like a loser, you half expect God to squash you like a bug. You're well aware of your failures and shortcomings, and you feel like a hopeless case. God specializes in hopeless cases. He binds up the broken. He gathers up the lost and the scattered. He gives strength and healing to the sick. There is hope for you. The prophet Isaiah said the same thing in a different way: "A bruised reed He will not break, and smoking flax He will not quench" (Isaiah 42:3 NKJV). The NASB reads, "a dimly burning wick He will not extinguish." That's a great image. From time to time you feel as if your flame is nearly out. But where there's the least little fire still smoking, there is hope. God won't extinguish your light, but will nurture it back into something that can again shine brightly for His glory.

what others say

LeRoy Eims

Why did Jesus choose men with very human tendencies and failings? Suppose He had chosen only those who were highly cultured, of great intellect and wealth, who never had any doubts or fears, men who never made mistakes or said things they later regretted. . . . Where would that put us?[2]

Unusual Behavior by Old Testament Prophets

Prophet	Behavior	Scripture
Isaiah	Went naked for three years to depict the coming shame of Egypt and Cush.	Isaiah 20
Jeremiah	Smashed pottery to signify the coming destruction of Jerusalem.	Jeremiah 19
Ezekiel	Ate bread cooked over cow dung to symbolize the defilement of God's people.	Ezekiel 4:9–17
Hosea	Married a prostitute to symbolize the spiritual adultery of God's people.	Hosea 1–3

Receive the Suffering Servant

> **JOHN 1:12** ***But as many as received Him, to them He gave the right to become children of God, to those who believe in His name. (NKJV)***

When Isaiah looked down the corridors of time to see the Messiah, what he saw was a suffering Servant: "He is despised and rejected by men, a Man of sorrows and acquainted with grief. And we hid, as it were, our faces from Him; He was despised, and we did not esteem Him" (Isaiah 53:3 NKJV). It's an amazing thing to think about. The people of God waited for centuries for the promised Messiah who would deliver them from oppression. They longed for this Messiah. But when He came, they rejected him. They hid their faces from Him and did not respect Him.

Indeed, one of the first things John said about Jesus, in the very first chapter of his Gospel, was that "His own did not receive Him" (John 1:11 NKJV). Rejection marked Jesus' life at every point. He got kicked out of village after village, including His home village of Nazareth. His own brothers didn't follow Him. The same mob that welcomed Him to Jerusalem as a hero with shouts of "Hosannah" turned on Him less than a week later, shouting "crucify Him." When Pilate gave them a chance to grant Jesus their annual pardon in honor of the Passover, they rejected the offer and pardoned the murderer Barabbas instead. On the cross, Jesus experienced the most painful rejection of all. His Father turned His face away from Him, and Jesus cried out, "My God, My God, why have you forsaken Me?"

go to

home village of Nazareth
Luke 4:16–30

brothers didn't follow Him
John 7:5

pardoned the murderer Barabbas instead
Matthew 27:15:1–26

For Jesus the suffering Servant, life on earth was one rejection after another. But there were (and still are) those who receive Him rather than rejecting Him. The Bible makes a special promise to them: "But as many as received Him, to them He gave the right to become children of God, to those who believe in His name" (John 1:12 NKJV). If you receive Christ—that is to say, if you believe He is who He says He is and submit to Him as the King of your life—you are one of God's children. That's your right. That's the promise that He made.

Jesus was a Man of sorrows. Those sorrows were multiplied by the constant rejections He experienced in His earthly life. But now He sits at the right hand of God, and there He welcomes you into His happy family. His sorrows are over. And His joys are multiplied by those who resist the trend of the world's rejection and receive Him as Lord and King.

what others say

Howard Hendricks

That's the wonder of the Gospel—that God, in love, broke into human history and made a way where there was no way. . . . What astounding news! Christ, the God-Man, acted to rescue a race of creatures that had turned against their Creator![3]

Some of Isaiah's Messianic Prophecies (NKJV)

Scripture	Prophecy
Isaiah 40:3	Foretold John the Baptist, "A voice crying in the wilderness"
Isaiah 53:3	The Messiah to be a "Man of sorrows, and acquainted with grief"
Isaiah 53:7	The Messiah would be "led like a lamb to the slaughter" and yet not open His mouth.
Isaiah 61:1	The Messiah would be sent "to heal the brokenhearted, to proclaim liberty to the captives, and the opening of the prison to those who are bound."

self-righteous confident of one's own righteousness or holiness as attained by one's own efforts

Born Again

2 CORINTHIANS 5:17 ***Therefore, if anyone is in Christ, he is a new creation; old things have passed away; behold, all things have become new.*** ***(NKJV)***

The idea of being "born again" is common enough in Christian circles that we don't usually think twice when we hear it. But consider how strange it must have sounded the first time Jesus said it. The first time we know of Jesus using the phrase was when a man named Nicodemus came to Him. By all outward appearances, Nicodemus had it all together. He was a prominent Jew, a Pharisee, and a member of the "the Jewish ruling council." But he knew something was lacking in his life. Nicodemus had heard Jesus preach—or, in any case, he knew something about Jesus and what He taught—so he approached Jesus in hopes of finding the missing piece. Nicodemus came by night; it wouldn't do for a Pharisee to be seen seriously investigating the teachings and the claims of this most unusual teacher.

Nicodemus got much more than he bargained for. He had devoted his whole life to obeying God. "Pharisee" wasn't an easily attained title, after all. He had always been interested in doing what was right, and he probably looked to Jesus to give him a few tips, maybe a few adjustments to make his holy life a little bit holier. He must have felt blindsided by Jesus' first remark: "Unless one is born again, he cannot see the kingdom of God" (John 3:3 NKJV). It kind of came out of nowhere. Nicodemus thought they were exchanging preliminary pleasantries, but Jesus said, in effect, "Forget about the **self-righteous** life you've been carefully constructing. You've got to start over with a completely fresh slate if you want to be a part of what God is doing."

Nicodemus was confused. "How can a man be born when he is old?" he asked. "Can he enter a second time into his mother's womb and be born?" (John 3:4 NKJV). It seems a naïve question to us. But do we really have a better grasp on the idea of being "born again" than Nicodemus did?

The Bible is the best commentary on itself. Thankfully, the Bible elsewhere clarifies exactly what it means to be born again. The very best biblical definition can be found in this promise: "If anyone is in Christ, he is a new creation; old things have passed away; behold, all things have become new" (2 Corinthians 5:17 NKJV). When someone makes the life-changing decision to follow Jesus, his or her life literally changes completely. Old sinful values, priorities, beliefs, loves, and plans change. New wholesome values, **priorities**, beliefs, loves, and plans take their place. New desires replace the old desires of the flesh, and the result is a new life, a rebirth.

go to

lusts
Romans 13:14

priorities
those things in life that enjoy the highest rank or attention

what others say

Johnny Cash

A few years ago I was hooked on drugs, I dreaded to wake up in the morning. There was no joy, peace or happiness in my life. Then one day in my helplessness I turned my life completely over to God. . . . My life has been turned around. I have been born again.[4]

A Matter of Control

ROMANS 8:9a ***But you are not in the flesh but in the Spirit, if indeed the Spirit of God dwells in you.*** *(NKJV)*

Paul took his commitment to Christ very seriously. He longed to please God in everything that he did. Obedience to the will of God was his all-consuming passion. But he had this problem: he was still a human being, with all of the frailties of humanity locked up in his body—something to which he frequently referred to as his "flesh," or the "sinful nature." That's why, at the end of Romans 7 we hear Paul wailing, "O wretched man that I am! Who will deliver me from this body of death?" (Romans 7:24 NKJV).

Paul's flesh, like our own, couldn't care less about pleasing God. Our sinful nature craves things. The flesh wants what it wants when it wants it. If we give in to our fleshly impulses, over time we can become controlled by those drives or desires—what the Bible calls "lusts." Food is a natural, normal fleshly desire. If we abandon ourselves to it, we can become gluttonous, and ruin our health in the process. Sex is a natural, normal, fleshly desire. If we abandon ourselves to it, it can lead to pornography, adultery, abuse. The desires themselves are not the problem. They are a problem when they become our masters.

This promise offered Paul the hope of victory over his flesh. He did not have to be dominated by his lusts. The Spirit of God was

surrender
to yield (something) to the possession or power of another

available to him. The same promise is ours. We can choose who will control us—our flesh or the Holy Spirit. As Christians, the choice is up to us. The desires of the flesh persist even after we have become new creatures in Christ. That's just the way God set things up. He doesn't set us free from all wrong desires the minute we receive Him. No, we still have to **surrender** to Him every day—every minute of every day—if we mean to be victorious over the flesh. Nevertheless, we can have victory over the flesh. As Paul said, you are not in the flesh but in the Spirit, if indeed the Spirit of God dwells in you" (Romans 8:9a NKJV). Sure, you're still in the flesh. But you don't have to give the flesh the final say.

apply it

If you are in Christ, the Spirit of God dwells in you. That means you don't have to be dominated by lusts. You can choose who will control you—your flesh or the Holy Spirit. If you are in Christ, the choice is yours. Day by day, moment by moment, we can say "No" to our flesh, and "Yes" to the Spirit, because "the Spirit of God dwells in [us]" (Romans 8:9b NKJV)." The way to victory is through surrender—constant surrender to the Spirit who gives you strength.

what others say

Fritz Ridenour

The Christian life is not merely a Sunday stroll with Jesus. It's a daily choice, a daily commitment to follow the Spirit, or a daily surrender to pleasing the old me, the sinful self.[5]

Made Holy!

HEBREWS 10:10 ***By that will we have been sanctified through the offering of the body of Jesus Christ once for all.*** *(NKJV)*

For the ancient Jews, "sanctification" was a defining issue. The idea behind *sanctification* is being "set apart." The Jews were "set apart" from other people-groups. They ate differently. They worshiped differently. They were forbidden from marrying people from other tribes, for that would cause them to become more like their neighbors, less "set apart."

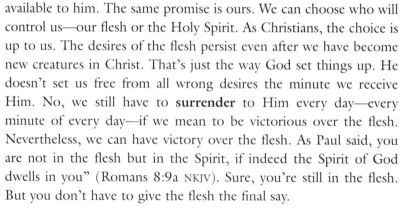

It wasn't just people who were sanctified, either. Objects could be sanctified. A pitcher, very much like other pitchers, might be sanctified or set apart for the purpose of serving in the temple. The idea is not merely being set apart, but more specifically, being set apart by a holy God as a holy object for a holy purpose.

The whole **sacrificial system** was based on this idea of sanctification. As the people of God went about their daily lives, they were soiled by accumulated sin. That is to say, they weren't as set apart from the world as they ought to have been. To offer up a sacrifice was to be cleansed of that sin, and once again to be sanctified, to have a clean slate. The problem was, the minute they left the altar, that sin started building up again; it wouldn't be long before they would have to go make another sacrifice.

The writer of the Book of Hebrews was committed to explaining the work of Jesus in terms that would make sense to Jews. It's not surprising, then, that he compares Jesus' death to the old system of sacrifice that the Jews still practiced at that time. The old means of sanctification was temporary. You could go to the altar to get sanctified, but you'd be back again. The blood of goats and bulls just didn't have what it took to effect a permanent cleansing. But the death of Jesus—that meant sanctification "once for all."

No one has ever been more sanctified, more "set apart" than Jesus. Among sinners, He was the sinless One. He made a way for us to be set apart once for all. Because the sanctified One died for us, we can be sanctified too. That's an incredible thing to think about. If you are in Christ, you are being conformed to His image. You have been set apart by a holy God as a holy object for a holy purpose. That is God's promise to you.

go to

conformed to His image
Romans 8:29

sacrificial system
the rules and regulations governing the offerings and sacrifices in the ancient Jewish tradition

what others say

Tim Hansel

We don't become holy by acquiring merit badges and Brownie points. It has nothing to do with virtue or job descriptions or morality. . . . It is a gift, sheer gift, waiting there to be recognized and received. We don't have to "be qualified" to be holy.[6]

Finders Keepers

MATTHEW **10:39** ***He who finds his life will lose it, and he who loses his life for My sake will find it.*** *(NKJV)*

dung
Philippians 3:8

orthodox
of, pertaining to, or conforming to beliefs, attitudes, or modes of conduct that are generally approved

Paul had it all—power, prestige, popularity, promise, and passion—everything an **orthodox** Jewish man could ever want. Talk about sterling credentials; try these on for size: "circumcised the eighth day, of the stock of Israel, of the tribe of Benjamin [Jacob's favored son], a Hebrew of the Hebrews; concerning the law, a Pharisee; concerning zeal, persecuting the church; concerning the righteousness which is in the law, blameless" (Philippians 3:5–6 NKJV). In terms of Paul's faith community and his chosen profession, he was a rising star. But as he stood on the pinnacle, he suddenly threw it all away.

The moment of truth came on the hot and dusty road to Damascus. Paul was on a mission to hunt down Christians living in that capital city, but something unexpected happened. "As he journeyed he came near Damascus, and suddenly a light shone around him from heaven. Then he fell to the ground, and heard a voice saying to him, 'Saul, Saul [his name before Jesus changed it to Paul], why are you persecuting Me?'" (Acts 9:3–4 NKJV). Paul knew that God had his number. You have to give him credit. Paul may have been bloodthirsty, but he seems to have been genuinely interested in serving God's purposes. When he found out that God's purposes weren't what he thought they were, he changed directions immediately. He surrendered on the spot, and it wasn't long before the persecutor of Christians became one of the persecuted, one of the most important figures in all of Christian history.

Think what Paul lost by becoming a Christian. A career that he had cultivated very carefully. A set of closely cherished beliefs by which he had shaped his whole life. Friendships. Security. Safety. Paul would say he had nothing to lose. He considered all that stuff to be the equivalent of dung compared to what he had found. Yes, the old Saul died on the road to Damascus. But that wasn't really a death. Paul would say that it wasn't until Saul died that Paul could live.

Jesus promised, "He who finds his life will lose it, and he who loses his life for My sake will find it" (Matthew 10:39 NKJV). Paul is living proof that Jesus keeps His promises. So is everyone who has ever found new life by allowing his or her old life to be lost in Christ.

what others say

Jim Elliot

He is no fool who gives what he cannot keep to gain what He cannot lose.[7]

Christology
an interpretation of the nature, person, and deeds of Christ

No Strings Attached

HEBREWS 13:16 ***But do not forget to do good and to share, for with such sacrifices God is well pleased.*** *(NKJV)*

As she felt frantically for her wallet, the desperation of her situation slowly sank in. She was in big trouble. Thirty-four years old, all alone, just her and her motorcycle, traveling across the United States. And somehow she had lost her wallet.

With a heart full of panic, she retraced her path back to the diner where she had last seen it. Only when she admitted to herself that the wallet was gone for good did she began to cry. Then for lack of another plan, she called her phone to receive her waiting messages. It was then that she heard: "Hi, Diane? This is Mike from Dubois, Wyoming. I found your wallet outside Grand Teton Park. Call me."

When she finally made contact, she offered Mike a reward. He replied: "No way. I can't do that. This is how we do things out here in Wyoming. We take care of each other. I just want you to get it back."[8]

something to ponder

Those are striking words: "We take care of each other." Mike did something good for someone else with no strings attached. You don't have to live in Wyoming to have that attitude, that willingness to bear one another's burdens. Isn't that exactly what the church is meant to do?

In Hebrews chapter 13 the writer to the struggling Hebrew believers was attempting to encourage them. He wrote a series of instructions that would make their lives more bearable despite their difficult circumstances. One of the most potent sounded so simple: "Do not forget to do good and to share" with others. It's kindergarten simple. Do good. Share. This promise comes in the middle of some pretty heavy theology. Lest you get lost in some of the most intense **Christology** in all of Scripture, the writer pauses to offer some very basic advice: Do good. Share.

go to

sacrifice that pleases God
1 Samuel 15:22

feeding of the five thousand
Matthew 14:13–21

cast out their nets
Luke 5:1–11

Why did the writer of Hebrews call sharing and doing good a "sacrifice"? Not because it usually takes a great deal of sacrifice to do good and share (though sometimes it does). He called it a sacrifice because it's a kind of offering. In serving others, you're really serving God. Forget about slaughtering bulls and goats on altars. The sacrifice that pleases God is service to others.

Have you ever wondered how to make God happy or what you could do that would bring Him pleasure? Wonder no longer. Hebrews 13:16 promises that God will be pleased with sacrificial acts of kindness performed by His children for those in need. It's great to know that when you share with others, you are bringing joy to the heart of Almighty God.

what others say

Ignatius of Loyola

Teach us, Good Lord, to serve Thee as Thou deservest; to give and not to count the cost; to fight and not to heed the wounds; to toil and not to seek for rest; to labor and not to ask for any reward save that of knowing we do Thy will.[9]

Good Measure

LUKE 6:38 ***Give, and it will be given to you: good measure, pressed down, shaken together, and running over will be put into your bosom. For with the same measure that you use, it will be measured back to you. (NKJV)***

Abundance is God's specialty. Consider the feeding of the five thousand. It was miracle enough that Jesus fed five thousand people with five loaves and two fish. But what about those leftovers? Twelve baskets full. There were a hundred times more leftovers than there was food to start with! Or consider the time Jesus instructed Simon and his fishing partners to cast out their nets one more time after a night of unsuccessful fishing. The boat was nearly swamped, so great was the catch!

So when God promises to give you abundance, you might want to pay attention. "Give, and it will be given to you," He promises. "Good measure, pressed down, shaken together, and running over" (Luke 6:38 NKJV). That's a great image. As the cereal boxes say, "contents may settle during shipping." Let them settle. God keeps pouring on the blessings until they run over the top.

This is one of those conditional promises, however. That kind of generosity is promised to those who are themselves generous. Jesus said, "With the same measure that you use, it will be measured back to you." If you're dishing out blessings with a teaspoon, how can you expect to be blessed by the gallon? Go ahead, be generous when you give of your time, your resources, your money. You will receive back according to your own generosity.

key point

It takes serious faith to give that way. You've really got to believe God's promises. It goes against your human nature to give more than you can afford to give. It probably goes against the advice of your financial planner—maybe even against the desires of your spouse. But God has made a promise to you. He will always give you what you need and more. True, there's no guarantee that if you give away a hundred dollars you're going to get a hundred dollars back. If that were certain, generosity wouldn't take faith, would it? You might get your hundred dollars back, you might not. You can be sure, however, that you will get more than a hundred dollars' worth of blessing for your trouble. It may be in the joy of obedience and the joy of seeing a needy brother or sister be provided for. How do you put a price tag on that? God has riches that don't have anything to do with money, and He longs to pour them out on you—pressed down, shaken together, and running over.

what others say

W. A. Criswell

If the war is won, God has to win it. If there is strength to do it, God has to give it. . . . For our enemies are not material or corporeal. . . . They are unseen. They are spiritual and God must help us.[10]

Power to the Powerless

2 Timothy 1:7 ***For God has not given us a spirit of fear, but of power and of love and of a sound mind.*** (NKJV)

Young pastor Timothy faced a hornet's nest of hostility. False teachers had infiltrated his Sunday school, wreaking all kinds of havoc. The men failed to assume spiritual leadership and wouldn't even pray. Some women were disruptive during the worship services; others became distractions due to their immodest dress. Some of

go to

stomach problem
1 Timothy 5:23

Nero
one of the most sadistic of the Roman emperors; he ruled from AD 54-68. He instituted some of the cruelest of all persecutions of the early church

Timothy's elders weren't biblically qualified. The widows were in an uproar because they were being neglected. The rich lorded it over the poor. Timothy suffered a stomach problem—probably an ulcer—and no wonder. He was young and did not command the respect of the people. He was shy of temperament and had allowed his spiritual gift to fall into disuse. Quite frankly, Timothy wanted to quit. That's what was going on *internally.*

Externally, Ephesus had erupted into an uproar during Paul's tenure there, so much so that Paul was prevented from preaching in the theater lest he be killed by the crowd. Added to that, the ever-present threat of Roman persecution, escalating under **Nero**, forced Timothy to face the very real possibility of imminent imprisonment and even death. You can understand why Timothy might have "a spirit of fear" or timidity.

Paul reached out to his young disciple. He didn't send him to a career counselor or provide him with the latest set of motivational tapes. Timothy needed something far more substantial. So Paul provided the promise of the Holy Spirit. He knew that this was the only lasting answer to the anxiety and pressure that threaten a believer's personal assurance and effectiveness.

apply it

Power, love, and a sound mind. That, according to Paul, was the answer to a spirit of fear. Think about it. To live in fear is to feel powerless against your problems. If you have God's Spirit within you, you can experience the joy of the promise, "He who is in you is greater than he who is in the world" (1 John 4:4 NKJV) But power by itself isn't the whole answer. You've probably known people—schoolyard bully types—for whom the exercise of power is simply a cover-up for fear and feelings of inadequacy. What really casts out fear is love. To be loved—and particularly to be loved by God—is to know a security that overwhelms fear.

Finally the Spirit gives us sound minds. Have you ever noticed how fear confuses you? Fear convinces you that you're just being "realistic" when in fact you're looking at a warped and tiny view of yourself and your situation. God's presence sets you free from all of that craziness and gives you a clear mind to meet your problems head-on. Do you live in fear? Trust God to give you power, love, and peace of mind.

what others say

R. A. Torrey

If it was in the power of the Holy Spirit that Jesus Christ, the only begotten Son of God, lived and worked, achieved and triumphed, how much more dependent are we upon Him at every turn of life and in every phase of service.[11]

Chapter Wrap-Up

- The truly sanctified One makes it possible for us to be sanctified.
- The sacrifice that pleases God the most is to do good and share.
- God promises to reward generosity with generosity.
- God promises victory over sin if we live by the Spirit rather than the flesh.

Study Questions

1. How does God use the foolish to shame the wise and the weak to shame the strong?
2. How does losing your life make it possible for you to find it?
3. Why does Paul use the word "sacrifice" to describe doing good and sharing?
4. Why doesn't God take away your fleshly desires the minute you receive Christ?
5. What is God's answer to fear and timidity?

Chapter 16: Promises to Meet Physical Needs

Chapter Highlights:
- **God's promise of joy in every circumstance**
- **Promise of strength**
- **Promise of healing**
- **Promise of long life**

A Matter of Priorities

LUKE 12:31 ***But seek the kingdom of God, and all these things shall be added to you.*** *(NKJV)*

Like a lot of preachers, Jesus sometimes preached His sermons more than once. You may be familiar with this promise from the Sermon on the Mount: "But seek first the kingdom of God and His righteousness, and all these things shall be added to you" (Matthew 6:33 NKJV). You may not remember that He made this very same promise in a slightly different context.

Jesus was preaching to a crowd when one of His hearers broke in with a request: "Teacher, tell my brother to divide the inheritance with me." No doubt this man had heard that Jesus was a problem-solver. He had money problems, so he went to Jesus looking for a solution. Maybe he was a younger brother, not entitled by law or tradition to receive much of an inheritance. He had heard that Jesus was bringing in a whole new way of doing things—releasing people from some of the burdensome laws of the Old Testament. Maybe this Jesus would be willing to release them from the laws of **primogeniture** while He was at it!

go to

releasing people
Matthew 12:1-12

primogeniture
the system of inheritance or succession by the firstborn, specifically the eldest son

The man made this surprising request. Actually, it wasn't a request. It was a command: "Teacher, tell my brother . . ." He didn't ask, "Teacher, what do you think about inheritances?" No, this man had an agenda, and he wanted Jesus on board. But Jesus, as He was inclined to do, changed the subject. He told a story about a man who placed all his hopes in riches. The man built barns to hold all his excess crops and goods. He envisioned years of ease and pleasure. But he died before he had a chance to enjoy any of it.

Then Jesus launched into a proper sermon. *Do not worry about food or clothes or anything you need,* He preached. *Birds don't build barns or plan ahead, but God provides for them. Flowers don't make or buy clothes, but they are more beautifully dressed than kings.* It's a matter of priorities. "seek the kingdom of God, and all these things shall

something to ponder

be added to you" (Luke 12:31 NKJV). Sure, you need clothes and food and shelter. But if you put those material needs first, you miss out on God. For that matter, in your worry you also miss out on the pleasure to be had from having clothes and food and shelter. But if you put God first, you get God and, *as promised*, you get everything else!

what others say

D. Martyn Lloyd-Jones

Here we are worrying about food and drink and clothing! The trouble with us is that we do not realize that we are children of our heavenly Father. If only we realized that, we should never worry again.[1]

What Jesus Says About

Riches	Scripture
"It is easier for a camel to go through the eye of a needle than for a rich man to enter the kingdom of God."	Matthew 19:24 (NKJV)
[From the parable of the sower]: "The cares of this world, the deceitfulness of riches, and the desires for other things entering in choke the word, and it becomes unfruitful."	Mark 4:19 (NKJV)
[Speaking of the poor widow who gave an offering of mere pennies]: "that this poor widow has put in more than all those who have given to the treasury; for they all put in out of their abundance, but she out of her poverty put in all that she had, her whole livelihood."	Mark 12:43–44 (NKJV)
"Woe to you who are rich, For you have received your consolation."	Luke 6:24 (NKJV)

The Confidence of Joy

PHILIPPIANS 4:19 ***And my God shall supply all your need according to His riches in glory by Christ Jesus. (NKJV)***

The Book of Philippians is fairly bursting with joy. "Fulfill my joy" (Philippians 2:2 NKJV). "I am glad and rejoice with you all" (Philippians 2:17 NKJV). "Rejoice in the Lord" (Philippians 3:1 NKJV). "I know how to abound" (Philippians 4:12 NKJV). Paul calls the Christians at Philippi "my joy and my crown" (Philippians 4:1 NKJV). All this joyful abounding comes, remember, from a man who is languishing in a Roman prison.

If the Roman authorities meant to dampen Paul's exuberant spirit, they weren't doing a very good job of it. They might have had Paul captive, but in so doing, they provided Paul with a captive audience. The guards who kept watch over Paul had no choice but to hear the gospel from him. In fact, Paul believed that his imprisonment, rather than discouraging the other Christians, actually emboldened them.

go to

guards
Philippians 1:13

living meant serving Christ
Philippians 1:21

Where does that kind of joy and confidence come from? In Paul's case, it came from the ability to see God at work in his everyday life. Paul's physical accommodations weren't ideal. But Paul's life wasn't grounded in his physical accommodations. For Paul, living meant serving Christ—and dying was no big deal. That meant there was very little the Romans or any other enemy could do to get at Paul. They could take what they wanted; Paul knew that God was going to keep giving him everything he needed.

Paul had learned "in whatever state I am to be content: I know how to be abased, and I know how to abound. Everywhere and in all things I have learned both to be full and to be hungry, both to abound and to suffer need" (Philippians 4:11–12 NKJV). How could he be satisfied in any condition he found himself? Because rich or poor, full or hungry, God had promised to meet his every need. That attitude of contentment was a mark of Paul's maturity.

key point

No wonder the believers found encouragement in Paul's imprisonment. If he could be so joyful in his circumstances, they could be joyful in theirs. Paul was confident that the God who had been so good to him would be just as good to the rest of His people: "And my God shall supply all your need according to His riches in glory by Christ Jesus" (Philippians 4:19 NKJV). That phrase, *according to His riches in glory*, is a big one. God doesn't just supply *out of* his riches, but *according to* his riches. If Bill Gates were to give you a nickel, he would be giving *out of* his riches, but not *according to* his riches—not in proportion to his riches. To say that God gives according to His riches is to say He gives richly indeed! And He gives the *kind* of riches that are truly valuable. God will provide for you according to His riches, just as He provided for Paul. That's His promise, and it means you can live a life of genuine joy.

what others say

Luci Swindoll

Are you feeling long on need and short on resources today? Let me encourage you to do what I do when I feel that way: go to the One who has promised to provide everything you need, in abundance. He may not give you the answer you had envisioned, but you can trust it to be the perfect provision.[2]

Day by Day

PSALM 34:10
The young lions lack and suffer hunger;
But those who seek the LORD shall not lack any good thing. (NKJV)

"I will bless the LORD at all times; His praise shall continually be in my mouth" (Psalm 34:1 NKJV). David had good reason to praise the Lord. God had just spared his life.

David was a man on the run, hounded and hunted by the most powerful person in the land, the notorious King Saul. Saul hated David with a passion, and pooled his vast resources in a desperate effort to stalk David down and kill him.

David was on his own, with no more possessions than the supplies he was able to carry on his back. He hid in caves, wore disguises, scrounged for food, and did whatever was necessary in order to survive. He got so desperate (1 Samuel 21:10–15 NKJV) that he went to King Achish of Gath, to hide in the hometown of his defeated foe Goliath. When the king's men recognized him, David naturally feared that Achish would imprison him, turn him over to his pursuer, Saul, or perhaps even execute him as a threat. David survived by pretending to be insane. He "scratched on the doors of the gate, and let his saliva fall down on his beard" (1 Samuel 21:13 NKJV)!

something to ponder

Achish viewed this "crazy" man as a problem he didn't need. He threw David out of town. As the words of a song go, he was "on the road again." Suddenly, David realized something. Even when he was running for his life, he lacked nothing. Out there in the desert, he had seen lions, securely situated on top of the food chain, grow weak and hungry. Yet David, alone, penniless, fleeing like some fugitive from the murderous whims of a hate-filled king, had everything that he needed. God sustained David day by day, providing food, shelter, water, and protection even when he was not aware of it. Psalm 34 is the song he wrote in honor of God's watch-care.

We all forget God's attentiveness from time to time, but He provides for us whether we are aware of His vigilance or not. "The eyes of the LORD are on the righteous, and His ears are open to their cry" (Psalm 34:15 NKJV). God is the giver of good gifts. You may lack some of the things you think you want, but God promises that you will never lack for the things that are truly good.

go to

God is for us
Romans 8:31

prospects
the outlook for the future

> what others say
>
> **Larry Burkett**
>
> God will keep his promise to provide every need we have through physical, material, and spiritual means, according to His perfect plan. . . . What a great relief it is to turn our burdens over to *Him.*[3]

What More Could He Give?

> **ROMANS 8:32** ***He who did not spare His own Son, but delivered Him up for us all, how shall He not with Him also freely give us all things? (NKJV)***

Romans 8 is surely one of the most-quoted chapters in all the Bible. And no wonder. It is a chapter of hope, depicting Paul's ascent out of the darkness of sin and into the light of God's grace. Romans 7 shows what happens when we focus on our own problems and shortcomings. Remember Paul's lamentation: "O wretched man that I am! Who will deliver me from the body of this death?" (Romans 7:4 NKJV). As long as he is looking at himself, Paul sees no way out of his troubles. But his gaze shifts to God in the last verse of chapter 7 and throughout chapter 8, and his **prospects** change utterly.

"There is now no condemnation to those who are in Christ Jesus" (Romans 8:1 NKJV). This is the same Paul who, earlier on the same page, was wallowing in self-condemnation. That changed perspective changed everything. *Sure*, Paul admitted, *I can't whip Satan in my own power.* But he doesn't have to. None of us has to. We have God on our side. And if God is for us, who can be against us? That's an incredible realization. The Almighty is for us!

And lest anyone should doubt that God is actually for us, Paul offers up the most convincing evidence imaginable: God "did not spare His son, but delivered Him up for us all" (Romans 8:32 NKJV). God didn't even love His own son more than He loved us. He who possesses all power over life and death, sin and judgment, is on our side.

When God has given us so much—secured eternal life and happiness for us by the death of Christ—how is it that we worry over so many things that are so much smaller? How is that we fret over rent payments and medical tests and social pecking orders? It's human nature to worry about such things, but even that isn't a legitimate excuse. God has allowed us to live above those things. If you dwell on your problems, they fill up your frame of reference until they look to be a hundred times bigger than you. But God calls us to constantly size them up against Him.

God holds nothing back. God has promised to do whatever it takes that we might be "more than conquerors through Him who loved us" (Romans 8:37 NKJV).

And beside Him, our troubles are mighty small. He gave us His son. Why would He withhold anything else we might need?

what others say

A. W. Tozer

With the goodness of God to desire our highest welfare, the wisdom of God to plan it, and the power of God to achieve it, what do we lack?[4]

What the Bible Says About

Worry	Scripture
"Do not fret—it only causes harm."	Psalm 37:8 (NKJV)
"Which of you by worrying can add one cubit to his stature?"	Matthew 6:27 (NKJV)
"Be anxious for nothing, but in everything by prayer and supplication, with thanksgiving, let your requests be made known to God."	Philippians 4:6 (NKJV)
"[Cast] all your cares upon Him, for He cares for you."	1 Peter 5:7 (NKJV)

Strength and Song

Psalm 118:14

The Lord is my strength and song,
And He has become my salvation. (NKJV)

Psalm 118 is located at the "geographical center" of the Bible. If you were to count the total number of verses in the Old and New Testaments put together (there are 31,174 total, according to J.M. Boyce's commentary on the Psalms) and divide by two, you would find that the middle verses are found in Psalm 118—verses 8 and 9. That is very appropriate. For Psalm 118 has a very broad reach, from near the beginning of the Bible to near the end. With one hand Psalm 118 reaches all the way back to the Book of Exodus for much of its subject matter. It contains a word-for-word quotation of Moses' victory song after the defeat of the Egyptians. (Many scholars, in fact, believe that Moses actually wrote Psalm 118). With the other hand, Psalm 118 reaches forward to the New Testament. No other Old Testament chapter is quoted more often in the New Testament.

quotation
Exodus 15:2

monotheism
the belief that there is only one true God, not multiple gods (as is the belief in polytheism)

"The Lord is my strength and song," Moses declared. Strength and song. You don't always put those two together. Strength is about hardness, military might. Music is a softer thing; it's about art, beauty, the finer things in life. Other religious traditions might have had gods of music and gods of war. But they wouldn't have been the same gods. Moses' pairing of strength and song is, in effect, a declaration of **monotheism**. The God of war and the God of music is One God. He is also the God of agriculture and nature and commerce and family and work. He is the Giver of every good and perfect gift. He is before all things, and in Him all things hold together.

But more to the point, Moses understood God to be his salvation. When Moses first spoke these words, remember, he had just seen God deliver him and his people from an impossible situation. They were almost literally between the devil and the deep blue sea—Pharaoh's army coming up behind, the Red Sea in front of them—when God opened the sea and the children of Israel walked across dry land to the other side. It was a defining moment in Jewish history.

It came as no surprise to Moses that God gave him the strength he needed. God has promised His strength—"The Lord will give strength to His people" (Psalm 29:11 NKJV) —to *all* His people, just when they need it.

Perhaps that's why the repeat of Moses' song appears in the very center of the Bible. The one God—God of war, God of music, God of all—is our great Deliverer. That is surely a promise worth rejoicing in.

go to

Epaphroditus
Philippians 2:25; 4:18

context
the parts of a written or spoken statement that precede or follow a specific word or passage, usually influencing its meaning or effect

what others say

Artur Weiser

It is *God* who is "his strength" and "his song", a confession which shows the humility and the joyous gratitude of a man who knows he owes everything to God.[5]

Just in the Nick of Time

PHILIPPIANS 4:13 ***I can do all things through Christ who strengthens me. (NKJV)***

It's a favorite verse among athletes: "I can do all things through Christ who strengthens me" (Philippians 4:19 NKJV). *Our team can win this game because we can do all things through Christ who strengthens us.* But what happens if the other team is claiming that same promise? What about the marathoner who claims this promise, then gets shin splints and can't finish the race? Does the promise of Philippians 4:19 mean that person could or should keep running in spite of an injury? A look at the **context** of this promise helps to answer those questions.

At the end of his letter to the Philippians, Paul included a thank-you note for a gift that the Philippians had sent him. Apparently it was a monetary gift that arrived in a time of great need for Paul, and it was carried by Epaphroditus, one of the members of the Philippian church. The Philippians had chosen to "share in [Paul's] distress," and he was grateful. But Paul was careful not to sound as if he were feeling sorry for himself. "I have learned in whatever state I am, to be content," he wrote. "I know how to be abased, and I know how to abound. Everywhere and in all things, I have learned both to be full and to be hungry, both to abound and to suffer need. I can do all things through Christ who strengthens me" (Philippians 4:12–13 NKJV).

Sometimes people claim that promise—"I can do all things"—as if it's supposed to mean, "I can succeed at anything as long as I have Jesus on my side." That's not what Paul was saying. Paul was saying, *sometimes I'm called upon to be hungry, sometimes I'm called upon to have plenty. Whatever my lot in life, I can get through because Christ is there with me, giving me strength.*

So when the coach in the home team's locker room says "We can do all things through Christ who strengthens us," and the coach in the visiting team's locker room says "We can do all things through Christ who strengthens us," there need not be anything contradictory about that. Christ promises to strengthen one team to win well, and one team to lose well. You aren't promised any particular outcome in your endeavors. You are, however, promised the strength to be content with the life God gives you.

go to

Good Samaritan
Luke 10:34

submission to the Holy Spirit
1 Samuel 16:13

> what others say
>
> **Marjorie Holmes**
>
> "Help me," I kept crying to my God . . . He came in the quiet of the night; he was there in the brilliance of the morning. He touched my senses with hope; he healed my despair.[6]

Praying for the Sick

JAMES 5:15a ***And the prayer of faith will save the sick, and the Lord will raise him up.*** **(NKJV)**

James' readers, as we have discussed before, suffered quite a bit. Besides suffering persecution, apparently some were sick as well. James offered, therefore, a simple pattern for healing:

1. The sick person should ask his or her elders to pray for him.
2. The elders should "[anoint] him with oil in the name of the Lord" (James 5:14 NKJV).
3. God promises that "the prayer of faith will save the sick" (James 5:15a NKJV).

In biblical times, to anoint a person with oil had both a medicinal and symbolic significance. The Good Samaritan, you will remember, applied oil to the wounds of the man who had fallen among thieves. That would have been a strictly medicinal use of oil. It is possible that James is directing the elders to administer some medical care to the sick person when he instructs them to anoint the sick person with oil. Whatever the medical significance of the oil, however, it is certain that the oil has a spiritual significance. To anoint a person a person with oil was to symbolize their submission to the Holy Spirit.

something to ponder

God's promise was to "save the sick." Sound too good to be true? Is perfect health just one prayer away?

go to

miraculous physical healing
Matthew 8:5–13; Matthew 12:22; Matthew 15:21-28; Mark 5:22–34

The word translated "save" is the Greek word *sozo*. It occurs over a hundred times in the New Testament, and though it can refer to physical healing, it is overwhelmingly used in the sense of spiritual salvation. God does grant miraculous physical healing, of course; He does it all the time. But we should be careful not to read this passage as a promise that every sick person who receives prayer and anointing from their church leaders will be healed of their sickness. Death, too, is a kind of healing; for those who are in Christ, death is the final healing of all hurts. James remarks that "if he [the sick person] has committed sins, he will be forgiven" (James 5:16 NKJV). That suggests that there is a very strong spiritual component to the healing that is being promised here.

key point

When you aren't well, you are very aware of the fact that you are needy, that you can't do it all on your own. That's why there is so much spiritual healing that happens when people are sick—whether they experience physical healing or not. When God heals, He heals the deepest, most serious problem; and that's not always your physical ailment. There are times when God's will is best accomplished through sickness, rather than health (2 Corinthians 12:9 NKJV). God promises a condition of inner vitality that supersedes our physical infirmities.

what others say

David Seamands

God is the great Alchemist who can take every damage, every hurt, every crippling infirmity, and turn it all into spiritual gold.

When you cooperate with the Holy Spirit in this process of deep prayer and inner healing, God will reweave the design of your life and recycle it into a means of serving others.[7]

Biblical Figures Who Were Anointed

Anointed	Anointer	Scripture
Aaron and his sons, anointed for the priesthood	Moses	Exodus 28:41
Saul, anointed for kingship	Samuel	1 Samuel 9:16
David, anointed for kingship	Samuel	1 Samuel 16:12–13
Solomon, anointed for kingship	Nathan	1 Kings 1:34–39
The sick people of Galilee, anointed for healing	The Disciples	Mark 6:13
Jesus, his feet anointed with perfume	"a sinful woman"	Luke 6:38

Down but Not Out

PSALM 41:3
The LORD will strengthen him on his bed of illness;
You will sustain him on his sickbed. *(NKJV)*

God has a special place in His heart for the hurting. David should know. At the time he wrote Psalm 41, not only was David plagued by some kind of illness. His enemies used the occasion to whisper behind his back that he would never recover: "'An evil disease,' they say, 'clings to him. And now that he lies down, he will rise up no more.'" That kind of gossip is a serious problem for a king. A king needs to be strong all the time; if he is perceived as weak—even temporarily—his enemies have the opportunity to hurt him. It's hard enough to protect yourself from rumors when you're in perfect health. When you're lying on your sickbed, it's that much harder to answer your enemies.

In that moment of need, David couldn't even count on friends. David complained that one of his trusted friends—a friend who had eaten his bread—"lifted up his heel against me" (Psalm 41:8–9 NKJV). Isn't that how life is so much of the time? It's one thing for people to be friendly to us when we're on top of our game and everything is going well. But when the chips are down, we discover who our friends really are. David had little he could cling to.

But he did have this: He knew that the Lord would "strengthen him on his bed of illness," and "sustain him on his sickbed" (Psalm 41:3 NKJV). David placed his absolute, unshakable confidence in the fact that God would reestablish him, or raise him up, to a place of usefulness in spite of his illness. What a great promise; when you've been sick for a while, you forget what it feels like to be healthy. It gets hard to imagine a life beyond your illness. That's why you have to rest in the objective truth of promises like Psalm 41:3. God restores and sustains.

When we understand that God's objective is restoration of the soul, sickness is no longer something to dread. Illness is a normal part of the human condition. Everyone gets sick. Each of us will go through seasons of physical frailty. Most of us will some day die of one disease or another. But whether we live or die, sickness will not be the victor. We will be the victor. Illness is merely another tool with which God continues to conform us to the image of His Son.

go to

will not be the victor
1 Corinthians 15:55

conform us
Romans 8:29

something to ponder

go to

burning bush
Exodus 3

predicate adjective
an adjective following a linking verb that describes the subject, such as 'roses are red.'

what others say

Joni Eareckson Tada and Steve Estes

From time to time God, in His mercy, may grant us healing from disease as a gracious glimpse, a 'sneak preview' of what is to come. It is my opinion that He sometimes does. But, in view of the fact that the kingdom has not yet come in its fullness, we are not to automatically expect it.[8]

The Power of His Name

ISAIAH 46:4
Even to your old age, I am He,
And even to gray hairs I will carry you!
I have made, and I will bear;
Even I will carry, and will deliver you. (NKJV)

When Moses stood before the burning bush, he asked the name of the God who spoke to him. The answer was "I AM." All the promises of God begin with that name. He IS. He exists beyond the confines of time. He Will Be, and He Was; that is true enough. But past tense and future tense are simply grammatical constructions to help time-bound creatures like us to put things into words. God lives in the eternal Now: I AM. That name is itself a kind of promise. *Your past is gone, you cannot see your future, but I AM!*

Jesus nearly started a riot when He said to the Pharisees, "Before Abraham was, I AM" (John 8:58 NKJV). The Pharisees were very sensitive to the name of God; by applying that name to Himself, Jesus was claiming to be God. We could learn something from the Pharisees here. We would do well to pay attention when God uses the words "I am" in the Scriptures. God says something interesting: "Even to your old age, I am He" (Isaiah 46:4 NKJV). "I am He." The grammar is just a little unexpected. You expect God to say, "I am here," or "I am good," or "I am on your side." To put it in grammatical terms, you expect a **predicate adjective**. But God doesn't give us one. We don't need one. It is enough to know that God is God. As much as things change here on earth, God doesn't change. He is forever God, forever the same.

Why does God talk about gray hair in this passage? Because gray hair represents the truth of our condition. Things are always in flux for us. Our strength ebbs away. We are bound by time. We *were* helpless babies. We *will be* old and infirm (God willing). But God IS. That is a promise to cling to when you look in the mirror and see gray hairs. God is, and He has a lifelong interest in you. He will not abandon you with indifference when you pass a certain age. He doesn't view you as useless or past your prime. He will "carry" you, even through all the trials and tribulations associated with the inevitable aging process. And He has pledged to you His wholehearted assurance by backing up this promise with the authority of His own name.

what others say

Robert Browning

Grow old with me!
The best is yet to be,
The last of life, for which the first was made:
Our times are in His hand
Who saith, "A whole I planned,
Youth shows but half; trust God: See all,
Nor be afraid."[9]

What Jesus Said About Who He Was

Jesus' "I AM" Statements	Scripture
"If you do not believe that I am He, you will die in your sins."	John 8:24 (NKJV)
"When you lift up the Son of Man, then you will know that I am He."	John 8:28 (NKJV)
"Most assuredly, I say to you, before Abraham was, I AM."	John 8:58 (NKJV)
"Now I tell you before it comes, that when it does come to pass, you may believe that I am He."	John 13:19 (NKJV)
Jesus said to them, "I am He." And Judas, who betrayed Him, also stood with them.	John 18:5 (NKJV)

All Things Being Equal

PROVERBS 10:27
The fear of the Lord prolongs days,
But the years of the wicked will be shortened. (NKJV)

The promise of "prolonged days" in Proverbs 10:27 is one of those "all things being equal" promises. We know from experience

go to

appointed time
Hebrews 9:27

Jesus asked
Matthew 6:27

that sometimes the wicked live to a ripe old age and that the righteous sometimes die young. Jesus Himself died in His early thirties. God does not guarantee anyone a long life to those who serve Him well. Everybody has an appointed time to die; God alone establishes the exact date. "Which of you by worrying can add one cubit to his stature?" Jesus asked. The length of our lives is out of our control, and rests securely within God's sovereign control. We each have an appointment with death, and you can be sure that for that appointment we won't be late.

Do we have the freedom, then, to live a devil-may-care lifestyle, taking crazy risks and making careless choices? Not at all. Quite the opposite, in fact. It's precisely *because* our days are numbered that we will want to maximize our days on earth, taking advantage of every opportunity to serve the Lord as faithfully as we possibly can.

That's where the promise of Proverbs 10:27 comes in. Here's the principle: *All things being equal,* someone who makes wise choices will live longer, healthier, and enjoy a better quality of life than someone who makes wicked choices.

The psalmist named Asaph finally came to understand that. One dark, doubt-filled day, Asaph wrestled with the fact that the wicked sometimes seem to get off scot-free. They have no real worries in life or at the time of death. Of the wicked he lamented, "There are no pangs in their death, but their strength is firm" (Psalm 73:4 NKJV). They mock God, live like the devil, and are yet always carefree. For Asaph, something just didn't add up. Until he had a brilliant burst of God-given insight: "Oh, how they are brought to desolation, as in a moment! They are utterly consumed with terrors" (Psalm 73:19 NKJV). Their end comes swift and sure. And once time is up, the wicked enter eternity empty-handed. Finally, Asaph understood the destiny of the wicked. For his own part, he rejoiced that he had personally made God "the strength of my heart" (Psalm 73:26 NKJV).

something to ponder

We will not be late to our appointment with death. But if we determine to make wicked choices, we may well be early.

what others say

Eugenia Price

The Bible clearly states, "As you sow, so shall ye reap." There is no promise anywhere that any human beings will be exempt from the consequences of sin, past or present....If we break ourselves over his moral laws, we must be willing to submit to the consequences.[10]

Chapter Wrap-Up

- Even when we forget about God's watch-care, He is faithful to watch over us.
- If God didn't even spare His own son for our sakes, why would He spare us anything else we need?
- God gives us strength to "do all things"—everything He would have us do.
- We move from the weakness of childhood toward the weakness of old age, but God doesn't change.

Study Questions

1. What does it mean to say, "If you put God first, you get God *and* everything else"?
2. Why were the early Christians encouraged by Paul's imprisonment rather than being discouraged?
3. What happens when you allow problems to fill your frame of reference? What happens when you set your problems beside God?
4. What does it mean to say that God is "my strength and my song"?
5. How does the context of Philippians 4:19 ("I can do all things through Christ who strengthens me" NKJV) shed light on what Paul was really saying?

Chapter 17: Promises to Meet Eternal Needs

Chapter Highlights:
- Promise of freedom from sin
- Promise of acceptance
- Promise of living water
- Overflowing blessings

A New Master

COLOSSIANS 1:13 ***He has delivered us from the power of darkness and conveyed us into the kingdom of the Son of His love. (NKJV)***

In his letter to the Colossians, Paul applied his considerable powers of persuasion to the subject of the preeminence of Christ. Perhaps the book could be best summed up in the declaration, "He is before all things, and in Him all things consist" (Colossians 1:17 NKJV). Christ first, last, and in the middle. Paul's prayer for the Colossians was that they would be "filled with the knowledge of His will in all wisdom and understanding" (Colossians 1:9 NKJV). That is to say, the way to spiritual blessing is an understanding of who Christ is. To know Christ is to love Him; the result is a life that is "fully pleasing to Him, and "fruitful in every good work" (Colossians 1:10 NKJV).

Even more importantly, when you seek to know God, you receive a new citizenship. You are no longer subject to "the power of darkness," but are joined to "the kingdom of the Son of His love" (Colossians 1:13 NKJV). To join the kingdom of God is to have freedom for the first time. Paul spoke elsewhere of "slavery to sin." He simply meant that you if you aren't in Christ, you don't really have the choice to do what is right and good. As you know from experience, you still sometimes choose badly when you are in Christ. But at least you have the choice.

Freedom in Christ is a bit of a paradox. You only experience that freedom when you're willing to acknowledge that you aren't your own boss. In Romans, Paul writes, "having been set free from sin, you became slaves of righteousness" (Romans 6:18 NKJV). You might say you'd prefer not to be anybody's slave. But we human beings don't have that choice. If you're not willing to submit to God's will, you're going to submit to the will of Satan. Any sovereignty of the self is only an illusion.

go to

His yoke is easy
Matthew 11:30

eternal
without beginning or end; existing outside of time

God insists we submit to His yoke. But here's the good news: Jesus promised that His yoke is easy and His burden is light. Sin is a hard master. Sin allows you to believe you are your own master; but that doesn't make the servitude any less harsh. God, however, welcomes you into His kingdom with the promise of a lightened load. He promises to set you free from the power that enslaved you—even the power of the self—and welcome you into His rest.

what others say

John Stott

Only one act of pure love, unsullied by any taint of ulterior motive, has ever been performed in the history of the world, namely the self-giving of God in Christ on the cross for undeserving sinners.[1]

God's Free Gift

Romans 6:23 ***For the wages of sin is death, but the gift of God is eternal life in Christ Jesus our Lord.*** *(NKJV)*

The promise of Romans 6:23 is the gospel in a nutshell: we sinners deserve death, but instead we have been given life as a free gift. That word "wages" refers to something we earn by the things we do—by our life's work, you might say. Death is the paycheck we rightfully deserve. Instead of giving us our just desserts, God offers us the gift of **eternal** life. It's an astonishing thing. It's exactly the sort of thing God delights to do.

This well-known promise comes in the middle of a discussion about slavery and the law. Apart from Christ, we are under the dominion of sin, and we are also under the dominion of the law. There were plenty of people in Paul's world who viewed the law of God as a kind of scorecard. They learned the law and obeyed it in order to score points and earn God's favor. To those people, Paul said, in effect, *You want what's coming to you? You want what your performance has earned with regard to the law? What you've earned is death!* On the other hand, there were people who had tried their hardest to follow the law and simply couldn't. For them, the law wasn't a way of building themselves up. No, the law was beating them down, reminding them how far they fell short. That's one of the main purposes of the law, by the way—to remind you how far you are from God's standard. God meant for the law to be a constant reminder of just how much we need Him. Those people for whom the law was a source of pride just didn't get it.

To both of those groups—the self-righteous law-keepers and the self-condemned lawbreakers—Paul communicated the same promise: God freely offers the eternal life that you cannot earn for yourself. Stop your striving. Stop your worrying. Eternal life is a gift to be received, not a wage to be earned.

Have you received God's free gift? If not, why not? Why would anyone turn his or her back on a gift so freely given, so wonderfully provided, so lovingly offered? There's no better time than now to receive this wondrous gift of God.

go to

Stop your striving
Psalm 46:10

fill their souls
Psalm 81:10

something to ponder

what others say

William Barclay

Paul uses two military words. For *pay* he uses *opsonia*. *Opsonia* was the soldiers pay, something that he earned with the risk of his body and the sweat of his brow . . . For gift he uses *charisma*. The charisma or, in Latin, the *donativum*, was a totally unearned gift. . . . On special occasions, for instance on his birthday . . . an emperor handed out a free gift of money to the army.[2]

Full Acceptance

JOHN 6:37b ***The one who comes to Me I will by no means cast out. (NKJV)***

The people had gathered on the shore of the Sea of Galilee to see the Son of God in action. But they got more than they bargained for. They were hungry, and there was no food available. So Jesus produced food on the spot, right before their eyes, in an obvious display of the power of God. With five little loaves and a couple of fish, Jesus miraculously fed some twenty thousand people!

After filling their stomachs, Jesus sought to fill their souls. Jesus said to them—and to *us*: "He who comes to Me shall never hunger, and he who believes in Me shall never thirst" (John 6:35b NKJV). Feeding that many people with earthly food was impressive enough, but Jesus was offering something of infinitely more value—spiritual food, living water. All spiritual nourishment begins with Him—and ends with Him too.

no rejection
Matthew 15:21-28

told him to leave his home
Genesis 12:1–4

Jesus went on to promise an open-arms welcome to every sincere seeker: "The one who comes to Me, I will by no means drive out" (John 6:37b NKJV). We all fear rejection. We all know how it feels to approach someone whose opinion of us matters, only to have him or her turn away. We have felt the sting of unreturned phone calls, unanswered mail, or turned-down invitations. But Jesus promised that there would be no rejection with Him. No turning His back. No sending us away. No walking the other direction.

The offer that Jesus made to the people was an offer of Himself. "I am the bread of life," He said (John 6:48 NKJV). Actually, He put it in much more extreme terms than that "Unless you eat the flesh of the Son of Man and drink His blood, you have no life in you" (John 6:53 NKJV). We've had two thousand years to get used to that kind of language, but it still strikes us as extreme. Can you imagine how extreme it sounded to people who were hearing it for the first time? Perhaps it's not surprising that immediately after this episode, "many of His disciples went back and walked with Him no more" (John 6:66 NKJV). Jesus made an incredible promise never to reject His followers, but many of His followers rejected Him.

The offer Jesus makes is a pretty intense one. He offers His body and blood as your spiritual food. Included in that offer is a promise never to cast out those who are willing to accept it.

what others say

Billy Graham

Your personal faith begins when you resolve: I will face myself now, my problems, my hang-ups, my assets, my faults. Now—right now—I turn myself over to God. I know that He will accept me as I am because of Jesus Christ.[3]

A Promise About a Promise

GALATIANS 3:29 ***And if you are Christ's, then you are Abraham's seed, and heirs according to the promise.*** (NKJV)

Abraham's life took quite a turn when God told him to leave his home and travel to a whole new country he had never seen before. Put yourself into Abraham's sandals for a moment, and try to imagine what that must have been like—to uproot your family, load all your worldly possessions onto pack animals, and begin a treacherous journey over unfamiliar terrain, only to end up in a place completely foreign to you. Add to that the sad fact that Abraham's father died along the way.

One thing Abraham had going for him: God did not abandon His pilgrim patriarch along the way. Quite the contrary. God made him a remarkable promise. God assured Abraham that He would bless him. It all added up to a promise God made not only to Abraham but to the rest of us as well, "in you all the families of the earth shall be blessed" (Genesis 12:3 NKJV).

prone to lie
Genesis 12:11–14; 20:1–13

God's Promises to Bless Abraham

Promise	Fulfillment
God would make Abraham's descendants into a great nation.	Fulfilled in the great nation of the Jews
God would make his name great.	Fulfilled by the fact that Abraham's name is known in three great religions—Christianity, Judaism, and Islam
God would bless those who blessed Abraham and curse those who cursed him.	Fulfilled repeatedly during Abraham's life

If you are in Christ, you are evidence that God is fulfilling that incredible promise to bless all the families of the earth through Abraham. If you belong to Christ, you are Abraham's seed. Forget about genealogies and family trees. You are Abraham's descendant in the most important way: you are a participant in the promise of God's deliverance that was delivered by way of Abraham.

Abraham "believed in the LORD, and He accounted it to him for righteousness" (Genesis 15:6 NKJV). The moment Abraham placed his faith in God's promise, God declared him righteous. This Abraham, remember, had done some pretty shocking things. He was prone to lie. He could be a coward. He had moments of real doubt. But the most important thing to know about Abraham was that he believed God. That was enough. God counted him as righteous on the strength of that belief.

That is the essence of God's promise in Galatians 3:29. God promises everyone that the moment we place our faith in Christ, we become Abraham's descendants or "seed," spiritually if not physically. And just as He did for Abraham, God has declared us righteous.

came in groups
Genesis 24:11

object lesson
a practical or concrete illustration of a principle

what others say

F. F. Bruce

He is as much the Gentiles' God as the God of the Jews, for in the gospel one and the same way of righteousness is opened up for both. He will accept Jews by virtue of their faith, and He will accept Gentiles on exactly the same basis.[4]

Filled to Overflowing

JOHN 4:14 ***But whoever drinks of the water that I shall give him will never thirst. But the water that I shall give him will become in him a fountain of water springing up into everlasting life.*** *(NKJV)*

The disciples did a double take. They couldn't believe that Jesus was talking publicly with a woman, especially a woman who was a Samaritan (an ethnic group especially hated by Jews), most especially an *immoral* Samaritan woman. But Jesus was on a search-and-rescue mission, even for sinful Samaritans.

Women usually came in groups to a well, in the early morning or late in the day to avoid the relentless heat of the Middle Eastern sun. That this needy woman came alone, and at noon, might indicate the public scorn and isolation to which she was subjected because of her immoral lifestyle.

Jesus was the master at moving a conversation in the direction He wanted it to go. By asking the woman at the well for a drink of water, Jesus established common ground with her. He then used the water as His **object lesson**, reaching way back in the Old Testament to do so. Through His prophet Jeremiah, God had condemned the disobedient Jews for rejecting Him—"the fountain of living waters" (Jeremiah 2:13 NKJV). This is the same "water" to which Isaiah referred when he said, "With joy you will draw water from the wells of salvation" (Isaiah 12:3 NKJV). Jeremiah further likened the Jew's rejection of God to making "broken cisterns that can hold no water" (Jeremiah 2:13 NKJV). When Jesus offered "living water" to the woman, He was promising to be the fulfillment of the promise given through Jeremiah hundreds of years earlier. Before the woman even understood how thirsty she was, this Man who had asked for a drink offered to quench her thirst forever. Thus, Jesus made a picture-perfect promise of "living water" to the sinful woman whose parched soul thirsted for the cleansing only Jesus could provide.

People don't usually take a drink of water until they know they are thirsty. Jesus made the Samaritan woman aware of the thirst in her life when He prodded her about her family life. "You have had five husbands, and the one whom you now have is not your husband" (John 4:18 NKJV). If she had been able to ignore her thirst before, the Samaritan woman couldn't ignore it now.

something to ponder

We are born thirsty. We are just as needy as that Samaritan woman. We need the living water that only Jesus has promised to provide. Aren't you glad that Jesus made His offer to anyone and everyone who "drinks of the water that I shall give him"? You don't have to be thirsty. When was the last time you took a drink?

what others say

Paul Tassel

A person must understand he is lost before he will desire to be found. He must realize he is alienated from God before he sees the need to be reconciled to God. . . . Jesus tactfully brought all of that into focus for her.[5]

Promises of Living Water, Bread of Life

Promise	Scripture
"Everyone who thirsts, come to the waters. Any you who have no money, come, buy and eat."	Isaiah 55:1 (NKJV)
"Whoever drinks of the water I shall give him shall never thirst again."	John 4:13–14 (NKJV)
"I am the bread of life. He who comes to Me shall never hunger, and he who believes in Me shall never thirst."	John 6:35 (NKJV)
"If anyone thirsts, let him come to Me and drink. He who believes in Me, as the Scripture has said, out of his heart will flow rivers of living water."	John 7:37–38 (NKJV)
"Let him who thirsts come. Whoever desires, let him take the water of life freely."	Revelation 22:17 (NKJV)

The Good Shepherd

> JOHN 10:10 ***The thief does not come except to steal, and to kill, and to destroy. I have come that they may have life, and that they may have it more abundantly.*** *(NKJV)*

go to

passing through Him
John 14:6

Lamb of God
John 1:29;
Revelation 5:6–14

The life of a shepherd was not easy. He was responsible for a flock of animals who were completely vulnerable if left to their own devices. Long nights in the desert left the sheep in a particularly precarious situation; predatory animals used the darkness to great advantage. Therefore, a shepherd often herded his sheep into a sheepfold—often simply a circular pile of rocks butted up against an indentation in the side of a cliff. For added protection, the shepherd would actually bed down for the night right in the opening of the rocks, literally becoming the gate of the sheepfold. The walls provided the sheep with shelter from cold night winds. In a well-positioned sheepfold, a rock ledge or overhang sheltered the sheep from winter rains. But the shepherd remained exposed to the elements. His first concern was not his own comfort or safety, but the safety of the sheep in his care.

So the shepherd was the sheep's main protection against natural predators—lions, bears, wolves, jackals, and hyenas—or thieves who wanted to steal the sheep. None of the sheep could leave the sheepfold, nor could an enemy enter and attack the sheep, without first passing through the shepherd. The sheep were thus afforded maximum protection and ultimate security.

Jesus was invoking this image when He said: "Most assuredly, I say to you, I am the door of the sheep . . . If anyone enters by Me, he will be saved" (John 10:7, 9 NKJV). He stands guard over our souls, the great Protector. No one comes in or goes out without passing through Him. Contrast that image of tender, shepherdly care to the picture He paints of the enemy: "The thief does not come except to steal, and to kill, and to destroy. I have come that they may have life, and that they may have it more abundantly" (John 10:10 NKJV).

something to ponder

Elsewhere in Scripture, of course, Jesus is described as the Lamb of God. But here He is the Good Shepherd, the One who is willing to lay down His life for His sheep. That's quite the opposite of our "adversary the devil (who) walks about like a roaring lion, seeking whom he may devour" (1 Peter 5:8 NKJV). Here in the Gospel of John, Jesus likens Satan to the thief who comes to steal, kill, and destroy. Contrast that with our Lord, the most loving and sacrificial of shepherds, who offers an abundant life. He has promised to provide us with everything we need; He offers us ultimate protection.

raised the stakes increased the costs or prices; caused more to be at risk

what others say

Lin Johnson

Jesus our shepherd promises to protect us, fight off our enemies, lead us, give us a satisfying life, and die for us. The picture of Jesus as a shepherd is comforting and encouraging . . . [6]

What Jesus Said About

His Sheep	Scripture
"Behold, I send you out as sheep in the midst of wolves. Therefore be wise as serpents and harmless as doves."	Matthew 10:16 (NKJV)
[At Judgment Day,] "All the nations will be gathered before Him, and He will separate them one from another, as a shepherd divides his sheep from the goats."	Matthew 25:32 (NKJV)
"And Jesus, when He came out, saw a great multitude and was moved with compassion for them, because they were like sheep not having a shepherd. So He began to teach them many things."	Mark 6:34 (NKJV)
"What man of you, having a hundred sheep, if he loses one of them, does not leave the ninety-nine in the wilderness, and go after the one which is lost until he finds it?"	Luke 15:4 (NKJV)
[To Peter]: "Feed my sheep."	John 21:17 (NKJV)

Safe in His Hands

JOHN 10:28–29 ***And I give them eternal life, and they shall never perish; neither shall anyone snatch them out of My hand . . . And no one is able to snatch them out of My Father's hand. (NKJV)***

Jesus the Good Shepherd taught often about His relationship with His sheep, He **raised the stakes** with regard to the protection and security He offered them. "I give them eternal life, and they shall never perish," He said. "Neither shall anyone snatch them out of My hand" (John 10:28 NKJV). If you ever had any doubts about your security in Christ, this passage should lay them to rest. Your security has nothing to do with your strength or ability to hold on to Christ. It has everything to do with His strength and ability to keep hold of you. When you place your faith in Him, He gives you eternal life.

go to

thieves nor robbers
John 10:1, 8

wolf
John 10:12

eternal
something that is everlasting, perpetual, and neverending

And just to make doubly sure that we understand just how secure we are, Jesus added the assurance: "No one is able to snatch them out of My Father's hand" (John 10:29 NKJV). It gets even better. When Jesus categorically stated, "I and My Father are one" (John 10:30 NKJV), He affirmed the fact that both the Father and the Son are equally committed to the absolute protection of Jesus' sheep and the preservation of their eternal life. Since the Father and the Son are one in essence, they are united in their protective power over us, guaranteeing beyond the shadow of any doubt our safety and security as members of the flock. It's a double team of protection and security; no thief can "kill, steal, or destroy" those who rest securely in the hands of the Father and the Son.

"I and My Father are one." Consider what a big deal (and how offensive) that claim was to the Jews who were listening to Jesus that day. They immediately "took up stones…to stone Him" (John 10:31 NKJV). When Jesus asked them why they wanted to kill Him, they responded, "Because You, being a Man, make Yourself God" (John 10:33 NKJV). There was a lot that they didn't understand about Jesus, but they understood that much: He was claiming to be God. He was making promises on behalf of God. Prophets had done that before, but Jesus was making those promises in the first person! "Neither shall anyone snatch them out of *My* hand." But to be secure in His hand, you first must come to terms with the huge claims He is making.

key point

When we place our faith in Him, He gives us **eternal** life. Our security as Jesus' "sheep" resides in the fact that as the "good shepherd" Jesus vows the eternal safety of His sheep. Neither thieves nor robbers, nor the wolf, symbolic of Satan, demons, and Satan's servants, can ultimately harm us.

what others say

Herschel Hobbs

Note that we do not hold on to Jesus or the Father. We are held by them. And before either man, thing, or devil can recapture to destroy us, such must overcome both the Son and the Father. And, of course, that is impossible.[7]

Money-Back Guarantee

2 Corinthians 1:21–22 ***Now He who establishes us with you in Christ and has anointed us is God, who also has sealed us and given us the Spirit in our hearts as a guarantee.*** (NKJV)

In ancient times—and even later—a king carried an official seal, often a signet ring, which served as his "signature" or badge of authority. When sending an official letter or document, he would seal it with a drip of candle wax, then use the signet ring to make his unique impression in the soft wax. That official seal spoke of the **authority** of the contents of the document. The seal ensured that the document was treated with the utmost care. It ensured that it got where it was going and was opened only by the person to whom it was addressed. It said, "This is no ordinary letter, to be jostled around with the others in the mail bag." The king's seal guaranteed that all the power of the king's office stood behind whatever the document said.

According to 2 Corinthians, we have the seal of the King of heaven on us. That seal represents all the authority of God's faithfulness to us. It guarantees that we are going to arrive in the place where God would have us to be. And though it may feel that we are being jostled around here on earth, our delivery is sure: we have the King's seal on us.

If we have God's seal on the outside, what we have on the inside, according to Paul, is "the Spirit in our hearts as a guarantee." That word "guarantee" is translated from the Greek *arrabon*. Some translations use the word "pledge" here. The word means "down payment," or "earnest money"—an amount paid when a deal is struck, as a guarantee that the full amount will be paid later. The experience of the Holy Spirit in our hearts is a down payment on the experience of God that we will enjoy more fully in heaven.

The seal of God on you is the guarantee that He is going to make good on His promise. All His power, all His riches stand behind that seal. Don't gloss over the significance of the fact that God is the One who makes the pledge in this deal. We human beings aren't the ones who are making the down payment. We aren't being a little bit obedient today with the promise of being even more obedient in the future. No, God makes a promise to us, and He seals it with the His Spirit as a down payment!

go to

experience of the Holy Spirit
Acts 1:8

authority
the right to control, command, or determine

something to ponder

go to

killed a man
Exodus 2:12

humble servant
Exodus 32:32

bizarre events
Jonah 1:17

what others say

John Walvoord and Roy Zuck

A seal on a document in New Testament times identified it and indicated its owner, who would "protect" it. So too, in salvation, the Holy Spirit, like a seal, confirms that Christians are identified with Christ and are God's property.[8]

Under Construction

PHILIPPIANS 1:6 ***Being confident of this very thing, that He who has begun a good work in you will complete it until the day of Jesus Christ. (NKJV)***

We are all works in progress, undergoing a radical overhaul of our lives from the inside out. It's easy to get discouraged in the Christian life. There are times when you feel as though you aren't making any progress. You fall back into old habits. You give in to things you thought you had conquered. Try as you might, you just can't or don't live the way you want to live. You feel like giving up. But you have this promise: God will never give up on you.

God never gave up on Moses, even though he had a violent, uncontrollable, explosive temper—so much so that he killed a man in cold blood. God sent him to the back side of a blistering hot desert to herd sheep, quite a contrast from the plush surroundings in which he grew up as a member of Pharaoh's household. But in the crucible of that hardship, an impetuous angry man was gradually transformed into a humble servant. God was indeed bringing to completion the "good work" He had begun.

God never gave up on Jonah. Jonah recoiled at the thought that God might save the repentant Ninevites, whose violent ways were legendary. Yet God patiently continued to work in Jonah's life, even arranging some rather bizarre events in the process, all with the aim of bringing to completion the "good work" He had begun. For that matter, He completed an incredible work in the lives of the Ninevites too.

He is doing the same in you. The process might be painful at times. You may have some hard lessons to learn along the way. But you can always be confident in the knowledge that you are one day closer to perfection—because you're one day closer to the "day of Christ Jesus." You can be confident that no matter what happens to you, no matter how tough your challenges or distressing your difficulties, "He who has begun a good work in you will complete it" (Philippians 1:6 NKJV).

Paul's confidence isn't based on a belief that his Philippian friends have "got what it takes," or that they possess the character and perseverance to perfect themselves. His confidence is in the God who is at work in their lives. It's a theme we've seen over and over in these promises: God is faithful to carry through on what He promises, to finish what He's started.

> **what others say**
>
> **Gerald Sittser**
>
> We do not know how things will work out, but we know that God will work them out. . . . Sometimes we will choose to put God first; sometimes we will choose not to. Still, somehow, God will work things out for our good, both because that is his nature and because that is his will for our lives.[9]

Living Well; Dying Well

2 Timothy 4:18 ***And the Lord will deliver me from every evil work and preserve me for His heavenly kingdom. To Him be glory forever and ever. Amen! (NKJV)***

Paul lived well. He also died well. Paul's secret to victorious living and dying is very simple: He understood his role, and understood God's role in his life. As Christ's servant, Paul willingly submitted himself to whatever God wanted to do in and through his life. When things went well, he praised God for His goodness in blessing him with such good fortune. When things went badly for the apostle, he praised God for His goodness in sustaining him through the trials. In a word, whatever life threw at him, he took it—and he took it with joy! God either did it or allowed it, all for Paul's ultimate good.

Paul's willing submission to God is most obvious in the closing chapter of 2 Timothy. Many scholars believe that this is the last of Paul's letters, written in the same year he was executed by the Emperor Nero. This was a much harsher imprisonment than some of his earlier imprisonments. He wasn't under house arrest, but rather he was chained in a dungeon, perhaps the famous Mamertine prison in Rome, where he was treated as a common criminal. His

go to

ultimate good
Romans 8:28

go to

deserted him
2 Timothy 4:16

imminent execution
2 Timothy 4:6

friends deserted him. Onesiphorus was one of the few friends who "was not ashamed" of Paul's chains and came to visit him in prison. The fact that Onesiphorus had to seek Paul out "very zealously" (2 Timothy 1:17–18 NKJV) suggests that Paul was pretty hard to find, deep in the prison.

Paul knew that he was facing imminent execution. But he was completely comfortable with what was happening. He spoke of his coming death as one would speak of an upcoming departure for an exciting journey. Paul was heaven-bound. He would close his eyes here, and open his eyes there. And if God wanted to take him to heaven now, that was just fine with Paul.

He could view life with such perfect submission because his confidence was unshaken that God would deliver him in safety to his ultimate destination. He knew God was faithful, even in that cold, damp prison. You, too, can learn to live with that liberating assurance. It begins by coming to grips with the faithfulness of God, who promises to "deliver you from every evil work, and preserve [you] for His heavenly kingdom" (2 Timothy 4:18 NKJV). Once you do, you will live well, and one day die well.

what others say

Larry Richards

The confident Christian does not see himself or herself as perfected. . . . Our confidence is not in ourselves or our achievements, but in his power to constantly lift us beyond ourselves.[10]

Dr. Lawrence J. Crabb, Jr.

Godly character can be defined as confidence in God that one day things will be as they should be. In this present life we groan—something is wrong with everything. But in the life to come, we will feast—nothing will be wrong with anything.[11]

Chapter Wrap-Up

- Sin is a hard master; but when Christ is your master, you find that His yoke is easy and His burden light.
- The pay we have earned with our deeds is death. God doesn't pay us according to what we deserve, however. He promises and freely gives us eternal life.
- Your security is based on God's grip on you, not your grip on God.
- God is always working in your life to complete what He has started.

Study Questions

1. In what way is "slavery to obedience" actually a kind of freedom?
2. Why did so many disciples desert Jesus after He said, "Unless you eat the flesh of the Son of Man and drink His blood, you have no life in you"?
3. What does it mean to say "You are Abraham's seed"?
4. Why did Jesus ask such embarrassing questions of the woman at the well?
5. What is God's down payment on eternal life?

Chapter 18: Promises to Meet Emotional Needs

Chapter Highlights:
- Promise of healing
- Promise of joy
- Promise of plenty
- Promise to protect
- Promise of peace

Healing for the Heartbroken

PSALM 147:3
He heals the brokenhearted
And binds up their wounds. *(NKJV)*

After years of weeping, the people of Psalm 147 were now singing. They'd had a lot to weep about. Because of their hard-hearted rebellion, God had removed His protective hand and allowed the Babylonians to march through their cities, level their beloved Jerusalem, destroy their temple, and take many of them as captives to Babylon. Of course, there remained a remnant who loved the Lord and remained faithful to Him. But they got caught in the whirlwind of the Babylonian invasion and were taken hostage along with everyone else. For seventy years the people of God languished in a foreign land, cut off from the land of the promise that had been so central to their sense of self.

go to

remnant
2 Kings 19:30

Jeremiah
Jeremiah 25:11

We get a glimpse of just how heartbroken these faithful people were when we observe Daniel defying the king's decree and praying three times a day, every day, with his windows opened, facing Jerusalem. Daniel, like everyone else, wanted desperately to go home. Psalm 137 is one of the great poems of that period of exile. "By the rivers of Babylon, there we sat down, yea, we wept when we remembered Zion. How shall we sing the LORD's song in a foreign land?" they lamented (Psalm 137:1, 4 NKJV).

God heard their cries. Just as He promised through the prophet Jeremiah, He brought his people back into the land. The weeping of the exile psalms gives way to the joy of Psalm 147.

"The LORD builds up Jerusalem; He gathers together the outcasts of Israel" (Psalm 147:2 NKJV). Sobs were replaced by singing. Depression gave way to delight. The Israelites now knew for sure that God "heals the brokenhearted and binds up their wounds" (Psalm 147:3 NKJV).

key point

God "counts the number of the stars; He calls them all by name" (Psalm 147:4 NKJV). He certainly is "mighty in power" (Psalm 147:5 NKJV). He can handle our problems when we cannot. This is the God who promises to heal the brokenhearted, to bind up the wounds of those who are hurting.

When your heart is broken, things look bleak and hopeless. But just wait. God knows your needs. He hears your cries. Even when His people were in exile—and even though it was their own fault—God did not abandon His people. He has promised He will not abandon you either. God is powerful enough to scatter the stars into space, yet gentle enough to heal your broken heart.

what others say

Ray Stedman

So God is forever putting us in situations where we are way over our depth and are forced to abandon hope in all human resources and cry out, "Lord, save me." . . . The God who loves us is delivering us up to death in order that we might trust, not in happy circumstances or pleasant surroundings, but in the Lord of life . . . [1]

Joy in His Presence

Psalm 16:11
You will show me the path of life;
In Your presence is fullness of joy;
At Your right hand are pleasures forevermore. (NKJV)

David was an emotional man. He knew exhilarating highs and debilitating lows. Many of his psalms take the reader on an emotional roller-coaster ride. Psalm 16 is one of them.

David's was not an easy life; he was constantly aware of the fact that he depended on God for his protection. Psalm 16 is one of four psalms that begins with the plea, "Preserve me" or "Preserve my life." He was a man hunted by his enemies and hounded by his fears. Yet he had God, and that made all the difference. When he turned his gaze toward God, his confidence was renewed. "I have set the LORD always before me," he wrote. "Because He is at my right hand I shall not be moved" (Psalm 16:8 NKJV). That confidence leads to genuine joy and delight: "In your presence is fullness of joy; at your right hand are pleasures forevermore" (Psalm 16:11 NKJV).

But how could he be so sure that his God was the right God? What was the source of such confidence in the face of continual conflict, such determination in the face of nagging doubts? The hope of the resurrection. Look at verse 10: "You will not leave my soul in **Sheol**, nor will You allow Your Holy One to see corruption" (NKJV). Peter, in his famous sermon at **Pentecost**, interpreted Psalm 16:10 as a prophetic utterance regarding the resurrection of Christ: David, Peter argued, "spoke concerning the resurrection of the Christ, that His soul was not left in Hades, nor did His flesh see corruption. This Jesus God has raised up, of which we are all witnesses" (Acts 2:31–32 NKJV). No other god, guru, or prophet could claim those credentials.

Sheol
the place of dead or departed spirits; Hades or hell

Pentecost
a Jewish feast held fifty days after Passover. During the Pentecost immediately after Jesus' death and resurrection, the Holy Spirit descended on Peter and the other disciples, and they "spoke in tongues."

David knew in whom he believed! So do we. Because of Christ's resurrection, we know that we are on the path of life—an abundant life today and eternal life tomorrow. When we enter His presence, God promises to flood our souls with a joy potent enough to sustain us even during the times of our deepest despair and discouragement. Strength for today; "pleasures forevermore" for tomorrow. That is what God promises to all who place their faith in the resurrected Christ. At His right hand are pleasures forever. In the meantime, because God is at our right hand, we stand firm and will not be moved (Psalm 16:8). No matter what!

something to ponder

what others say

Gene Getz

David was not a perfect man. But he had a proper view of God, which affected his own heart and caused him to be a person God could use, in spite of his human weaknesses. What about you? What is your view of God?[2]

The Not-So-Lonely Leader

DEUTERONOMY 31:8 ***And the LORD, He is the One who goes before you. He will be with you, He will not leave you nor forsake you; do not fear nor be dismayed.*** *(NKJV)*

Joshua was given a huge responsibility—to carry on the legacy of leadership laid down by Moses. It had been forty years since Joshua first distinguished himself in the eyes of Moses and the rest of the children of Israel. Of the twelve spies who first scouted out the Promised Land, only Joshua and Caleb believed God's promises and voted to invade, regardless of the fortified cities and the giants in the land. The people demanded furiously to return to Egypt, then they threatened to stone Joshua, but he stood his ground: "The LORD will bring us into this land," Joshua insisted, "[He] is with us" (14:8–9 NKJV). Neither Moses nor God ever forgot Joshua's faithfulness.

go to

Joshua and Caleb
Numbers 13—14

milk and honey
Numbers 14:7–8

A new day was about to dawn on the people of Israel. Finally they were ready to possess the land their parents should have possessed forty years earlier—a land flowing with milk and honey. As their years of wilderness wandering gradually ground to a halt, so did Moses. Now well advanced in years, he knew he was about to die. He needed to make it official: Joshua was to be his successor.

Joshua was a bold one. Nevertheless, the thought of leading the nation of Israel had to be daunting even for Joshua. Having been Moses' right-hand man for decades, Joshua surely understood what he was getting into. He must have faced the loneliness of this leadership position with hesitation. So Moses made him this promise: "The LORD, He is the One who goes before you. He will be with you, He will not leave you nor forsake you; do not fear nor be dismayed" (Deuteronomy 31:8 NKJV). Moses, in effect, was speaking back the same promise to Joshua that Joshua had spoken to the Israelites so many years before: *God is with you! You have nothing to fear! Go forward boldly!*

something to ponder

God makes this same promise to us, "He Himself has said, 'I will never leave you nor forsake you'" (Hebrews 13:5 NKJV). Because of His affirmation, we can say with confidence, "The LORD is my helper; I will not fear. What can man do to me?" (Hebrews 13:6 (NKJV). God makes an indelible point: There is absolutely no way whatsoever that He will ever leave, abandon, turn His back, forget, or ignore you. In the words of Jesus, "Lo, I am with you always, even to the end of the age" (Matthew 28:20 NKJV).

what others say

John Marrant

(when seized by a Cherokee warrior during colonial times): He asked me how I did live. I said I was supported by the Lord.

> He asked me how I slept. I answered that the Lord provided. He asked what preserved me from being devoured by wild beasts? I replied, the Lord Jesus kept me from them. He stood astonished, " . . . He must be a fine man; where is he?" I replied, "He is here present."[3]

rhetorical question
a question asked solely to produce an effect or to make an assertion and not to elicit a reply

Some of the Israelites' Grumblings

The Situation	The Complaint	Scripture
An angry Pharaoh makes the Israelite's lives harder	"You have made us abhorrent in the eyes of Pharaoh."	Exodus 5:20 (NKJV)
Pharaoh's army approaching to kill the Israelites	"Because there were no graves in Egypt, have you taken us away to die in the wilderness?"	Exodus 14:11 (NKJV)
Food shortage	"Oh that we had died by the hand of the LORD in the land of Egypt, when we sat by pots of meat, and when we ate bread to the full."	Exodus 16:3 (NKJV)
Water shortage	"Why is it you have brought us up out of Egypt, to kill us and our children and our livestock with thirst?"	Exodus 17:3 (NKJV)
Tired of eating only manna without any meat to go with it.	"We remember the fish which we ate freely in Egypt, the cucumbers, the melons, the leeks, the onions, and the garlic."	Numbers 11:4 (NKJV)

Lingering Lonesomeness

PSALM 27:10
When my father and my mother forsake me,
Then the LORD will take care of me. (NKJV)

Psalm 27 begins with two questions and ends with two commands—actually, one question and one command, each repeated twice. David asks, "The LORD is my light and my salvation: Whom shall I fear? The LORD is the strength of my life; Of whom shall I be afraid?" (Psalm 27:1). It's a **rhetorical question**, of course. The obvious answer is, "nobody." David's life, you will remember, was full of people of whom he might have been afraid, and nobody would have blamed him. Goliath. Saul. His own rebellious son Absalom. But with the Lord as his light and his strength, David had

imperative mood
mood of the verb used in commands, requests, etc., as in *Listen! Go!*

no one to fear. Indeed, he lived a remarkably brave life, which is one of the reasons he has always been such a well-loved figure.

Having begun with the question "Whom shall I fear?" Psalm 27 finishes with a command that is repeated for emphasis: "Wait on the LORD; be of good courage, and He shall strengthen your heart; Wait, I say, on the LORD." We aren't very good at waiting. That must be why this sentence is in the **imperative mood**. It's not an observation, but a command.

David, as you know, was called upon to wait on the Lord more than most of us. When Samuel anointed him as king, David was probably sixteen or so. He was about thirty before he actually wore the crown and sat on the throne of Israel. That was almost fourteen years of living with an unfulfilled destiny. That was a lot of waiting. Meanwhile, most of the time David's life was in danger from one enemy or another.

But the light of God's presence always broke through, both before David became king and after. The Lord *was* his "light and…salvation," the "strength" of his life (Psalm 27:1 NKJV). He watched as his enemies stumbled and fell (Psalm 27:2 NKJV). He faced his enemies' attacks with confidence (Psalm 27:3 NKJV), for God always rose to the occasion and kept David safe, allowing him to sing songs of victory even in the presence of his enemies (Psalm 27:6 NKJV). Even when those closest to him rejected him and he felt the ache of loneliness—even if his parents were to forsake him—David could confidently rest in the promise of God: "the LORD will take care of me" (Psalm 27:10 NKJV). David knew that God always keeps His promises. He could know beyond the shadow of any doubt that God never would forsake him (Psalm 27:10 NKJV).

something to ponder

Fear and loneliness don't have to be our enemies. They can be our friends *if* in the midst of our fear and loneliness we learn to wait.

what others say

Dr. F. B. Meyer

David's lifelong habit of waiting upon God for direction and guidance is instructive and stimulating. Notice that the successive steps of his career were taken after waiting upon God. The advice which he gives to us all in the psalm which dates from this period was the outcome of his own deepest experience: "Wait on the Lord . . ."[4]

Seeing Through a Different Set of Eyes

Psalm 17:15
As for me, I will see Your face in righteousness;
I shall be satisfied when I awake in Your likeness. *(NKJV)*

go to

awesome presence of God
1 Samuel 17:26

vision dazzled
Acts 9:3, 9

They each saw something. And what they saw changed their lives forever.

Abraham "waited for the city which has foundations, whose builder and maker is God" (Hebrews 11:10 NKJV).

Moses "looked to the reward" that awaited him (Hebrews 11:26 NKJV).

The writer to the Hebrews joined the party by looking for the city "to come" (Hebrews 13:14 NKJV).

Paul was granted an ever-so-rare glimpse into heaven, and blurted out the refrain, "Eye has not seen, nor ear heard, nor have entered into the heart of man the things which God has prepared for those who love Him" (1 Corinthians 2:9 NKJV).

Peter got into the act, looking "for new heavens and a new earth in which righteousness dwells" (2 Peter 3:13 NKJV). He even invited us, his readers, to live a blameless life, since we are "looking forward to these things," our future, eternal home (2 Peter 3:14 NKJV).

When John saw laid out before his bedazzled eyes the panorama of prophecy, he was so overcome with his heavenly vision that he stopped mid-sentence and "wept much" (Revelation 5:4 NKJV), because he still couldn't see as much as he wanted to see.

Then there's King David. He glimpsed something so grand and glorious it made his trials and tribulations melt away into insignificance, because of the grandeur and glory of what was to come. David could be content in the present because he counted on the future fulfillment of the promise that "I will see Your face in righteousness; I shall be satisfied when I awake in Your likeness" (Psalm 17:15 NKJV).

David had a knack for seeing what other people couldn't see. When the Israelite army was overawed by the presence of Goliath, David saw the much more awesome presence of God, and it made Goliath look rather puny. Nevertheless, David longed for the day when his vision of God would be completed with a face-to-face encounter. He was ready to have his vision dazzled.

go to

Absalom
2 Samuel 13–19

forty days fasting
Matthew 4:1–11

One day we, too, will see God's face. And when we do, "we shall be like Him, for we shall see Him as He is" (1 John 3:2 NKJV). In the meantime, what do you see? Do you see the magnitude of the problems you face, or do you see the magnitude of God? Everything depends on what you choose to look at. There's another world that's even more real than the world you see around you. When you get a glimpse of it—a little foretaste of the full vision you'll get in heaven—it changes everything about the way you live here on earth.

what others say

Harold Fickett

As Christians you and I have heard the voice of Jesus through the ministry of the Holy Spirit in our lives. And this has been wonderful. But when he comes for us, it will be even better. For then each of us will be privileged to look into His face.[5]

Food for Thought

Psalm 63:5
My soul shall be satisfied as with marrow and fatness,
And my mouth shall praise You with joyful lips. (NKJV)

Marrow and fatness. For David, his soul's communion with God was a source of incredible richness. You wouldn't have known it from looking at his outward situation, though. As you may remember from the *Prayers* section of this book, David wrote Psalm 63 while he was in the Judean wilderness, having been run out of his capital city by his own rebellious son Absalom. In the hills near the Dead Sea, the wilderness of Judah is some of the most forbidding terrain in the world. Desert conditions prevail; in the summertime, temperatures above 110 degrees Fahrenheit are common. So are snakes and scorpions. Trees, on the other hand, are exceedingly uncommon. There is some shade to be had in the caves of the region, if you're willing to share it with the snakes and scorpions. The wilderness where David found himself, by the way, was the same wilderness where Jesus spent forty days fasting before He began His ministry.

You can understand why David described his situation as "a dry and thirsty land where there is no water" (Psalm 63:1 NKJV). You can take it figuratively if you want to, but there was a very literal truth to what he was saying. In the middle of that land, where the earth seemingly yielded up no good thing, David enjoyed fatness and marrow. Spiritually, he couldn't have enjoyed richer fare if he had still been in his palace.

Once he was stripped of power, position, palace, and perks, once he was forced to flee like a fugitive, once he had nothing else to hold on to, not even his own family, *that's* when he learned: "My soul follows close behind You; Your right hand upholds me" (Psalm 63:8 NKJV).

Sometimes when you have been reduced to nothing, you discover that all along you had everything . . . and still do. God shows Himself strong in our weakness. He reveals His riches in our poverty. Every now and then, you find yourself in a "dry and weary land where there is no water." The thirst you experience in that place may be just what you needed to spur you on to seek out the living water that God promises. The hunger you experience in that place may be just the thing that sends you God's promise of the bread of life. God promises to satisfy your soul, not with dry crusts, but with marrow and fatness.

apply it

what others say

Stuart Briscoe

When you find yourself in prison, or in a hospital bed, or tied to a kitchen sink, or anchored to an office desk, it's a good thing to remember what God has been doing in your life instead of moaning about your present status.[6]

Yours for the Asking

JAMES 1:5 ***If any of you lacks wisdom, let him ask of God, who gives to all liberally and without reproach, and it will be given to him.*** *(NKJV)*

There are certain requests that contain their own answers within themselves. In the Wizard of Oz, the Scarecrow, the Tin Man, and the Lion each asked for what he already had. The Scarecrow asked for a brain, but he had already demonstrated considerable intelligence simply to find the Wizard in the first place. His request for a brain was evidence that he already had one. The Tin Man asked for a heart, because he wanted to be able to love. But that desire to love

liberally
freely or generously

present perfect tense
the verb tense indicating an action that is already over and done at present moment

was evidence that he already had a heart that was already loving; otherwise, why would he be interested in love at all? The Cowardly Lion's bravery had already seen the traveling foursome through many dangers; when he asked the Wizard for courage, the Wizard had only to point out to the Lion how he had already displayed it.

The request in James 1:5 (NKJV) works in a similar way. "If any of you lacks wisdom, let him ask of God, who gives to all **liberally** and without reproach, and it will be given to him. Do you desire to be wise? Then you have already headed down the path to wisdom. Having the right desires—and pursuing them—is a large part of wisdom. When God granted Solomon one request, Solomon asked for wisdom. The fact that he asked for wisdom above anything else he might have asked for demonstrates that he was already pretty wise. Sure, the Scriptures quote God as saying plainly, "Because you have asked this thing...I have done according to your words" (1 Kings 3:11–12 NKJV). Notice the **present perfect tense** there—*I have done*. It's already accomplished. Perhaps God gave Solomon wisdom *before* he asked for it, not *because* he asked. Perhaps Solomon's request did not *result* in wisdom, but merely *revealed* that God had already given it.

something to ponder

James promises those of us who are overwhelmed with "various trials" (James 1:2 NKJV) that if we ask God for wisdom He will respond generously. Yet anyone wise enough to ask God for insight is no doubt already trying to see his situation from God's perspective. God gives wisdom "to all liberally." And why wouldn't He? God desires that His children should be wise. If you ask Him for the very thing He most wants to give you, surely He will give it gladly.

what others say

J. Grant Howard

God has revealed in His Word through precept and principle what He wants us to be and do. He has made it clear to us, and our responsibility is to know it and do it. At the same time, we live in His world and He has furnished us with numerous other factors that He uses to call our attention to the precepts and principles in His Word.[7]

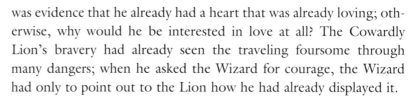

A Preserving Promise

Psalm 119:50
This is my comfort in my affliction,
For Your word has given me life. (NKJV)

hostile environment
Daniel 3:8–30

Psalter
another name for the book of Psalms

Psalm 119 is the longest psalm in the **Psalter**; indeed, it's the longest chapter in the entire Bible, by a pretty wide margin. Its theme is the wondrousness of God's Word—"your Law" as it usually phrases it. The psalm shows the benefits of God's Word from every possible angle. Many scholars believe the author of this psalm is Ezra. A little background information on this important Old Testament figure helps explain why this seems a good conjecture.

When God's people returned to Jerusalem from their Babylonian exile, it was the priest and scribe Ezra who reintroduced them to the Scripture that had been so long neglected. "All the people gathered together as one man in the open square" (Nehemiah 8:1 NKJV) to hear Ezra the priest read from the Scriptures. "Ezra opened the book . . . and when he opened it, all the people stood up" (Nehemiah 8:5 NKJV). Every day for seven days, Ezra stood in the square to read, and every day the people stood to listen. Such was the magnitude of their seventy-year-long hunger for God's Word. Ezra shared their hunger, and he was devoted to helping to satisfy it.

Psalm 119 was obviously written by a person who revered the Scriptures. The psalmist "delighted in" God's Word, "loved" it, "obeyed" it, "mediated on" it, and "rejoiced in" it. Throughout the psalm it is evident that the psalmist had lived under life-threatening duress, as he notes—"They almost made an end of me on earth" (Psalm 119:87 NKJV). Such language suggests life in the religiously hostile environment of Babylon, again pointing to Ezra as the possible author.

When he felt overwhelmed, when life seemed confusing to him, when he didn't know where else to turn, the psalmist turned to the promises of the Bible: "This is my comfort in my affliction, for Your word has given me life" (Psalm 119:50 NKJV). There's a priceless principle for us in those words. When you hold the Bible, you are holding a book of God's promises. When the circumstances in your life become overwhelming, when everything in your world seems confusing, do what Ezra did. Review and remind yourself of God's promises. There you will find God's strength. There you will discover truth to which you can cling. There you will receive refreshment for your weary soul. There, in His promises, God will meet you, comfort you, and preserve and hold your life together.

> **what others say**
>
> **Tim LaHaye**
>
> If you read the writings of men or look at the problems that surround you, joy will turn to fear, dread or sometimes depression. . . . It is the Word of God that puts joy in your heart, regardless of the circumstances.[8]

Shalom!

JOHN 14:27 ***Peace I leave with you, My peace I give to you; not as the world gives do I give to you. Let not your heart be troubled, neither let it be afraid.*** *(NKJV)*

The streets of Jerusalem and other Israeli cities resound with the word "Shalom." It's the common greeting among Israelis, and it means "Peace." It's so much a part of the Jewish culture that their capital city has the word built right into it—Jeru*salem*, the city of peace. Tragically, it remains to this day a city of war.

The world cannot produce lasting, life-sustaining peace. That's why Jesus offered His disciples a different kind of peace. "Peace I leave with you, My peace I give to you; not as the world gives do I give to you" (John 14:27 NKJV). It's a good thing He didn't give peace as the world gives it. The world's fickle, fragile, fleeting peace doesn't ultimately do us a whole lot of good. Jeremiah complained of the false peace of the world, which doesn't really address conflict at its source: "They have also healed the hurt of My people slightly, Saying, 'Peace, peace!' When there is no peace" (Jeremiah 6:14 NKJV).

When Jesus offered His promise of peace to the disciples, His timing was perfect. It was the night before He went to the cross. Their lives were about to be completely upended. They would shortly be in desperate need of Jesus' unique brand of peace. So that's what He gave them. Later, on the evening of His resurrection, He greeted them with the words, "Peace to you" (Luke 24:36 NKJV). Sandwiched in between was the death and burial of their master and friend. The whole point of that violent, seemingly senseless death and that incredible resurrection was peace—a reconciliation between God and man after centuries of conflict and struggle.

We cannot produce this kind of peace; we can only receive it. The peace that Jesus offers is not based on our own passive temperament or the tranquility of the life we live. It is based solely on the trustworthiness of His Word. The disciples were about to live through the horror of their leader's execution and the very real possibility that they would share His fate. Nevertheless, Jesus offered them peace—and not just the superficial healing that says "Peace, Peace" when there is no peace. When you come to terms with God's trustworthiness you can, to use a popular cliché, "let go and let God." He *will* carry us through the tough times. And it's precisely because of this promise that our hearts need not be troubled; we need not be afraid.

something to ponder

what others say

Josh McDowell

A few months after I made that decision for Christ, a kind of mental peace developed. Don't misunderstand... What I found in this relationship with Jesus wasn't so much the absence of conflict but the ability to cope with it. I wouldn't trade that with anything in the world.[9]

What the Bible Says About

Peace	Scripture
"When a man's ways are pleasing to the LORD, he makes even his enemies to be at peace with him."	Proverbs 16:7 (NKJV)
The Messiah called "The Prince of Peace."	Isaiah 9:6 (NKJV)
"Blessed are the peacemakers."	Matthew 5:9 (NKJV)
"He Himself is our peace."	Ephesians 2:14 (NKJV)
The peace "that surpasses all understanding."	Philippians 4:7 (NKJV)

No God, No Peace; Know God, Know Peace

ISAIAH 26:3

You will keep him in perfect peace,
Whose mind is stayed on You,
Because he trusts in You. *(NKJV)*

As a whole, the people of Israel in the north and Judah in the south were a rebellious lot. Because of their stiff-necked and flagrant

go to

reconciliation
Colossians 1:20

need not be afraid
1 John 4:18

stiff-necked
Exodus 32:9;
Deuteronomy 9:13;
2 Chronicles 30:8;
Psalm 75:5;
Jeremiah 17:23

go to

suffer the same fate
Matthew 5:45

disobedience, judgment would hit the two nations with the full force of a sledgehammer. As the morality of the two countries continued to slide unabated, the menacing Assyrian Empire continued to expand—an expansion that would swallow up Israel and disperse its people throughout the empire.

A similar judgment would follow in the south. The Babylonians crushed Jerusalem along with its temple, and forced her inhabitants into exile. Talk about a threat to world peace! Tragically, as so often happens, the remaining righteous were forced by circumstance to suffer the same fate as the wicked.

But not forever! Isaiah assured God's people that they could have inner peace even while in the grip of a brutal war and exile. He comforted them with the promise of God's peace: "You will keep him in perfect peace, whose mind is stayed on You, because he trusts in You" (Isaiah 26:3 NKJV). You might say that to have your mind stayed on God *is* perfect peace.

Isaiah told the faithful few not to focus on their immediate pain, but to look higher, to see farther to a hope that burned brighter than anything they were experiencing down here. When their minds settled on God and His purposes, everything they were going through, as hopeless and horrible as it was, would ultimately fade away into irrelevance. A new day was coming. God's will would prevail.

something to ponder

Paul, who would himself lose his head to a Roman sword, wrote to the Christians living under the oppressive of the Roman regime, "I consider that the sufferings of this present time are not worthy to be compared with the glory which shall be revealed in us . . . If we hope for what we do not see, we eagerly wait for it with perseverance" (Romans 8:18, 25 NKJV). Paul knew exactly what Isaiah was talking about. Hope for a better future. Perseverance in the meantime. Those are the words of a man who knew the promise of God's peace! It had everything to do with sharing God's vision. The example set by Paul and Isaiah is worth following. He forces you to ask some important questions: On what is your mind stayed? Where is your trust? Where is your focus?

what others say

Elisabeth Elliot

Our enemy delights in disquieting us. Our Savior and Helper delights in quieting us. . . . The choice is ours. It depends on

> our willingness to see everything in God, receive all from His hand, accept with gratitude just the portion and the cup He offers.[10]

Chapter Wrap-Up

- When your heart is broken, everything looks bleak. But God never abandons His people.
- When God is present, you have nothing to fear. And God is always present.
- When we ask for wisdom, God promises to supply it every time.
- God's Word is a source of comfort in affliction.

Study Questions

1. How does a vision of the eternal change the way you live your life on earth?
2. On what grounds do you have confidence that God always answers prayers for wisdom?
3. Why do scholars believe that Ezra wrote Psalm 119?
4. What was Jeremiah talking about when he complained of those who say "Peace, Peace" when there is no peace?
5. What does is it mean to say, "To have your mind stayed on God is perfect peace"?

Chapter 19: Promises to Meet Spiritual Needs

Chapter Highlights:

- **Promise to forgive**
- **Promise to provide**
- **Promise of belonging**
- **God's promises never pass away**

Escape Route

1 CORINTHIANS 10:13 ***No temptation has overtaken you except such as is common to man; but God is faithful, who will not allow you to be tempted beyond what you are able, but with the temptation will also make the way of escape, that you may be able to bear it.*** *(NKJV)*

Corinth could truly be called, "Sin City." It was a wealthy city, and a port city, with every vice you might imagine in a place where sailors come for shore leave. Idolatry flourished, fueled by Corinth's dozen pagan temples employing over a thousand religious prostitutes. Such was Corinth's reputation for debauchery that elsewhere in the ancient, pagan world, especially wicked people were referred to as displaying "Corinthian morals."

The Christians in Corinth must have felt that they were under constant attack. Just walking down the street would have been a barrage of sensual stimulation. It was to these believers that Paul wrote the reassuring, and yet challenging, words, "No temptation has overtaken you except such as is common to man; but God is faithful, who will not allow you to be tempted beyond what you are able, but with the temptation will also make the way of escape, that you may be able to bear it" (1 Corinthians 10:13 NKJV). *I know it seems impossible,* Paul is saying. *But God does not put you in situations in which the temptation is genuinely too much to bear. He always provides a way out.*

When it comes to temptation, we are all in the same boat. Sometimes when you are faced with an opportunity to sin, it feels as if nobody could possibly understand what you're going through—as if you've got nobody to talk to. But whatever it is, it's a common temptation. Others have fallen, others have resisted. You have no reason not to be among those who resist. On the flip side, this truth tells us that we ought to be encouraging one another. When others fall, you can and should lift them up, realizing that it could have been you.

experienced every temptation
Hebrews 4:15

succumb
to give way, yield, or surrender

Secondly, God is faithful to strengthen you if you turn away from the temptation and toward Him. It also helps to know that when He walked the earth, Jesus experienced every temptation you face. There is always a way out. You always have the option of saying "No." There's no reason you have to fall into the shame and disappointment of surrendering to temptation.

There's an important point to be made here. In the encouragement of this promise, there is also implied a challenge and a warning. "The devil made me do it" simply won't fly. When you **succumb** to temptation, it's because you choose to surrender, not because we have been overcome.

God promises to give us the capacity to "say 'no!'" Although the appeal to sin may seem too enticing to resist, the power is ours to stand firm. God will always provide us with "a way out," an escape route. At times, in the face of especially strong and relentless temptations, we will have no choice but to "flee" (2 Timothy 2:22 NKJV).

what others say

Paul Van Gorder

> Not only does God put a limit, a boundary upon the temptation, but He also makes a way of escape. . . . if the heart condition is right, and we are in utter dependence upon Him, the temptation will not be too strong for us.[1]

One-Two Punch

JAMES 4:7 ***Therefore submit to God. Resist the devil and he will flee from you.*** *(NKJV)*

God promises that you have the ability to put Satan on the run. It's a two-step process, a one-two punch. First, "submit to God." Second, "resist the devil." The result is inevitable: the devil will flee from you.

That word "submit" was originally a military term. It speaks of men aligning themselves under their commanding officer, ready to obey his every order. We usually think of submission as a kind of passivity, but this definition reminds us that there is a submission that is actually a readiness for action. As is clear from this passage, to submit to God means you're ready to resist, or take a stand against the devil.

Some wildlife experts have said that if it becomes obvious that you can't avoid a conflict with a shark or a bear, your best bet is to stand your ground and punch it in the nose in hopes that it will flee. A similar principle is at work in this promise. The difference is that whereas you *hope* the grizzly runs away, you have all the confidence of God's Word that the devil will flee if you stand your ground. The word James used was *feugo*. It's the root of the English word "fugitive." Submit to God, resist the devil, and the devil has no choice but to run and hide, like an outlaw fleeing from a posse.

Jesus underwent intense temptation during His forty days in the wilderness. But he sent Satan running by submitting to God and resisting Satan's overtures. Not relying on His own arguments against the devil's temptations, He resisted by answering each temptation with a quotation from the Old Testament.

Living in the will of God won't prevent us from Satanic attack. Quite the contrary. Obedient living virtually guarantees that we *will* be tempted by the devil. Satan doesn't worry about disobedient believers; it's the obedient ones that pose a threat to him.

This same submit-resist formula will work for you. You can send Satan spinning out of your life by beginning each day with the prayer: "Lord, help me to live in Your will today." Ask Him to make you aware of seemingly innocent indulgences that will in time form an irresistible pull on your resolve. Then, when the devil does attack, quote Scripture. Jesus quoted verses directly related to the specific temptation. If you don't know the perfect verse, quote James 4:7, reaffirming your submission to God and your will to resist the devil.

go to

quotation from the Old Testament
Matthew 4:4, 8, 12

Satanic attack
Ephesians 6:12

Satan Tempts Jesus

Temptation	Scripture
Told Jesus to prove he is the Son of God by commanding stone to become bread	Luke 4:3–4
If Jesus would worship Satan, Satan would give Jesus authority over all the kingdoms of the world	Luke 4:5–7
Told Jesus to throw himself from pinnacle of the temple, and have the angels save him to prove He is the Son of God	Luke 4:9–12

what others say

Martin Luther

When I find myself assailed by temptation, I forthwith lay hold of some text of the Bible, which Jesus extends to me.[2]

go to

sorrow that God feels
Ephesians 4:30

godly sorrow
2 Corinthians 7:10

don't want to continue in sin
John 14:15

compound word
a word made by combining two other words

self-flagellation
the practice of punishing oneself—literally, whipping oneself

Forgiveness of All, for All

1 John 1:9 ***If we confess our sins, He is faithful and just to forgive us our sins and to cleanse us from all unrighteousness. (NKJV)***

To confess literally means "to say the same thing as another." The Greek word is *homologeo.* It's a **compound word**—*homo* ("same") + *logos* ("word"). When you confess your sins, you are saying the same things about your sin that God says. Confession is a matter of coming back to your senses. You are leaving your warped perspective behind and seeing things from God's perspective—which, of course, is the only true perspective. You stop with your willful blindness, with your self-justification, and you say, "You're right, God." When David confessed his grievous sin with Bathsheba, he acknowledged, "Against You, You only have I sinned" (Psalm 51:4 NKJV). He was seeing things from God's perspective, saying the same thing God said about his sin.

That's where repentance begins—not with a commitment to do better, or with a round of **self-flagellation**. When you are willing to see your situation the way God sees it, God promises to forgive you and to cleanse you from all unrighteousness (1 John 1:9). In true confession, you identify your sin and you begin the process of feeling the same sorrow that God feels as the result of your sin. That kind of "godly sorrow" includes a desire not to repeat the sin. When you love God, after all, you don't want to continue in sin. When you confront your sin with an honest attitude of humble, sorrowful sincerity, God promises to forgive your sins.

Like the rest of the promises of the Bible, this one depends on God's character, not yours. God is *faithful.* He will keep His promise. He is *just.* He always does what's right. The promise doesn't depend on your ability to muster up enough sincerity or enough sorrow. Your feelings aren't the key factor here. Begin to see things the way God sees them, and leave the rest to Him.

something to ponder

There's no reason for you to berate yourself over past sins. If you have confessed them, God has forgiven you and cleansed you from that unrighteousness. You need not fear that God will cast you out of His presence or put you on a shelf with a big label that reads "unusable" every time you fail. God knows how often we fail. That's why He made us this promise.

what others say

Greg Johnson

What if you could start anew each day? As a Christian, of course, you can. The bricks of sin that form a wall between you and God can be torn down and thrown away. A close, open relationship with him is achieved the moment you confess your sins and humbly ask God to forgive you. The slate is supernaturally erased.[3]

go to

Nathan confronted David
1 Samuel 12:1–15

A Point to Ponder

PSALM 32:5
I acknowledged my sin to You,
And my iniquity I have not hidden.
I said, "I will confess my transgressions to the LORD,"
And You forgave the iniquity of my sin. Selah (NKJV)

Selah is an important word to understand when interpreting the psalms. It could be translated, "Pause, and carefully consider what I just said." *Selah* is the psalmist's way of alerting us to the fact that he just made a profound statement, a point to ponder. In Psalm 32, that *Selah* draws our attention to the importance of the promise that comes before.

Psalm 51 is the most familiar of the psalms that came out of David's adultery with Bathsheba and his later repentance. But Psalm 32 is worth a look too. Like Psalm 51, it reflects on David's egregious sin and his repentance.

At least nine months passed between the time David's affair with Bathsheba began and the time he confessed and repented. In the biblical record it appears that the prophet Nathan confronted David right about the time Bathsheba gave birth to the child of their adultery. That time gap is what David is describing in Psalm 32 when he writes, "When I kept silent, my bones grew old through my groaning all the day long. For day and night Your hand was heavy upon me; my vitality was turned into the drought of summer" (Psalm 32:3–4 NKJV). That's what unconfessed sin does to you. It drains the life out of you.

David couldn't take it any longer. He finally broke down and confessed his sin. Psalm 51 records the resulting prayer. How did God

go to

nobody knows
Matthew 25:13

will not pass away
Isaiah 40:8

asymmetry
disproportion of two or more parts

respond to David's earnest confession? David tells the tale: "I said, 'I will confess my transgressions to the LORD,' and You forgave the iniquity of my sin" (Psalm 32:5 NKJV).

There's a striking imbalance in the story of David's sin and repentance. Watching David's sin unravel is like watching a train crash in slow motion. It just gets worse and worse, and you know there's going to be some serious damage before it ever stops. Casual lust gives way to adultery, which results in an inconvenient pregnancy, which leads to murder, which leads to a major cover-up, which surely affected the king's ability to rule effectively.

And then, much more suddenly than it started, it's all over. David confessed his transgression. God forgave the iniquity of his sin. Yes, there are lingering consequences. But the heart issue that gave rise to this cascade of trouble is dealt with, just like that. It's the **asymmetry** of God's promise of forgiveness. He doesn't promise us the opportunity to work off our wrongdoing. He promises to forgive. It doesn't quite add up in our human ledgers. But it doesn't have to. It's the way God chooses to do things. Selah.

what others say

David Seamands

There is no forgiveness from God unless you freely forgive your brother from your heart. And I wonder if we have been too narrow in thinking that "brother" only applies to someone else? What if YOU are the brother or sister who needs to be forgiven, and you need to forgive yourself?[4]

Standing Tall and True

MARK 13:31 ***Heaven and earth will pass away, but My words will by no means pass away.*** (NKJV)

Heaven and earth will pass away. If you doubt it, just turn on the news. between wars and storms and environmental disasters and pandemics and outrageous injustice, this world doesn't look like the kind of place that can last forever. That's not to say that the Apocalypse is just around the corner; nobody knows when that will be. But whether it's ten thousand years from now or tomorrow afternoon, you can be sure this world is coming to an end.

But the Word of God will not pass away. As promised in Scripture, while everything around it shakes to rubble or melts in fire, the

Word of God will stand firm. It's the only firm foundation on which to build your life.

Consider Jesus' parable about the wise and foolish builders. The foolish man built his house on sand. "The rain descended, the floods came, and the winds blew and beat on that house; and it fell. And great was its fall" (Matthew 7:27 NKJV). But the wise man built his house on the rock—not just any rock, but *the* rock. "The rain descended, the floods came, and the winds blew and beat on that house; and it did not fall, for it was founded on the rock" (Matthew 17:25 NKJV). What is that rock? Jesus identified it as "these sayings of Mine." A wise builder builds "his house on the rock" (Matthew 17:24 NKJV).

If you've ever seen a demolition crew, you realize what seems to be a perfectly sturdy and unshakable house is actually a collection of pieces—two-by-fours, sheets of drywall, nails, screws, pipes, wires—held together in just the right way. It's surprising how easily a demolition crew can take a structure apart. It doesn't take much force to see how fragile a sturdy, stable house actually is. It's a miracle it stands when it's built on a rock. On sand, or on a fault line? Forget about it.

When you trust a house to stand, what you're really trusting is its foundation. What are you building your life on? The most careful attention to detail won't do you a bit of good if the whole structure is sitting on shifting sand. Your life is going to last forever. It's going to outlast this world by eons. You'd better take care that you're building on a foundation that will last as long as your life will.

something to ponder

What Jesus Said About

The Word	Scripture
"One jot or one tittle will by no means pass from the law till all is fulfilled."	Matthew 5:18 (NKJV)
"Scripture cannot be broken."	John 10:35 (NKJV)
"Your word is truth."	John 17:17 (NKJV)

what others say

John MacArthur

In a strong statement concerning Scripture, Jesus said, "Scripture cannot be broken." He meant that what God said was true and what was prophesied would take place. He even compared the duration of Scripture to the duration of the universe.[5]

nuances
a subtle difference or distinction in expression or meaning

Four for One

PSALM 19:7–8
The law of the LORD is perfect, converting the soul;
The testimony of the LORD is sure, making wise the simple;
The statutes of the LORD are right, rejoicing the heart;
The commandment of the LORD is pure, enlightening the eyes.
(NKJV)

Psalm 19 reflects God's greatness as revealed in God's world (Psalm 19:1–6 NKJV) and God's Word (Psalm 19:7–11 NKJV). In writing it, David described in some detail the what the Bible contains, the qualities which makes up its character, and God's commitment as to what the Bible can do in our lives—Four Promises for the Price of One.

What the Bible Says

The Bible's Content	The Bible's Character	God's Promise
Law	Perfect	Converts the soul
Testimony	Sure	Makes wise the simple
Statutes	Right	Rejoices the heart
Commandment	Pure	Enlightens the eyes

This passage in Psalm 19 is characterized by "thought rhyme." In what we call "rhyming poetry" in the English tradition, line structure is organized around words with similar sounds—cat–mat, spoon–June–honeymoon. In "thought rhyme," the line structure is organized around words with similar *meanings*. In the chart, you can see that the four lines of Psalm 19:7–8 each begin with a synonym for God's Word: *law, testimony, statutes, commandment.*

In the second column, the four descriptions of the Bible's character are mostly synonymous (though not as closely synonymous as the words in the first column). The Word of God is perfect and pure, right and sure. Looking at the passage this way does two things: First, it demonstrates how carefully and meditatively David dwelled on the Word of God, turning it over and over in his mind. Secondly, the repetition allows the reader to see slight **nuances** of meaning. Rather than having to choose between the idea that God's Word is perfect and the idea that God's Word is sure, the psalm gives us both.

It's that third column of the chart that allows us really to delve into the multi-faceted benefits of the Scriptures' perfect, sure, pure righteousness. It converts the soul. It makes new people out of us. It brings wisdom to those who lack wisdom. The result is a joyful heart and clear vision.

go to

hard-headed
Ezekiel 2:4

In this Psalm, David takes his time. He doesn't mind being redundant. Reading through this book, you may have noticed that the promises of God *are* often redundant. God has a way of promising the same things over and over. There are reasons for that. One is simply that we human beings are hard-headed and need to have things repeated to us. Just as importantly, God repeats His promises because they are so deep and rich you couldn't possibly get to the bottom of them in one try. Meditate on the promises of God. Roll them over and over in your mind and see what new depths you discover. God promises that the Bible will revive us, make us wise, bring joy to our hearts, and teach us how to live—Four for One!

something to ponder

what others say

Elisabeth Elliot

The Scriptures encompass the whole man, his whole world, and reveal the Lord of the universe. In them we have not only a perfect frame of reference, but specific and practical instruction, reproof when it's reproof we need, correction when we've gone wrong.[6]

Everything We Need

2 Peter 1:3 ***As His divine power has given to us all things that pertain to life and godliness, through the knowledge of Him who called us by glory and virtue.*** *(NKJV)*

Advertising is aimed at convincing us that no matter how much we have, we do not have enough. Every commercial, ad, billboard, or telemarketing phone call attempts to get us to believe that there's one more product or service we need to make our lives better. When Paul and Peter wrote to their brothers and sisters in Christ, they frequently took the opposite approach. They worked at convincing fellow believers that they already had everything they needed to live a victorious, dynamic Christian life.

You have everything pertaining to life and godliness. That's an amazing promise to consider. How often do you feel defeated? How often do you feel that you just don't have the resources to live the kind of life you want to live? God's promise is that you already have more than enough resources. His resources are your resources. His power is your power. It's the very same power that Jesus promised to His disciples just before He ascended into heaven; the same power that is greater than all the power Satan can muster; the same power that enabled Jesus to defeat the devil when He was tempted in the wilderness; the same power that raised Jesus from the dead. *That* same power is at work in your life giving you "everything you need" to live a godly life—a life that is loyal and obedient to God.

go to

ascended into heaven
Acts 1:8

all the power Satan can muster
1 John 4:4

defeat the devil
Luke 4:14

raised Jesus from the dead
Romans 1:4

one of Peter's favorite themes
2 Peter 1:2, 5, 6, 8; 2:20; 3:18

We develop the quality of this kind of life by deepening our "knowledge of Him." The knowledge of God is one of Peter's favorite themes. Here he used the word *epignosis*. The word denotes not just a casual knowledge, but a thorough knowledge. One definition is "recognition"—the ability to know God when you see Him or hear His voice. That knowledge is what unlocks the treasure chest that God has hidden in those who believe.

something to ponder

The glorious God of "divine power" is the One who called us "by glory" (2 Peter 1:3 NKJV). The good God who generously blesses our lives with "all things that pertain to life and godliness" is the One who called us, by His "virtue" (2 Peter 1:3 NKJV). You already have everything you need to lead a victorious, dynamic Christian life. Anyone who tries to tell you otherwise just has something to sell!

what others say

Abraham Lincoln

I trust that as He shall further open the way, I will be ready to walk therein, relying on His help and trusting in His goodness and wisdom.[7]

A. W. Tozer

With the goodness of God to desire our highest welfare, the wisdom of God to plan it, and the power of God to achieve it, what do we lack?[8]

Groaning Inwardly; Waiting Eagerly

ROMANS 8:29 ***For whom He foreknew, He also predestined to be conformed to the image of His Son, that He might be the firstborn among many brethren.*** (NKJV)

A potter begins with the end in mind when she sits down to make a pot. She envisions something beautiful, something useful. Something that looks very different from the gray lump of raw material she has to work with. She works the clay—kneads it, pokes it to soften it into something she can shape. She puts it on the wheel and spins it. With deft fingers she stretches the clay out of its "natural" shape—which was no shape at all—and into a shape that looks more like the object she has in mind. She paints it, glazes it, then sticks it in the oven to harden and toughen and become waterproof. If the clay had feelings, surely it wouldn't enjoy the process of becoming a pot. That's a lot of stress and strain, tugging, and prodding. If the clay could think, it would have to come up with a whole new way of thinking about itself. If the clay could choose, it might choose not to go through all that. But it would be making a big mistake. Because clay doesn't do anybody any good in its natural state.

go to

Potter
Isaiah 29:16

beautiful
Isaiah 61:3

God is the Potter. When He looks at you, he doesn't see a lump of raw material, but the beautiful vessel He intends you to be. That's what Paul meant when he said "whom He foreknew, He also predestined to be conformed to the image of His Son." All the stresses and strains of life on earth are the Potter's way of tugging you into the shape He envisioned for you long before you were born.

key point

Paul never sugarcoated the fact that just like everybody else, Christians experience what he called "the sufferings of this present time" (Romans 8:18 NKJV). Most people live as victims of their sufferings, regarding pain as an uninvited intruder. Christians, however, are able see purpose in it. They understand that sin is the cause of grief and suffering in the world; but through the power of God's Spirit, they live in victory in the midst of their sufferings, and they anticipate the day when they will suffer no more. For a believer, there is no such thing as meaningless suffering. God will always bring blessing out of suffering and subject our personal pain to this practical promise: "For whom He foreknew, He also predestined to be conformed to the image of His Son" (Romans 8:2 NKJV).

- "Predestined" means to order in advance the events of our lives in order to bring about a predetermined result.
- "Conformed" can refer to a potter molding a lump of clay into an object of beauty based upon an image or likeness that he has in his mind.
- "His Son" is just that likeness.

Just as a skilled craftsman applies pressure to squeeze or fashion the clay into a predetermined image, so God uses the pressures of this life to shape us into the image of His Son.

angels sit back and watch us
1 Peter 1:12

If we have ever prayed to be more like Jesus, sung lyrics to that effect, asked ourselves the question, "What Would Jesus Do?" or longed to have God change us from what we are into the what He wants us to be, remember: the road that leads to spiritual growth is paved in pain. So, while we may "groan within ourselves," we are "eagerly waiting" for that glorious day when the process will be complete (Romans 8:23 NKJV).

what others say

Martin Luther King, Jr.

I may not be the man I want to be; I may not be the man I ought to be; I may not be the man I could be; I may not be the man I can be; but praise God, I'm not the man I once was.[9]

People of God; People of Mercy

1 PETER 2:10a ***[You] once were not a people but are now the people of God.* (NKJV)**

The desperate desire to belong seems to be an innate need, a part of human nature. We cover our cars with bumper stickers, plaster logos all over clothes and baseball caps, learn secret handshakes, endure hazing all because we want to know we belong to something—and want others to know we belong too.

If you are in Christ, you do belong to something so fantastic, so awesome, so incredible, so large, so powerful, that even the angels sit back and watch us in wonder. We belong to the church!

Jesus made this promise: "I will build My church" (Matthew 16:18 NKJV). Today, He is actively fulfilling that promise. The moment you placed your faith in Jesus to save you, you became a part of His church—the worldwide company of Jesus' followers. For the time being, we are what theologians have called "the church militant," still struggling, still expanding the territories of God's kingdom here on earth. But one of these days, we will be "the church triumphant," enjoying the rest brought about by Christ's victory over our enemies.

Peter reassures us, "But you are a chosen generation, a royal priesthood, a holy nation, His own special people, that you may proclaim the praises of Him who called you out of darkness into His marvelous light" (1 Peter 2:9 NKJV). Think of it! We have been handpicked by God to be His people. We were nobodies: "You once were not a people." But God, for reasons known only to Him, made us His people. We didn't belong. Now we belong to God and to each other. We were misfits. Now we are fitted together like the parts of a body or the stones in a building.

go to

parts of a body
Romans 12:4–8

stones in a building
1 Peter 2:5

Out of darkness. Into glorious light. Why did God do such an incredible thing for people such as us? Because He wanted to. We once were strangers to God. Now we are strangers to the world. It's a good thing we "strangers and aliens" have each other. That's an important part of what it means to be the church. God has called us out of the world. That could be a very lonely situation. But because we belong to God, we belong to one another. It's our greatest calling to love one another, to spur each other on, to bear one another's burdens.

key point

what others say

William Sanford LaSor

The church has passed through many generations and undergone many changes. There have been changes in ritual, changes in language, changes in forms of government, and in many other elements. But it is still the same fellowship with the Lord Jesus Christ and with all who are His.[10]

It Took a Miracle

EPHESIANS 2:19 *Now, therefore, you are no longer strangers and foreigners, but fellow citizens with the saints and members of the household of God.* (NKJV)

Peter had a problem. He hated Gentiles.

Indeed, the entire infant church had a problem. While they remained essentially a Jewish sect, nobody thought a thing about it. But as soon as Gentiles started showing up to the Sunday morning worship services, the centuries-old racial divide between Jew and Gentile threatened to kill the baby church in its crib. The wide gulf that existed between Jew and Gentile is perhaps best illustrated through the ministry of Peter.

go to

demanded an explanation
Acts 11:2–3

apostle to the Gentiles
Romans 11:13

Cornelius was a Gentile. When he invited Peter to his home, Peter didn't want to go. It took nothing less than a supernatural vision from God to convince Peter just to set foot in the Gentile's house. After Cornelius prayed to receive Christ, the racial barrier began to break, but not without a price. As soon as Peter got back to Jerusalem, church leaders demanded an explanation. It was a big deal. The church leaders still didn't get it. Actually, even Peter didn't fully get it himself. In Galatians, Paul mentions that he had to rebuke Peter to his face because Peter was choosing not to eat with the Gentiles in the church when certain Jewish Christians were there. There's a real irony in that scene. The man who first broke through the ethnic divide being rebuked for prejudice—and by a man who once built his career on violently protecting the purity of the Jewish faith. It shows just how hard it is to overcome long-held prejudices.

Paul had such a change of heart concerning non-Jewish believers that he even identified himself as "an apostle to the Gentiles." Indeed, he so whole-heartedly embraced them that he penned this promise to them in Ephesians 2:19 (NKJV), "Therefore, you are no longer strangers and foreigners" (as far as the things of God are concerned), "but fellow citizens with the saints" (the Jews), "and members of the household of God" (united with them as one).

something to ponder

Prejudice is far from over in the church. It has been remarked that Sunday morning is the most segregated time of the week in America. This faith is about reconciliation, the breaking down of barriers between people. According to God's promise, we aren't strangers to anyone who believes. If God could reach out to sinners like us, who are we to refuse to reach out to others simply because they come from a different socio-economic class or are of a different ethnicity or were born in a different country? Prejudice of any kind is abhorrent to God and has no place in the body of Christ. Jesus died for the sins of "the whole world" (1 John 2:2 NKJV).

> **what others say**
>
> **Luci Swindoll**
>
> Don't bypass the potential for meaningful relationships just because of differences. Explore them. Embrace them. Love them.
>
> *"You have left me in this world, Lord, because there are people here you love and to whom I can become your representative. Make me a loving ambassador for this divine mission."*[11]

Chapter Wrap-Up

- If you submit to God and resist the devil, the devil will flee.
- Hiding sin drains the life out of you. Confessing sin gives you a new lease on life.
- You already have everything you need to live a life that pleases God.
- God already has in mind the person He is shaping you into.

Study Questions

1. What is the significance of the statement, "No temptation has overtaken you but such as is common to man?
2. How is "submission" different from "passivity" in James 4:7?
3. What sets you free from the compulsion to berate yourself for past failures?
4. Why are God's promises sometimes repetitive?
5. As church members, how does our status as "strangers and aliens" in the world impact our fellowship with one another?

Chapter 20: Promises to Meet Ministry Needs

Chapter Highlights:
- Promise of the Holy Spirit
- Promise of a firm foundation
- Promise of judgment

A Matter of Trust

PROVERBS 3:5–6
Trust in the LORD with all your heart,
And lean not on your own understanding;
In all your ways acknowledge Him,
And He shall direct your paths. (NKJV)

Even though God gave him very clear instructions, King Saul had a habit of "leaning on his own understanding." God's instructions, after all, were often **counterintuitive**. Saul had his ideas regarding how kings should behave themselves, and God's instructions often didn't square with those ideas.

When the Philistines prepared to attack Saul and his men, they all panicked The men ran and hid in caves and cellars and thickets. Never mind that God had assured Saul of His presence and protection. Saul didn't know what to do. He needed guidance from God, but he found it hard to wait for that guidance. After seven days of waiting for the prophet Samuel to come perform the sacrifice, Saul gave up waiting and performed the sacrifice himself—something he had no business doing! The ways of God were hard, so Saul leaned on his own understanding. Samuel arrived about the time the unauthorized sacrifice was over, and he told Saul what was at stake: if only Saul had waited on God, "the LORD would have established your kingdom over Israel forever. But now your kingdom shall not endure."

When the Israelites fought the Amalekites, God ordered that Saul and his army destroy them completely. The Amalekites were a notoriously wicked and barbaric people who terrorized other nations, plundering whole cities of their wealth while killing the men, raping the women, and enslaving the sons. Indeed, they were the first to attack the Israelites as they entered the Promised Land. But total annihilation made no sense to Saul. He refused to obey God. He spared the Amalekites' cruel king; perhaps he viewed it as some sort of professional courtesy. Because Saul "leaned on his own understanding," the Amalekites continued to torment Israel for years.

go to

presence and protection
1 Samuel 12:22

destroy them completely
1 Samuel 15:1–9

counterintuitive
going against common sense, but nevertheless accurate

something to ponder

God's straight path and crystal-clear directions continued to remain an enigma to Saul throughout his troubled life—all because he never learned to trust in the Lord and acknowledge Him. Saul eventually lost everything that was important. He even committed suicide as the last desperate act of a wasted life (1 Samuel 31:4 NKJV). To quote Saul's own words, "I have played the fool" (1 Samuel 26:21 NKJV).

"My thoughts are not your thoughts, nor are my ways your ways," says the Lord (Isaiah 55:8 NKJV). We can't always make sense of God's way of doing things. How could we? We are mere human beings. But whether we understand or not, God commands us to trust in Him with all our hearts, not to lean on our own understanding. The command comes with a promise: He will give us straight paths to walk in. The path gets crooked when we travel it by our own understanding. God's commands are always right, even when they make no sense to us.

what others say

Gerald Sittser

God does have a plan for our lives. We will discover that plan, however, as we simply do the will of God we already know in the present moment. Life will then gradually unfold for us.[1]

The Spirit of Truth

JOHN 16:13a ***However, when He, the Spirit of truth, has come, He will guide you into all truth.*** **(*NKJV*)**

DaVinci's famous painting The Last Supper depicts a scene of serenity and intimacy shared by a teacher with his students. That's not really what that evening looked like. The disciples were confused and confounded by events that were rapidly spinning out of their control. The week had begun with Jesus' (and the disciples') triumphal entry into the city of Jerusalem. They were welcomed in the manner of conquering heroes. Their ambitions had been stoked by the seemingly obvious fact that Jesus was getting ready to usher in the kingdom of God. Who knew what kind of power the disciples would enjoy in that administration! But on the other hand, Jesus kept referring to His own death. It was very complicated, and most perplexing.

Jesus saw right through the disciples. He saw clearly the hardness of their hearts, their lingering preoccupation with their own preeminence in the earthly kingdom they thought Jesus was about to establish, their obvious dismay over Jesus' pronouncement that one of them would soon betray Him, and their gut-wrenching fear every time He alluded to His imminent death. These were men living in abject denial. He had to admit, "I still have many things to say to you, but you cannot bear them now" (John 16:12 NKJV).

But then He made this promise: "However, when He, the Spirit of truth, has come, He will guide you into all truth; for He will not speak on His own authority, but whatever He hears He will speak; and He will tell you things to come" (John 16:13 NKJV). In all their confusion—confusion that would grow more profound before things ever became clear again—Jesus offered the promise of help and clarity. He promised them the Holy Spirit. This Spirit would guide them in truth, teaching them things they never could have known otherwise. This Spirit would even strengthen their hope by showing them the future—something that would be a big help, given the future they faced.

In a nutshell, Jesus promised inspiration. The word "inspiration" literally means "breathing in"—the breath of God breathed into a human heart. And the breath of God is the Spirit of truth. It's an amazing thing to consider that, if you are in Christ, God's Spirit dwells in you. The same Spirit that by which the Bible was written, the same Spirit by which the disciples performed miracles, the same Spirit who was there when the universe was formed lives inside you, giving you wisdom and insight that you couldn't get any other way.

key point

Pathway to Blessing

what others say

J. Grant Howard

> The believer who is properly programmed with the Word is ready to process the data from his world in a proper and understanding way.... As the mind is renewed, the believer becomes more qualified to examine all the facts in a life situation and discover and do the will of God.[2]

JAMES 1:25 ***But he who looks into the perfect law of liberty and continues in it, and is not a forgetful hearer but a doer of the work, this one will be blessed in what he does.*** *(NKJV)*

go to

boldly proclaimed
Matthew 3:1–2;
John 1:12

steal the limelight
John 1:19–20

James offers us a three-step program for blessing:

1. Look into the law of liberty.
2. Continue in it.
3. Do what it says, and don't be a forgetful hearer.

The person who can do that "will be blessed in what he does." James isn't saying that we can count on any sort of material prosperity as a result of obedience. He *does* promise that if we live in continual obedience to the Word of God, we will be free from sin's grip—what we like to call these days "addictions." He *does* promise that God blesses obedient believers.

John the Baptist obeyed the law of God. He boldly proclaimed the arrival of the Messiah to a people who were not ready to receive Him. He adamantly denied being that Messiah when presented with a golden opportunity to steal the limelight from Jesus. When Herod, a ruthless Roman leader of considerable power, married a woman who wasn't his to have, John confronted him with his sin (Matthew 14:4 NKJV). John was a man of impeccable integrity and uncompromising conviction. Yet, he was thrown into prison and left to languish there until Herod had him beheaded. He was stripped of everything he had, including his freedom and ultimately his life. Where is the blessing in that?

But note what Jesus said about him: "Among those born of women there has not risen one greater than John the Baptist" (Matthew 11:11 NKJV). God's blessing in this case was not measured in the size of his house, the kind of chariot he owned, the holdings in his portfolio, or his position in the community. God's blessing was measured by the kind of man he was and the lasting impact he made on everyone who knew him.

something to ponder

Righteousness is its own reward. If you stick to an exercise program, you don't look for somebody to give you a cookie for your reward. You understand that the exercise contains its own inherent rewards. You feel better. You look better. You have more energy. Those are the proper rewards for exercise. The proper rewards for righteousness aren't material riches or comfort. That's not to say that you won't have money or comfort. Maybe you will, maybe you won't. But that has nothing to do with a reward for a righteous life.

God promises that the reward of continuing in the law of liberty is, well, continuing in the law of liberty.

John learned to store up for himself "treasures in heaven" (Matthew 6:20 NKJV). He's enjoying them now. Blessings for others and blessings for himself. He couldn't do better than that!

> **what others say**
>
> **J. Oswald Sanders**
>
> If the worth of praise is to be measured by the lips from which it falls, no mortal man was ever praised so greatly . . . our Lord marked John out not only as the greatest man of his day, but the greatest man of all days up to that time . . .[3]

Something Not to Be Ignored

PROVERBS 1:25–26
[Wisdom speaking]:
Because you disdained all my counsel,
And would have none of my rebuke,
I also will laugh at your calamity;
I will mock when your terror comes. (NKJV)

This is an unusual promise—a warning promise. "Wisdom"—for Solomon wrote these words as if he were quoting Wisdom, as if she were a person who could actually speak in an audible voice—promises to laugh at and mock those who ignore her. Too bad Solomon didn't listen to her.

It's hard to make sense of Solomon's life. He was revered as the wisest man who ever lived, and yet he did some things that were so unwise as to be disastrous. He should have been an example to us all. Instead, Solomon's life ends up more cautionary tale than the example of a model citizen. He shows how little you can take for granted.

Early in his life, Solomon's star rose at an amazing pace. He was young, privileged, godly, and extremely wise. His ruling concerning the two women who both claimed to be the mother of the same child, became the stuff of legend. The Queen of Sheba traveled some twelve hundred miles to hear for herself the wisdom of this man. When she got through grilling him with tough riddles, Solomon's wise answers left her breathless. His reputation spread like wildfire.

go to

a person who could actually speak
Proverbs 1:20

breathless
1 Kings 10:5

defile
to make filthy or dirty; pollute

But somewhere along the way Solomon lost his way. His vaunted wisdom failed him. Solomon eventually crashed and burned.

Solomon entered into many agreements with foreign leaders by marrying their heathen wives, a common practice in biblical times. Common but unwise. In order to appease his wives, Solomon allowed them to turn his loyalty away from God, even to the point of unwisely erecting altars to their false gods. Solomon, whose splendor far outshone every other king, unwisely burdened his people with excessive taxation while forcing many into slave labor. Solomon knew better. But he chose worse.

You wonder what stage of life Solomon was in when he put that chilling promise in the mouth of the lady Wisdom: "Because you disdained all my counsel, and would have none of my rebuke, I also will laugh at your calamity; I will mock when your terror comes" (Proverbs 1:25–26 NKJV). Solomon had even more opportunity than most of us to heed the teachings of Wisdom. But he disdained her. And he became a laughingstock.

apply it

God promises to give wisdom to anyone who asks for it. Cling to that promise. And don't disdain God's wisdom when you receive it. You don't want Wisdom to have to keep her promise to "mock when the terror comes."

what others say

LeRoy Eims

Dr. Howard Hendricks told of a man who came to him with this...problem. The man said, "Howie, years ago I put my ladder up against the wall and began to climb. For all these years since then I have struggled to make it to the top. Now I've arrived only to discover that fifty years ago I placed my ladder against the wrong wall.[4]

You Are What You Say

MATTHEW 12:36 ***But I say to you that for every idle word men may speak, they will give account of it in the day of judgment. (NKJV)***

You know the old saying, "You are what you eat." That's not what Jesus said. Jesus said you are what you say. "There is nothing outside the man which going into him can **defile** him; but the things which proceed out of the man are what defile the man" (Mark 7:15 NKJV). Think about how concerned we are with what goes into our minds and bodies: the things we eat, the things we watch, the things we read. Those are all important, of course, but Jesus was more concerned with what comes out of us than what goes in. He was concerned even with the idle words we give almost no thought to.

heart
1 Samuel 24:13

When it comes to watching what you eat, no diet guru can hold a candle to the Pharisees, who had rules for everything from what foods were acceptable to how they were cooked to how they washed before eating them to the utensils they used. But they had enormous blind spots. Their hearts were sick. They didn't know how to love anybody; they didn't even seem very good at loving themselves. Jesus, in His ongoing war with the Pharisees, nailed them on the subject of the words they spoke. "Brood of vipers! How can you, being evil, speak good things? For out of the abundance of the heart the mouth speaks" (Matthew 12:34 NKJV). It's not even the words themselves that matter. They are only the symptoms of the heart.

There they stood, the Pharisees, exposed, unmasked, fully revealed as the self-righteous, self-serving hypocrites that they were. Based on their "every idle word" they condemned themselves to the point where Jesus had to promise them, "For by your words you will be justified, and by your words you will be condemned" (Matthew 12:37 NKJV).

The promise of Matthew 12:36 is another one of those warning promises: God promises to hold you accountable for every idle word you speak. Ouch! The authenticity of our faith and the quality of our commitment to Christ can best be measured by our words. God sees our hearts. Sometimes it's hard for us to see our own hearts. But if you want to know what kind of shape your heart is in, listen to yourself. Think about the idle words you say, when you aren't really thinking about what you're saying, or when you don't think anyone will hear. What you say conveys far more than the message you want to communicate. Your speech betrays the condition of your heart.

what others say

Billy Graham

Each of us has a tongue and a voice. These instruments of speech can be used destructively or employed constructively.

magistrate
civil officer charged with the administration of the law

> I can use my tongue to slander, to gripe, to scold, to nag, and to quarrel; or I can bring it under the control of God's Spirit and make it an instrument of blessing and praise. . . . Only God can control it, as we yield it to Him.[5]

The Pharisees vs. Christ

The Pharisees	Scripture
Condemned Jesus for reaching out to sinful people	Luke 15:1–2
Demanded that Jesus give them a supernatural sign	Matthew 12:38
Bombarded Jesus with nonstop questions	Matthew 19:3
Scrutinized Jesus' every move in a vain attempt to discredit Him	Luke 6:7
Challenged Jesus' teachings	Luke 16:14
Plotted and planned for an opportune moment to seize Jesus and kill Him	John 11:47, 53, 57

Building to Last

1 CORINTHIANS 3:12–14 ***Now if anyone builds on this foundation with gold, silver, precious stones, wood, hay, straw, each one's work will become clear; for the Day will declare it, because it will be revealed by fire; and the fire will test each one's work, of what sort it is. If anyone's work which he has built on it endures, he will receive a reward.*** *(NKJV)*

When Paul was arrested in Corinth, he was hauled before the *bema*. The *bema* was a raised platform where a **magistrate** sat and passed judgment. There the Roman proconsul Gallio sat in judgment of Paul considering the charges the local Jews had leveled against him. (Gallio threw the case out of court) The judges' table in an athletic event—for example, the Isthmian Games, which also were held in Corinth—was also known as a *bema*. In the Bible, the word *bema* is translated "judgment seat." Paul used the word several times in the Bible to speak of the judgment seat of Christ, before which we will all stand someday.

When, Paul spoke of Christ's *bema* in his letters to the Corinthians, you wonder if he was picturing the *bema* in Corinth where he stood before Gallio. Though the *bema* of Corinth a threatening, ominous place for Paul, he actually spoke of Christ's *bema* in order to encourage the Corinthians. Those who are in Christ have nothing to fear from the judgment seat.

Though Paul doesn't specifically mention the judgment seat in 1 Corinthians 3:12–14, he does speak of the day when Christ will judge the works of each person's hands. Paul likened our labors for the Lord to someone building a building. If we are serving Christ faithfully, it's as if we're building with "gold, silver, precious stones" (1 Corinthians 3:12 NKJV). If, however, we are frittering our lives away, we're building with "wood, hay, straw" (1 Corinthians 3:12 NKJV). It will all burn away on that day of judgment, leaving you with nothing to show for a whole life. Those who choose to live their lives for the Lord will be rewarded at the *bema*. And when we are, our hearts will swell with joy because we were able to accomplish great things for the glory of our Lord.

go to

condemned by Pilate
John 19:13

trees as symbols
Jeremiah 17:7–8; Ezekiel 19:10

Make no mistake about this: God promises that we will stand before the *bema* seat for the purpose of reward, not condemnation (Romans 8:1). Interestingly enough, the apostle John used the same term to refer to the place where Jesus was condemned by Pilate to die. He took our place, received the punishment we deserved so we could lay hold of the reward that He deserved. Because he went to a *bema* seat of judgment, we look forward to God's promise of a *bema* seat of reward.

something to ponder

what others say

Charles R. Swindoll

God, you see, is primarily interested in the quality of our fruit. He looks behind our hustle and bustle...He probes and penetrates down to our motive, our inner purpose...and on the basis of that discovery, He plans our eternal rewards.[6]

Deeply Rooted

PSALM 1:3
He shall be like a tree
Planted by the rivers of water,
That brings forth its fruit in its season,
Whose leaf also shall not wither;
And whatever he does shall prosper. (NKJV)

Biblical writers often used trees as symbols of God's blessing. Trees are taken for granted in many parts of the world, but in the arid conditions that characterize so much of the Holy Land, trees are some-

go to

honor God and serve others
Galatians 5:22–23

thing very special. They bring to an often bleak landscape the dual blessings of beauty and much-needed shade. Think of the root system that would be required to sustain a plant the size of a tree in a place with so little water. Any tree that manages to survive is soaking up every drop of water that's available to it. Even when a dry spell comes, it survives because its roots are deep. It is fitting that the Psalter begins with a discussion of trees. Those whose "delight is in the law of the LORD" are like healthy trees.

The trees of which the psalmist speaks have been planted along nourishing streams of life-giving water. Here that water is a metaphor for the spiritual nourishment to be found in the Bible. The vitality of such trees can be measured by the fruit they produce when in season. Prosperous trees produce good fruit.

The prosperity God promises those who daily meditate upon the Scriptures has nothing to do with material wealth. There is no promise here that we will somehow attain a comfortable life. Every healthy tree must learn to withstand the blowing winds of adversity. But as a tree soaks up water and bears luscious fruit, so we too can soak up God's Word, producing actions and attitudes that honor God and serve others. We will achieve true prosperity as we discover the value of God's Word in our lives and meditate on it daily. That fruit, those words and actions, are the result of an intricate root system that provides both nourishment and stability. When you dive into the Word, you are strengthening that network of roots.

something to ponder

That little phrase "in its season" is worth noting. Trees don't bear fruit year-round, but only in season. At other times of the year they are dormant, deepening their roots in preparation for the next fruit-bearing season. You may feel as if your life is in a period of dormancy. Be of good cheer. Perhaps this is just a time for you to deepen your roots, drink in God's Word, and await the arrival of your next fruit-bearing season.

what others say

A. W. Tozer

The bough that breaks off from the tree in the storm may bloom briefly and give to the unthinking passerby the impression that it is a healthy and fruitful branch, but its tender blossoms will soon perish and the bough itself wither and die. There is no lasting life apart from the root.[7]

"Hmmmmm . . ."

JOSHUA 1:8 ***This Book of the Law shall not depart from your mouth, but you shall meditate in it day and night, that you may observe to do according to all that is written in it. For then you will make your way prosperous, and then you will have good success. (NKJV)***

go to

totality of the Bible
2 Timothy 3:16

The big day had finally arrived. After God's appearance to Moses in the burning bush, the Ten Plagues, the parting of the Red Sea, the thundering atop Mount Sinai, the pause at the edge of the Promised Land, the mutiny of the ten spies, the endless years of wilderness wandering, the death of a generation, the raising of a new generation, the death of Moses, and the inauguration of Joshua, Israel would finally occupy the land that God had given them.

God made Joshua a promise: "As I was with Moses, so I will be with you. I will not leave you nor forsake you" (Joshua 1:5 NKJV). God challenged Joshua to "be strong and of good courage" (Joshua 1:6 NKJV). Then He gave Joshua the single most important piece of advice the new commander-in-chief would need to lead the new nation, advice that carried the promise of guaranteed success: "This Book of the Law shall not depart from your mouth, but you shall meditate in it day and night . . . For then you will make your way prosperous, and then you will have good success. (NKJV)

The "Book of the Law" referred to the totality of Scripture as it existed in Joshua's day—the Pentateuch or the five books that Moses wrote, Genesis through Deuteronomy. We can now extrapolate this promise to include all sixty-six books of the Bible. Indeed, whenever a biblical writer refers to the Law or Scripture, he is making reference to the totality of the Bible as it existed at the time of his writing.

The Hebrew word translated "meditate" literally means "to moan or growl." The same word is used to describe the growling of a lion. Seems a strange way to put it, doesn't it? The connection is probably the "hmmmmm . . ." sound people often make when they're lost in thought. It sounds a little like a low growl. God is encouraging Joshua to ponder His word that earnestly, just as if he were trying to solve a problem or plan out his future. "Hmmmm. . . ." God is calling Joshua to engage in the careful, deliberate process of mulling over biblical truths time and time again. He calls all of us to

go to

our minds
Romans 12:2

Nicodemus
John 3:1–21

not to tangle with the Pharisees
Matthew 15:12–14;
Matthew 16:6;
Mark 8:15;
Luke 12:1

discipline our minds to *think* biblically, and thus train ourselves to *act* biblically. It's a slow process. But it's well worth it. By meditating on God's Word, we lay hold of God's surefire promise for absolute success.

what others say

Oswald Smith

When the Word of God becomes your meat and drink, your daily study and a very part of yourself, then, and not until then, will you be able to use it as He intends.[8]

Robert E. Lee

In all my perplexities and distresses, the Bible has never failed to give me light and strength.[9]

A Vast Right-Winged Conspiracy

LUKE 12:11–12 ***Now when they bring you to the synagogues and magistrates and authorities, do not worry about how or what you should answer, or what you should say. For the Holy Spirit will teach you in that very hour what you ought to say. (NKJV)***

"Do not worry," Jesus said. But the disciples, it would seem, had good reason to worry. The Pharisees were on their case. They were a cold, calculating group of self-absorbed, self-righteous men. And they had the power to do real harm to their enemies. Until Jesus showed up, things had been going more or less their way. So the Pharisees were determined to get rid of Jesus and His followers once and for all. They made enthusiastic and dogged enemies. But Jesus always managed to sidestep them.

Jesus called the Pharisees "an evil and adulterous generation" (Matthew 12:39 NKJV), "blind guides" (Matthew 23:16 NKJV), "whitewashed tombs" (Matthew 23:27 NKJV), and for good measure, a "brood of vipers" (Matthew 23:33 NKJV). He bested them in every confrontation, but they never relented in their efforts to trap him. And, with the exception of Nicodemus, the Bible gives no indication that they ever considered the possibility that Jesus may be speaking the truth, that perhaps they had sins of which to repent. Jesus continually warned His disciples not to tangle with the Pharisees; it's not hard to see why.

But Jesus also encouraged His followers with the promise that when the inevitable happened, when they got hauled before these treacherous teachers, God would be there with them. "When they bring you to the synagogues and magistrates and authorities, do not worry about how or what you should answer, or what you should say." At the moment of testing, the Holy Spirit would give them the words and the courage they needed to meet their challenge head-on.

go to

we should not fear human beings
Psalm 56:4

God's Spirit will do the same for you. The world is opposed to the values of God, and if you are living out a life that pleases God, you can be sure you will experience opposition. And the truth is, some of your opponents will be more articulate, better educated, better prepared, and better looking than you. Under your own power, you might not know how to answer such people. Aren't you glad you don't have to answer them under your own power? God promises to be by your side giving you the words and the courage you will need to face your opposition head-on. He *will* be with you, even to the end of the age (Matthew 28:20 NKJV).

something to ponder

what others say

F. Kefa Sempangi (pastor persecuted under the dictator Idi Amin)

There was no human being to whom I could appeal . . . My mouth had frozen and I had no clever words to speak. In that moment, with death so near, it was not my sermon which gave me courage, or an idea from Scripture. It was Jesus Christ, the living Lord.[10]

Losing Is Not an Option

Psalm 118:6
The Lord is on my side;
I will not fear.
What can man do to me? *(NKJV)*

"What can man do to me?" Well . . . a lot. The stories of the early Christian martyrs show just how much the faithful throughout history (and even today) have suffered at the hands of the church's enemies. Nevertheless, the Bible is insistent that we should not fear human beings. Jesus taught His disciples, "Do not fear those who kill the body but cannot kill the soul. But rather fear Him who is able to destroy both soul and body in hell" (Matthew 10:28 NKJV). That was a Man who would be executed on a Roman cross, speaking to men who would suffer and die for their faith.

go to

grows at an accelerated pace
Philippians 1:12

So, sure, there's a lot people can do to your body. Books like *Foxe's Book of Martyrs* or even the publications of the Voice of the Martyrs organization demonstrate how creative the enemies of the church can be in inflicting pain on those who would follow Christ. But the suffering of the martyrs isn't the whole story of martyrdom. It's not even half the story, or a quarter. The real story of martyrdom is the story of a church that grows at an accelerated pace when its enemies try to stop it through violence. As John Foxe put it, every time there were persecutions, the church continued to grow, being "watered plenteously with the blood of saints."[11]

The apostles and brethren of the first century had no reason for dread because the same Lord Jesus who had already suffered for them, gave them the courage to suffer for Him in return. In addition, He was *with them* in the middle of every violent encounter. Evil men could never take that away!

something to ponder

You're probably not going to be called upon to die a violent death for the sake of the gospel. That's not the biggest challenge facing the Western church. It's not even on the top ten list. Nevertheless, you've probably experienced fear with regard to the public expression of your faith. You may fear rejection or funny looks. You may fear lost prospects in your career if you're too bold about the gospel. God promises you that you need not fear what any human being can do to you. If you want something to fear, fear the timidity of a halfway commitment to Christ. If anything is going to stop the progress of God's kingdom, it's timid Christians, not open opposition by the church's enemies!

what others say

Richard W. DeHaan

Though the wicked have mercilessly tortured followers of Jesus and have cruelly taken the lives of many, they have been unable to put an end to the witness of the Gospel.[12]

Deaths of Early Christian Martyrs (according to *Foxe's Book of Martyrs*[13])

Name	Manner of Death
Stephen	Cut to death with stones
James, the son of Zebedee	Beheaded
Philip	Whipped, imprisoned, and finally crucified
Matthew	Hacked to death with an ax
James, the Lord's brother	Beaten to death with a club
Matthias	Stoned, then beheaded
Andrew	Crucified
Mark	Dragged to pieces
Peter	Crucified upside-down
Paul	"Gave his neck to the sword"
Jude	Crucified
Bartholomew	Beaten, then crucified
Thomas	"Thrust through with a spear"
Luke	Hanged on an olive tree
Simon	Crucified
John	"Cast into a cauldron of boiling oil," miraculously escaped, and banished to the island of Patmos

Chapter Wrap-Up

- Through His Spirit, God promises to give help and clarity to His people.
- God promises to judge every idle word we speak—for those words are the overflow of our hearts.
- For believers, the judgment seat will be a seat of rewards—thanks to Jesus' willingness to face a judgment seat of punishment.
- When you meditate on God's Word, God promises strength and sustenance.

Study Questions

1. How do you keep from "leaning on your own understanding" when your idea of how things ought to go just doesn't square with God's?
2. In light of John the Baptist's life and death, what are the blessings of obedience?
3. What did Jesus mean when He said it is not what goes into a person that defiles him, but what comes out?
4. God calls us not to fear what human beings can do to us, but we all struggle with fear nevertheless. Why is it that even the most faithful believers sometimes experience fear?
5. Why do stories of Christians' suffering turn out to be stories of hope for Christians?

BE SMART • BE INSPIRED •

Appendix A—The Answers

Chapter 1

1. By remaining mindful of God's mercy; it is *only* God's mercy—not our own worthiness—that makes it possible for us to approach His throne. Remembering that keeps you humble. But it also gives you boldness. After all, if God in His mercy invites you to His throne, you can be sure you have a place there.
2. Ultimately, God's plan for us is to change *us*, not to change our circumstances. Silence—making us wait—is one of the ways in which God works on our character.
3. A "foxhole prayer" grows out of a specific (and desperate) situation: things have grown so dire that even a non-praying person flings up a prayer. The "prayer of a settled heart" grows out of a person's habitual prayerfulness, whatever situation that person finds himself or herself in.
4. A "God preserve" is a little corner of your life where you try to keep God penned in—a place where you can come see Him when you feel like it, but where He won't cause trouble in the rest of your life. "God preserves" are dangerous because they reflect a complete misunderstanding of who God is and how He works in people's lives. He is Lord of all, and He will not be limited to a small "God preserve."
5. Just because a human being has good intentions doesn't mean he or she can carry out on those good intentions. And just because a human being has power to do good, that doesn't mean he or she has the inclination. But when God intends to do good to you, His plans cannot be thwarted. He has both the power and the intention to do good.

Chapter 2

1. When you don't know what to say, speechlessness is the most honest kind of prayer. In that situation, the Holy Spirit is praying on your behalf. Better to stay silent than try to come up with words with which to impress God.
2. David prayed that prayer at a time when he had no earthly props left to him. The only goodness left to him was the goodness of God.
3. Sanctification is a slow, daily process. It requires that you strive constantly to be more like Christ. Daily prayer is an important component of being consistently faithful for the long haul. Bear in mind also that sanctification isn't something you do on your own, no matter how hard you work at it. It requires the intervention of God—another reason to approach it prayerfully.
4. When you pray for people, God turns your heart toward them. Perhaps that's why He calls us to pray for our enemies. It's doesn't even matter whether a person knowing you're praying for him or her. When you pray, your attitude toward that person begins to look more like God's attitude toward him or her.
5. Paul was praying not that their circumstances would change, but that they would be able to see the incredible things that were *already* true in the spiritual realm.

Chapter 3

1. God's "dwelling place" used to be a temple on a hill in Jerusalem. But now it is in the hearts of the faithful. God makes His presence known in the world through the lives of His people.
2. God wanted His people to be a manifestation of His power and goodness. As He delivered them, protected them, did marvelous things in their lives, He wanted it to be obvious that His power was at work, not the power of earthly allies. Today, it is tempting to put our trust in riches or influence or some other earthly power. But God wants us to rely on His power.
3. Praise begins with the acknowledgement of God's greatness, and our own reliance on His grace and mercy. A spirit of self-sufficiency blinds us to the fact that we owe God for every good thing in our lives.

4. When you lose yourself in prayer, you are doing (on a very small scale) what you will be doing for eternity. You practice the praise of God, and you learn to forget about yourself and your worries as you focus on the glory and the sufficiency of God.
5. Praise reminds you of how big, how good, how gracious God is. It takes your mind off the worries and pre-occupations of the world, replacing them with the comfort of knowing you serve a great God.

Chapter 4

1. A broken bone is a painful thing. But if that pain is God's means of restoring you to fellowship with Him, it's well worth it. For David, the pain of seeing his own sin—and the punishment for that sin—gave way to the joy and relief of being restored to God.
2. We voluntarily choose to sin. But that choice leads to situations in which our choice is severely limited. Bad financial choices lead to the slavery of debt. The choice to take drugs leads to the slavery of addiction. Whatever the sin, the pattern is the same.
3. Even in the days of the Old Testament laws of ritual cleansing—when God appeared to be such a stickler—it was still the heart that mattered. The Israelites desired to be in communion with God; that was the important thing. They would have time later to figure out the ritual cleansing.
4. A healthy fear of God grows out of an understanding of who God is and how He interacts with His people. Even when God punishes His people, He does so out of love, with a view to restoring them to fellowship with Him. So there is hope, not despair, in God's correction.
5. When you come face-to-face with your sin, it's your job to turn away from it, not to punish yourself. There may be lingering consequences of your sin, and you have to deal with them. You may be called upon to make amends to the people you've hurt. But there is no point in beating yourself up. Repentance is about turning back to God and enjoying restored fellowship. Self-punishment just gets in the way.

Chapter 5

1. The psalms of complaint have a way of turning into psalms of praise when the psalmist takes his eyes off himself and starts looking at God.
2. At Jericho, the Israelites conquered because they were obedient to God in what appeared to be an impossible situation. At Ai, they believed they could conquer in their own strength. The difference wasn't God's presence or absence, but the Israelites' attitude of prayerlessness in the Ai debacle.
3. When you pray, you're "pouring out" your heart before God. That's what a sacrifice is: rather than holding on to your goods, holding on to your very self, you pour them out, offer them to God for His use.
4. He was probably just exhausted—physically, mentally, spiritually. It happens to everybody, no matter how faithful. Elijah prayed a crazy prayer in his exhaustion; but God didn't answer that prayer—or, in any case, he didn't answer "yes." Instead of killing Elijah as Elijah asked, God sustained him.
5. Down in the green valley, it's easy to place your trust in man-made things. It's hard going in the "high places," or in "a dry and thirsty land," but there you find that what you really need is God. And it is a blessing to know that He is there for you when all else fails.

Chapter 6

1. The prayer of the Pharisee is "Thank you that I am better than other people." That is the opposite of a Christian view of yourself, the world, and God. And it's hard to turn to God when you think you're doing fine on your own. That simple prayer, "Have mercy on me, a sinner," on the other hand, is exactly what God is looking for.
2. A life of character—a willingness to live honorably, to live for others and not just for yourself—puts you in a position to receive the blessings of God. Before we attempt to convince God of what He should bless us with, we should first ask for and work toward a godly character.
3. Throughout history, as the enemies of the Church have sought to stamp out Christianity through persecution, the Church has only spread. The courage of the martyrs in the face of death is an encouragement to other believers and actually strengthens the Church. Also, when persecutions cause Christians to scatter, they carry the gospel with them.
4. These "thorns" keep us humble and reliant on God. They help us see that it is God's strength in our lives that matters, not our own strength.
5. If you have a sense of your own righteousness that leads you to believe that you don't need God, you need to turn away from that righteousness just as surely as you need to turn away from your sin.

Chapter 7

1. An intercessory prayer is a prayer in which you are making requests on behalf of another person.

2. A benediction is a special kind of intercession, usually spoken by a person with some authority over the people for whom it is spoken. A benediction says, in effect, "I'm going to use my authority to be a blessing to you, not to use you for my own gain or gratification."
3. The importance of looking forward is pretty self-evident: You pray in hope, confidently looking forward to what God is going to do. But it's also important to look back at what God has already done in your life. It is a great encouragement as you pray for Him to come through for you again.
4. A life of love and wisdom doesn't just "disapprove" of things that are bad in the world. It "approves the things that are excellent." That is to say, it demonstrates the rewards and blessings of serving God so that everyone can see.
5. Love includes the habit of seeing the best in people. That can get you in trouble when you love people who are manipulative or mean or even just overly needy. Knowledge and discernment help to protect you from the damage such people can cause. They also help you to love those people in ways that actually help them rather than just perpetuating their worst tendencies.

Chapter 8

1. There are at least two ways to answer this question: first, we pray because God commands us to pray. It's true that He is fully capable of working His holy will without anybody's help, but He has chosen to use prayer as a component of that work. It is a privilege and a joy to partake in that. Secondly, the point of prayer isn't to persuade God to change His will nearly so much as it is to change the will of the person praying. As you pray, your will and desires come into conformity with those of God.
2. Sometimes God speaks "directly" to people, but more often He speaks through the scriptures, through conversations, through circumstances. The important thing is to be quiet and still long enough to hear God's voice in those things.
3. Prayer changes your desires. It brings your will more into line with God's will. And that's the first step in doing God's work in God's way.
4. The world is constantly presenting you with ways to get by without having to trust in God: credit card offers, office politics, mind-numbing entertainment, materialism. But as you put your trust in those things, you miss out on the opportunity to see that the battle truly is the Lord's.
5. Gideon's prayer was a sign of humility. He didn't trust his own discernment, so he asked God to confirm what His agenda actually was. Saul was only interested in his own agenda and was using "God-talk" to justify what he wanted to do anyway.

Chapter 9

1. The Kingdom of God has not yet come in its fullness, and yet it asserts itself every time God's people are motivated by God's love rather than selfish ambition, every time they pursue God's will rather than the will of the world.
2. Sometimes there is a disconnect between your will and God's will. That's just a part of being a human being—even a godly human being. The question is, are you going to submit to God's will, or are you going to insist on getting your way? Thankfully, as you submit to God's will, you find that your own will begins to change; you begin to want what God wants.
3. When you come to terms with how much God has forgiven you, how can you be less than loving or forgiving in your relationships with other people?
4. When it comes to our physical needs, God promises to give us what we need, but He doesn't promise us wealth. He gives us daily bread. The marrow and fatness God promises is a spiritual abundance, not a material abundance. And if you want to experience that spiritual abundance, one of the first steps is learning to find joy in daily bread, not requiring material wealth to be happy.
5. Temptation isn't sin. It's a test. When you pass a test, that's a good thing. It only becomes a bad thing when you fail the test. Getting through temptation without falling into sin builds your character and makes you more like Christ.

Chapter 10

1. Martyrdoms and persecutions were never very effective at thwarting the spread of the Church. They're no fun, but they aren't really a threat to the march of the Gospel. But when believers are seduced by the world and begin to be indistinguishable from the world, that's when the spread of the Gospel begins to stall out.
2. Faith is never easy. If it were, it wouldn't be faith. It is a strain for us human beings to believe what we cannot see. There's no better way to live than a life of faith, but it's still a strain and a burden. That burden will be lifted, however, when we see God face to face.
3. The reason for Jesus' death on the cross wasn't just because the Romans and the Jews conspired to crucify Him. He died on the cross because of all of our sins. His willingness to forgive those who "did this to Him" must include all of us...we all did it to Him.
4. We know from Jesus' prayer in the Garden that

His human nature cried out for what it wanted. His perfection derived not from the fact that he *couldn't* sin, but from the fact that he submitted His human will to the will of the Father.

5. While it's nice to think good thoughts about somebody, if they're just thoughts or feelings, they don't really go beyond your head. When those thoughts and feelings become a prayer, suddenly you're hitching them to the most powerful force in the universe!

Chapter 11

1. Our confidence derives from God's character, God's faithfulness, not our own.
2. Even more important than character is the knowledge that God is faithful. You can stand firm without fear because you know He keeps His promises. Whatever happens to you—even if it's death—God can make it good.
3. God cannot lie. He cannot die or sin or change. Or break a promise. But those are all limits that God imposed on Himself. What the angel Gabriel meant was that when it comes to the limits that are imposed on us human beings, nothing is impossible with God.
4. Satan is like a lion on a leash, but he's still a lion. He still prowls about looking to do harm to God's people, and he still can.
5. Our hope is the realization that God is slow to anger and abounding in love. God's mercy is our hope, especially when the realization of our sin makes us feel hopeless.

Chapter 12

1. Lazarus still died. His physical resurrection was a source of joy to him and his family and friends, but it was only temporary. The real point of the story, the promise that really matters, is the fact that Jesus exercises power over death itself. Lazarus' physical resurrection was temporary, but his spiritual resurrection—and yours—is eternal.
2. When you truly love God—when you want what He wants—you find that the world doesn't have the same power over you that it used to have. The world's real power over you isn't the power to hurt you or kill you. It's real power is its ability to steal your heart away from the things of God. If you love God with all your heart, soul, mind, and strength, the world no longer has that power over you.
3. Conviction points you upward toward God. It causes you to repent and enjoy a restored fellowship with Him. Condemnation drags you down into a spiral of self-hatred.
4. According to the principle of "double jeopardy," you can't be convicted of the same crime twice. Because Jesus has already taken the punishment for our sins and crimes, those who are in Christ cannot be found guilty of them.
5. Though you were born here on earth and have spent all your life here, your true citizenship is in heaven, if you are in Christ. You may look like the locals, but in fact you're just passing through on your way to your true home in heaven.

Chapter 13

1. Suffering causes us to rely on God rather than on our own resources. It is a means by which God gets our attention and draws us to Himself.
2. Our difficulties here on earth are real enough, but they aren't nearly as real and substantial as the rewards that await us in heaven. Just as earthly pleasures are flimsy in comparison to those of heaven, earthly sorrows also seem as light as a feather.
3. Many of the early martyrs died by fire. Peter compared those fires to the refiner's fire, by which the impurities of gold or silver are burned away, leaving something much purer and more beautiful.
4. "Counting it all joy" is about deciding to view the circumstances of your life as occasions for rejoicing. Happiness is something that you have to take as it comes; sometimes your circumstances are happy, sometimes they aren't. But joy is a choice. You have it or don't have it because of a decision you've made, not because of your circumstances.
5. For Paul, living and dying both were all about his relationship with God in Christ. Death, for Paul, was the ultimate deliverance from the troubles and hardships that marked his life on earth.

Chapter 14

1. Elijah was a superstar when it came to performing miracles, but he was also subject to fear and failure, just like the rest of us.
2. We can't see the whole picture from here. From here, life often looks like a tragedy. But God knows things that we don't know. He has a bigger plan, one in which the future is bright indeed. Every now and then, you get a glimpse of that future; you get a taste of "great and mighty things, which you do not know," and that new knowledge gives you strength to carry on.
3. We are creatures of time. That means we are by nature impatient. To learn to wait on God is to learn to have a more heavenly, less time-bound perspective. And that is a source of true strength.

4. The presence of God is the most awesome kind of wealth imaginable. When you are aware of His presence, how can you covet the earthly riches of another person? If you understand the riches of God's presence, how could you be less than content?
5. There's nothing very beautiful about the back side of a tapestry. It's messy and chaotic, with strands going here and there in a seemingly random fashion. But when you turn it over, a beautiful picture is revealed. From where we are, we can only see the back side of the tapestry that God is weaving. But one of these days, He's going to invite us to see the front side, and we will marvel at what He has been doing all along.

Chapter 15

1. God shames the wise and the strong when He uses the foolish and the weak to do His work in the world. When the foolish and weak do great things, it is obvious that God is at work.
2. As long as you are clinging to your old life, including all the things in which you have always found your self-worth, you won't be able to lay hold of the abundant life that God has in mind for you. You have to die to that old life before you can live a better one.
3. Paul wasn't necessarily talking about sacrifice as in something that is hard to do. (Sometimes it is difficult to do good and share, sometimes it isn't). Rather, he was speaking of sacrifice as an offering to God. Serving others is a way of serving God.
4. If you didn't have to worry about sinning, you wouldn't really need God any more. Turning to God would be a one-shot deal. But God would have us turn to Him every day—every day to say, "God, I can't do this without You. I can't please you without your help."
5. Love is the only thing that perfectly casts out fear. As you are secure in God's love, you don't have anything to fear from anybody.

Chapter 16

1. When you look to the things of earth to give you satisfaction, they disappoint you every time. They simply can't satisfy, even though they promise to. When you understand, however, that there is true satisfaction in seeking God's kingdom—and that the things of earth can be used as a means of glofifying God—suddenly the things of earth *can* have true significance and can give you a proper satisfaction.
2. When they saw that Paul could still choose joy in spite of his extremely difficult situation, they had reason to be encouraged. Beyond that, they could also see that the progress of the gospel was not hindered, but actually helped by Paul's imprisonment.
3. When you focus on your problems, they appear bigger than they actually are. They fill your frame of reference. On the other hand, if you expand your frame of reference so that you can see God's greatness (or at least as much of His greatness as you can see), your problems start looking pretty small.
4. God is all in all. He's the God of battle and the God of beauty. He is the God of everything. And He is on your side.
5. That verse follows Paul's declaration that he has learned to be content in whatever situation God has placed him in—in wealth or in poverty, in safety or in danger. Paul isn't saying, "With God's help, I can do anything I put my mind to." He's saying, "In Christ, God strengthens me to get through whatever He has put in front of me.

Chapter 17

1. When you are enslaved to sin, freedom is just an illusion. You think you're free to choose, but in fact you can't choose to do good. When you are a "slave to Christ," you're actually able to choose whether to please God or not.
2. It's one thing to follow a Man who's healing people and sticking it to the "powers that be." But things got a little too intense for a lot of people when Jesus said they had to eat His flesh and drink His blood. They simply weren't ready for that kind of radical commitment.
3. For the Old Testament Jews ethnic purity was an extremely important concept. They believed being one of "God's people" meant having the right genealogy. In truth, being one of "Abraham's seed" means participating in the covenant God established with Abraham—through faith, not through literal bloodlines.
4. Nobody takes a drink until they realize they're thirsty. Jesus would rather embarrass the woman than let her continue in her sin.
5. The Holy Spirit in our hearts is a little foretaste of heaven. God's pledge of greater things to come, it reminds us and reassures us of the blessings of heaven that await us.

Chapter 18

1. An eternal perspective makes the difficulties of our earthly existence seem manageable. It's not that our problems aren't real; it's just that there are things that are much *more* real.
2. The most important grounds of this confidence is simply the fact that the scriptures clearly state that God gladly gives wisdom to anyone who asks.

Beyond that, there's the fact that God wants us to be wise even more than we want to be wise ourselves. Of course He's going to give us what we ask for when it's what He wants for us anyway!

3. The towering respect for the Word of God that motivated Ezra's life come through in Psalm 119. Other small clues—such as the fact that the psalmist apparently lived in a religiously hostile climate—also suggest Ezra's authorship.
4. The peace of the world is no real peace because it doesn't deal with the human heart, the real source of strife. If by "peace" you mean the absence of war, you're not really talking about real peace.
5. It's not just that God promises to give you peace if you can stay focused on Him. Being focused on Him *is* a kind of peace because it means your thoughts are where they ought to be, not running here and there.

Chapter 19

1. This statement has a double significance. On the one hand, it reassures you that, whatever temptation you're struggling with, plenty of people have faced it before. Some resisted, some didn't, but the ones who resisted demonstrate that it can be done. On the other hand, the knowledge that everybody struggles with the same temptations helps you to be more supportive of those who fall. You realize that it could have been you.
2. That word "submit" is actually a military term. It speaks of soldiers forming up under the command of an officer. There's nothing passive about that!
3. The knowledge that God is faithful to forgive your sins and cleanse you from your unrighteousness. Confessed sins are over and done with. It's not up to you to beat yourself up over them.
4. There are a couple of reasons that God's promises can sometimes be repetitive. One is that we are hard-headed people and need to hear things more than once before we really listen. Secondly, even when we are really listening, the promises of God are so deep that they deserve to be stated and restated just so we can see more and more of their richness.
5. Our "alien" status means we have all the more reason to live in community with one another. It can be isolating to live as a Christian in the world. We need each other.

Chapter 20

1. It's a matter of trusting God and taking Him at His word. He doesn't require that we understand everything, only that we follow His lead. To insist on understanding God's ways is really just another way of leaning on your own understanding.
2. Obedience is its own reward. God's blessing is not measured in material terms. It is measured by the kind of person you are and the lasting impact you make on everyone who knows you.
3. Your heart is the real issue. Corruption settles there, and it has nothing to do with what you eat. The words you say are the overflow of your heart. If they are unclean, you can be sure your heart is defiled.
4. Soaking your mind and heart in God's word is like soaking a piece of meat in marinade. The flavor soaks all the way through; it's not just on the surface.
5. Persecutors never seem to succeed in halting the progress of Christ's Church. The more Christians suffer, the more the Church grows. For those who love the Church, that's a source of incredible encouragement.

Appendix B—The Experts

Bailey, Robert W.—The pastor of the First Baptist Church of Concord, North Carolina, author of several books on pastoral care.

Banks, Vickey—A popular conference speaker and author of *Sharing His Secrets, & Love Letters to My Baby.*

Barclay, William—A professor of Divinity and Biblical Criticism at Glasgow University, best-selling author, broadcaster on radio and television, and a regular contributor to widely circulated newspapers.

Baxter, J. Sidlow—A prolific writer, Bible teacher, and pastor from London, England.

Benson, Robert—A popular speaker and author on the subject of prayer. His books include *Living Prayer* and *The Night of the Child.*

Boom, Corrie ten—The world-famous author of *The Hiding Place*, spent her life sharing her experiences and faith with people all over the world.

Bottke, Allison Gappa—The originator and editor of the *God Allows U-Turns* series.

Bouchier, Barton—He was the author of *Manna in the House*, published by Reed and Pardon Printers, 1852.

Bridges, Jerry—The treasurer for the Navigators and Navigator Field Ministries before becoming Vice President for corporate affairs for the Navigators, also the author of several books.

Bright, Bill—The founder and president of Campus Crusade for Christ, author of numerous books, columns and articles.

Briscoe, Stuart—The pastor of Elmbrook Church in Waukesha, Wisconsin, director of "Telling the Truth" tape ministry, and author of many books.

Browning, Robert—He is credited as being the most important Victorian poet after Tennyson.

Bruce, F. F.—A former Rylands professor of biblical criticism and exegesis at Manchester University, England, and author of numerous books and commentaries.

Burkett, Larry—The founder and president of Christian Financial Concepts, Incorporated, well-known author and host of a nationally syndicated radio talk show.

Cash, Johnny—The legendary country-western singer known for his deep, distinctive voice recorded more than 1,500 songs.

Chafer, Lewis Sperry—The founder and first president of Dallas Theological Seminary, his books on Systematic Theology are considered classics.

Chambers, Oswald—He was born in Scotland and his ministry of teaching and preaching took him for a time to the U.S. and Japan. The last six years of his life were spent as principal of the Bible Training College in London and as a chaplain to the British Commonwealth troops in Egypt during WWI.

Chilton, Bruce—A professor at Bard College, a priest, and the author of many titles including *Rabbi Jesus* and *A Galilean Rabbi and His Bible.*

Crabb, Dr. Lawrence J., Jr.—A psychologist and professor at Colorado Christian University, he is a popular conference speaker, and author.

Criswell, W. A. (1909-2002)—He was pastor of the First Baptist Church in Dallas, Texas for forty-seven years.

Daly, Richard—An ordained minister in Gloucestershire, England and the author of *A Little Book of Bible Promises, God's Little Book of Calm, God's Little Book of Promises for Children*, and *Healed.*

DeHaan, Richard W.—The radio pastor of the Radio Bible Class, a part of RBC Ministries, contributor to the devotional series *Our Daily Bread*, and author.

Dobson, Dr. James C.—A psychologist, best-selling author and Founder/President of Focus on the Family Ministries.

Donihue, Anita Corrine—She is a wife, mother,

grandmother, and author of the best-selling devotionals *When I'm on My Knees* and *When God Sees Me Through.*

Edman, V. Raymond— He was missionary in Ecuador and president of Wheaton College for twenty-five years.

Eims, LeRoy—He is the director of Public Ministry Worldwide for the Navigators, a speaker, seminar leader, and author.

Elliot, Elisabeth—The wife of martyred missionary Jim Elliot; she is a well-known speaker, and author.

Elliot, Jim—One of five missionaries martyred for his faith among the Auca Indians in Quito, Ecuador.

Fickett, Harold L.—The former pastor of the ten thousand-member First Baptist Church of Van Nuys, CA, more recently the president of Barrington College in Rhode Island.

Getz, Dr. Gene—A professor of practical theology at Dallas Theological Seminary, his is the founder/pastor of Fellowship Bible Church in Dallas, Texas.

Graham, Billy—Dr. Graham has touched more lives with the good news of Christ than anyone in history. His crusades have taken him to every continent, and he has had the privilege of knowing heads of state throughout the world. He lives with his wife, Ruth Bell Graham, in the mountains of North Carolina. He is a best-selling author.

Hakewill, George (1579–1649)—The author of *An Apologie, or Declaration of the Power and Providence of God in the Government of the World*, England 1627.

Hansel, Tim —Stanford graduate, founder of Summit Expedition (a wilderness adventure ministry), author, and conference speaker

Hanegraaff, Hank—The author of *The Prayer of Jesus* (with Lee Strobel) and *The Covering: God's Plan to Protect You from Evil.*

Harrison, Nick— Editor and author of such titles as *Magnificent Prayer* and the best-sellers *Promises to Keep: Daily Devotions for Men Seeking Integrity* and *365 WWJD: Daily Answers to "What Would Jesus Do?*

Heavilin, Malilyn Willet—A popular speaker and author, including the best-seller, *Roses in December.*

Hendricks, Howard—A professor and chairman of the Department of Christian Education at Dallas Theological Seminary.

Henry, Matthew—The highly respected seventeenth and early eighteenth century minister from Chester, England who died in 1714. His commentaries have inspired Bible scholars and teachers for hundreds of years.

Hession, Roy—An internationally beloved evangelist, Bible teacher, NS author whose works have been translated into more than forty languages.

Hobbs, Herschel—The past president of the Southern Baptist Convention, speaker on the Baptist Hour radio program, and former pastor.

Holmes, Marjorie—A columnist for *Women's Day* magazine and the *Washington Star*, she has been called America's favorite inspirational writer.

Hopkins, Mark—He was an educator, a professor of philosophy, and the President of Williams College from 1836–1872.

Howard, J. Grant, Jr.—The chairman of ministerial studies at Western Conservative Baptist College in Portland, OR.

Humbert, Cynthia Spell—The author of *Deceived by Shame, Desired by God*, has coauthored three books and contributed to several others.

Hybels, Bill—He is founder and pastor of Willow Creek Community Church, and the author of several books, including *Honest to God?, Fit to be Tied* and *Too Busy Not to Pray.*

Ignatius of Loyola—A crippled Jesuit who worked for the conversion of the heathen during the early 1500's and wrote a book of devotions called *Spiritual Exercises.*

Ironside, H. A.—The pastor of Moody Memorial Church in Chicago for many years, an internationally loved Bible teacher and preacher, and writer on all the New Testament books.

Jakes, T. D.—He is the assistant presiding prelate of the Higher Ground Assemblies as well as senior pastor of Temple of Faith Ministries in West Virginia. Bishop Jakes is much sought after as a speaker and travels extensively ministering to both clergy and laity.

Johnson, Greg—He is a literary agent for Alive Communications, founding editor of Breakaway magazine, served 10 years in Youth for Christ/Campus Life, and is an author of numerous books.

Johnson, Lin—The managing editor of the *Christian Communicator, Advanced Christian Writer*, and *Church Libraries*; is also an author and Bible curriculum writer.

Jordan, Rebecca Barlow—A conference speaker and the author of *At Home in My Heart*, and *Daily in Your Presence.*

King, Dr. Martin Luther, Jr.—The prominent black civil rights leader who advocated nonviolent methods to bring about change.

LaHaye, Dr. Beverly—The founder and chairman of Concerned Women for America, a nationally recognized advocate, author and spokesperson for traditional family values.

LaHaye, Dr. Tim—The best-selling author of the Left Behind series, founder and president of Family Life Seminars.

LaSor, Dr. William Sanford—A professor of Old Testament at Fuller Theological Seminary, and a writer of biblical commentary for the lay Bible student.

Lee, Robert E.—A confederate general in the "War between the States," known for his impeccable Christian testimony.

Lincoln, Abraham—President of the United States from 1861–1865, during which time he held the nation together through the Civil War, the bloodiest conflict in our nation's history.

Lindsey, Hal—The author of best-selling books, fre quent speaker on Christian cable television about end-time events.

Lloyd-Jones, D. Martyn—An author, physician, and minister at Westminster Chapel in London.

Lockyer, Herbert—A pastor in Scotland and England for twenty-five years, lecturer for the Moody Bible Institute, and conference speaker throughout the United States and Canada.

Lucado, Max—The pastor of Oak Hills Church of Christ and the author of a number of works for both children and adults, including *Traveling Light* and *No Wonder They Call Him Savior*

Luther, Martin—The instigator of the Protestant Reformation in the early 1500's, who promoted the concept that salvation was by faith alone, he nailed his thesis of 95 statements on the door of the Wittenberg Church.

MacArthur, Dr. John F., Jr.—The pastor of Grace Community Church in Sun Valley, California, president of The Master's College, best-selling author and radio preacher.

Marrant, John—A teenage missionary to the Cherokees, former resident of Charleston during colonial times, converted by the preaching of George Whitefield.

Marshall, Peter—He was pastor of the New York Avenue Presbyterian Church in Washington, D.C. and Chaplain of the U.S. Senate. He is known as one of America's greatest preachers.

Matheson, George—A blind, well-loved pastor in Scotland in the late 1800's who wrote the words to the famous hymn, "O Love that Wilt not Let Me Go."

McDowell, Josh—The author of numerous best-selling books, traveling staff member for Campus Crusade for Christ, speaker at more than 580 Universities in 57 countries.

McGuffey, William Holmes—Former president of Ohio University, considered the "Schoolmaster of the Nation" whose reading textbook was a mainstay in American education through the 1920s.

McHenry, Janet Holm—She is a prolific author and high school English teacher. She is the author of *PrayerWalk* and *Daily PrayerWalk*. She is affectionately known as "The PrayerWalk Lady."

McVey, Steve—He is the President of Grace Walk Ministries, a discipleship-training ministry in Atlanta, GA, as well as a sought-after leader of Grace Walk conferences. Steve and his wife, Melanie, have four children and reside in Atlanta.

Mermann, Alan C.—He is the author of *Some Chose to Stay: Faith and Ethics in a Time of Plague.*

Merritt, James—The president of the Southern Baptist Convention.

Meyer, Dr. F. B.—British Bible teacher whose writing has enriched readers for over one hundred years.

Moody, D. L.—Premier evangelist and soul-winner of the late 1800's in Great Britain and the U.S., founder of Moody Bible Institute.

Moore, Beth—A popular conference speaker and teacher and the author of a number of books and study guides including *Jesus, the One and Only.*

Morris, Leon, B.Sc., M.Th., Ph.D.—The vice-principal of Ridley College and author of *The First Epistle of Paul to the Corinthians.*

Mother Teresa—The winner of the Nobel Peace Prize, was known worldwide for her work with "the poorest of the poor."

Mueller, George—Founder and maintainer of orphanages in England in the late 1800s, caring for over ten thousand orphans and raising millions of dollars through prayer alone.

Murphey, Cecil "Cec"—The author of more than sixty books, including *Invading the Privacy of God* and *The God Who Pursues.*

Murray, Andrew—He was one of four children. He studied for three years at a theological school in Holland before going as a missionary to Africa. He is a well-known author of such works as *Experiencing the Holy Spirit.*

Myers, Warren—A well-known Christian author and the author of many books on prayer, including *How to Have a Quiet Time* and *Discovering God's Will.*

Nee, Watchman—He gave his life to Christ in China

in1920. He was both a Bible teacher and author of such works as *God's Overcomers* and *The Glorious Church.* For twenty years he was imprisoned for his faith, dying in China in1972.

Ogilvie, Lloyd John—Former Chaplain of the United States Senate and the 1988 "Preacher of the Year" (National Association of Religious Broadcasters).

Omartian, Stormie—A best-selling author and well-known speaker in the Christian community. She has written such books as *The Power of a Praying Wife* and *The Power of a Praying Parent.*

Palms, Roger—Editor of *Decision* magazine, former pastor and director of a campus ministry at Michigan State University.

Peterson, Eugene H.—A retired professor of spiri tual theology at Regent College in Vancouver, BC. He was a founding pastor of Christ Our King Presbyterian Church in Bel Air, Maryland. He is the author of the highly acclaimed translation of the Bible, *The Message*, as well as *Allegories of Heaven*, and many others.

Pink, Arthur W.—A British scholar who served in pastorates in Australia and the U.S. during the early 1900's, originator of *Studies in Scripture*, a magazine on biblical exposition.

Price, Eugenia—Successful script writer for major television networks before becoming a popular writer (particularly of southern romances) in the Christian marketplace.

Rice, Donna—The cofounder and president of The Book of Life Bible Institute, an attorney, wife, mother, and the author of *The Secret of the Garden Prayer.*

Richards, Lawrence O.—Author of nearly 100 books, including textbooks used in Bible colleges and seminaries, and a Bible teacher to all age groups.

Richter, Stephen—A German Christian author who professes the Protestant faith.

Ridenour, Fritz—Former youth editor for Gospel Light publications, and best-selling author

Roberts, Frances J.—A poet, musician, hymn writer, and author of nine titles including the best-selling *Come Away My Beloved.*

Robison, Betty—The cohost of the Life Today show with her husband James Robison. She is the mother of three children and the grandmother of eleven. She resides in the Dallas-Fort Worth area.

Sanders, J. Oswald—Former director of Overseas Missionary Fellowship (OMF), principal of New Zealand Bible Training Institute, and author of many books.

Seamands, David A.—Professor Emeritus at Asbury Theological Seminary, former missionary and pastor, and best-selling author in the area of Christian psychology.

Sempangi, F. Kefa—Founder and pastor of the four teen thousand- member Redeemed Church of Uganda, and the director of the Africa Foundation, Inc., an organization to help Ugandan refugees.

Sittser, Gerald—An author and professor of religion and philosophy at Whitworth College in Spokane, WA.

Smith, Oswald J.—Pastor of the People's Church in Toronto and a best selling author in the mid 1900s.

Solzhenitsyn, Alexander—Recipient of the Nobel prize in literature, called the greatest living master of the Russian language, imprisoned for his stand on human rights.

Sproul, R. C., Ph.D.—The founder and principal teacher for Ligionier Ministries. He has spent the last thirty years writing more than fifty books and recording hundreds of messages on video and audiocassettes to provide Christian material to hurting people.

Spurgeon, Charles Haddon—Called the "prince of preachers," his sermons held throngs spellbound at the Metropolitan Tabernacle in London in the 19th century. He wrote over 3,500 sermons and is the author of *The Treasury of David.*

Stedman, Ray C.—Nationally recognized expositor, author of several well-known books, and a pastor.

Storms, C. Samuel—He is an associate professor of theology at Wheaton College and the author of several works including *The Beginner's Guide to Spiritual Gifts.*

Stott, John R. W.—Famous lecturer, author of numerous devotional books, and the rector of All Souls Church in London.

Swindoll, Charles R.— Chancellor of Dallas Theological Seminary, host of the nationally syndicated radio program "Insight for Living," and author of many books

Swindoll, Luci—Vice-president of public relations at *Insight for Living*, popular speaker, and author

Tada, Joni Eareckson—Artist, speaker, and author of over twenty books, founder and president of Joni and Friends (JAF)Ministries which advances Christ's kingdom among the disabled.

Tassell, Paul—Former national representative of the General Association of Regular Baptist Churches and author of several books.

Torrey, R. A.—An evangelist, teacher, president of Moody Bible Institute, author of over forty books and former dean at what is now Biola University.

Tozer, A. W.—Pastor, longtime editor of what is now called *Alliance Life*, the official magazine of the Christian and Missionary Alliance church, and author of many books.

Vamosh, Miriam Feinberg—She holds a Bachelor's Degree in Jewish education, has been a tour guide in Israel since 1975, and is the author of *Daily Life at the Time of Jesus.*

Van Gorder, Dr. Paul R.—Associate teacher of the *Radio Bible Class*, speaker on the TV series *Day of Discovery*, contributing writer for *Our Daily Bread*, and well-known author.

Vischer, Lukas, PhD—The author of *Growth in Agreement* and the editor of *The Reformed Family Worldwide: A Survey of Reformed Churches, Theological Schools, and International Organizations.*

Walvoord, Dr. John F.—Former president of Dallas Theological Seminary for thirty-four years, author, and co-editor of *The Bible Knowledge Commentary.*

Weiser, Artur—A German professor and theologian during the mid 1900s whose works on the Psalter have been translated into English.

Wesley, John—The founder of Methodism.

Wilkinson, Bruce—The founder and president of Walk Thru the Bible Ministries and is the author of the best selling *The Prayer of Jabez.*

Willard, Dallas—A professor of philosophy at the University of Southern California. He is the author of *The Divine Conspiracy* and *The Spirit of the Disciplines.*

Endnotes

Part 1

PRAYERS ENDNOTES

Chapter 1—THE DYNAMICS OF PRAYER

1. R. C. Sproul, *The Holiness of God* (Wheaton, IL: Tyndale House Publishers, 1985),
2. Stephen Richter, *Metanoia-Christian Penance and Confession* (New York, NY: Sheed and Ward, Inc., 1966), 81.
3. C. Samuel Storms, *To Love Mercy* (Colorado Springs, CO: NavPress, 1991), 179–180.
4. Nick Harrison, *Magnificent Prayer* (Grand Rapids, Michigan: Zondervan), 242.
5. Lloyd John Ogilvie, *The Power of Prayer* (Novato, CA: New World Library) edited by Dale Salwak, 96.
6. Rebecca Barlow Jordan, *Daily in Your Presence* (Uhrichsville, OH: Barbour Publishing), 15.
7. R.C. Sproul, *The Holiness of God* (Wheaton, IL: Tyndale House Publishers, Inc.,1998), 38.
8. John Wesley, *A Plain Account of Christian Perfection* Chapter 11, (http://www.worldinvisible.com/library/wesley/8317/8317c.htm).

Chapter 2—PRAYERS OF AN AWAKENED HEART

1. Dallas Willard, *Hearing God* (Downers Grove, IL: InterVarsity Press, 1984).
2. Lukas Vischer, *Intercession* (Geneva, Switzerland: World Council of Churches, 1980), 40.
3. Billy Graham, *Time with God* (Dallas, TX: Word Publishing, Inc., 1991) edited by Amanda and Stephen Sorenson, 595.
4. Nick Harrison, *Magnificent Prayer* (Grand Rapids, Michigan: Zondervan), 282.
5. Janet Holm McHenry, *Daily PrayerWalk: Meditations for a Deeper Prayer Life* (Colorado Springs, CO: WaterBrook Press, 2002), 175.
6. John Gill, *John Gill's Exposition of the Bible* (http://bible.crosswalk.com/Commentaries/GillsExpositionoftheBible.) Commentary on Ephesians 3:19.
7. Matthew Henry, Commentary on 1 Thessalonians 5. *Matthew Henry Concise Commentary on the Whole Bible.* (http://bible.crosswalk.com/Commentaries/MatthewHenryConcise/mhc-con.cgi?book=1th&chapter=005). 1706.

Chapter 3—PRAYERS OF PRAISE

1. Warren Myers *Time with God* (Dallas, TX: Word Publishing, Inc., 1991) edited by Amanda and Stephen Sorenson, 555.
2. Alan C. Mermann, *The Power of Prayer* (Novato, CA: New World Library) edited by Dale Salwak, 18.
3. C. Samuel Storms, *The Grandeur of God* (Grand Rapids, MI: Baker House Publishers, 1984), 149.
4. Frances J. Roberts, *Come Away My Beloved* (Uhrichsville, OH: Barbour Publishing, 2004).
5. Leon Morris, *Tyndale New Testament Commentaries 1 Corinthians* (Grand Rapids, MI: Wm. B. Eerdmans Publishing Co., 1983), 103.
6. Corrie ten Boom, *He Sets the Captives Free* (Old Tappan, NJ: Fleming H. Revell, 1977), 75.
7. Nick Harrison, *Magnificent Prayer* (Grand Rapids, MI: Zondervan, 2001), 189.

Chapter 4—PRAYERS OF REPENTANCE

1. Vickey Banks, *Sharing His Secrets* (Sisters, Oregon: Multnomah Publishers, Inc.), pg. 85.
2. Billy Graham, *Time with God* (Dallas, TX: Word Publishing, Inc., 1991) edited by Amanda and Stephen Sorenson, 163.
3. Cynthia Spell Humbert, *Deceived by Shame* (Colorado Springs, CO: NavPress 2001), 171.
4. Max Lucado, *No Wonder They Call Him Savior* (Sisters, OR: Multnomah Publishers, Inc., 1986), 34.

5. Matthew Henry Commentary on Ezra 9. *Matthew Henry Concise Commentary on the Whole Bible.* (http://bible.crosswalk.com/Commentaries/MatthewHenryConcise/mhc-con.cgi?book=ezr&chapter=009), 1706.
6. Allison Gappa Bottke, *God Allows U-Turns* (Uhrichsville, OH: Promise Press, 2001), 13.
7. Beth Moore, *Let Us Bow Before Him* (Spirit Led Woman, June/July 2002), Strang Communication, 13.
8. T. D. Jakes, *Can You Stand to Be Blessed?* (Shippensburg, PA: Destiny Image Publishers, Inc., 1994), 41.

Chapter 5—PRAYERS OF PERSONAL DISTRESS

1. Oswald Chambers, *My Utmost for His Highest* (Westwood, NJ: Barbour & Co., Inc., 1963), 104.
2. Andrew Murray, *The Best of Andrew Murray on Prayer* (Uhrichsville, OH: Barbour Publishing, Inc., 2000), Page Heading: March 16.
3. Betty Robison, *Women at the Well* (Ft. Worth, TX: Life Publishing, 2001), 62.
4. Peter Marshall, *Wonderful Thoughts to Live By* (Augusta, GA: William Kuhlke Co., 1975), 188.
5. Bill Hybels, *Too Busy NOT to Pray* (Downers Grove, IL: InterVarsity Press, 1988).
6. Steve McVey, *Grace Walk* (Eugene, OR: Harvest House Publishers, 1995), 120.
7. Barton Bouchier, *The Treasury of David by C. H. Spurgeon* (Peabody, MA: Hendrickson Publishers, 1993), Volume II, 540 (1855).
8. Miriam Feinberg Vamosh, *Pathways Through the Land of the Hart* (Jerusalem, Israel: 1993/5753), 5.
9. Joni Eareckson Tada, *Joni Eareckson Tada, Her Story* (New York, NY: Inspirational Press, 1990), 281.

Chapter 6—PRAYERS OF PETITION

1. Bruce Wilkinson, *The Prayer of Jabez* (Sisters, OR: Multnomah Publishers, Inc., 2000), 24.
2. Charles Haddon Spurgeon, *Morning and Evening Devotions, June 24, PM* (http://devotionals.crosswalk.com).
3. James Merritt, *God's Prescription for a Healthy Christian* (Wheaton, IL: Victor Books, 1990), 399.
4. Joni Eareckson Tada, *Joni Eareckson Tada, My Story* (New York, NY: Inspirational Press, 1990), 542.
5. Bruce Wilkinson, *The Prayer of Jabez* (Sisters, OR: Multnomah Publishers, Inc. 2000).
6. Nick Harrison, *Magnificent Prayer* (Grand Rapids, MI: Zondervan), 247.
7. Word Publishers, Inc. *Prayers That Avail Much* (Tulsa, OK: Harrison House, 1989), 84.
8. Alan C. Mermann, *The Power of Prayer* (Novato, CA: New World Library, 1998) edited by Dale Salwak, 17.
9. Mark Hopkins, *Creative Quotations from Mark Hopkins* (http://www.creativequotations.com/one/1449.htm).
10. Max Lucado, *No Wonder They Call Him Savior* (Eugene, OR: Multnomah Publishers, Inc., 1986), 18.

Chapter 7—PRAYERS OF INTERCESSION

1. Andrew Murray, *The Best of Andrew Murray on Prayer* (Urhichsville, OH: Barbour Publishing, Inc., 2000), 433.
2. Anita Corine Donihue, *When I'm On My Knees* (Barbour Publishing, Inc., Uhrichsville, OH), 106.
3. Robert Benson, *Living Prayer* (New York, NY: Penguin Putnam, Inc., 1998), 139.
4. Richard Daly, *Healed* (Waynesboro, GA: Paternoster Lifestyle) pp.133–134.
5. Stormie Omartian, *Heaven Your Real Home* (Grand Rapids, MI: Zondervan Publishers, 1995) 181.
6. Eugene H. Peterson, *The Message, The New Testament, Psalms and Proverbs* (Colorado Spring, CO: NavPress, 1995), 315.
7. George Hakewill, *The Treasury of David by C. H. Spurgeon* (Peabody, MA: Hendrickson Publishers, 1993), Volume II, 245.

Chapter 8—PRAYERS FOR GUIDANCE

1. Dallas Willard, *Hearing God* (Downers Grove, IL: InterVarsity Press, 1984).
2. Mother Teresa, *The Power of Prayer* (Novato, CA: New World Library) edited by Dale Salwak, 6.
3. Matthew Henry, Commentary on 1 Samuel 23, *Matthew Henry Concise Commentary on the Whole Bible*, (http://bible.crosswalk.com/Commentaries/MatthewHenryConcise/mhc-con.cgi?book=1sa&chapter=023). 1706.
4. Hank Hanegraaff, *The Prayer of Jesus* (Nashville, TN:W Publishing Group, 2001), 19.
5. Charles R. Swindoll, *Time with God* (Dallas, TX: Word Publishing, Inc., 1991) edited by Amanda and Stephen Sorenson, 573.
6. Watchman Nee, *God's Overcomers* (Anaheim, CA: Living Stream Ministry, 1999) 14.

7. Richard W. DeHaan, *Pray, God Is Listening* (Grand Rapids, MI: Zondervan Publishing House, 1980), 37.
8. Richard W. DeHaan, ibid, 22.

Chapter 9—THE LORD'S PRAYER

1. Cecil Murphey, *Invading the Privacy of God* (Ann Arbor, MI: Servant Publications).
2. Cecil Murphey, *Invading the Privacy of God* (Ann Arbor, Michigan, Servant Publications, 1997), 46.
3. Watchman Nee, *God's Overcomers* (Anaheim, CA: Living Stream Ministry, 1999), 13.
4. Bruce Chilton, *Rabbi Jesus* (Doubleday, New York, New York), 195.

Chapter 10—THE PRAYERS OF JESUS

1. Matthew Henry, Commentary on John 17. *Matthew Henry Concise Commentary on the Whole Bible.* (http://bible.crosswalk.com/Commentaries/MatthewHenryConcise/mhc-con.cgi?book=joh&chapter=017). 1706.
2. Robert Benson, *The Game* (New York, NY: Penguin Putnum, Inc., 2001), 161.
3. Andrew Murray, *The Best of Andrew Murray on Prayer* (Uhrichsville, OH: Barbour Publishing, Inc., 2000.) Page heading July 24.
4. J. W. McGarvey and Philip Y. Pendleton, *The Fourfold Gospel* (1914), (http://www.ccel.org/m/mcgarvey/ffg/FFG000A.HTM), Section CXXXIII , Subsection C.
5. James Strong, *The Exhaustive Concordance of the Bible* (Riverside Book & Bible House, Iowa Falls, Iowa), Greek Dictionary of the New Testament pg. 55.
6. Robert Benson, *Between the Dreaming and the Coming True* (New York, NY: Jeremy P. Tarcher/Putnam, 2001), 122.

Part 2

PROMISES ENDNOTES

Chapter 11—PROMISES CONCERNING OUR GOD

1. Joni Eareckson Tada, *Secret Strength* (Portland: Multnomah Press, 1988), 331.
2. George Matheson, quoted in *Worship and Service Hymnal* (Carol Stream, IL: Hope Publishing Co., 1975), 323.
3. A. W. Tozer, compiled by Warren W. Wiersbe, *The Best of A. W. Tozer* (Harrisburg, PA: Christian Publications, Inc., 1978), 109.
4. Corrie ten Boom, *Each New Day* (Old Tappan: Fleming H. Revell, 1977), 25.
5. Bill Bright, *Believing God for the Impossible* (San Bernardino: Campus Crusade for Christ Int., 1979), 5.
6. Arthur W. Pink, *The Attributes of God* (Grand Rapids: Baker Book House, 1975), 77.
7. Jerry Bridges, *The Practice of Godliness* (Colorado Springs: NavPress, 1984), 249.
8. Charles Haddon Spurgeon, quoted by Tom Carter, *Spurgeon at His Best* (Grand Rapids: Baker Book House, 1988), 244.

Chapter 12—PROMISES CONCERNING OUR FUTURE

1. Herbert Lockyer, *All the Miracles of the Bible* (Grand Rapids: Zondervan Publishing House, 1965), 257.
2. Charles R. Swindoll, *Rise and Shine* (Portland: Multnomah Press, 1989), 174.
3. Dr. Paul R. Van Gorder, *The Church Stands Corrected* (Wheaton: Victor Books, 1976), 154.
4. Robert W. Bailey, *Ministering to the Grieving* (Grand Rapids: Zondervan Publishing House, 1980), 15.
5. Marilyn Willett Heavilin, *When Your Dreams Die* (San Bernardino: Here's Life, 1990), 141.
6. D. L. Moody, *Heaven and How to Get There* (Chicago: Moody Press, n.d.), 68–69.
7. Dr. John F. MacArthur, Jr., *Heaven* (Chicago: Moody Press, 1988), 10.
8. Lewis Sperry Chafer and John Walvoord, *Major Bible Themes* (Grand Rapids: Zondervan, 1976), 184.
9. Greg Johnson, *Life Is Like Driver's Ed* (Ann Arbor, MI: Servant Publications, 1996), 34.

Chapter 13—PROMISES CONCERNING OUR PROBLEMS

1. David Seamands, *Healing Meditations for Life* (Wheaton: Victor Books, 1996), 17.
2. Richard W. DeHaan, *Good News for Bad Times* (Wheaton: Victor Books, 1975), 125.
3. V. Raymond Edman, *The Disciplines of Life* (Minneapolis: World Wide Publications, 1948), 216–217.
4. Charles R. Swindoll, *Seasons of Life* (Portland: Multnomah Press, 1983), 164.
5. H. A. Ironside, *11 Corinthians* (Neptune, NJ: Loizeaux Brothers, 1974), 116–117.
6. Roy Hession, *My Calvary Road* (Grand Rapids: Zondervan Publishing House, 1978), 113.

7. John R. W. Stott, *Guard the Gospel* (Downers Grove, IL: InterVarsity Press, 1973), 124.
8. Roger Palms, *God's Promises for You* (Old Tappan: Fleming H. Revell, 1977), 61.
9. Alexander Solzhenitsyn, quoted by Marshall Foster and Mary-Elaine Swanson, *The American Covenant—the Untold Story* ((Roseburg, OR: Foundation for Christian Self-Government, 1981; Thousand Oaks, CA: The Mayflower Institute, 1992), 164.
10. Billy Graham, quoted by David Frost, *Billy Graham—Personal Thoughts of a Public Man* (Colorado Springs: ChariotVictor Publishing, 1997), 83–84.

Chapter 14—PROMISES CONCERNING OUR DEPENDENCE

1. R. A. Torrey, *Power and Peace in Prayer* (Westchester, IL: Good News Publishers, 1978), 18–19.
2. Beverly LaHaye, *Prayer—God's Comfort for Today's Family* (Nashville: Thomas Nelson Publishers, 1990), 90–91.
3. George Mueller, *Answers to Prayer* (Chicago: Moody Press, n.d.), 106–107.
4. Herbert Lockyer, *All the Promises of the Bible* (Grand Rapids: Zondervan Publishing House, 1964), 151.
5. Jerry Bridges, *The Practice of Godliness*, 213–214.
6. Charles Haddon Spurgeon, quoted by Tom Carter, *Spurgeon at His Best*, 296.
7. William Holmes McGuffey, *Eclectic First Reader—Lesson 37*, as quoted by Catherine Millard, *The Rewriting of American History* (Camp Hill, PA: Horizon House Publishers, 1991), 202.
8. Corrie ten Boom, *Each New Day*, 50.

Chapter 15—PROMISES CONCERNING OURSELVES

1. Dr. James Dobson, *Preparing for Adolescence* (Ventura: Vision House, 1978), 37.
2. Leroy Eims, *The Lost Art of Disciple Making* (Grand Rapids: Zondervan Publishing House, 1978), 29.
3. Howard Hendricks, *Say It with Love* (Wheaton: Victor Books, 1973), 14.
4. Johnny Cash, quoted by Billy Graham, *How to Be Born Again* (Waco, TX: Word Publishers, 1977), 153.
5. Fritz Ridenour, *How to Be a Christian Without Being Religious* (Glendale: Regal Books, 1972), 63–64.
6. Tim Hansel, *Holy Sweat* (Dallas:Word Publishers, 1987), 61.
7. Jim Elliot, quoted by Robert C. Girard, *Life of Christ—God's Word for the Biblically Inept* (Lancaster, PA: Starburst Publishers, 2000), 129.
8. Dee Gagnon, *DeeTours* (Brockton, Massachusetts: Pegasus Publishing, 2000), 109, 113.
9. Ignatius of Loyola, quoted by Elisabeth Elliot, *Let Me Be a Woman* (Wheaton: Tyndale House, 1967), 57.
10. W. A. Criswell, *Ephesians* (Grand Rapids, Zondervan Publishing House, 1974), 298.
11. R. A. Torrey, *The Person and Work of the Holy Spirit* (Grand Rapids: Zondervan Publishing House, 1974), 224.

Chapter 16—PROMISES TO MEET PHYSICAL NEEDS

1. D. Martyn Lloyd-Jones, *Studies in the Sermon on the Mount* (Grand Rapids, MI: Wm. B. Eerdmans, 1960), 131.
2. Luci Swindoll, et al., *Joy Breaks* (Grand Rapids: Zondervan Publishing House, 1997), 100.
3. Larry Burkett, *Your Finances in Changing Times* (Chicago: Moody Press, 1975), 69–70.
4. A. W. Tozer, *The Knowledge of the Holy* (New York: Harper & Row, 1961), 70.
5. Artur Weiser, *The Psalms* (Philadelphia: The Westminster Press, 1962), 727.
6. Marjorie Holmes, *To Help You Through the Hurting* (Garden City, NY: Doubleday and Co., 1983), 108–109.
7. David Seamands, *Healing Meditations for Life*, 170.
8. Joni Eareckson Tada and Steve Estes, *A Step Further* (Grand Rapids, MI: Zondervan, 1982), 133.
9. Robert Browning, quoted by Robert J. Morgan, *Stories, Illustrations, & Quotes* (Nashville: Thomas Nelson Publishers, 2000), 12.
10. Eugenia Price, *What Is God Like?* (Grand Rapids: Zondervan Publishing House, 1960), 121.

Chapter 17—PROMISES TO MEET ETERNAL NEEDS

1. John Stott, quoted by Morgan, *Stories, Illustrations, & Quotes*, 167.

2. William Barclay, *The Letter to the Romans* (Philadelphia: Westminster Press, 1977), 91–92.
3. Billy Graham, *The Jesus Generation* (Grand Rapids: Zondervan Publishing House, 1971), 125.
4. F. F. Bruce, *The Epistle of Paul to the Romans* (Grand Rapids: Wm. B. Eerdmans Publishing Co., 1963), 100.
5. Paul Tassell, *That Ye Might Believe* (Schaumburg, IL: Regular Baptist Press, 1987), 40–41.
6. Lin Johnson, *John—God's Word for the Biblically-Inept* (Lancaster, PA: Starburst Publishers, 2001), 137.
7. Herschel Hobbs, *Exposition of the Four Gospels* (Grand Rapids: Baker Book House, 1968), 170.
8. John Walvoord and Roy Zuck, editors, *The Bible Knowledge Commentary*, New Testament Edition (Wheaton: Victor Books, 1983), 557.
9. Gerald L. Sittser, *The Will of God as a Way of Life* (Grand Rapids: Zondervan Publishing House, 2000), 234.
10. Larry Richards, *The Bible—God's Word for the Biblically Inept* (Lancaster, PA: Starburst Publishers, 1998), 265.
11. Dr. Larry Crabb Jr., *Understanding People* (Grand Rapids: Zondervan Publishing House, 1987), 207.

Chapter 18—PROMISES TO MEET EMOTIONAL NEEDS

1. Ray C. Stedman, *Authentic Christianity* (Waco, TX: Word Books, 1975), 122–123.
2. Gene A. Getz, *David* (Glendale, CA: Regal Books, 1978), 26.
3. John Murrant, quoted by Robert J. Morgan, *From This Verse* (Nashville: Thomas Nelson Publishers, 1998), May 10th.
4. Dr. F. B. Meyer, *David* (Westchester, IL: Good News Publishers, 1960), 31.
5. Harold L. Fickett, Jr., *Keep On Keeping On* (Glendale, CA: Regal Books, 1978), 80.
6. Stuart Briscoe, *Bound for Joy* (Glendale, CA: Regal Books, 1977), 4.
7. J. Grant Howard, Jr., *Knowing God's Will and Doing It* (Grand Rapids: Zondervan Publishing House, 1976), 50.
8. Tim LaHaye, *How to Study the Bible for Yourself* (Irvine, CA: Harvest House, 1976), 18–19.
9. Josh McDowell, *More than a Carpenter* (Wheaton, Tyndale House, 1981), 125.
10. Elizabeth Elliot, *Keep a Quiet Heart* (Ann Arbor, MI: Servant Publications, 1995), 20.

Chapter 19—PROMISES TO MEET SPIRITUAL NEEDS

1. Paul Van Gorder, *The Church Stands Corrected*, 93.
2. Martin Luther, *Table Talk*, quoted by Morgan, *Stories, Illustrations, & Quotes*, 725.
3. Greg Johnson, *Life Is like Driver's Ed*, 174.
4. David Seamands, *Healing for Damaged Emotions* (Wheaton: Victor Books, 1981), 31–32.
5. John MacArthur, *Why I Trust the Bible* (Wheaton: Victor Books, 1987), 45.
6. Elisabeth Elliot, *Trusting God in a Twisted World* (Old Tappan: Fleming H. Revell Co., 1989), 67.
7. Abraham Lincoln, as quoted by Peter Marshall and David Manuel, *The Glory of America* (Bloomington MN: Garborg's Heart 'N Home, Inc., 1991), 6.23
8. A. W. Tozer, *The Knowledge of the Holy* (New York: Harper & Row, Publishers, 1961), 70.
9. Martin Luther King, Jr., quoted by Tim Hansel, *Holy Sweat* (Dallas: Word Publishers, 1987), 55.
10. William Sanford LaSor, *Church Alive* (Glendale, CA: Regal Books, 1973), 41.
11. Luci Swindoll, et al., *Joy Breaks*, 140–141.

Chapter 20—PROMISES TO MEET MINISTRY NEEDS

1. Gerald Sittser, *The Will of God as a Way of Life*, 34.
2. J. Grant Howard, *Knowing God's Will and Doing It*, 35–37.
3. J. Oswald Sanders, *Bible Men of Faith* (Chicago: Moody Press, 1974), 173.
4. LeRoy Eims, *The Basic Ingredients for Spiritual Growth* (Wheaton: Victor Books, 1992), 121.
5. Billy Graham, *The Secret of Happiness*, quoted by Max Lucado, *The Inspirational Bible* (Nashville: Word Publishing, 1995), 1412.
6. Charles R. Swindoll, *Come Before Winter* (Portland: Multnomah Press, 1985), 310.
7. A. W. Tozer, *The Best of Tozer*, quoted by Max Lucado, *The Inspirational Bible*, 576.
8. Oswald J. Smith, *The Man God Uses* (London: Marshall, Morgan & Scott, 1953), 12.
9. Robert E. Lee, quoted by Henry H. Halley, *Halley's Bible Handbook* (Grand Rapids: Zondervan Publishing House, 1965), 19.

10. F. Kefa Sempangi, *A Distant Grief* (Glendale, CA: Regal Books, 1979), 121.

11. William Byron Forbush, editor, *Foxe's Book of Martyrs* (Grand Rapids: Zondervan Publishing House, 1926), 2–5.

12. Richard W. DeHaan, *Good News for Bad Times*, 123.

Prayers in the Bible Index

Prayer and Who Prayed	Bible Reference	Page #
Prayer at the End of Stephen's life (martyred for his faith)	Acts 7:59	90
Prayer at the End of Jesus' life (Jesus)	Luke 23:46	68, 141
Prayer before Dying (Jesus)	John 17:13	133
Prayer for a Sign (Gideon)	Judges 6:17	110
Prayer for Bravery and Victory (Jehoshaphat)	2 Chronicles 20:9	66, 67
Prayer for Disciples to Join Him in Heaven (Jesus)	John 17:24	137
Prayer for Elisha's Servant (Elisha)	2 Kings 6:17	26
Prayer for Ephesian Believers (Paul)	Ephesians 1:18–20; 3:16–19	26–27
Prayer for Fire from Heaven; Elijah's Prayer against Prophets of Baal	1 Kings 18:26–29	65
Prayer for Friends in Thessalonica (Paul)	1 Thessalonians 3:12	29
Prayer for God's Blessings (Moses)	Numbers 6:24–27	98
Prayer for God's Blessings on Joseph's Children (Jacob)	Genesis 48:15–16	96, 97
Prayer for God's Forgiveness for Another's Sin (Moses)	Numbers 14:19	47, 48
Prayer for God's Goodness and Favor (David)	Psalm 25:7	87
Prayer for God's Goodness and Favor (thief on the cross)	Luke 23:32–43	87
Prayer for God's Goodness and Will (David)	Psalm 16:1	19, 20
Prayer for God's Will to Be Done (Jesus)	Matthew 26:39	138
Prayer for Guidance (Abraham's chief servant)	Genesis 24:12a–14	77
Prayer for Guidance (David)	1 Samuel 23:10–11	113
Prayer for Guidance (Jesus' disciples)	Acts 1:24a	121
Prayer for Guidance (King Saul)	1 Samuel 14:37	91
Prayer for Healing (Hezekiah)	Isaiah 38:15a–16	24, 26
Prayer for Healing (Jeremiah)	Jeremiah 17:14	42, 43
Prayer for Healing (leper)	Matthew 8:2	81
Prayer for Healing (Moses)	Numbers 12:13	99
Prayer for Healing of Jairus's Daughter (Jairus)	Luke 8:41–56	98
Prayer for Help in Leadership (Moses)	Numbers 11:14	61
Prayer for Ishmael (Abraham)	Genesis 17:18	98
Prayer for Israel (Nehemiah)	Nehemiah 1:6a	118
Prayer for Israel in the Wilderness (Moses)	Exodus 32:9–14	265
Prayer for Leadership (Moses)	Numbers 27:15–17	101
Prayer for Mercy (Hezekiah)	2 Chronicles 30:18b–19a	51, 52
Prayer for Mercy (Ezra)	Ezra 9:9–10	54
Prayer for Remembrance (Samson)	Judges 16:28	49
Prayer for Repentance (David)	Psalm 51	55, 150, 273
Prayer for Sanctification for the Disciples (Jesus)	John 17:17	69, 275
Prayer for Sodom (Abraham)	Genesis 18:22b–23	95
Prayer for the Jewish Nation (Nehemiah)	Nehemiah 1:6b	4
Prayer for the Philippians (Paul)	Philippians 1:9–10	107
Prayer for Unity (Jesus)	John 17:11b	132
Prayer for Unity of the Disciples (Jesus)	John 17:20–21	133
Prayer for Victory (Jehoshaphat)	2 Chronicles 20:6b	117
Prayer for Wisdom and Understanding (Solomon)	1 Kings 3:9a	80
Prayer from a Besetting Sin; Paul's Thorn in the Flesh	2 Corinthians 12:8–9	89, 230
Prayer from a Sorrowful Spirit; Hannah's Prayer of Sacrifice	1 Samuel 1:11	64
Prayer from a Troubled Heart; David's Prayer of Complaint	Psalm 31:9, 14–16	68
Prayer from David; Thirst Satisfied by His Heavenly Father (David)	Psalm 63:5	127, 260
Prayer from David; Thirsting for His Heavenly Father	Psalm 63:1	69, 260
Prayer from the Heart; Giving God the Glory (David)	Psalm 144:3	8
Prayer Instead of Retaliation (David)	Psalm 109:1–4	71
Prayer of a Settled Heart (David)	Psalm 89:26b	7
Prayer of Abandonment (Jesus)	Mark 15:34	69, 140

Prayer and Who Prayed	Bible Reference	Page #
Prayer of Blessings (anonymous writer of Hebrews)	Hebrews 13:20–21	105
Prayer of Blessings and Good Works (Paul)	2 Thessalonians 2:16–17	143
Prayer of Blessings for Solomon (David)	1 Kings 2:1–4	98
Prayer of Dedication for the Temple (Solomon)	1 Kings 8:59a	18
Prayer of Dedication of the Temple and for God's Faithfulness (Solomon)	1 Kings 8:56–58	103
Prayer of Dedication to the Temple (Solomon)	Psalm 11:4	3
Prayer of Despair (Elijah)	1 Kings 19:4	65, 66, 176
Prayer of Forgiveness for His Killers (Jesus)	Luke 23:33–34	139
Prayer of Forgiveness for Stephen's Killers (Stephen)	Acts 7:60	90
Prayer of God's Sovereignty (David)	2 Samuel 7:22	36
Prayer of Healing (Mary and Martha to Jesus about Lazarus)	John 11:3	104, 165
Prayer of Humility and Boldness (Abraham)	Genesis 18:30	95
Prayer of Humility and Repentance (as described in Jesus's parable)	Luke 18:13	78, 79, 172
Prayer of Humility; Request for God's Holiness and Mercy (David)	Psalm 5:7	5
Prayer of Impatience (David)	Psalm 141:1	88, 89
Prayer of Impatience (David)	Psalms 22:19; 35:22; 38:21–22; 70:5	89
Prayer of Intercession (Roman officer to Jesus)	Matthew 8:6	74
Prayer of Intercession for Job's Children (Job)	Job 1:5	98
Prayer of Jabez	1 Chronicles 4:9–10	83
Prayer of Praise	Psalm 119:171	40
Prayer of Praise (David)	1 Chronicles 29:11	37
Prayer of Praise (David)	Psalm 18:28	21
Prayer of Praise (David)	Psalm 30:2	22, 23
Prayer of Praise (David)	Psalm 89:26b	7
Prayer of Praise (Levites)	2 Chronicles 5:13c	38
Prayer of Praise (Moses)	Exodus 15:11	33, 34
Prayer of Praise and Worship to God Above All Others (David)	Psalm 138:1–2	23
Prayer of Praise at the End of David's Life	1 Chronicles 29:9–20	37
Prayer of Praise: God Is Enough (Habakkuk)	Habakkuk 3:17–19	72
Prayer of Protection from Persecution (Jesus)	John 17:14	135
Prayer of Protection from the Evil One (Jesus)	John 17:15–16	134
Prayer of Questioning (Jeremiah)	Jeremiah 12:1, 4–5	59
Prayer of Readiness (Samuel in response to God's voice)	1 Samuel 3:10b	111
Prayer of Readiness (Isaiah answers God's call)	Isaiah 6:8b	56, 57
Prayer of Rejoicing in God's Faithfulness (David)	2 Samuel 7:28	114
Prayer of Repentance (Children of Israel)	Judges 10:10	48
Prayer of Repentance (David)	Psalm 51:1–2, 8, 10	55
Prayer of Repentance (Jeremiah asks for mercy in judgment)	Jeremiah 10:24	57
Prayer of Reverence and Gratitude (David)	2 Samuel 7:18	34
Prayer of Safekeeping in Travel (children of Israel before moving ark)	Numbers 10:35b	109
Prayer of Safety and Comfort (David)	Psalm 3:3	120
Prayer of Sanctification (Paul)	1 Thessalonians 5:23	30
Prayer of Shame (Ezra)	Ezra 9:6	52
Prayer of Supplication for Solomon and the Children of Israel (Solomon)	1 Kings 8:52	102
Prayer of Surrender (David)	Psalm 139	18
Prayer of Thanks (Simeon)	Luke 2:29–32	10, 11
Prayer of Thanksgiving (David)	2 Samuel 22:29	116
Prayer of Thanksgiving (Hezekiah)	Isaiah 38:10–20	25
Prayer of Thanksgiving (Jesus)	Luke 10:21	131, 132
Prayer on Acceptability of Words (David)	Psalm 19:14	85
Prayer to Give Glory, Honor, and Thanks (angels in heaven)	Revelation 4:8–11	5, 45
Prayer to Hear God; Reminding God of His Promises to Israel (Isaiah)	Isaiah 64:12	9
Prayer to Intentionally Remember the God of Their Ancestors (David)	Psalm 145:4–5	41
Prayer to Question Defeat; Sin in Camp (Joshua)	Joshua 7:7a	62
Prayer to See God's Glory (Moses)	Exodus 33:18	17
Prayer upon Dying (Jesus)	Luke 23:46	68, 141
Prayer, Intercessory (Paul)	2 Thessalonians 1:11	14
Prayer, Intercessory (Paul)	Romans 1:7b	13
Prayer, the Lord's (Instructions on, from Jesus)	Matthew 6:8b–9a, 10–12	123–128
Prayer, the Lord's (Jesus taught to disciples)	Luke 11:2	12
Prayer, the Magnificat (Mary)	Luke 1:46–47	43
Prayers of Daniel After He Was Forbidden to Pray (Daniel)	Daniel 6:10	43, 84
Prayers Without Words (Angels in Heaven)	Revelation 8:1	26
Prayers Without Words (David)	Psalm 39:9	26
Prayers Without Words (Hezekiah)	Isaiah 38:15	26
Prayers Without Words (Job)	Job 40:4	26

Promises in the Bible Index

God's Promises	Bible Reference	Page #
Promise God Is On Our Side	Romans 8:1	170, 225, 293
Promise God Will Be Found When Sought	Jeremiah 29:13	159
	Jeremiah 33:33	194
	Matthew 7:7	196
	Hebrews 13:5	200, 201, 256
	James 4:8a	199
Promise God Will Crush Satan	Romans 16:20a	154
Promise God Will Deliver Us from Difficulty	Proverbs 3:5–6	285
	1 Corinthians 10:13	269
	2 Corinthians 4:17	175, 179
Promise God Will Help Us Endure	Proverbs 3:12	176, 177
	Hebrews 12:11	186
	James 1:2–4	182
	James 1:12	188, 203
	1 Peter 1:6b–7	180
Promise God Will Never Forget His People	Isaiah 49:15	148
Promise God Will Provide for Our Needs	Psalm 19:7–8	276
	Psalm 118:6	297
	Matthew 7:11	201
	Luke 12:31	221, 222
	Philippians 4:19	222, 223, 228, 235
Promise God Will Set Us Apart	Hebrews 10:10	212
Promise God's Promises Never Pass Away	Mark 13:31	274
	Psalm 19:7–8	276
Promise Nothing Is Impossible with God	Luke 1:37	62, 153
Promise of a Firm Foundation	1 Corinthians 3:12–14	292
Promise of Absolute Security	John 10:10	40, 243, 244
	John 10:28–29	245
	Philippians 1:6	22, 248, 249
Promise of Abundance	Luke 6:38	216
	Hebrews 13:16	215. 216
Promise of Acceptance	John 6:37b	239, 240
	Galatians 3:29	240, 241
Promise of Answered Prayer	James 5:16	143, 192, 230
Promise of Blessings	Psalm 46:1–2a	185
	James 1:25	287
	Psalm 1:3	293
Promise of Deliverance by God from Difficulty	2 Corinthians 4:17	175, 179
Promise of Difficulty	John 16:33b	175
Promise of Eternal Glory	2 Timothy 4:18	183, 184, 249, 250
Promise of Eternal Life in Heaven	Psalm 49:15	163, 164
	John 11:25	165
	1 Corinthians 15:52b	162
	2 Corinthians 1:21–22	247
	2 Peter 3:13	166, 259

God's Promises	Bible Reference	Page #
Promise of Faithfulness	Lamentations 3:22–23	151
	2 Corinthians 1:21–22	247
	Hebrews 10:23	147
Promise of Forgiveness and Grace	Psalm 32:5	273, 274
	Psalm 51:17	150
	1 John 1:9	272
Promise of Freedom from Sin	Romans 6:23	238
	Colossians 1:13	237
Promise of Future Judgment	Ecclesiastes 12:13–14	172
	2 Corinthians 5:10	171
Promise of God's Love	Psalm 30:5	178
	Psalm 103:7–8	156
	Romans 8:38–39	155
Promise of Healing for the Sick	Psalm 41:3	231
	James 5:15a	229
Promise of Jesus' Return	John 14:2–3	167
	Acts 1:11	161
	2 Corinthians 1:21–22	247
	Philippians 1:6	22, 248, 249
Promise of Judgment	Matthew 12:36	290, 291
Promise of Living Water, Bread of Life	Isaiah 55:1	127, 243
	John 4:13–14; 6:35; 7:37–38	
Promise of Long Life	Isaiah 46:4	232
Promise of New Life	Psalm 17:15	259
	Matthew 10:39	213, 214
	John 1:12	208, 209, 288
	Romans 8:9a	211, 212
	2 Corinthians 1:21–22	247
	2 Corinthians 5:17	210, 211
	2 Timothy 4:18	183, 184, 249, 250
Promise of Overflowing Blessings	Galatians 3:29	240, 241
Promise of Peace	Psalm 16:11	102, 110, 254, 255
	Isaiah 26:3	265, 266
	John 14:27	264
Promise of Power	Psalm 46:1	158
Promise of Strength for Every Circumstance	Psalm 118:14	226
	Romans 8:32	15, 225, 226
	Philippians 4:13	228
	2 Timothy 4:18	183, 184, 249, 250
Promise of Tenderness	Ezekiel 34:16	207
Promise of the Triumph of Llove	1 John 5:4	169
Promise of Wisdom	Proverbs 1:25–26	289, 290
	James 4:7	270, 271, 283
Promise to Give Us the Holy Spirit	Luke 12:11–12	296
	John 16:13a	286
Promise to Guard and Keep Us	Psalm 118:6	297
	Psalm 119:50	263
Promise to Heal the Brokenhearted	Psalm 147:3	253
Promise to Never Abandon Us	Deuteronomy 31:8	255, 256
	Psalm 27:10	257, 258
	Psalm 118:6	297
Promise to the Powerless	1 Corinthians 1:27	205
	2 Timothy 1:7	217
Promise to Uphold Those Who Fall	Psalm 145:14	195
	Isaiah 40:31	198
	Ephesians 3:11–12	96, 191
Promise We Belong to God	Romans 8:29	203, 213, 231, 278
	Ephesians 2:19	281, 282
	1 Peter 2:10a	280
	2 Peter 1:3	277, 278

Index

A

B

C

D

E

F

G

H

P

Q

R

S

T

U